# SCOON

## SURVIVAL FOR SERVICE

GW00770978

# SCOON

## SURVIVAL FOR SERVICE

### My Experiences as
### Governor General of Grenada

PAUL SCOON

MACMILLAN
CARIBBEAN

Macmillan Education
Between Towns Road, Oxford ox4 3pp
A division of Macmillan Publishers Limited
Companies and representatives throughout the world

www.macmillan-caribbean.com

ISBN 0 333 97064 0

First published 2003

Designed by Bob Elliott
Cover design by Gary Fielder, AC Design
Illustration by Peter Harper

All photographs supplied from the author's
private collection

### DEDICATION

*This book is dedicated to my wife, Esmai,*
*who lovingly and courageously stood beside me*
*during those eventful and turbulent years.*

Printed and bound in Malaysia

2007 2006 2005 2004 2003
10 9 8 7 6 5 4 3 2 1

# CONTENTS

# ACKNOWLEDGEMENTS

E VER since I stepped down from office, numerous people have been urging me to write about my experiences as Governor General of Grenada during my fourteen-year tenure. To have survived as Her Majesty's Representative for so long under unusual circumstances was worth recording. In addition, the feeling was that the telling of my story would greatly enhance one's understanding of an important phase of Grenada's history. I wish to thank all those individuals, too numerous to mention by name, for their encouragement.

In an undertaking of this sort, an author depends on help from others. In particular, I owe a great debt of gratitude to Esmai, my wife, who not only stood by my side through thick and thin while I was in office, but also gave me every encouragement and support while I was writing. Apart from typing the manuscript she was always there to offer useful criticisms on the contents and to remind me of certain episodes during our eventful stay at Governor General's House. In many respects, she was probably the most serious critic of my manuscript. I thank her publicly for her unswerving and generous support.

I am also grateful to former Prime Ministers, Nicholas Brathwaite (now the Rt. Hon. Sir Nicholas Brathwaite) and Ben Jones who gladly received me for interviews at various stages in my writing. My gratitude also goes to Keith Mitchell, George Brizan, and Daniel Williams (now Sir Daniel Williams) who served as Ministers in the Blaize administration (1984–1989) Interviews with them helped clarify for me the details of some of the decisions made in that administration that were crucial in my reconstruction of the larger picture. Sir Daniel Williams later helped me in other important ways. As Governor General he allowed me access to his office to check on certain documents for accuracy. The book is better because of the assistance these individuals provided

I have also benefited from the fruitful discussions I held with several Grenadians of all walks of life – not least some of those who were incarcerated without trial in Richmond Hill Prisons – about their personal experiences during the revolutionary period.

Lauriston Wilson Jr., who served as Permanent Secretary and Director of Finance before and during my term of office, painstakingly took me through the meandering economic and fiscal policies of the various administrations for whom he worked. I wish to thank him immensely.

Wellington T. Leonard, popularly known as Duke Leonard, also provided detailed information pertaining to the rescue of Esmai and me during those crucial moments in October, 1983. Duke was the commander of the Seals who came to my official residence on October 25, 1983, to protect and carry us to safety. My thanks go out to him for his kind assistance.

I am most grateful to David Montgomery, retired Deputy British High Commissioner to Barbados and the Eastern Caribbean, who read some of the chapters and gave me some useful hints as well as information about events leading up to the military intervention of October 25, 1983.

Grenadian-born Edward L. Cox, History Professor at Rice University in Houston, Texas, U.S.A. was kind enough to read my manuscript from the beginning. I am indeed grateful for his helpful suggestions at all times. I am equally grateful to him for writing the Foreword to this book.

While the book has benefited from the assistance of many individuals, I alone should be held accountable for whatever shortcomings might inadvertently later become apparent.

PAUL SCOON

*Grenada*
*May, 2003*

# FOREWORD

WHILE the careers of some Caribbean politicians have received extensive coverage either through their own writings or that of academics, the experiences of governors general have attracted scant attention from professionals and lay people alike. In a way, this is quite understandable. Under the parliamentary system of government that the English-speaking Caribbean nations have inherited from Great Britain, governors general normally perform mostly ceremonial and rather limited constitutional duties. With the exception of Guyana, the same is true even for those countries that have embraced a republican form of government. Hardly performing an activist or executive constitutional role, the president's role pales in comparison to that of the powerful prime minister. Often, the head of state is viewed as a figure-head. This perception, however, masks the reality of the enormous power the head of state enjoys in handling major constitutional issues that require his own deliberate judgement.

Sir Paul Scoon's book on his experiences as governor general of Grenada over a fourteen-year period demonstrates the potential enormity of the head of state's constitutional role. First appointed as the Queen's representative when the flamboyant Eric Matthew Gairy was prime minister, Sir Paul managed to survive Gairy's idiosyncrasies and the People's Revolution of 1979 to 1983. In the uncertainties following what he terms the six day "rule of terror" when General Hudson Austin sought to rule by force of arms, Sir Paul's assumption of almost plenipotentiary powers helped stabilize the floundering ship of state. Whatever his political ideology might have been, none can doubt that in all his actions, he was actuated first of all by his love of country and his understanding of his constitutional role. A dedicated patriot of the highest order, Sir Paul took his task seriously. Subordinating his personal interests to the larger goal of doing what he considered right and best for Grenadians, this longest serving governor general in independent Grenada's history paid a huge personal price on behalf of his country. His willingness to share with us some of his experiences will help demystify the role of the governor general during the revolutionary period. More importantly, this book finally answers questions concerning Sir Paul's relationship with Eric Gairy and Maurice Bishop, and the factors that influenced some of the decisions he made from late 1983 onwards.

*Survival for Service* takes us through the unique challenges Sir Paul had to face during the closing years of his public service career. Beginning as a teacher at his *alma mater*, the Grenada Boys' Secondary School, his eventual move to the Ministry of Education where he held the position of Chief Education Officer seemed then to many to be the culmination of a life that was to be dedicated solely to the educational realm. After all, his students saw in him the perfect educator and role model whose strength rested in his willingness and ability to provide them with intellectual food and instil in them the essential moral fibres on which society rested. His elevation to the post of Cabinet Secretary and eventual appointment as governor general after a six-year sojourn in London as an international civil servant left many sceptics wondering whether he possessed the fortitude and resiliency to work so closely with Gairy. Time proved that he possessed them, and more.

To me, the most interesting and revealing aspects of *Survival for Service* is the perspective Sir Paul provides on the revolutionary and post-revolutionary phases of Grenada's history. Whatever Bishop's goals for the office of governor general might have been, he failed to see the tensions inherent in maintaining an office that was obviously at variance with the revolutionary political ideology and tradition. We may never know with certainty what Bishop's eventual plans for the governor generalship might have been had the revolution stayed its course. What is patently clear, however, is that in the early days of the revolution, Bishop perceived the office as potentially reassuring to politically conservative Grenadians. According to Sir Paul, cordial relations between himself and Bishop in the Revolution's early days eventually became somewhat lukewarm as the years progressed. The quality of reports he received regarding cabinet meetings and decisions also deteriorated. Was Cabinet becoming less important than the Central Committee in the decision-making process? Was a movement afoot to marginalize the governor general? Sir Paul seems to think that eventually his office would have been abolished. As one scholar wrote some years ago, how can one justify a revolutionary governor general?

And yet, the governor general stepped boldly into the breach occasioned by the events of October 25, 1983. The contents of conversations between General Austin and Sir Paul have finally become part of the public consciousness. From Sir Paul's accounts, we are left with the picture of an army commander lacking the wherewithal for effectively ruling civil society. Austin's prevarication regarding the disposal of the bodies of his murdered colleagues and the planning of a burial for them suggests that he was probably either carrying out instructions from others or that he was not sufficiently aware at the time of the political implications of his statements to the governor general.

Sir Paul seems convinced that General Austin and his associates can and should now clear the air regarding the disposal of the bodies. Convinced that he had to take action to stabilize the situation and free Grenadians from what he perceived to be impending despotic military rule, Sir Paul invoked his powers under the 1973 constitution to marshal foreign military aid. Under no circumstances was he prepared to permit a military junta to frustrate the will of the people.

Now that the facts are finally out, Sir Paul has confirmed what a number of persons have long suspected regarding his role in the summoning of outside military relief. Through David Montgomery, a British diplomat based in Barbados with responsibility extending to the Eastern Caribbean, Sir Paul received a message from Barbados's Prime Minister Tom Adams regarding the desirability of seeking outside help. Sir Paul eventually agreed to seek such aid. The irony, of course, is that a British diplomat was privy to sensitive information of an international and possibly diplomatic nature about which his government was for some time apparently kept in the dark. Sir Paul was undoubtedly painfully aware of the gravity of the local situation and the implications of taking the action he did. His was a stressful and lonely plight at that time, and concern for the welfare of Grenadians and the sanctity of the 1973 constitution seemed uppermost in his mind. I find convincing his argument that he relied on Montgomery's oral communication in preference to a written document which, if falling into the wrong hands, could have compromised his efforts and even endangered the lives of himself and countless other Grenadians.

*Survival for Service* also sheds light on the strained relationship between Sir Paul and his erstwhile legal advisor, Anthony Rushford, whose boorish behaviour and political indiscretions ran afoul of the generally accepted norms of etiquette that the urbane governor general had come to expect of such a high functionary. The actions of Richard Hart, the attorney general at the time of the dénouement, also comes in for harsh criticism. A strict interpreter of constitutional matters and one who was fully aware of civil service protocol, Sir Paul simply could not understand why neither individual paid him the deference expected of his office.

In the end, a governor general whose functions prior to 1983 had been largely circumscribed suddenly found himself entrusted with almost unlimited executive authority. In justifying his action, he invokes both the 1973 constitution and the People's Laws of the revolutionary era. According to his reasoning, the killing of Bishop and many of his cabinet colleagues whose legitimacy to office rested on laws promulgated in 1979 deprived the island of its prime minister and government. Because the revolutionary government had remained silent on the governor general's role, it became necessary for Sir Paul to invoke the 1973 constitution, which had prescribed his duties in the absence of a government. When he appointed the Advisory Council to help him in administering the country and pave the way for a return to democratic government, he rightly failed to chair it. Yet there is no doubt that his was a highly centralized government. Witness, for example, the manner in which he handled the election preparations in 1984.

Grenadians interested in the administration of justice have for a long time been baffled over the manner in which the matter of the commutation of the death sentence for the convicted killers had been handled. Sir Paul makes it clear that in his view politicians improperly interfered with and compromised the process. Few persons realized that Sir Paul had already signed and handed over to the commissioner of prisons the warrants for the executions. Regardless of what one thinks of the death penalty, one is left with the distinct impression that some training in constitutional and governmental procedures would serve our politicians well. Considerable public embarrassment and unnecessary anxiety for the convicted could have been avoided had things been done sooner and differently.

It is unlikely that a governor general who remained in office for some fourteen years would not have a fair sense of the strengths and weaknesses of the various prime ministers with whom he worked. Sir Paul seems to consider Blaize the most disciplined, politically sensitive, fiscally responsible, and concerned with the country's welfare. Politically flamboyant Gairy and Bishop in their own ways energized the citizenry into achieving some of their true potential. Somewhere in between stood Brathwaite and Jones. As chairman of the Advisory Council, Brathwaite performed exceptionally well. Each politician, naturally, had peculiar problems with which to contend and challenges to face. It is now the lot of a different set of politicians to move the nation forward.

We owe an enormous debt of gratitude to Sir Paul for making available to us his thoughts, perspectives, and experiences on a wide range of issues.

EDWARD L. COX
Associate Professor of History
*Houston, Texas*                                    Rice University

# LIST OF ABBREVIATIONS

| | |
|---|---|
| ADC | Aide-de-camp |
| AIFLD | American Institute of Free Labour Development |
| CARICOM | Caribbean Community |
| CDB | Caribbean Development Bank |
| CIDA | Canadian International Development Agency |
| FAO | Food and Agriculture Organization |
| GCMG | Knight Grand Cross of the Most Distinguished Order of St. Michael and St. George |
| GCVO | Knight Grand Cross of the Royal Victorian Order |
| GIDC | Grenada Industrial Development Corporation |
| GNP | Grenada National Party |
| GULP | Grenada United Labour Party |
| IESC | International Executive Service Corps |
| IFAD | International Fund for Agriculture Development |
| IMF | International Monetary Fund |
| JEWEL | Joint Endeavour for Welfare, Education and Liberation |
| MAP | Movement for Assemblies of the People |
| MBPM | Maurice Bishop Patriotic Movement |
| NDC | National Democratic Congress |
| NEC | National Economic Council |
| NEWLO | New Life Organisation |
| NJM | New Jewel Movement |
| NNP | New National Party |
| OECS | Organisation of East Caribbean States |
| PRA | People's Revolutionary Army |
| PRG | People's Revolutionary Government |
| RFG | Radio Free Grenada |
| RMC | Revolutionary Military Council |
| SERVOL | Service Volunteered for All |
| TNP | The National Party |
| UNCTAD | United Nations Conference on Trade and Development |
| USAID | United States Agency for International Development |
| WTO | World Trade Organisation |

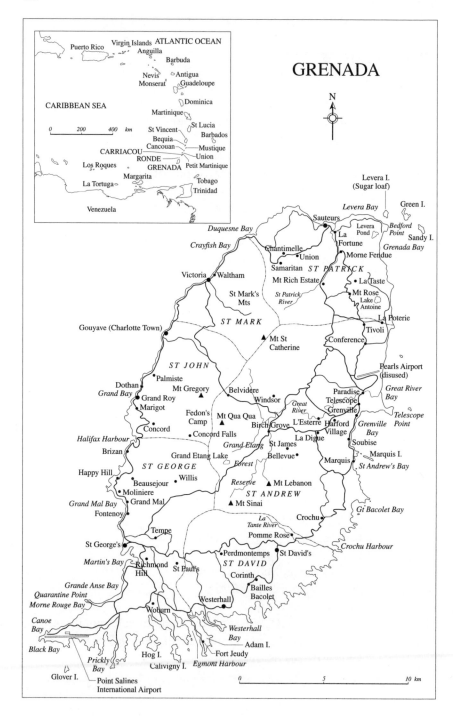

# GRENADA

# 1

## A New Beginning

IT was exactly 6.30 p.m. on a bright sunny day in June, 1978, when a black Daimler pulled up outside our London home, 27 The Avenue in Kew. Alighting from the car was the Rt. Hon. Sir Eric Gairy, Prime Minister of Grenada. He was accompanied by my old school friend, Lauriston Wilson Jr., Permanent Secretary in Grenada's Ministry of Finance. Also in the car was a security officer from Scotland Yard. Before entering our home Sir Eric had advised the security officer that he was about to visit "territory" which was safe and secure, and there was no need for a security presence inside the house. My family and I had left Grenada in 1973 for London where I took up the post of Deputy Director of the Commonwealth Foundation on secondment from the Government of Grenada. My substantive position at home was Secretary to the Cabinet.

Grenada was not without its anxieties and uncertainties in the months leading up to its independence on February 7, 1974. Indeed, signs of mounting instability filled the air. Hopes of any semblance of unity faded as anti-government demonstrators took to the streets almost daily. Amid growing personal animosity and rising tension, Grenadians were abandoning their homes, albeit temporarily, for abodes in neighbouring islands or for unplanned vacations in more distant lands. Those who had the courage to remain or who could not afford to travel abroad continued to grapple with the uncomfortable effects of what seemed to be a never ending dock strike in St. George's, the nation's capital, and an equally devastating electricity strike. There was growing concern, not least in the British House of Commons, about personal safety and national security on this tiny island soon to be elevated to the status of a fully independent sovereign state within the Commonwealth.

Arrangements had already been made for the Duke of Gloucester to hand over the instrument of Independence on behalf of Her Majesty the Queen, and Government House was suitably refurbished to accommodate the royal visitor. However, because of the potentially explosive situation as far as security was concerned, all plans for his visit to Grenada were cancelled at the instance of the British government. Hon. Peter Blaker, Parliamentary Under-secretary in the Foreign and Commonwealth Office was the leader of the British delegation at the independence celebrations, and in the absence of a royal personage he was given the responsibility of handing over the constitutional instruments. At the midnight ceremony when the flag of independent Grenada was hoisted for the first time the island was still without electricity and it was against this dismal backdrop that the nation of Grenada (which includes the three islands of Grenada, Carriacou and Petit Martinique) was born.

Prime Minister Gairy, the father of the nation, was in no way daunted by the action of the striking workers. In his view the withdrawal of labour was politically inspired, but he was firm in his resolve to see the celebrations through. He had arranged for alternative lighting at Fort George where the flag raising ceremony took place in the presence of visiting and local dignitaries and a large and enthusiastic Grenadian crowd. Soon after the Grenadian flag was hoisted, *H.M.S. Bacchante,* which was in port for the celebrations, fired a 21-gun salute to greet and honour the new nation. At precisely 10.33 a.m. on the same day, Hon. Peter Blaker, at a special parliamentary meeting at York House, handed a personal message from the Queen together with the constitutional instruments to His Excellency Leo Victor Degale, Grenada's first Governor General.

Since the granting of adult suffrage in 1951, political growth had been atrophied by personal rancour. Little wonder, then, that the parliamentary opposition and various non-governmental organizations while not being averse, as they widely asserted, to political independence for Grenada, were nevertheless vehement in their opposition to such a significant advance with all the concomitant political, economical, and social consequences under the leadership of Eric Gairy. Independence yes, but under Gairy no – that was the current collective wisdom of the Grenadian middle class. Such a posture, of course, could not be described as compatible with democratic propriety. Entrenched in any democracy is the right of the people to elect their political leaders, and while democracy is accommodating to all shades of thinking, the views of the majority must prevail.

It was under Gairy's leadership that the Government of Grenada sought independence from Britain. In response the British Government promised to comply, provided that the victorious party at the next general elections had Independence as its main election plank. I was present when Mr Joseph Godber, Minister of State in the Foreign and Commonwealth Office so advised Gairy at the official residence of the Premier. Needless to say Gairy never looked back. In its 1972 election manifesto, Gairy's party, the Grenada

United Labour Party, put forward independence as its main plank. Gairy went on to win the 1972 elections convincingly. His party annexed thirteen out of the fifteen seats contested for in the House of Representatives. The other two seats went to the Grenada National Party. Gairy's party got 58.9% of the popular vote while the other party got 41.1%. The total votes cast was 34,241. Again in the general elections of 1976 – the first since the attainment of Independence – Gairy was returned to power although with a reduced majority. On this occasion his party was able to muster only nine seats while the combined opposition parties contesting under the banner of the People's Alliance captured as many as six. The People's Alliance obtained 48.2% of the 40,777 votes cast while the Grenada United Labour Party got 51.8%.

Obviously I wanted to hear from Sir Eric himself how Grenada was coping with the teething economic problems peculiar to small independent states with very limited resources, bearing in mind that Grenada was the first of the East Caribbean states to become independent. Sir Eric gave me every assurance that the prospects for growth were good, that the people had settled down to work again, and the country was proceeding apace economically and socially. Never one to be pinned down to answering questions, it soon became clear that Sir Eric was not going to make any exception on this occasion. In his usual ebullient manner he came straight to the point. He asked whether I would accept the offer of the post of Governor General that was soon to become vacant. If I were interested, he would recommend me to Her Majesty the Queen. Although this came like a bolt from the blue, I subsequently learnt that there had been a certain measure of speculation in Grenada that I would assume the mantle of that high office at the end of my assignment with the Commonwealth Foundation.

Mr Wilson succinctly outlined the terms and conditions of the office. I in turn thanked Sir Eric and asked him to give me some time to think about it and to discuss it with my family. I was scheduled to leave for Canada on duty in two days' time. I would be in touch with him on my return. One week after my return to London, I informed Sir Eric that I had agreed that my name be placed before Her Majesty. In early September I got news of my appointment. Only then did I break the news to my director, John Chadwick, who warmly congratulated me adding that he thought something was brewing as only recently he had to report confidentially on me in response to a request "from certain quarters." John Chadwick, former Colonial Office administrator and diplomat, while expressing deep satisfaction and happiness over my appointment, in his cynical way interjected that I should always be prepared to face a coup. In all my years working with

John, I never considered him a man of prophetic propensities, and so I sharply retorted that this was not part of our political tradition in the English-speaking Caribbean. The man was endowed with such a incisive mind that he at once spotted my displeasure, and so in typical fashion he quickly changed the subject and went on to discuss arrangements for my departure from London.

The first three weeks in September were exceptionally busy for us, what with attending farewell functions, saying good-bye to friends and colleagues and giving up the house in Kew. By then news of my appointment had spread as evidenced by the number of congratulatory telegrams and letters that came pouring in. The telephone, too, had never been busier. My wife and I finally left London on Wednesday, September 27, on an Air Canada flight for Toronto. Leaving Toronto four days later we flew on British West Indian Airways (BWIA) to Port-of-Spain, Trinidad, where we spent a couple days before embarking for Grenada on Leeward Islands Air Transport (LIAT). After an uneventful thirty-minute flight, we landed quietly and without ceremony at Pearls Airport. As we disembarked we were met by a young, well-dressed gentleman whom I easily recognized as one of my erstwhile students of the Grenada Boys' Secondary School. Now Senator the Hon. Henry Bullen, he was there to welcome me in his capacity as Minister of State for Home Affairs, Foreign Affairs, Information and Public Relations. With the minimum of delay we were escorted from the VIP lounge to our car for the forty-minute drive to St. George's. On arrival at Governor General's House, we received a cordial welcome from the Acting Governor General, Mrs Marie-Josephine McIntyre and her husband Colin. The staff gave us a rousing welcome as we entered the House. Prime Minister Gairy later dropped by to greet us and to hold discussions with me.

For close on two hundred years, York House, a quaint but impressive two-storey building, has stood guard on the horse-back ridge overlooking the city centre of St. George's. This historic building serves as the repository of two most important pillars of the Grenada constitution, namely, the Legislature and the Judiciary. The Legislature is bi-cameral consisting of a fifteen-member elected House of Representatives and a Senate whose thirteen members are wholly nominated. These together comprise the Houses of Parliament that occupy the top floor of York House where all legislative matters are discussed and voted upon. On the lower floor resides the High Court of Justice jealously guarding the rule of law and zealously interpreting the laws formulated by the Parliamentarians on the upper floor. There can be no denying that the hallowed walls of York House for decades have echoed and re-echoed the joys and fears of the Grenadian people.

It was in this historic building that I took the Oath of Allegiance and the Oath of Office on Wednesday, October 4, 1978. Present at this impressive and awe-inspiring ceremony was a wide cross section of specially invited guests including my mother., representatives from the public and private sectors, dignitaries from the church and the judiciary, members of the diplomatic corps, and a visiting World Bank team. The occasion was a special joint sitting of both Houses of Parliament with all the pomp and ceremony associated with a state opening of a parliamentary session. In the absence of the Hon. the Chief Justice, Sir Maurice Davis, who was out of the island, Mr Justice Winsley Bruno administered the Oaths. In accordance with the Order Paper, welcome and congratulatory speeches were made by the Leader of Government Business in the House of Representatives, Hon. George Hosten, and by the Leader of the Senate, Senator the Hon. Derek Knight. I must admit how disappointed I was when I read the Order Paper the previous evening and observed that the opposition was not down to speak. Frankly I thought the proceedings would be dismally hollow without a contribution from Her Majesty's Opposition, and I kept wondering whether such an omission was symptomatic of the lack of unity in the country. Further the office of Governor General is above partisan politics. His role is by no means divisive. Rather his is to unify the nation both by example and by persuasion, and nothing should be done, not least in Parliament and in his very presence, to diminish his stature as the symbol of national unity. I was, therefore, very much relieved when the Hon. Alison Reason, Speaker of the House of Representatives, invited Hon. Maurice Bishop, Leader of the Opposition, to speak, even though he emphasized that his speech should be limited to associating himself with the congratulatory remarks made by the two previous speakers.

From all appearances Mr Bishop's speech was well received by members of both Houses of Parliament. For my part I thought he made a statesmanlike speech. The last speaker on the Order Paper was the Prime Minister. In his own inimitable style, he followed the pattern of the previous speakers by extending felicitations and a warm welcome to my wife and me and offered best wishes for every success in my new role. But he did not stop at that. He embraced the opportunity, as he was wont to do before such a captive audience, to outline some of the current projects undertaken by Government and to heap praises on the self-help efforts of the people. And, as if pointing an accusing finger at the Opposition, he firmly and unreservedly denounced communism and strongly vowed to nip it in the bud whenever and wherever it reared its ugly head in Grenada.

My first public duty was the presentation of awards to those Grenadians whose names appeared on Her Majesty's 1978 Birthday Honours List. These awards are usually presented at Governor General's House, but to add to the grandeur of the occasion, and in my anxiety to get on with the job, I agreed to hold this particular Investiture as part of the inauguration ceremony. At the conclusion of the Investiture and just prior to the adjournment, I took leave of the Honourable Houses of Parliament. Within minutes I posed with members of Parliament in the courtyard for a group photograph before proceeding to Melville Street (a street named after Brigadier General Robert Melville, the first British Governor of Grenada) in the city centre for a review of the troops that included contingents of the local army and police.

All members of Parliament accepted my invitation for pre-lunch drinks at Governor General's House that gave me an opportunity to get to know the parliamentarians better. What was most significant was that the Government and the Opposition members were meeting together for the first time since Independence to socialize. I was forcibly struck by the relaxed atmosphere, the interaction between Government and Opposition, not least between the Prime Minister and the Leader of the Opposition, and the apparent camaraderie. It was even mooted by members of both sides that such social occasions could enhance the growth of the body politic, and they looked forward to meeting at regular intervals outside of Parliament to converse informally and to relax in a social setting. I quietly hoped that this truly marked a new dawn for the forging of national unity and I entertained the thought of making this a regular feature when I make my annual visit to Parliament to read the Throne Speech and declare the new session of Parliament open.

# 2

## Getting Acquainted

Thursday, October 5, was my first full day in office. I was at my desk precisely at eight o'clock that morning – the regulation time for the commencement of work in Government offices – but to my astonishment I could find no one in any of the offices. I subsequently learnt that lateness in reporting for work was not peculiar to the Governor General's office; nevertheless, it was my firm view that this office should set the tone in matters of punctuality, and, if the staff had grown accustomed to enjoying a special privilege of reporting late for work, that was totally unacceptable to me. By way of an excuse, I learnt that the driver was late in collecting a staff member that morning. I immediately gave orders that this privilege of using drivers and transport belonging to the Governor General's house be terminated forthwith. In response to a verbal inquiry, my secretary advised me that work began in the Governor General's office as in all Government departments at 8 a.m., but gently added that this was not for the Governor General. And when the staff was presented to me that same day, I made it abundantly clear that I expected everyone without exception to be at work on time. Apart from the office staff I had a domestic staff of seven, eleven gardeners and a police contingent of eight performing duties as orderlies, drivers and security personnel.

The office staff was small. It comprised a personal assistant, a full-time aide-de-camp, a secretary and an accounts clerk. This was a far cry from the days when the Governor's office was buzzing with activity: the Governor, resident in Grenada, was the Governor of the Windward Islands of Grenada, Dominica, St. Lucia and St. Vincent. With constitutional changes over the years, each of the Windward Islands had its own Governor and on attaining independence they each had a Governor General with the exception of Dominica that opted for a republican form of government with a ceremonial President as Head of State. The British Monarch is the Head of State of sixteen Independent Commonwealth countries including Grenada. In these countries, with the exception of Britain where the Monarch resides, the Queen is represented by a Governor General who acts in Her name on the advice of the local Cabinet of Ministers. The Governor General has direct access to Buckingham Palace and does not take directives from the British Foreign and Commonwealth Office or indeed from any arm of the British Government. His allegiance is to the Queen, not to Her Majesty's Government in Britain. In the normal course of his duties, he is not expected to receive instructions from the monarch, nor does he consult the monarch before he takes any decision. The Governor General must use his discretion. He takes action and then reports to the monarch depending on the magnitude or the significance of the action taken.

With the advent of the ministerial system of government and subsequent political independence, responsibility for the day-to-day execution of government business shifted from the Governor General to the Cabinet of Ministers who, to all intents and purposes, constitute the Executive and are answerable and accountable to Parliament. The ministers control the departments of government, and in administering a wide range of laws and policies they have the support of the civil service, statutory boards and commissions. Each minister has a portfolio consisting of a group of subjects for which he or she is responsible. Various Acts of Parliament empower ministers to make regulations that can have far reaching effect on the lives of the Grenadian people. The ministers formulate policy within the framework of the Constitution and the laws made by Parliament, they issue directives on economic and social programmes, and they control expenditure that has been approved and appropriated by Parliament.

Presiding over the Cabinet of Ministers is the Prime Minister who is appointed by the Governor General. In selecting a Prime Minister, the Governor General as stipulated by the Constitution appoints a member of the House of Representatives who appears to him likely to command the support of the majority of the members of the House. Other ministers are appointed by the Governor General, acting in accordance with the advice of the Prime Minister, from among the Senators and the members of the House of Representatives. Conversely, the Prime Minister at any time can advise the Governor General to revoke the appointment of any of the ministers or to assign new duties to them. There is no obligation on the part of the Prime Minister to give any reason to the Governor General or to anyone else for such action. Thus the Prime Minister has the constitutional authority to hire and fire ministers at will. Clearly the Prime Minister is not on equal footing with the other ministers: a fact that ministers of Government do not always seem to appreciate. As head of government he is responsible to the Governor General for ensuring that there is good and orderly government in the country, and he must keep the Governor General fully informed concerning matters of state. Decisions taken in Cabinet are the collective responsibility of the members of Cabinet, and if any Cabinet minister feels very strongly about a decision taken by Cabinet and in conscience, or for some other reason, is unable to go along with that decision, he should resign. For the doctrine of collective responsibility is central to the proper functioning of Cabinet. Once Cabinet takes a decision every Cabinet member is party to that decision and is bound by it even though he might have vigorously opposed the measure during the Cabinet discussions.

In Grenada Cabinet meets once a week to consider submissions and take decisions on these submissions. Simply a submission is a case made out by a minister for approval by Cabinet. A great deal of work is to be done by the ministry involved before the matter is taken to Cabinet. For example, a request may come from a non-Grenadian who is desirous of obtaining a licence to own property in Grenada. The civil servant in the ministry dealing with this subject must get all the information necessary and must make out a case based on such information and inquiries and indeed on the relevant laws and regulations as to whether or not this particular request should be granted. He should then send up the written paper with the full story about the matter in hand to his permanent secretary who is the administrative head of the ministry and the minister's chief adviser. In a large ministry, the memorandum will be channeled to the permanent secretary through the senior assistant secretary who will add his own comments to the memorandum. The permanent secretary in turn will study the proposal and make any alterations before advising the minister to take the matter to Cabinet. The minister concurs by signing the memorandum that now becomes a Cabinet submission to be forwarded to the Secretary to Cabinet for circulation to members of Cabinet as part of the agenda for the ensuing meeting. A decision by Cabinet whether by way of approval or rejection or deferral is known as a "conclusion." The permanent secretary has a very important role to play by way of advising the minister properly if Cabinet is to take decisions which are reasonable and which are for the common good. Once a conclusion is reached, it is passed to the appropriate ministry for implementation and it is the business of the permanent secretary to act on the conclusion that is now a Government decision with dispatch, with loyalty and with diligence.

While Cabinet is the chief executive body in the land it is nevertheless not without its limitations. Its role is neither legislative nor judicial, and Cabinet must never appear to be encroaching on what is distinctly and separately the province of either parliament or the judiciary. There must be no undue interference by Cabinet with certain bodies like the Public Service Commission or certain functionaries such as the Director of Public Prosecution, or the Director of Audit, or the Supervisor of Elections. It must be emphasized that Cabinet cannot make laws.

But it is the role of Cabinet to initiate the passage of legislative measures. For example it is the Cabinet that must take a decision, say, to control the development of land resources. Such decision is then taken to Parliament in the form of a bill that after debate and passage by both Houses of Parliament is assented to by the Governor General and then becomes law.

Without briefing, without advice, and devoid of any special gubernatorial knowledge or experience, I entered upon the office of Governor General. The only document available to me was a confidential memorandum from Buckingham Palace with guidelines on certain procedural matters mainly in the area of protocol. In the circumstances I had to draw heavily on my administrative experience and at the same time exercise unusual patience and tolerance as I observed closely what was going on around me. My earlier posting as Secretary to Cabinet gave me the opportunity to appreciate the importance of the relationship between the Governor's office and the office of the Premier, and my frequent visits to Government House to brief the then Governor, Dame Hilda Bynoe, were still fresh in my memory. Similarly the Constitution presented no problem to me. I had a working knowledge of the pre-independence Constitution that, it would seem, was more or less updated to formulate our independence Constitution. The latter so strikingly resembled the former that it looked very much as if the learned constitutional expert diligently and dutifully did a superb pasting job in order to clothe the old constitution in a new dress. However, with limited background knowledge and learning resources, I was determined to discover from the very outset what the office of Governor General was all about and indeed how the people of Grenada perceived that office. It did not take me long to realize that the success of my tenure would depend on the extent to which the people of Grenada perceived me as a leader, as a man of dignity, and as a man who fully understands the mood of the people. Further it was my responsibility to uphold the dignity of the Crown at all times, and to see to it that the constitution of Grenada was strictly adhered to. By vigilance, by persuasion and by keeping myself informed, I was to ensure that there was good governance continuously. In the final analysis the success or failure of my office would depend on my own efforts.

Constitutionally the office of Governor General is primarily a ceremonial one. The Governor General is not actively involved in the day to day running of government. Apart from taking pride of place on ceremonial occasions or presiding over major State functions, he supports good causes and so lends his patronage to charitable and voluntary organizations, service clubs and youth movements. He attends many and varied social functions in any one year, and delivers speeches particularly to non-governmental organizations. Among his multifarious duties he summons, prorogues and dissolves Parliament, he assents to bills passed by Parliament thus giving them the force of law, he goes down to Parliament at the opening of every new session to read the Throne Speech. Prepared by the Government this speech outlines their legislative and other programmes for the year. Parliament, of course, is the law-making body of the State, but the legislative process is complete only when the Governor General gives his assent to the parliamentary bill. In this sense, therefore, Parliament is made up of the Head of State as represented by the Governor General, the Senate and the House of Representatives. The Governor General also appoints Ministers of Government, Senators, certain heads of department in the civil service, Justices of the Peace, members of the Public Service Commission and certain other special commissions. Nearly all the Governor General's actions are done in accordance with advice given to him by the Prime Minister or some other appropriate person or commission as the case may be. The Prime Minister is his principal adviser. However, in his own deliberate judgement, that is without the obligation to take advice from anyone, he appoints the Prime Minister, the Leader of the Opposition, the Supervisor of Elections and the Chairman of the Public Service Board of Appeal. A very significant aspect of his work is to receive Heads of State and other visiting dignitaries as well as to receive ambassadors and accept their letters of credence on behalf of Her Majesty. He also executes conveyances of Crown lands and he reads all Cabinet papers and Parliamentary papers. He receives regular visits from the Prime Minister who must keep him informed of all matters pertaining to Government in particular and to the country in general.

Following the pre-independence upheaval Grenada had become so politically polarized that it was well nigh impossible to get an objective or well-considered view on the prevailing political, social or economic condition in the tri-island State. Political affiliations, hatred for Gairy, rising expectations particularly among the youth, the alleged level of prosperity among the business community all influenced opinion forming and, sad to say, personalities rather than issues constituted the dominant factor in any discussion on Grenada. Even professional people were split down the middle politically and seemed to have abandoned their role as opinion formers. In fact many of them saw their civic role as an adversarial one and spent much of their time, energy and resources fanning the flames of dissent. Families were divided. Parents who supported the old-established order found that there was a growing chasm between themselves and their children who were in the vanguard of a new political movement that was sweeping through the land under the vigorous though subtle direction and tutelage of Maurice Bishop, Bernard Coard and others. The young people up to the age of twenty-five constituted approximately 60 per cent of the population. This teeming youthful population was a force to be reckoned with as they became more and more restless in their search for some sort of direction. They were old enough as not to be insensitive to the deceit and dishonesty of everyday life and they were smart enough to question the moral decrepitude of political and other leaders of our society. Our youngsters could no longer find comfort in the old-established order and even their parents could not persuade them to follow the existing political and social pathways. They became more vocal and more active in their youth groups and embraced every opportunity to make their voices heard. One such opportunity was Assembly '78 when for some months the Roman Catholic Church brought its members together in various committees to take a critical look at the church in Grenada, to evaluate and to chart a course for the future of the church. The youth organizations of the church were high in their commitment to Assembly '78 and played an active and meaningful role in its proceedings. This resurgence of youthful vigour in the church was very much in evidence when my wife and I attended the concelebrated mass that marked the official opening of Assembly '78. That was on Friday, December 1. The mass was held at the geodesic dome that had been specially built near the Grand Anse beach in 1976 for a General Assembly meeting of the Organization of American States. Also attending holy mass on that occasion were Prime Minister Gairy and leader of the Opposition, Maurice Bishop. When the two men shook hands at the peace sign, the congregation burst forth in loud and rapturous applause. Assembly '78 deliberated on the findings of the various committees for the next ten days and concluded with another concelebrated mass, but this time at Queen's Park on the afternoon of Sunday, December 10. The young people participated with equal exuberance. At the secondary schools the students got every encouragement and support for their new behavioural pattern from the younger teachers some of whom were more rebellious than the students themselves and were leading lights in the movement that Maurice Bishop and Bernard Coard were pushing ever forward. When I attended the Speech Night exercises of a leading girls' school in December, 1978, I was horrified to find one of the teachers so unkempt and so shabbily dressed as if she had just returned from rambling through the Grand Etang forest. Her mode of dress was truly revolutionary. One week later on a similar occasion, at a boys' school this time, I took the unusual step to properly adjust the necktie of a student before I presented his prize to him.

Instinctively soon after I assumed office, I felt compelled to do my own analysis on Grenada, and during my first three months in office, I unobtrusively and quietly did so. My office was inundated with requests for courtesy calls from quite a variety of people representing different fields of endeavour on the island, and I made myself available to receive them. Thus I received ambassadors and high commissioners, local religious leaders, and representatives of non-governmental organizations including the service clubs and national sporting organizations. I attended Sunday mass in different churches throughout the island and visited as many institutions as time and circumstances allowed. At Christmas time, my wife and I visited hospitals, homes for senior citizens, and children's homes. This was to become an annual feature. As most of these visits took me outside St. George's, I took this opportunity to observe my fellow citizens at work and at play and to appreciate rural Grenada.

Expectations ran high with the announcement of my proposed visit to Carriacou on Thursday, December 7. For some years the people of the sister isle had felt left out of the mainstream of national activities. Thus an early visit by a new Governor General was well received with a sense of honour and a deep feeling of satisfaction. In true Carriacouan tradition, my wife and I were given a very warm and friendly welcome on our arrival at Lauriston Airport. Accompanying us were Captain Michael Campbell, my aide-de-camp, and Senator the Hon. Wellington R. L. Friday, the Minister for Education. Prior to the start of our journey to Belair Park, the official residence of the Governor General when in Carriacou, a number of prominent residents were presented to me. Among them was the veteran politician, Herbert Augustus Blaize, who was the parliamentary representative for Carriacou and Petit Martinique.

My day-long programme was a packed one. It consisted of visits to schools, to the Belair hospital, to the main administrative building and to other places of interest. The school visits, though fleeting, brought back fond memories of my earlier career. The classrooms and in many cases familiar faces vividly reminded me of the enthusiasm and verve of students and teachers as I knew them some ten years previously in my capacity as Chief Education Officer. But my visit to Hillsborough Government School took me even further down memory lane. It was in August, 1955, that I slept on the hard wooden benches in that school for ten nights on end while camping with a group of cadets from the Grenada Boys' Secondary School. One month after, on September 22 to be exact, Hurricane Janet, a most devastating hurricane, struck with all its fury and flattened the Hillsborough Government School.

Whatever one may say of Carriacou and its 7000 inhabitants, it must be emphasized that their friendliness is second to none, their family ties are so closely knit as to be unbreakable, their industry and their courteousness are worthy of emulation, and they are generous to a fault. As I journeyed across Carriacou that day, I could not help but feel that years of neglect by the government in St. George's were mainly responsible for the lack of certain amenities on the island and the non-maintenance of certain infra-structural works and buildings. The roads in particular were in a deplorable condition.

# 3

## *Five Years of Independence*

ERIC MATHEW GAIRY, whether in government or in opposition, was undoubtedly the dominant figure in Grenadian politics for almost thirty years. And even when at one stage he had lost his franchise for the offence of disturbing an electioneering meeting of a rival candidate, his political power never dwindled, nor did his supporters forsake him. In fact, during his temporary absence from the legislature his party members rendered with increased emotion and with more than usual gusto the theme song of their party, "We'll never let our leader fall." As if to emphasize that his political party was based on the doctrine of strict obedience, he continued to call all the political shots from outside the legislative chamber and, like lambs, those of his party in Parliament followed the instructions of their good shepherd without question, without demur.

Gairy always remembered, though at first not fondly, Justice Elvin St. Bernard, who made the court ruling to deny him of his franchise, thus rendering him ineligible for a seat in the Legislative Council (the precursor of the House of Representatives). However, with the passage of time he recommended the same judge for the insignia of Commander of the Most Excellent Order of the British Empire (CBE), which the latter politely but firmly declined. Justice St. Bernard, a master at the Grenada Boys' Secondary School during my school-boy days, told me that he believed it was wrong for judges to accept honours on the recommendation of politicians. Yet Justice St. Bernard later acceded to Gairy's request to chair a function marking the opening of a Senior Citizens' home at Laborie, St. George's, on Sunday, December 24, 1978. By then Gairy's premiership was experiencing some hard knocks and it was a feather in his cap to secure the services of so respected and so erudite a retired judge. However, it was quite clear that the learned judge obliged out of a show of solidarity with the elderly people in his neighbourhood rather than out of any desire to enhance Gairy's egoistic tendencies. He clearly knew that Gairy would have sought to make capital of the fact that, by honouring the judge, he bore no ill-will towards him. It is even possible that Gairy would have used the honour to remind the judge and the Grenadian population that he was truly the overlord of our dear little island.

Ever since he was exiled from Aruba in 1950 and returned to his native Grenada, Gairy set out to realize his ambition of making himself a leader of the people. Articulate, smartly dressed, endowed with a powerful memory and a sound understanding of the psyche of the Grenadian people, particularly the agricultural workers, he found that agricultural wages were abysmally low and working conditions awfully stifling. Social mobility for agricultural workers was effectively blocked while the plantocracy enjoyed a standard of living that generally speaking they did not merit on grounds of either good labour relations or industriousness, let alone vision. They unashamedly lived off the fat of the land, depending heavily on the toil and sweat of the labourers whose low wages were deliberately kept at an indecent level.

Born and bred in a rural community, Gairy was well fortified with a profound knowledge of the plight of the agricultural workers. His formal education did not go beyond the all-age primary school. Although many of his adversaries, who were not as richly endowed with common sense, took a delight in reminding him of his educational limitations, it is instructive to note that one of Grenada's outstanding sons, Theophilous Albert Marryshow, Father of West Indian Federation and one of Grenada's best orators of all times, never had the experience of a secondary education. Indeed, many successful Grenadian men and women, whether in business or the profession, never had the privilege, the opportunity or the means to pursue a course of studies at the secondary-school level. But Gairy was an avid reader who continued to educate himself in the hard school of life and became quite capable of holding his own among men and women of proven intellectual ability. He always boasted of a sermon he delivered at the age of twelve while serving as an acolyte in the Roman Catholic church. He was specially chosen by his parish priest to do this assignment. "After mass that Sunday the priest highly commended me," he would so often recall. He became a primary school teacher before migrating to Aruba where in a short time he was flirting with trade unionism and trying to organize workers, much to the annoyance of the authorities. The Aruban authorities were glad to see the back of him in 1950. He was an ardent disciple of the Rosicrucian Order, always feeding his mind on the voluminous literature coming out of that organization. His skilful manipulation of people – his supporters as well as his detractors – gave the impression that he was a well-trained psychologist, and the way he was able to sway his listening crowd seemed to indicate that he was second to none in the art of crowd psychology. Suffice it to say he had no such training. He knew his people intuitively. Somehow he clearly understood their needs, their hopes and their fears and he seemed to know how to deal with them. He was a forceful and effective communicator.

It was not without significance that Gairy targeted the sugar estates of the southern part of the island to start his labour movement. Sugar was king in the West Indies in the 17$^{th}$ century, and sugar still held vestiges of its regal pomp in Grenada in 1950, not so much for its contribution to the overall economy of the country but rather in terms of the archaic operations in the cane belt and the meagre, almost non-existent, benefits accruing to workers. In a sense, too, the exploitation of workers still present in the sugar industry reflected the economic exploitation and social stratification that existed on the island from the days of slavery. This system Gairy was determined to overturn. The trade union fervour of the sugar workers so well ignited by Eric Gairy spread like wildfire to workers on other estates throughout Grenada. The hapless workers embroiled in a morass of social discontent, suffering from chronic impecuniosity and virtually imprisoned within a cocoon of increasing economic deprivation, woke up under Gairy's charismatic and dynamic leadership and released their pent-up energies which erupted like a volcano. Spared the labour disturbances that neighbouring St. Vincent, St. Lucia, Barbados and Trinidad had experienced in the 1930's, Grenada was therefore ripe for the type of labour agitation that Gairy initiated. Trade Unionism, though started in the 1920's, had remained somewhat limited while working class conditions deteriorated.

The road workers were in a similar plight with poor housing, inadequate clothing, improper nutrition, and low self-esteem. Equally aggrieved, they joined forces with the labourers on the estates. No amount of prompting from the Labour Commissioner could deviate the workers from their strike-bound path. The joint appeal by the heads of the four leading religious denominations – the Roman Catholics, Anglicans, Methodists and Presbyterians – to prevent the much-talked about island-wide strike was to no avail. As if to say that such an appeal was not Christ centred but rather promoted by members of the plantocracy, these suffering workers rejected it outright. After all, they were Christians too.

On Monday, February 19, 1951, a month-long island-wide strike of agricultural and road workers began, and three days later a state of emergency was declared by George Conrad Green, who was administering the affairs of Grenada in the absence of Sir Robert Arundell, the British Governor. The strike left behind it a trail of destruction – looting, burning of schools and other government buildings as well as private homes. There was also much damage to crops and estate buildings. Four persons were reportedly shot by the police.

Events took place with amazing rapidity, and mesmerized the members of the powerful plantocracy who always felt that Gairy could not succeed in calling an island-wide strike. Grenada was then a Colony of Great Britain and the era of gun-boat diplomacy was still very much in vogue. It was no surprise, therefore, that two battleships, the *H.M.S. Devonshire* and the *H.M.S. Snipe*, were quickly on the scene to bear evidence of imperial power and to restore law and order in this part of the far-flung Empire. Governor Arundell quickly returned to his headquarters in St. George's to take control of the affairs of the troubled colony. In addition, police were brought in from some of the neighbouring islands to augment the local constabulary, the allegiance and adequacy of whom were apparently questioned.

Gairy was arrested, and so was his chief lieutenant, Gascoigne Blaize, not to be confused with Herbert Augustus Blaize who later became Prime Minister of Grenada – a mistake that has crept into the writings of some of the instant foreign experts on Grenada and unfortunately repeated by some reputable institutions. Roberts, a young police officer from the St. Lucian constabulary, was the individual who arrested Gairy. By a cruel twist of fate, years later, the same Roberts was recruited into the Royal Grenada Police Force by the Herbert Blaize Administration, this time as Chief of Police. When Gairy assumed office after winning the general elections in August, 1967, he kept Roberts as Police Chief. Gairy grasped the earliest opportunity to remind Roberts of the 1951 arrest and to comment on qualities that Roberts had exhibited even then. "You arrested me in 1951. To be able to do so you must have had in you the makings of a first-class policeman. I am therefore retaining you as my Chief of Police."

It was in this manner that Premier Gairy greeted the Chief of Police at a meeting of Senior Civil Servants soon after the 1967 Elections. Gairy under arrest on the *H.M.S. Devonshire* was taken to the neighbouring island of Carriacou – then a dependency of Grenada, now an integral part of the sovereign state of Grenada. He was placed under guard at the Government Rest House at Top Hill and with a sense of humour and as if in a mood for celebration having made his maiden voyage on one of Her Majesty's ships, he had no hesitation in asking for his comforts of wine and women. Sadly for Gairy, it was neither practicable nor proper to grant his request. The looting and burning of property continued unabated and certain people were living or, perhaps more correctly, hiding in fear. Meanwhile a contingent of the Welsh Fusiliers landed in Grenada to maintain law and order.

Gairy's arrest did very little to lessen the confrontational zeal of the striking workers. On the contrary this aggravated the situation as the level of the workers' commitment and enthusiasm seemed to have risen even higher with the removal of their hero. Only Gairy could appeal to the good sense of the people. The state of emergency ended on March 5, the same day Governor Arundell returned to Grenada. Gairy was released from detention, returned to Grenada, and was requested by the Governor to make a broadcast appealing for calm. Indeed it was only when he spoke to the people on radio urging them to stop the burning and the looting that some semblance of order and safety was brought back to the island.

By any reckoning a social revolution had begun. Existing relationships on the estates would never be the same again. The workers would no longer be subservient; they would speak up for their rights and would seek better housing, proper clothing and a higher level of nutrition for themselves and their families. The task of reconciliation and reconstruction was not an easy one. The planters who were smarting under a false sense of security never imagined that Gairy, whom they regarded as nothing but an upstart, could bring Grenada to a standstill. They were shocked and they panicked. In meetings with the Governor they referred to Gairy as communist, a standard tactic used in other islands to discredit labour leaders from at least 1920 onwards, and, as they were wont to do in such circumstances, they lay all the blame for the current upheaval at Gairy's feet. The plantocracy and their representatives urged the Governor to act decisively and in a draconian manner against Gairy and his minions. The Governor could not agree with their views and they in turn lost their composure and threatened to take the law into their own hands. Some of these planters could not face reality, and refused to examine themselves. Others could not, or did not, understand the causation of this social revolution with which they were suddenly faced and for which they were mainly responsible. Still others could not come to terms with having to abandon the luxurious life style that they had enjoyed at the expense of the toil and sweat of the poor labourers on the estates.

E. W. Balthrop, Labour Adviser to the British Secretary of State for the Colonies, was sent out by the British Government to mediate and report on the situation. Balthrop, like the Governor, did not agree with the sentiments expressed by the planters. The strike was settled by the offer of increased wages and better working conditions to the workers. There was a certain degree of dislocation on the estates and many of the estate owners and managers packed their bags and left the country to take up residence abroad. The workers became members of the newly-established Grenada Manual and Mental Workers' Union of which Gairy was President General. To the workers Gairy was their new-found messiah who delivered them out of the depths of poverty and want and enabled them to acquire better clothing, food and shelter. All of a sudden, their self-esteem was inflated. The working class, particularly the agricultural workers on the estates, would never forget what their leader did for them in 1951, and they affectionately called him "Uncle" – a name from which he gradually shied away as he grew in stature politically and socially.

For Gairy the island-wide strike was a total success. Brimming with confidence, he entered the political arena with the launching of his Grenada People's Party, later to be called the Grenada United Labour Party (GULP). This evidently was his ultimate ambition. His GULP was destined to be a force to be reckoned with for a long time. Like a high priest, adorned in a white cape, he would start his political meetings with prayers and hymn singing before pontificating to the massive crowds. The artificial barriers between the plantocracy and the rest of the country began to weaken. As windows of educational opportunities were flung open, an increasing number of children of agricultural workers began to rub shoulders at the secondary-school level with children of middle-class parentage.

Gairy's contribution to the development of education has often been overlooked. It was during his premiership that I served as Chief Education Officer and I can vouch for his great interest in the education of the nation's children and his leadership role in increasing the number of free places in secondary schools, in the school-building programme, and in ensuring that opportunities for scholarships abroad were well publicized to attract eligible applicants. It was the Gairy administration that had taken the decision to introduce free secondary education at the beginning of the school year in September, 1979.

But perhaps his greatest legacy in the field of educational development was his pivotal role in the creation, encouragement and support of pre-primary schools. While in opposition in 1962–1967, Gairy went all over the country establishing these little one-room, one-teacher schools for children aged three to five. In many cases, he used his own resources to pay a small stipend to the teachers who though not qualified, displayed a high level of dedication and a deep sense of commitment. When Gairy regained power in 1967, he brought all these pre-primary schools under the umbrella of the Ministry of Education. The teachers were paid by government, and special training courses were organized for them. Early childhood education has since become an important element in Grenada's educational system.

The St. George's University School of Medicine, later to be transformed into a full-fledged university, the St. George's University, had a rough and difficult teething period in 1976 and for some years afterwards. The establishment of the university was the subject of widespread opposition, from professionals and intellectuals, from our own University of the West Indies, from our local doctors and from Gairy's political opponents. Amid all the opposition both locally and regionally, it was Eric Gairy who stood tall, and with unwavering resolve, piloted the bill through Parliament for the establishment of the university. He insisted that the university be located in Grenada and promised that government would do whatever it could to help it along. While all the caustic and illogical arguments were being leveled against the university, the early faculty members got down to serious work under the enlightened and scholarly guidance of Vice Chancellor, Dr. Geoffrey Bourne, well known and widely respected in academic circles, particularly in the United Kingdom, the U.S.A. and Australia. Today, the magnificent buildings at the True Blue campus replete with its cricket academy, the university's growing reputation for scholarship, and a student body representative of over fifty nationalities bear eloquent testimony to the vision of Prime Minister Gairy. He was right in defying his critics by allowing Chancellor Charles Modica to establish an institution of higher learning in Grenada.

As the years went by, Gairy's domineering style was more pronounced. Nevertheless, he was never forgiven in certain influential quarters for the confusion he had caused in Grenada in 1951. Sadly, he also grew in vindictiveness. He set up himself as the undisputed boss of the tri-island state of Grenada. He caused much distress to families by interfering with the working of the Civil Service, thus causing people to leave prematurely in disgust or blatantly having their services terminated.

By 1978 Prime Minister Gairy was behaving as if Grenada was his private estate and felt competent to interfere with every aspect of life in Grenada – governmental as well as non-governmental. He was in control of every ministry and gave orders direct to Civil Servants even at times bypassing heads of departments to reach subordinate officers. He, like the estate owners against whom he had earlier rebelled, was a man for luxurious living. He liked orderliness, but it must be according to his own whims and fancies. Although he insisted on correct protocol, yet he would attend a function and make changes to the carefully-arranged seating plan there and then if he did not want a certain individual to sit too close to him. His idiosyncracies were many. Some were laughable. When travelling abroad he would never depart or return on a Tuesday. He would not be driven in a red car. I can well remember when in my presence he upbraided his High Commissioner in London for meeting him at Heathrow Airport in a red Daimler, and he bluntly refused to be driven in it. Or he would ask for police escort in London as he did not wish to spend too much time on the road getting to his appointments. Every Grenadian knew that Gairy loved the spectacle of police outriders.

He was obsessed by the honorific system. At the constitutional conference in London in 1973, he sought a Knighthood by using veiled threats to withdraw Grenada from the Commonwealth if Her Majesty did not bestow the honour of Knighthood upon him. As it turned out, he was made a Knight Bachelor in 1977. But prior to that he used a string of letters behind his name indicating honorary degrees from institutions unheard of and unknown by Grenadians. His actions, as he so often claimed, were motivated by divine connection, if not by divine right.

When I assumed the office of Governor General, Gairy was 56 years old. I quickly discerned that he no longer possessed his former glory. A vociferous, potentially dangerous and politically active younger generation never heeded his oft-repeated ranting and raving. They wanted change and worked both clandestinely and openly towards that end. He appeared not to be as mentally alert as he once was, but Government was more and more centred around his personage. There was little initiative on the part of his Ministers, still less on the part of civil servants. They all waited on directives from the "big man" himself. Some of his most loyal and influential supporters were beginning to distance themselves from him. Those who continued to cling to him did so out of fear rather than out of admiration. Many of them did not want to become victims of his increasingly appalling vindictiveness. Others did not want their business concerns to be less profitable. Meanwhile, his own business ventures were flourishing. He had shares in Portofino Restaurant. He owned Hibiscus Inn, a small hotel. He also was the owner of Rock Gardens and Evening Palace, the former a guest house *cum* nightclub and the latter a nightclub. Among his assets, he also included the plantation house at Point Salines, as well as lands in the vicinity of the Golf Course in Woodlands. Evidently he had reached his pinnacle. But perched on his high pedestal, he did not and could not recognize that things were falling apart in the country. People were losing confidence and were getting restless. He had won the 1976 General Elections with a reduced majority. Cracks began to show in the body politic, and there were signs of instability.

It would appear that there were observers both in Grenada and outside closely monitoring political and other developments in the country. Very early in my tenure in office, I surmized that all was not well with state security, notwithstanding official advice to the contrary. My discernment was confirmed when on Thursday, November 9 – some five weeks after my inauguration – E. H. Jones, Senior Security Liaison Officer attached to the British High Commission, called on me to exchange views on the security of the State.

During the latter part of 1978, there were some rather strange, and, in some cases, inexplicable occurrences. The residence of the manager of Barclays Bank in the residential area of L'anse aux Epines was the target for homemade

Molotov cocktails. Irie Bishop, a policeman, went missing and was never found; there was on-going speculation over the fate of the four young men from Carriacou who went on a fishing expedition on one of the nearby islets. The Hon. Ben Joseph Jones suffered loss of his boucan by fire of an unknown origin, and in December of that year the town of Grenville was the scene of a massive conflagration when Nyack's business premises were razed to the ground. Meanwhile barrels of guns purporting to be barrels of grease were entering Grenada. One such barrel was intercepted and, instead of allowing the police to deal with this matter, Prime Minister Gairy thought he himself was competent enough to handle it . This, of course, proved futile.

If Gairy was losing sway in the country, he still doubtlessly held dominance in Cabinet as he was still able almost effortlessly to bamboozle his ministers into agreeing with him on any matter for which he sought approval. He never failed to make it abundantly clear by action or words that he was the undisputed leader, and to dispel any doubt he tried to convince everyone that he was sent by God. His latest craze was an obsession with unidentified flying objects (UFOs). He took time off to speak at length in the United Nations about UFOs and these mysterious objects featured prominently in the first Throne Speech I delivered – incidentally a speech that took forty-five minutes. He considered Cabinet supreme, and any casual observer of Grenadian parliamentary practice would easily discern that Cabinet was in the ascendancy, and it was the dictates of Cabinet rather than parliamentary approval mattered. Many Cabinet matters that should have been properly debated in Parliament were implemented without any recourse to parliamentary scrutiny.

As Governor General I took an oath to protect and preserve the Constitution of Grenada. Fully cognizant from past experience of Gairy's *modus operandi* in Cabinet, I was very watchful of any move intended to place Cabinet conclusions over the supremacy of the Constitution. On January 12, 1979, an instrument for the appointment of an acting Chairman of the Public Service Commission was placed before me. The instrument originated in the office of the Attorney General. After carefully perusing the document, I felt unable to approve it as the person recommended to act as Chairman was not a member of the Commission. I immediately sought advice from the acting Attorney General and wrote to him *inter alia*:

"a) What is my authority to appoint an Acting Chairman of the Public Service Commission under subsection (1) (a) of Section 83 of the Grenada Constitution Order 1973?

b) Bearing in mind subsections (9) and (10) of section 83 of the Grenada Constitution Order, do I have the authority to appoint as Acting Chairman of the

Public Service Commission a person who is not at present a member of the said Commission?

Would you also be good enough as to advise me whether an acting member of the P.S.C. can be appointed to act as Chairman?"

Meanwhile my office staff pointed out to me that there was precedence for such an appointment, and they placed before me the file that clearly told the story. Some days earlier I had granted the incumbent Chairman leave of absence for a visit abroad. The Commission was due to meet early the following week. Thus the acting appointment was seemingly a matter of urgency. Indeed the same Claude Morrison now recommended for an acting appointment was appointed previously in similar circumstances on more than one occasion. While I agreed that there was precedence for appointing Morrison acting Chairman, I could not defend something that I believed to be wrong. I felt certain that my interpretation of the Constitution was correct. This was confirmed when the acting Attorney General promptly replied in the following terms:

"My opinion on the strict interpretation of Section 83 of the Grenada Constitution Order 1973 is as follows:-

a) Section 83 (1) (a) contemplated the situation where the Governor-General is constituting the Commission and has nothing to do with acting appointments. As such there is no authority to make an acting appointment under this Sub-section.

It is clear that the appointment of someone who is not an existing member of the Commission to act as Chairman where the office of Chairman was not vacant etc. was not contemplated by the framers of the Constitution. Until the existing Chairman or person holding that office has resumed those functions as the case may be, they shall be exercised by such one of the other members of the Commission as may for the time being be designated in that behalf by the Governor-General, acting on the advice of the Prime Minister.

As to whether an acting member of the Public Service Commission can be appointed to act as Chairman, my opinion is that such a procedure was not also contemplated by the framers of the Constitution due to the provisions of Sub-sections (9) and (10) of Section 83. Any appointment of an acting member to act as Chairman would be manifestly repugnant to the intention of Sub-section 9 of Section 83 of the Constitution."

The acting Attorney General in this instance was a public officer, not a politician. His advice was quite clear and, in my estimation, was in keeping with the provisions of the Constitution. Yet I could never understand why he sent such a document to me for signature. Be that as it may, the meeting of the Public Service Commission could not be held as scheduled. I learnt later that at its weekly meeting, Cabinet had been engrossed in considering the matter of Claude Morrison's appointment as acting Chairman of the Public Service Commission. The Attorney General was called into Cabinet for these deliberations. I have always been curious to know what advice, if any, the Attorney General could have given to Cabinet. Was his advice to Cabinet at variance with the advice he gave me? Or did he proffer similar advice? Whatever happened in the Cabinet room, Sir Eric and his Cabinet obviously had their way. For close on the heels of this meeting, I was sent a recommendation that Morrison be appointed to act as a member of the Public Service Commission.

I immediately approved the recommendation. Twenty-four hours later I received a further document from the Attorney General, this time an instrument for Morrison to act as Chairman of the Commission. Whatever the latest legal advice might be, I still felt my interpretation of the provisions of the Constitution in this regard was correct. However, guided by the advice of the chief legal officer, I reluctantly signed the instrument. This whole episode I thought was ominous and for the first time I began to entertain thoughts of curtailing my term of office. In my view the Constitution would always be sacrosanct and should never be sacrificed on the altar of political expediency. To so tamper with the Constitution is to strike at the very foundation of the State, and when Cabinet would go all out to bend the constitutional provisions in order to satisfy the whims and fancies of the Prime Minister, the integrity of the body politic must be called into question. The Constitution is the supreme law and must prevail over any other law in the country, let alone Cabinet conclusions.

Parliament under the Westminster model is that it is this august body which accommodates divergence of opinion, respects the voice of dissent, and listens to the views of the people as presented by their representatives. It is the forum for the staging of many a verbal battle all in the name of the people of the State. Men and women who make up this honourable band of lawmakers are supposedly citizens of dignity, honour and trust. Through debates and questions they protect the national interest, uphold the rule of law, and keep the government on their toes. Dignity and decorum in Parliament must be of the highest order. Respect for one another and especially respect for the presiding officer must be without question. Parliament has its own rules regulating its procedure and the presiding officer is the guardian of those rules, applying them as circumstances demand. In Parliament the presiding officer is in control, not the Prime Minster who like any other member is subject to discipline from the Chair. Parliamentary practice in Grenada has its origin in the old House of Representatives that cowardly surrendered itself in 1877 to give way to Crown Colony government.

It is against this backdrop that I took a hard look at the working of Parliament in Grenada during my first five months in office. The Parliament of Grenada is replete with all the ceremonial trappings associated with the Westminster model. The mace carried into the Chamber by the Sergeant-at-Arms is the symbol of authority. The Speaker and the President are fully regaled as if they are presiding in the palace of Westminster, and even the clerk of Parliament resplendently enrobed in wig and gown failed not to outdo the lawyers themselves who have long since abandoned their wigs. All these and more are all part of the mystique of the parliamentary establishment. In my first five months in office, Parliament met three times. Two of the three meetings were joint meetings, one on the occasion of my inauguration and the other marked the start of a new parliamentary session. So in point of fact there was only one " business" meeting between October, 1978 and March, 1979.

The infrequent meetings of Parliament were a source of discontent, not least among the members of the Opposition. Although according to the parliamentary rules, Parliament must meet at least once a month, this was manifested more in the breach than in the observance. No wonder why many plans were put in train without parliamentary debate or sanction. Meanwhile, Cabinet progressively inched its way in the pecking order to gain supremacy over Parliament and, sadly, there was a growing perception, certainly among members of the ruling party, that once Cabinet took a decision, it was not necessary to take the matter to Parliament. With an egoistic leader, the Cabinet was becoming more and more powerful, blocking the opportunity for the people's voices to be heard through their elected representatives. Cabinet dictatorship was on the ascendancy while Parliament seemingly bore a closer affinity to a social club which was disorganized and with no clear objectives.

On the rare occasions when Parliament did meet, there were frequent complaints about agenda papers getting to members late, with little or no time to study them. Additionally, the Opposition constantly complained that such actions stifled debate and reduced Parliament to a rubber stamp to give blanket approval to the decisions of the executive. In such a situation it is all too easy for members of Parliament not to study the order paper, comforted in the thought that their paramount duty is simply to vote for or against the measure before the House. The Government proposes and the Opposition opposes. Hon. Bernard Coard, Member for the town of St. George, aptly summed up the situation when at a meeting of the House of Representatives on July 14, 1978, he said *inter alia*:

"I just wanted to draw it to the attention of this Honourable House that every time we come to Parliament, nearly every single occasion, Bills are rushed through from the first reading, second reading, committee stage, third reading, all in a matter of minutes all in the space of one day, frequently with the Opposition having got the bill 24 hours before, or 48 hours before, sometimes right here on the table. We have protested many times."

His observations, and the complaints of the opposition as a whole, were certainly on target.

Accountability for public expenditure was always a sore point under the Gairy administration. He had a penchant for unauthorized spending, and he would not be curbed. One would recall that the Grenada Constitution was suspended in 1961 because of Government's reckless spending and non-compliance with the financial rules and regulations. In any analysis of the functions of Parliament, accountability of public expenditure must stand high. Grenadians have a right to know how their taxes are spent; and expenditure of public funds is the one area that has to be jealously guarded by the representatives of the people. Therefore, in a democracy, structures must be in place to test the propriety of public spending. One such structure is the Public Accounts Committee that is made up of members of the House of Representatives who do not hold ministerial portfolios. Its function is to examine the annual audited accounts and to report to Parliament on the propriety or otherwise of moneys spent. The Committee may summon before it senior civil servants for questioning. At a meeting of the House of Representatives on September 8, 1978, almost two years after the 1976 general elections, Hon. Bernard Coard reiterated his call for the setting up of the Public Accounts Committee in these words:

"The Minister of Finance has failed in his duties to the Constitution and the Standing Rules of this House to set up as is required of him by a motion in Parliament the Public Accounts Committee. We therefore once more call again for its implementation as the Constitution requires that it be set up at the earliest possible opportunity after a general election."

Even a cursory glance at Hansard, the official record of parliamentary debates, would reveal that these Honourable men and women looked upon their attendance at Parliament as a pastime devoutly to be observed with pomp and ceremony rather than a serious obligation which entailed prior preparation for logical and well reasoned debate. They were obviously overwhelmed by the dictatorial tendencies of Gairy as they failed to discharge effectively their bounden duty of looking after the people's business in Parliament. In fact, debate was often a purposeless and quarrelsome clash of words between the government and the opposition. Shrouded by party politics nearly every debate degenerated into accusations that one side was communist and the other was fascist. It was the communist bogey that was plaguing the benches on the government side. In Parliament there was a marked absence of back benchers. This was partly because the complement of the House of Representatives, fifteen all told, was small. But more significantly the Prime Minister seemed almost obligated to give a ministerial appointment to every party member who had been successful in the general elections. This was also a way of rewarding them financially. Thus, every ministry had either a Minister of State or a Parliamentary Secretary to assist the Minister who was in overall charge. In a sense, therefore, the House of Representatives became Cabinet enlarged. Similarly, the Senate was more often than not packed with unsuccessful candidates in the general elections through the good offices of both the Prime Minister and the Leader of the Opposition upon whose recommendations the Senators are appointed. Some of these Senators who failed to get the people's confidence in the elections were subsequently made Ministers, Ministers of State or Parliamentary Secretaries. In point of fact they were placed in positions of great influence after they had been rejected by the people. This was the ugly face of parliamentary democracy as practised in Grenada.

Amid the growing discontent in Parliament and the seething dissatisfaction in the country over the conduct of parliamentary business, Prime Minister Gairy found it necessary to use whatever political skills he could muster in order to regain the confidence of the people in the democratic process. Evidently people were losing faith in Parliament and parliamentarians were looked upon with scant regard. The alienation between people and Parliament was a cause of great concern to the Prime Minister. Gairy's answer was to bring Parliament to the people. He therefore devised a plan to move Parliament temporarily out of the confines of York House and place it in a more accessible area even for one day. What better occasion to do this than on the fifth anniversary of independence. And if the sitting of Parliament could be incorporated with some of the independence activities, so much the better as a captive audience would be ensured.

At the instance of the Prime Minister, it was agreed by Cabinet that the ceremonial opening of the third session of the second Parliament would take place at Queen's Park in St. George's on Wednesday, February 7, 1979, beginning at 9.30 o'clock in the forenoon. I was accordingly advised and in turn issued the necessary proclamation. But more than that I was further advised that the sitting of Parliament would not be held in isolation. It would be an integral part of the programme of the fifth anniversary of independence with the accent on Parliament on the one hand and on children's participation on the other hand. All this was to take place in the presence of dignitaries and representatives of all walks of life, including, of course, both resident and non-resident diplomats accredited to Grenada. For the first time, Parliament was to be held on the grounds of the premier playing field of Grenada and on a bank holiday. Sir Eric always boasted of the many firsts for Grenada under his premiership. For example, during his term in office there was the appointment of Hilda Bynoe as the first Lady Governor in the Caribbean, the winning of the Miss World contest by a Grenadian, Jennifer Hosten, the holding of the first Carifta Expo in the island, and now the moving of Parliament to Queen's Park so that thousands of Grenadians might witness the proceedings. One wondered what or who would be the causation of the next first.

A week-long Agricultural Exhibition and Trade Fair was opened by me on February 6. As dawn broke on Wednesday, February 7, 1979, Queen's Park was already humming with activity according to reports from my aide-de-camp who had made an early morning reconnaissance journey to the temporary parliamentary site. Finishing touches were being put to the preparations for what promised to be a grand extravaganza of pomp and ceremony, a grand display of patriotism and an unusual togetherness of the various political factions. Such was the level of Sir Eric's expectations. People from all parts of Grenada soon began converging on Queen's Park despite the torrid heat of the morning sun that seemed not to have flagged either their curiosity or enthusiasm. As usual on occasions like this the school children were overly excited, and oblivious of the possibility of fainting in the blazing sun.

The day's proceedings began with a short ecumenical service. After this I returned to Governor General's House to change into clothing more appropriate for Parliament where I was to read the traditional Throne Speech – my first since assuming office. The Throne Speech is prepared by the Government of the day, and it simply outlines the Government's programme for the ensuing year, including the main legislative measures to be placed before Parliament. A Throne Speech should be precise, clear and to the point. This speech, however, was not. In addition to an opinion on the significance of unidentified flying objects (UFOs), there was also included a litany of the achievements of the Government over the years. The speech was not clear as to what measures Government intended to place before Parliament in the year ahead.

While this historic and unique sitting of Parliament was taking place, hundreds of school children stood in deep silence and, resplendent in their school uniforms, waited patiently and devotedly to play their own part in the morning's proceedings. But as time went by the blazing sun poured forth more and more heat, thus causing dozens of youngsters to faint. The Prime Minister had to seek a brief adjournment and ordered the restless children to find shelter wherever they could in the environs of the pavilion. That was the end of the school children's rally. A reception on the grounds of Governor General's House and later a state dinner hosted by me brought the curtain down on the day's celebration.

To ensure greater people's participation, rallies and other activities were held in each of the parishes and in Carriacou and Petit Martinique. All these rallies were well attended. So too was the Military Parade which was splendidly executed on the Tanteen playing field and which drew loud applause and generous commendation from visiting diplomats and other dignitaries. The members of Her Majesty's Opposition took no part in the celebrations and were conspicuous by their absence from the joint sitting of the Houses of Parliament at Queen's Park. Some days later both Herbert Blaize and Bernard Coard apologized in person to me, categorically stating that their absence was not intended either to insult or offend me. It was felt in some quarters that Gairy was making Parliament a political football and Herbert Blaize, once an outstanding athlete and an upholder of parliamentary principles, would not be tempted to participate in this ball game.

There were varying views as to the merits and demerits of taking Parliament to Queen's Park. Some thought that having a parliamentary sitting at Queen's Park was to debase the great institution of Parliament. Others were of the view that it was just another of Sir Eric's political ploys to recapture some of his support, while still others in solidarity with the Prime Minister felt it was a courageous initiative. No doubt Sir Eric himself believed that he was inspired by God to do this. I, for one, thought that it was the quintessence of parliamentary mockery. Nevertheless, most of the visiting diplomats felt that Gairy was still a formidable force to reckon with, and his support in the country was still very strong. Many of them quietly expressed this view not out of politeness but because of what they had seen during the celebrations. If one were to judge by the massive spectator interest in the celebrations throughout the country, one was bound to conclude that Sir Eric was well-entrenched as Prime Minister and he and his Ministers had nothing to fear.

# 4

## *Another First*

I was already awake when my bedside telephone rang at half past five on the morning of Tuesday, March 13, 1979. The chirping of the birds and the rustling of the leaves outside my bedroom window seemed to have stopped momentarily in due deference to this unusual early morning call. "Good morning, Your Excellency. Corporal Scott speaking. Your Excellency, you have a new Government. The elected Government has been overthrown by Maurice Bishop and his New Jewel Movement. Nearly all the police stations have surrendered and the Commissioner of Police has left for his home." In a well-measured and deliberate tone, Corporal Scott spoke without any semblance of emotion. I thanked him in equal measure. Scott was in fact delivering a message from Osbert James, Police Commissioner, who had abandoned his post and then driven to my residence to inform me of the existing state of affairs in the country. In his anxiety to get to his home in Mamma Cannes, some twenty miles away, and because he was hesitant to disturb me so early in the morning, Commissioner James decided to beat a hasty retreat to the safety of his home, leaving Scott, one of my orderlies, to pass on the startling news.

I was totally nonplussed and my initial reaction was one of disbelief. Although I had recent intelligence that all was not well with state security and that there was growing dissension and dissatisfaction within the Police Force, yet I could not conceive of the idea that any group of men or women, small and ill-equipped, could so easily seize control of a country. The vulnerability of Grenada in terms of security was no longer in doubt, and the efficacy of political independence for small island states was at once called into question. Our democratic way of life at one fell swoop came in for a rude awakening, if not a smashing defeat. Then I remembered John Chadwick's prophetic words to me some six months earlier when he warned me that amid the ever-growing political turmoil and rising social discontent in so many former colonies, I should be prepared for a coup. Grenadians, who had been accustomed for years to change their governments peacefully by use of the ballot box, woke up on the morning of March 13 to hear that their democratically elected government suffered a demise at the hands of a few rebellious young men and a new government established by force of arms. "The dictatorship of Eric Gairy has been overthrown and a new revolutionary government is in control." These were the words that greeted me when I turned on my radio only to be reiterated joyfully by the revolutionary voices as they beamed their sensational message to audiences far and near.

As news of the coup came to hand, I showed no sign of emotion but remained absolutely calm. My wife and I said our morning prayers as usual. Then I began to receive telephone calls with all sorts of unsolicited advice. Prime Minister Gairy had left for the United States of America the previous day with Senator Wellington Friday, Minister for Education, and Miss Gloria Payne, the Acting Cabinet Secretary. Sir Eric had never disclosed to me the purpose of his visit, but I learnt from the Acting Cabinet Secretary that he was looking forward while in America to holding discussions with Mrs Andrew Young, Chairperson of the International Year of the Child Commission. As previously arranged, Sir Eric held discussions with the American Ambassador Frank Ortiz in the VIP lounge at the Grantley Adams Airport in Barbados. Ortiz took the opportunity to introduce to Sir Eric two FBI agents who were on their way to Grenada to assist with investigations into the importation of illicit firearms from the United States of America. These two men landed in Grenada and at once started their investigations, but with the turn of events on the following day, they quickly packed their bags and left the island.

Soon after the departure of Sir Eric and his advisers, I received the Hon. Herbert Preudhomme who took the oaths of allegiance and of office before me to fulfil the functions of Prime Minister during the latter's absence. I took the opportunity to discuss the security of the country with Mr Preudhomme who was overly confident that all was well and that measures were in place to deal with any disturbance that might occur. "Your Excellency, we have those boys well covered. They cannot try anything funny" – a clear reference to the New Jewel Movement which was formed in March, 1973, as a result of a merger of JEWEL (Joint Endeavour for Welfare, Education and Liberation) and MAP (Movement for Assemblies of the Peoples). JEWEL had been founded in March, 1972, and six months later MAP was organized. This was to be my last conversation with Herbert Preudhomme for another four years.

Among the first to be taken into custody on that historic morning was Preudhomme himself. Unhappily for him, his telephone was immediately disconnected and the revolutionaries were cunning enough to commandeer his number, thus placing themselves at a vantage point to receive any calls meant for Preudhomme. The rapidity with which the telephone numbers of Cabinet were transferred to those who seized power was a clear manifestation of the high level of support and loyalty that Bishop and the New Jewel Movement enjoyed at the telephone company. Senator Derek Knight, a clever and experienced lawyer and politician, telephoned me to suggest that I declare a state of emergency. I in turn sought his advice as to the enforcement of a state of emergency when nearly all our police had already "surrendered" to the new leaders. I told Senator Knight that it was both pointless and dangerous – exceedingly dangerous – to declare a state of emergency and that I was not prepared to do so. I called George Hosten, Minister for Finance, and a close personal friend whom I considered the most level-headed Cabinet Minister. Hosten was resigned to the fact that the Gairy administration was truly toppled and nothing could be done to reverse it. By mid morning, the coup leaders had almost the whole Cabinet arrested. One notable exception was Senator Derek Knight QC, a seasoned campaigner, and another was Senator Henry Bullen, young and in-experienced. When Senator Knight called a second time, he too concluded that all was lost and there was nothing he could usefully do but to leave the island immediately. He further told me that he and Senator Bullen were about to leave the island by boat and he rang to say farewell. I wished them well as these two brave men set out on a fishing boat for the little island of Union, one of the St. Vincent Grenadines. Once they landed on Union Island, they could very easily move on to mainland St. Vincent and from there further afield. Their escape was obviously well planned and well executed with the help of friends in St. Vincent.

The army headquarters in True Blue was attacked and seized and almost simultaneously the Radio Station in Morne Rouge – both places were south of the capital, St. George's.

I pondered over the lovely phrases about our new democracy and freedom which were coming from the lips of our revolutionary leaders out of Radio Grenada, now firmly in their hands and renamed Radio Free Grenada. I could not help feeling that all this was a smokescreen for an ideological change that was already firmly entrenched. All the verbiage smacked of classical communist propaganda, and I firmly believed that our new leaders as well as their younger followers were well schooled in the communist philosophy and practice long before this fateful day.

A telephone call confirmed that the coup was not entirely bloodless as was first rumoured. Two people had lost their lives. One was Lieutenant Brizan who had left his home in Perdmontemps about six miles away for the army headquarters shortly after he had heard that there was unrest in the

True Blue barracks. Another victim was Constable Pysadee of the Fire Department who was shot in the line of duty. News also reached me that Assistant Superintendent Raymond and Inspector Desousa who had held on at Police Headquarters for some hours after the Commissioner of Police had abandoned his position had at last surrendered to the revolutionary forces.

As to whether or not Commissioner James had acted irresponsibly by abandoning his post is debatable. Here is a man who is suddenly faced with a novel and rather unique situation. He does not know where to turn. He cannot speak to the Prime Minister who is not at home, his support staff has vanished, and his police stations in domino fashion are surrendering one after another. One could well imagine the consternation and panic at the various police stations around the country – some of them with contingents as small as three or four – when confronted by groups of armed, trigger-happy youngsters zooming with exuberance and confidence and ordering the dejected policemen to put up a white flag as a sign of surrender. James, however, simply delayed his arrest when he hastened to his country residence.

The ease and rapidity with which the New Jewel Movement captured the Army Headquarters was incredible and raised more questions than answers. When hardly more than a score of young men, ill-equipped and untrained for any warlike engagement, swooped down on the army barracks, they met little or no resistance from the men in green. Green was the colour of the army uniform and the men acquired the sobriquet "green beasts." Information reaching me indicated that in less than half an hour, the army capitulated and the buildings were set ablaze. This swift action must have pleasantly surprised Maurice Bishop who reportedly had been somewhat cautious in sanctioning the attack. Bearing in mind the consequences of possible failure, he had justifiable reservations. For Coard and Austin it was then or never and their views tilted the balance of opinion to take the plunge without further delay. So they did, with Austin in the vanguard.

Prime Minister Gairy, whose portfolio included responsibility for national security, had directed that warrants be issued for the arrest of the hierarchy of the New Jewel Movement during the weekend preceding the coup. However, word to that effect reached the leadership of the group who forthwith went into hiding. It was also reported that on the day before the departure of Gairy for the U.S.A. someone with a ham radio intercepted a broadcast that stated "all towns being searched. Assistance requested." The reply was "Help arriving soon by" ... followed by three names which appeared to be Spanish. It was not clear whether they were names of boats or of individuals. This no doubt gave rise to the speculation that there was a

Cuban boat in Grenadian waters standing by to take away the leaders in case the coup had failed. The question arises as to the state of preparedness of the army in a situation when it was generally known that guns were being smuggled into Grenada in barrels purporting to be barrels of grease and when the New Jewel Movement were intensifying their efforts with a view to taking over the Government by force. They made no secret of that. Were the upper echelons of the army so naive that they had no intelligence of what was happening among the New Jewel Movement, particularly during the days of the 10th to the 12th of March? Were the top brass of the army happy about the loyalty and devotion of their men? Or were they so frustrated that they had virtually abandoned all control? Curiously some days before the coup, most of the ammunition had been moved from the army headquarters to the police headquarters in Fort George. What a strange and untimely occurrence! The reason for this movement of arms has never been made clear. As to whether the removal of the arms was a directive from the political directorate or whether it was done on the initiative of the senior army officers is open to conjecture. But the fact remains that ranks in headquarters on that fateful morning could not adequately defend themselves as they had the barest minimum of arms and ammunition. But what was even more bizarre was that earlier that night there was a drinks party in camp when the men were properly plied with intoxicating beverages. I have never been able to ascertain beyond a doubt what was the *cause célèbre* for such extravagant merriment and who was responsible for paying the bill.

On the very morning of the coup, my ADC who was an army captain observed some of his ranks in revolutionary uniform on duty in the city centre. He actually spoke to some of them. It would appear that Bishop and his associates were able to implant spies and sympathizers for the New Jewel Movement into the military in late 1978 and early 1979. From Bishop's point of view, this was obviously an extremely good strategy. These spies were used to find out the number and types of weapons, quantities of ammunition, exact strength, periods of greatest vulnerability, number of soldiers remaining in camp at night and the whereabouts of the soldiers generally. Bishop and his men even tried to infiltrate the senior echelons of the army and perhaps partly succeeded. My own ADC was approached on three occasions to join the movement, the last time being three days before the revolution by a leading member of the New Jewel Movement who tried hard to persuade him to join in the struggle. In similar manner, Bishop and his comrades were able to recruit persons from key establishments and institutions for membership in the New Jewel Movement.

From all reports army discipline was abysmally low even in normal circumstances. There were a few energetic and intelligent young men at the officer level, but their hands were tied as political dictates constituted the determining factor when it came to managing the affairs of the army. The ranks, on the other hand, left much to be desired in terms of loyalty, devotion to duty and intelligence. Deplorable was the manner in which recruits were drafted. All that was required was for a prospective recruit to go to one of the Ministers of Government or top party official and indicate a desire to be a member of the military and he was then forwarded to army headquarters at True Blue. "Sometimes a call from Mt. Royal (the Prime Minister's official residence) or even a call from Tita, the caterer for meals for the army, would suffice. Very little screening could have been done. Referral took precedence over vigorous testing and thorough investigation of the applicant's background," said one senior army officer.

Soon after their mission was accomplished at army headquarters, the rebels almost effortlessly captured Radio Grenada which they immediately renamed Radio Free Grenada and indeed this was to be their headquarters for the next three days. It was from there at precisely 10.30 o'clock that morning, Maurice Bishop, the revolutionary leader, made his first national broadcast. He made a rallying call for unity. He further appealed to Grenadians for their support, assured supporters of the former Gairy Government of their safety as long as they did not resist the new Government violently, and issued some broad policy statements:

*"All democratic freedoms, including freedom of elections, religious and political opinion will be fully restored to the people; personal safety and property of individuals will be protected; foreign residents are quite safe and are welcome to remain in Grenada and we look forward to continuing friendly relations with those countries with whom we now have relations."*

These were the assurances of Maurice Bishop and he went on to state the purpose of the revolution in these words:

*"People of Grenada, this revolution is for work, for food, for decent housing, and for health services; for a bright future for our children and grand children. The benefit of the revolution will be given to everyone regardless of political opinion or which political party they support.*

He ended this historic speech thus:

*"Long live the people of Grenada! Long live freedom and democracy! Let us together build a just Grenada!"*

Fine words, but after listening to the speech I at once began to question the sincerity of the man, and for the rest of the day one question was firmly implanted in my mind. Will he keep those promises? In my first three months in office, I was able to bring myself up-to-date on the activities of the New Jewel Movement and to familiarize myself with some of the literature they had produced in recent years, not the least of which was their 1973 manifesto which had all the ingredients of communist philosophy and practice. True to form, the manifesto was characteristically a document that was anti-imperialist, anti-capitalist and anti-Gairy. It called for genuine independence, self-reliance and agrarian reform. It advocated the national-ization of banks, insurance companies, foreign-owned hotels and foreign-owned housing development projects. Existing political institutions were to be replaced by people's assemblies which would send delegates to a National Assembly, and that Assembly would become the main legislative and executive institution. It was my understanding that the manifesto was written in the main by Bishop, Unison Whiteman and George Brizan with an input by Bernard Coard to whom the draft was sent for review. This was verified when I consulted one of the authors of the manifesto. Shortly afterwards, George Brizan ceased to be associated with the New Jewel Movement. Any allegation that the members of the New Jewel Movement were a bunch of communists was neither confirmed nor denied by Bishop and his revolutionary colleagues. Whether this accusation was pre-revolutionary or post-revolutionary, it evoked a response that was neither positive nor negative. Perhaps a casual listener would have thought that this well-articulated speech showed Bishop as a great believer in the democratic process and a champion of the freedoms inherent in this process. He made no mention of communism or even socialism. In the midst of an unusually perplexed situation which suddenly surrounded me, I fear I could not be a mere casual listener. I weighed his words carefully, and I was not convinced about his stated intentions.

The clock ticked on and neither Bishop nor any of his comrades from the revolutionary high command saw it fit to make any contact with me. Nor did I make any attempt to get in touch with them. I adopted a "wait and see" attitude. A number of people called enquiring about my personal welfare and reassuring me of their loyalty and support. Surprisingly, one man, who was obviously living in the past and could only see the Governor General in the role of a colonial administrator, in all seriousness wanted to know what plans I had for running the government. What a man! The revolutionary fervour seemed to have eluded his grasp. Members of my domestic staff expressed concern about their own future, and some of them who evidently did not take Bishop's words seriously began to wonder aloud what would become of Grenada. The clandestine operations and unbecoming behaviour of supporters of the New

Jewel Movement were well known to some of my police staff. In the years just prior to the revolution there was a more pronounced police presence at key buildings and installations, particularly at night as a precautionary measure against the throwing of incendiary devices.

Cautious indeed I was when my ADC just after 9 o'clock that evening knocked at my bedroom door to inform me that I had some unusual visitors. A convoy of vehicles carrying armed men and women pushed open the locked gates at both ends of the driveway, swarmed the grounds and surrounded the building as if in readiness for an assault. These gates were unprotected following the disintegration of the police force from whom my guards came. The only protection I had consisted of my ADC and one of his fellow army colleagues and trusted friend Lieutenant Charles George who from that morning, for his own safety, had come to take sanctuary in Governor General's House. Also on the premises were four of my Orderlies. Captain Campbell, my ADC with the help of Lieutenant George, acted very sensibly and bravely that evening to avoid what could easily have been a bloody shoot-out as some of these intruders were in a belligerent mood and one impatient guy from the time he entered the building threatened to shoot through to the floor upstairs with his AK47. While Captain Campbell was talking with the leader of the men, Lieutenant George quickly got all the police staff who were on the premises to sit in the foyer where they were visible. He made sure that they were unarmed.

Orders had been given by Ralph Thompson to pick me up and take me to the Radio Free Grenada in Morne Rouge in South St. George to meet with the High Command. I knew this was a polite way of saying to arrest the Governor General as Cabinet Ministers had already been "in protective custody" at the radio station. Ralph Thompson was a man of little consequence but an ardent and fearless supporter of the New Jewel Movement. I had never met him but sadly his name again surfaced three years later when he fell ill as a detainee in the Richmond Hill Prison and later died in the General Hospital much to the embarrassment of the People's Revolutionary Government, particularly the leader, Maurice Bishop, and the deputy leader, Bernard Coard. A man of unflinching loyalty prior to and during the first few months of the revolution, Ralph Thompson, like so many others, fell foul of the revolutionary leaders and was incarcerated as a counter revolutionary. On his dying bed, a despondent and disappointed man, he would welcome neither Bishop nor Coard who were nervously anxious to be at his bedside in the twilight hours of his life.

My ADC tried hard to reach Maurice Bishop at Radio Free Grenada to ascertain the veracity of those orders but with no success. In hindsight, perhaps, just as well for the occasion might have proven more eventful if the large contingent with their new found arms were told that their mission had been aborted. Although the Commander of the contingent agreed with the ADC that I should travel in my official car I told my ADC that I would rather not, and so I was driven in a vehicle belonging to the revolutionary forces with a stevedore nicknamed "Mary Boy Child" at the wheel. Before leaving Governor General's House I asked my wife to telephone our lawyer, Sir Denis Henry, and apprise him of my predicament.

Dressed in a grey suit with my rosary in my pocket and escorted by my ADC and two men armed with AK 47 rifles, I left for the journey which was noticeably much less than under normal circumstances when my own driver was at the wheel. Before leaving Governor General's House my attire provoked a remark from one of the revolutionaries: "How he dress up so!" It is my view that one must be on one's dignity in good times as well as in bad. On arrival at the Radio Station I was confronted by a fleet of cars all carefully parked with known Gairy supporters including Ministers of Government who were "in protective custody." Of these supporters I well remember young Anthony Cherman, a well-known Gairy supporter who shouted to the two men escorting me to the High Command upstairs, "You better be careful with the Governor General. Don't touch this man." The scene in the Radio Station reminded me of a busy sidewalk with people, people, everywhere, and these were just milling around as if in utter disarray. When Maurice Bishop saw me his face fell in astonishment. He was livid and wanted to know under whose instructions I was there. He apologized profusely, promised to call on me within a day or two and ordered that I be returned to my official residence immediately and he personally saw to it that I was put in a car for my return home – not the same vehicle in which I made the onward journey.

My arrest was a bit of an embarrassment for Bishop and understandably so, as I learnt later that Michael Manley of Jamaica and others had advised him not to touch the Governor General who should be left in post. Further, I know that Bishop asked journalist, Alister Hughes, not to report it either inside or outside Grenada. This whole episode should be treated as a non-event. If for me the ride to the Radio Station were unusually fast, as I recall it returning to Governor General's House was the ride of my life. I had never been driven so recklessly on the roads in Grenada and all I could do was to quietly surrender my life entirely to God and from the depths of my heart seek His grace and guidance for my safe return home.

The toppling of the Gairy administration evoked very little sympathy from Grenadians at home and abroad. Even a casual observer on the morning of the coup would agree that the ousting of Gairy brought joy to the hearts of most Grenadians. Amid the spontaneous rejoicing throughout Grenada on that historic day there were some who expressed regrets at the way the Government fell, but very few shed tears. Conscious of the fact that life must go on, most Grenadians including even some of Gairy's staunchest supporters breathed a sigh of relief. For some it was the end of victimization in the public service, for others it was the return of, or compensation for, lands and other property that were compulsorily acquired, and still for others it was the end of the too frequent calls on their diminishing resources for financial and other contributions. And for all it was a welcome break from the constant egoistic outpourings and the political gobbledygook from Radio Grenada which the Government monopolized and which Sir Eric considered as an essential piece of equipment for the furtherance of his overlordship on his beautiful estate of Grenada, the Isle of Spice.

Two days after the coup, Mr Bishop telephoned me. He advised me of his intention to suspend the Constitution. However, the Queen would remain as titular Head of State and he would like me to continue in the post of Governor General if it were agreeable to me. There would be no Parliament for the time being. Changes were also to be made in the judicial system, and he was contemplating the establishment of a Grenada High Court. On enquiry he informed me that all was well with those in protective custody. Conscious of the workload he had ahead of him, I extended to him my best wishes and assured him that I would endeavour to give of my best in the interest of the Grenadian people.

On that same day I made a nationwide broadcast in these words:

"Fellow Grenadians, Greetings. I am speaking to you from Governor General's House. You have been kept fully aware of the events of the past two days. As your Governor General I want to thank all of you who sent me good wishes for my personal welfare and well being and I want to let you know that I have been treated with every respect and courtesy, and I should like to congratulate all of you on the calm and peaceful manner with which you greeted this period of change. I want also to commend all those who have assumed the burden of ensuring that law and order is maintained.

It is my understanding and in fact I have been given the assurance that all those in custody are being treated with the greatest care and attention. I have also been given the assurance that there is absolutely no cause for alarm among our friends from abroad who have made their homes in our beautiful country.

At the earliest time and with the appropriate advice and cooperation I shall do everything possible to ensure that we have a working arrangement of which all Grenadians can be justly proud. Meanwhile, as representative of Her Majesty the

Queen, who is the constitutional Head of State, I shall continue to watch the situation.

I love my country and so do you and I want you to know that in any discussions about our future I shall see to it that the interests of the country and its people are paramount. Let us look to the future with confidence and hope. We shall move forward together. May God bless you all."

At his first Rally at Queen's Park a few days after the coup, Bishop announced to the massive crowd that he had got news that Sir Eric Gairy had resigned from office. The crowd went into a wild frenzy with clapping, dancing, singing and shouting when Bishop made the announcement. Earlier in the day in response to a personal enquiry from Bishop, I made it clear that I had received no such resignation from Sir Eric. The proceedings of the Rally were broadcast on radio and I listened with intense interest. The people's reaction to this announcement confirmed my view that the euphoria in the aftermath of the coup was not because of the *coup d'état* per se but because the coup effectively wiped out the Gairy regime. Enough was enough for Grenadians. Needless to say, regional media reports had triggered off Bishop's announcement.

Admittedly, on the morning of Tuesday, March 20, Hon. John Compton, Prime Minister of St. Lucia, called from the Holiday Inn in Antigua to inform me that Sir Eric had asked him to let me know that he had resigned as Prime Minister of Grenada and that confirmation would be reaching me within a few hours from Sir Eric through the good offices of the British High Commission in Port-of-Spain. It was expected that Sir Eric, who was then in New York, would use the facilities of the British Mission to convey the message to me. About half an hour later, Hon. Lester Bird of Antigua phoned me to confirm that Sir Eric had passed that message to Hon. John Compton. Mr Bird also advised me to apprise Mr Maurice Bishop of that development and promised that he (Bird) would get in touch with him. At lunchtime Hon. John Compton called again to enquire whether I had received any further word from Sir Eric. I replied in the negative. An enquiry also came from the secretariat of the West Indies Associated States (later renamed the OECS Secretariat). I did pass on the information to Mr Bishop in compliance with Mr Bird's request. Whatever facts the media might have had at their disposal, let it be clearly understood that I received no resignation from Sir Eric and I would have been surprised if one had reached me. Gairy never submitted a resignation but rather all along considered himself to be the Prime Minister in exile waiting with anxious expectation for the reversal of fortune which would enable him to resume his premiership.

It was manifestly clear that Bishop and his New Jewel Movement had been preparing to take over the government. They had carefully recruited supporters in key areas of employment in both the public and private sectors. If Deputy Prime Minister Herbert Preudhomme thought that the government had the New Jewel Movement covered, as he indicated to me the day before the coup, he was totally off the mark. But what was more he and his colleagues were not sufficiently clever enough to realize that they had been providing an umbrella for covering up subversive activities in the public service by either recalcitrant or ostensibly faithful civil servants whose main task was to expose the flanks of government day by day. Many of these were in very sensitive positions in the civil service. From day one of the coup, one of Sir Eric's police drivers was gleefully driving Maurice Bishop. He was rapidly promoted to the officer rank in the Police Force. One of Sir Eric's secretaries immediately jumped on the revolutionary bandwagon to become a top secretary in Bishop's office. Among those who immediately either joined the revolutionaries as army officers, became members of the government, or were given special assignments all in the cause of the revolution were teachers, bank clerks, civil servants and commercial clerks. In fact, many of these simply abandoned their jobs and joined "in the struggle." Policemen who had been supporters of the New Jewel Movement were singled out early for courses in Guyana and/or were promoted as officers. No wonder the top echelons of the Police Force, prior to the Revolution, had been constantly frustrated in their efforts to get evidence of criminal wrong doings once the New Jewel Movement was involved. Bishop and his men were always a step ahead of Gairy and his government as the former was furnished with information well in advance by cells of workers in almost every area of the Grenadian working population. The rapidity with which the Telephone and Electricity Services came to the aid of the revolutionaries on the morning of March 13 suggests that the New Jewel Movement had successfully infiltrated both departments. Throughout the revolutionary period Bishop and his men never loosened the grip on these two essential services.

Grenadians are religious and God-fearing people. The revolutionary leader knew this. He was well aware of the great influence the Church exerted on the lives of Grenadians. Therefore, an unofficial alliance with the Church, however tenuous or non-transparent, would be of immense help to Bishop and his followers. They therefore proceeded to exploit a situation in which the Church was beginning to speak out against the excesses of Gairy. What Bishop and his colleagues did was to have private meetings with individual members of the clergy and to cultivate friendships with many of them. This was made easy as many key supporters of the New Jewel Movement were also practising churchmen and women. Members of the youth arm of the Roman Catholic Church, in particular, who were for the most part New Jewel Movement supporters, were in the vanguard of church activities during the months leading up to the revolution. At best it was important that the church should appear to be on the side of the New Jewel Movement during the pre-revolutionary period and at worst they should refrain from criticizing the potential revolutionaries from the pulpit.

Maurice Bishop and others frequently held private talks with members of the clergy including the Roman Catholic Bishop, Monsignor Sydney Charles and the Vicar General, Monsignor Cyril LaMontagne. The Venerable Archdeacon of Grenada, Father Hoskins Huggins, had little love for Gairy, whom he thought was a tyrant. Gairy was fully aware of Archdeacon Huggins' opinion of him. I well remember how displeased Gairy was when I asked Archdeacon Huggins to say the grace at the State Banquet celebrating the Fifth Anniversary of Grenada's Independence six weeks before the revolution. At that time I had no knowledge that the love that these two Christian men had for each other was almost non-existent. The zeal of some of the younger clergymen was already propelled by the gale force winds of liberation theology which was sweeping across the Latin American countries.

While all these pre-revolutionary manipulations were taking place, Gairy continued to antagonize the clergy and actually threatened to deport certain members of the Dominican Order and others who were not demonstrative of their support for him. All this, of course, was very helpful to Bishop as he relentlessly tried to woo the clergy and the faithful. At the same time, that strong attachment which previously prevailed between the clergy and the working class supporters of Gairy was beginning to loosen. Some months after the revolution, Father Bernard Kadlec, the longest serving Roman Catholic priest on the island, told me that the older folk were most annoyed with the clergy whom they blamed for the fall of Gairy. People whom Fr. Bernard knew to be so gentle and kind over the years now refused to greet the priests as they once did and some of them displayed downright hostility.

It is no wonder, then, that the Church in Grenada did not speak out against the revolution on the morning of March 13, 1979, or indeed for months after. Maurice Bishop would certainly have been surprised if it were otherwise. The church seemed to have either temporarily made a diversion from the path of building God's Kingdom or, confused by the pre-revolutionary activities in Grenada, seemed to have placed new interpretation on sacred scriptures. It may also be that the church leaders, ignorant of the true import of communism, were completely outsmarted by Bishop and his colleagues. Whatever their reasons, they did not remain neutral and some of the clergy were supportive of the New Jewel Movement and went so far as to use the pulpit in an effort to gain the congregation's acceptance of the revolution. In my very presence, Father Austin Milner, preaching at the Blessed Sacrament Church in Grand Anse, St. George's, on the first Sunday after the coup sought to do just that. Others tried to justify the coup. Father Oliver Leavy, an Irish Keltigean priest, displayed great enthusiasm for the new government. So did Father Sean Doggett of the same Order. From the pulpit at the church in Gouyave, Fr. Leavy tried to impress upon his congregation that the revolution was not only necessary but also legitimate and justified. And as if to re-echo Maurice Bishop's slogan, "Forward ever, backward never," he quoted from the prophet Isaiah: "No need to recall the past, look to the future." Father Martin Simmons, a Dominican priest, had great admiration for Maurice Bishop and his work and gave his fullest support to the New Jewel Movement and subsequently to the People's Revolutionary Government. It was the same Father Martin who kept me as Governor General waiting for over half an hour in Munich during the revolutionary period on the occasion of the opening of the Munich Community Centre, a Roman Catholic project. He obviously allowed his commitment to the revolutionary leader to cloud his sense of protocol. When it became clear to me that I was kept waiting because Prime Minister Bishop who was expected to be present had not yet arrived, I gave the nod to my ADC. We took leave of Father Martin and then left the building before the function started to make our way back to St. George's. Within a fortnight of the revolution, Fr. Bernard Kadlec, who was then resident in Jamaica, wrote a congratulatory letter to Maurice Bishop stating *inter alia*: "It is a marvel how you succeeded in overthrowing Gairy's autocracy and reign of terror and bribery."

Grenadian Judy Williams, once in training to become a Roman Catholic nun, slowly but surely transformed Pope Paul's Camp, a Catholic Centre for youth activities, into a communist den. She too was a great supporter of Maurice Bishop. Another English Dominican priest, Father Gilbert Coxhead, mistaken in his belief that the New Jewel Movement really cared for the poor and the oppressed, allowed them to conduct weekly seminars at his Rectory prior to the revolution. While Bishop

Sydney Charles, Head of the Roman Catholic Church in Grenada, greeted the events of March 13 with cautious optimism, he was not unhappy that the coup had occurred. The Anglican Archbishop of the West Indies and Bishop of the Windward Islands, Grenadian-born Cuthbert Woodroffe, quite diplomatically and without emotion concluded that the *coup d'état* was "regrettable but inevitable." The Methodist Minister, an Englishman, was discreetly silent, but his Church was somewhat divided over the political upheaval. There were at least two lay preachers and the son of a very prominent Methodist who occupied leading positions in the revolution. The Presbyterian Church while adopting a strictly non-partisan posture would have been the last to shed any tears for Gairy, even with the most violent prodding.

Gairy always had some measure of support from individuals in the business community. The special favours meted out to businessmen by Gairy varied directly with the level of financial contribution donated to the Grenada United Labour Party over which Gairy was solely and fully in control. It was not unusual for Government to grant monopolies to certain businessmen for the importation of basic foods such as sugar or rice. This had always infuriated the New Jewel Movement. They were equally infuriated by the callous way in which certain people engaged in commercial activities were placed on Statutory Boards, and in some cases in very sensitive positions which gave them unfair advantage over other businessmen. However, the coup had the support of the Chamber of Commerce which is the official organ of the business community. Members saw the ousting of the Gairy government as an opportunity to build something new and different in the Caribbean. Similar sentiments were re-echoed by the Employers Federation who were also supportive of the overthrow.

Regionally the news of the *coup d'état* was received with little or no reaction from official quarters. John Compton, Prime Minister of St. Lucia, was demonstrably upset and boldly expressed his displeasure at this whimsical manner of uprooting a democratically elected government. But there was little else that he could do. Grenada was an independent sovereign state and no amount of pleading by any CARICOM leader could cause British warships to race to its shores to restore law and order as they did in 1951. This was a new ball game and gun-boat diplomacy was no longer appropriate or justifiable. Nor could it stand up to the test of legality in the absence of a request from the *de jure* authorities on the island. Eric Williams, the Prime Minister of Trinidad and Tobago, obviously did not like the turn of events in Grenada but kept a discreet silence and maintained an equally discreet distance. In fact, he directed his Ministers and senior officials to keep away as much as possible from the revolutionary leaders in Grenada. But Bishop had the tacit support of Michael Manley, the democratic socialist leader of Jamaica, and of Forbes Burnham, the socialist President of Guyana, both of whom were not sorry to see the back of Gairy and both of whom were willing and ready to provide any support within their power and resources whether in training, in the loan of personnel, or advice. Gairy's relationship with many of the CARICOM leaders was strained. Gairy felt that he was way above the leaders of the OECS in ability and political astuteness while most of the leaders of the East Caribbean Associated States resented his egoistic tendencies and the leaders of the larger Caribbean territories signed him off as a waste of time. His autocratic manner at home was well known in the region and his infrequent forays in the international area were in recent times greeted by derision and scorn. The only subject he could speak on with a certain modicum of conviction was UFOs (Unidentified Flying Objects). He clearly did not understand the ramifications of the changing global situation nor was he any longer capable of making any constructive contribution to the more serious debates on regional or global economic issues.

Many Grenadians abroad who had left home because they could no longer accept the leadership of Gairy were happy to learn that at last he was removed from office. However, one of the sad effects of the revolution was that Grenadian communities whether in the United Kingdom, in the U.S.A. or to a lesser extent in Canada became acutely polarized. Once the Revolution was accomplished the New Jewel Movement, support groups came to the fore and in London they virtually took over the office of the High Commission from the outset. This left deep chasms in the Grenadian communities abroad and did not enhance the furtherance of investment at home.

The removal of the democratically elected government of Grenada by force of arms was not prejudicial to Grenada's membership in the Commonwealth. After all, Commonwealth leaders could point to precedent in this regard. While the revolutionary leaders were quick to discard certain sections of the Constitution, they were nevertheless cunning enough to retain those parts which gave to the revolution a certain degree of respectability and which enhanced the cause of acceptability and stability. Her Majesty Queen Elizabeth II retained the title of titular Head of State and her representative, the Governor General, remained in place. Thus the government changed but the State remained the same. In the afternoon of March 22, I received the British High Commissioner who informed me that a statement issued in London earlier that day indicated that the British High Commissioner to Grenada would call formally on Mr Bishop and with that call normal relations between the new government of Grenada and the British Government would commence. The question of recognition did not arise as there was no change in the Head of State. The following morning, I received the American Ambassador, Frank Ortiz, who intimated to me that he was formally calling on Prime Minister Bishop as an indication that his government was ready and willing to carry on normal relations with the government of Grenada. Ortiz, however, was particularly concerned about the quick return to constitutional rule with the emphasis on very early general elections. Canadian High Commissioner, Allan Roger, was next in line. I received him three days later. He too informed me that he had had instructions from his government to call on Prime Minister Bishop and to tell him that the Canadian government was ready to do normal business with him on the understanding that general elections be held at the earliest possible time. Trinidad and Tobago, through its President Ellis Clarke, made it clear that what happened in Grenada constituted a mere change of government and not a change of State. Their relationship had always been with the State of Grenada and would continue on that basis.

Shridath Ramphal, Commonwealth Secretary General, left his London desk to make a hurried trip to the Caribbean for the purpose of making his own assessment on the situation in Grenada. Over lunch at my residence, Ramphal and I discussed the events of March 13 and more. He was satisfied that the coup was holding, but he expressed regrets that this unfortunate syndrome had reached the English-speaking Caribbean and predicted that the second coup would be much bloodier. He, however, emphasized that there was no question of Grenada being expelled from the Commonwealth and indeed Grenada could continue to take up its position in the Commonwealth Heads of Government meetings and could participate fully in the various Commonwealth activities. He also promised to do whatever he and his colleagues at the Secretariat could towards the enhancement of economic and social growth of Grenada by way of technical advice and training. The Secretary General felt that Grenada needed all the help it could get, and the countries giving aid should offer more than they normally do to ensure stability of the country and provide new avenues for employment. Impressed by the calm and quiet of the country, he felt that with the promises made by Bishop the future should be encouraging. He was returning to London with a shopping list given to him by Maurice Bishop and his colleagues.

I had kept Her Majesty informed of the *coup d'état*. At an audience on Friday, May 4, 1979, at Buckingham Palace, I gave the Queen an up-to-date report on affairs in Grenada. She invested me with the insignia of Knight Grand Cross of the Most Distinguished Order of St. Michael and St. George (GCMG), an honour conferred on me only five days before the *coup d'état*.

# 5

## Constitutional Monarchy in a Revolutionary State

CONSTITUTIONAL monarchy is as far removed from the accepted definition of a "revolutionary" regime as God is from the devil. But, in March, 1979, in a rare and unique set of circumstances, the system of government adopted by Grenada following independence in 1974 – parliamentary democracy associated with constitutional monarchy – was brusquely swept aside. I, as Her Majesty's Representative, was allowed to remain *in situ*, but with the scope of my responsibilities effectively reduced. No such condescension was accorded to Grenada's elected Parliament that was abruptly and unceremoniously abolished. Thereafter, having dealt with these two basic symbols of freedom and democracy, the new regime quickly imposed the kind of State controls and constraints redolent of the totalitarian regimes in Eastern Europe (at that time), in the Far East, and of course in Cuba. And so the people of Grenada became the unwitting recipients of the first revolutionary socialist regime in the English-speaking Caribbean

The situation in which I found myself was both anomalous and unprecedented in a Commonwealth country. Governors General are expected to carry out their responsibilities conscientiously, impartially and with dignity. In normal times it is a privilege and an honour to do so, but in these adverse circumstances in 1979 (and throughout the immediately ensuing years), a new dimension was added, that is, it became a sacred duty to maintain the standard to the extent that this was possible..

During those uncertain days of March, 1979, I was aware of the likely challenge I should have to face if I were to remain as Head of State. I was much less sure of my ability to meet it with the necessary degree of courage, diplomacy, and sheer intellectual stamina – having regard to the probable no-holds barred, political poker game that lay ahead and the fact that the new, cock-a-hoop regime held virtually all the cards. In retrospect it was fortunate that I was blissfully unaware of the odds stacked against me.

Having had no experience of either political in-fighting or gambling, I might well have concluded that there would be no constructive role for me to play and advised the Queen accordingly – coupling such advice with a request that, in the circumstances, I might be relieved of my appointment as Governor General.

In a highly charged atmosphere, with the situation around me changing at bewildering speed, I considered my position with objectivity. I could turn to no precedent in the Commonwealth, and there was no relevant corpus of thought to which I could refer. A decision had to be taken. I decided, not without some misgivings, to remain as Governor General and face whatever music the Peoples Revolutionary Government chose to play. There would be no question of seeking guidance or receiving advice from Buckingham Palace as to what course of action I should take when confronted with the peculiar problems that were bound to arise. The Government had changed, not the State. Governors General are expected to get on with the job. In the midst of adversity, they are not expected either to abandon their responsibility or to cringe under unusual stress. Instead they must use to the maximum effect their tact and diplomacy, and they must act with courage, commonsense and dignity. Therefore, I went no further than keeping Her Majesty informed. The Queen in turn showed great concern about my personal well-being and safety as well as the welfare of my family during this very trying period.

I have always believed that it is wrong to capitulate when faced with seemingly insuperable problems and particularly so for anyone in a position of authority. In my view, such a person is of little mettle and therefore someone who is unfit for leadership. In the situation in which I found myself, the issues (as distinct from the practicalities) seemed to be startlingly clear, that is, only the Government of Grenada had changed. The State itself continued to exist as before and whatever policies the new regime chose to follow, they would be unlikely to conform to the accepted principles of constitutional government and parliamentary democracy. In these circumstances, the preservation of as many symbols and institutions that reflected that way of life must be accorded the highest priority. The Office of Governor General was clearly one such institution and this pointed unequivocally to my remaining as Her Majesty's Representative. But there was no shortage of other views. Many people voiced the opinion that I should relinquish my office immediately. On this score, I received much unsolicited advice and admonition. Others advocated that, as was customary in a revolutionary situation, I should simply be removed from office. People of this latter persuasion may have been influenced by the fact that

Prime Minister Gairy had recommended my appointment as Governor General. They may also have had in mind that only by removing me could the People's Revolutionary Government make a clean break with the past. Another view expressed was that the Governor General's Residence should be converted into a National Museum. One newspaper, the *Trinidad Express*, in its editorial column expressed the view that I should be ashamed of myself for clinging on to office. On the other hand a columnist in a Barbados newspaper felt that I should use all the authority at my command and work with Maurice Bishop, the revolutionary leader, for a better quality of life for all Grenadians. I lost no sleep nor did I suffer any perturbation as a result of these varying opinions. Clearly my mind was made up and I was determined in my resolve to carry on whatever the consequences might be.

The small size of Grenada makes intelligence gathering somewhat easy. I, therefore, had no difficulty in ascertaining what others were saying or thinking about the office I held. This divergence of opinion concerning the office of Governor General and its future reflected the absence of conformity in political thought and action among the people, their attitude towards the monarchy, and the seemingly profound loyalty which at the outset Bishop received from so many people, especially the youth. What surprised me greatly were the negative thoughts on western style democracy emanating not so much from the young revolutionaries but from supposedly responsible citizens who ought to have appreciated the niceties of the democratic way of life as distinct from the vagaries and uncertainties of a revolutionary regime. Although the revolution had come to roost, it soon became quite evident that its potential impact was not readily understood by the vast majority of Grenadians. In fact, during the early stages of the revolution, very few Grenadians imagined that the nation could be so easily brought into the Marxist/Leninist plexus with its accompanying suppression of personal liberty. In any case, amid the euphoria of those early revolutionary days, and no doubt duped by promises such as early elections, compensation for properties acquired by the Gairy administration, or return of those properties to their owners, Grenadians by and large genuinely felt that they would have better days under Bishop and his Revolutionary Government. Little did they know that they were well and truly trapped into what a select committee of the British House of Commons described as "a classic revolutionary movement in the Bolshevik mould."

Any suggestion that Bishop's immediate preoccupation was to find a way to legitimize the *coup d'état* within a democratic framework was nothing more than wishful thinking. Instead, his main concern was the consolidation of the revolution. He had in custody the Ministers of the Gairy administration with the exception of Lady Gairy, who was personally held in high esteem on both sides of the political divide. Although Lady Gairy's movements were closely monitored, at no time during the revolution was she detained. When she eventually left Grenada, she did so of her own free will, unmolested and unprovoked, to take up residence in the U.S.A. Also in custody were known political activists, including parliamentarians of Sir Eric's Grenada United Labour Party.

Without any political motivation, I was determined to do whatever I could to bring back normalcy to the country. In the process, I tried to persuade Bishop that all his efforts should be towards that end. My idea of normalcy entailed the early release of those detained, the return to constitutional rule and the holding of national elections within three months. While Bishop did not fully share my idea of normalcy, at least I had the satisfaction of assessing him as a patient and polite listener. He made it clear that he wanted to make absolutely sure that the revolution was holding, and as far as he was concerned, the threat of mercenaries landing in Grenada to overthrow revolution was not imaginary but real.

I suggested to Bishop that if he could cajole George Hosten and three other Ministers into resigning from Parliament, I could then appoint him (as Leader of the Revolution) Prime Minister. It might appear presumptuous of me to prefer George Hosten to the Deputy Prime Minister, Preudhomme, who had been performing the functions of Prime Minister during Sir Eric's absence. Preudhomme was no match for Hosten in terms of intellect and ability. Moreover, Preudhomme's longstanding blind loyalty to Gairy virtually made him, in my view, unsuitable to take the lead in any such negotiations.

I could see no problem in appointing Bishop as Prime Minister. He was an elected member of Parliament and Leader of the Opposition, and in my judgment would have been in a position to command the support of the majority of members in the House of Representatives. Under this proposal, Bishop would advise me to dissolve Parliament and call elections within three months. Whether this would have been constitutionally proper was open to question. Despite Gairy's well-known political and other shortcomings and the widespread unpopularity of his regime, I could not assume that the Commonwealth Governments would have accepted this manoeuvre which, in the view of some, would have been tantamount to their acquiescing in the armed overthrow of an elected Government. For my part I had to acknowledge that the incumbent Prime Minister was not in post, and it was in the highest degree unlikely that he would return to

Grenada in the foreseeable future. It would have been impracticable for me to consult him. Unquestionably, Maurice Bishop was the *de facto* Prime Minister.

Bishop did not reject the proposal. He indicated that he would hold discussions with the more senior Ministers among the detainees. He expressed the hope that, as a first step towards translating my plan into action, I would agree to chair a meeting at my residence. He also asked me whether I would be good enough to make the necessary arrangements for such a meeting. I was so elated that I readily consented, and immediately gave instructions to my staff to prepare one of the reception rooms for what was going to be an historic meeting. The participants would sit around the table – with Bishop and his comrades on one side and the detained parliamentarians, as chosen by Bishop, on the other. No specific date was fixed for the meeting except that, as proposed by Bishop, it was to take place in a day or two. The long mahogany table, shining at its brightest, was neatly arranged with paper and pencil as if prepared for an important Board of Directors meeting. My hope was that in our current political turmoil, we could at least demonstrate to our Caribbean brothers and sisters and, indeed, to the world that we were sufficiently mature to sit around the table in a spirit of goodwill and decide what was best for Grenada. Alas! Three days passed and I heard nothing further from Mr Bishop. On the fourth day in a telephone conversation, he informed me that he had changed his mind about the proposed meeting. Despite my bitter disappointment the table was left as set for the ensuing two weeks. I kept hoping that good sense would prevail and that a meeting would be convened at a moment's notice, but slowly, waking up to reality, I finally accepted that this was not to be. Thus an early opportunity to rectify the constitutional position was missed.

Bishop was not short of legal advice from the Caribbean and elsewhere. As a practising lawyer he had always collaborated closely with the Organization of Caribbean Bar Association, members of whom eagerly represented clients in any of the islands especially in matters dealing with alleged abuses of human rights and political victimization. For example, in 1970, during the impasse between the nurses and the Grenada Government, it was through the initiative of Maurice Bishop that attorneys from the other islands came to Grenada to defend the nurses in court. Bishop himself had undertaken similar visits to other islands to defend clients who were aggrieved because of some allegedly unconscionable or unjust action by government. It was no surprise, therefore, to observe a steady flow to Grenada of lawyers – many of them young and radical – from Trinidad, Barbados, Guyana and elsewhere to advise Bishop. Intelligence later reached me that it was these internationalist lawyers who advised Bishop that a revolution was a revolution and that he should do nothing which could be construed as a departure from it. To acquire the mantle of premiership via the constitutional route would be to presage the death-knell of the revolution. According to their thinking, a constitutional arrangement along the lines I had suggested should not even be treated as a matter for consideration.

One of the first acts of the Bishop regime was to suspend the Constitution. People's Law No. 1 was the mechanism used to achieve this end. Because of the prevalence of the powerful propelling ideological winds of change then affecting Grenada, there was no guarantee of the Constitution's resurrection in its current form. In his Declaration of the Grenada Revolution, Bishop clearly and emphatically placed "the violation and abuses of democracy committed by the Administration of Eric Matthew Gairy under the guise of constitutionality" as the *raison d'être* for the revolution. Further, the Declaration categorically stated that the Revolution was the work of the people. So was the appointment of the People's Revolutionary Government. Similarly, it was the people who empowered the said People's Revolutionary Government to issue such laws, orders, rules and regulations and to do all things it might deem necessary for the restoration and preservation of the peace, order and good government of Grenada. In short all Bishop's acts were purportedly done in the name of the people. The Declaration is silent as to where and when the people met to invest the Government with such far-reaching authority or what was the *modus operandi* for getting the consent of the majority of the Grenadian people. That said, it is instructive to note that a pledge by the People's Revolutionary Government to return to constitutional rule at an early opportunity was embodied in the Declaration. No date was given. The promise of the appointment of a Consultative Assembly to formulate a new Constitution that was to be submitted for approval in a referendum also featured prominently in the Declaration of the Grenada Revolution.

With the Declaration in place, Bishop set out to promulgate People's Laws in the form of Decrees. All these laws came into effect once they were signed by Bishop as Prime Minister and proclaimed on radio and/or in the Government Gazette. Thus from March, 1979 to October, 1983 – the period of the Revolution – I as Governor General had absolutely nothing to do with the various laws that came into effect, and my signature therefore was not appended to any of the People's Laws. People's Law No. 1 not only suspended the Constitution but also purported to legalize the actions of the revolutionaries as from March 13, 1979. Law No. 2 established, in accordance with the sovereign will of the Grenadian people, the People's Revolutionary Government in which it vested all executive and legislative powers including the authority to appoint a Prime Minister. Law No. 3 retained Her Majesty the Queen as Head of State and the Governor General as her representative, who would perform such functions as the People's Revolutionary Government may from time to time advise.

The judiciary did not escape the tentacles of that hydra-headed monster otherwise called the Revolution. The repeal of the West Indies Associated States Supreme Court Act 17 of 1971 led to the establishment of the Supreme Court of Grenada consisting of a High Court and a final Court of Appeal. One consequence of all this was the almost spontaneous removal of the headquarters of the West Indies Associated States Supreme Court from Grenada. In fact, the Chief Justice had fled from Grenada the day after the coup. Viewing the revolutionary process as outrageous, he could not see himself operating in accordance with revolutionary norms and usages.

People's Law No. 7 formally established the People's Revolutionary Army whose members were also given the powers of arrest and search. In this regard they were given parity of status with officers of the Royal Grenada Police Force.

The Revolution brought to the fore a number of instant experts on Grenadian affairs, some of whom were totally ignorant of even basic facts about Grenada. These self-appointed experts placed much store on the suspension of the Constitution as it affected the role of the Governor General. Few took the trouble to analyze with any degree of objectivity the efficacy of the suspended Constitution, and fewer still were concerned with ascertaining whether there was any modicum of affinity between the provisions of the Constitution and the contents of the so called People's Laws.

Indeed, Bishop kept the Constitution close to his breast. Despite his ideological stance, he never really shelved it. As a lawyer he obviously viewed it as a good reference point and useful tool in the formulation and subsequent promulgation of the new-styled People's Laws. Any serious observer who followed closely the peculiar pattern of the Bishop Administration would glean that in practice Bishop used the constitutional provisions to good effect as circumstances demanded. A study of the enactment of the various laws decreed by the Prime Minister would reveal that from time to time, he brought back into force sections of the suspended Constitution under the guise of People's Laws.

On no occasion during the revolutionary period did Prime Minister Bishop attempt to frustrate any of my activities. Nor could I personally complain that he was inaccessible, even though he did not see me on a regular weekly basis. In fact, he readily responded to any request I made of him. For example, when either by accident or design some revolutionary soldiers without warning removed the stand-by generator which served both my Residence and the former residence of the Prime Minister, Bishop had an equally powerful one replaced within hours and this time on Government House grounds, to serve my residence only. On another occasion, when my car would not start about twenty minutes before I was due to leave for a ceremonial occasion at Queen's Park, I telephoned Bishop to apprise him of the situation. He immediately sent me alternative and suitable transport to take me to Queen's Park on time. While in the pre-revolutionary period, such matters would have been handled by the Ministry of External Affairs, it is worthy of note that despite the changed situation the Prime Minister continued to do everything at his disposal to ensure that the dignity of the office of Governor General was maintained at all times.

I got to know Bishop well during his premiership. He was a product of the Presentation Boys College, a Catholic secondary school run by Irish religious brothers. He then proceeded to Britain where he read law and was qualified as a barrister. Though we did not always see eye to eye, his frequent calls on me always led to serious dialogue. From the very outset I could discern that he was genuinely concerned about the less fortunate in society. When it came to ideology, we were poles apart. He looked to the left while I felt more comfortable setting my sight in the opposite direction. Notwithstanding his role as champion of the people, I thought he had a long way to go in getting to understand the psyche of the Grenadian man and woman. As an urban dweller growing up with lower middle-class values, he never experienced the reality of living in the rural areas of Grenada. He also had to learn early in his premiership that Grenadians expect high standards of deportment from their leaders. Well do I remember one of Bishop's early appearances as Prime Minister before a massive crowd in Queen's Park watching a football match between a Grenada team and a visiting team from Trinidad and Tobago. It was a Sunday afternoon and Prime Minister Bishop not only arrived late but was very casually dressed in a T shirt and a pair of plimsolls, as if relaxing in his backyard. You could hear the murmurings all around the pavilion as he made his way to the official box. The commentary, in local parlance, that continued into the next day was: "He ain't ready yet!"

Bishop declined to move into Mt. Royal, the official residence of the Prime Minister. For some two weeks he continued to live in his private home on the St. Paul's main road. He then moved to Mt. Wheldale to reside in what used to be the official residence of the Chief Justice. Thus he was in close proximity to Governor General's House – a three-minute leisurely stroll away. No sooner had he moved into residence than Bishop sought my permission to play tennis on my grounds. I readily acceded to his request. In fact, I invited him to play with me. Our first encounter on the tennis court was at quarter past six one morning. I did not enjoy my tennis that morning though I had to endure it for one hour. For me it was an uneasy feeling trying to concentrate on a game while four men in uniform stood fully armed at each end of the court supposedly ready for action if the need arose. Bishop must have discerned that these armed men were a source of discomfort to me. On subsequent occasions they stood at a more discreet distance while tennis was in progress, and then their numbers were reduced to two and later to one.

The tennis court scene provided an interesting contrast in the perspectives and outlook of both Bishop and myself during the early period of revolutionary rule. The Governor General and the Prime Minister playing an early morning game of tennis in the Governor General's backyard, a location that must of necessity be a key security area. The Governor General walking around his grounds freely and unaccompanied by guards, in the firm knowledge that his environs are secure even for a revolutionary Prime Minister who is his next-door neighbour. The Prime Minister, on the other hand, is never without armed men around him. During the entire revolutionary period, Prime Minister Bishop, in my view, was too heavily guarded. Any form of protection which is overdone can send out wrong messages and misleading signals. Any person who is always heavily guarded is a potential target. Well do I remember the evening when the electrical power supply failed while the Prime Minister was visiting me. We were sitting in the small reception room downstairs when suddenly we were engulfed in darkness. By the time the stand-by generator was switched on, the reception room was full of security men who had obviously accompanied the Prime Minister. There was hardly any room to turn.

When I received Prime Minister Bishop on March 28, 1979, we held discussions on subjects ranging from the Constitution to the administrative problems of the Civil Service. All was not well with the staffing that he had inherited in various Government departments. Some people were not suitably qualified for the jobs they were doing; others who had the benefit of training were doing jobs well below their capacity; still others continued to wallow lazily in a mire of low productivity. I was well aware that the Civil Service was full of anomalies owing to the easy way of hiring so many individuals who did not have the required qualifications for entry into the

Service. This had been part of Gairy's strategy to increase employment opportunities, and he had used the Civil Service to achieve this objective. Some people had been taken on to do what was normally a clerical job which they simply could not handle, but, after many years, some of these recruits became proficient, and had been absorbed into the Civil Service.

But it was on the Constitution that we had lengthy discussions. Bishop explained why it became necessary to suspend the Constitution. He felt strongly that it was the only way to consolidate the Revolution and to ensure peace and stability in the State. However, he had since taken steps to bring back certain sections of the Constitution and all those would be gazetted by the end of the week. The sections of the Constitution dealing with the Governor General, the Public Service Commission, pension rights, Public Service Board of Appeal, citizenship were among those to be brought back into operation immediately. He further informed me that a new census of eligible voters would be taken within a fortnight.

For the first time since the introduction of adult franchise in 1951, Grenadians were denied their right to choose their parliamentary representatives. For many, this right had come to be regarded as inalienable, and for a people fashioned in the democratic mould it was painful to stand by helplessly and watch their brothers and sisters in other English-speaking Caribbean countries proudly exercising their right to elect their governments via the ballot box. The Grenadian hero, Theophilus Albert Marryshow, who in his lifetime had laboured relentlessly to ensure that the democratic principle of one man-one vote was the bedrock for proper governance, must have been turning in his grave. Ironically enough the People's Revolutionary Government often cited Marryshow not only as their national hero but also, and more importantly, as their political guru. I constantly, though riskily, reminded the comrades that Marryshow was a firm believer in parliamentary democracy.

Prime Minister Bishop, in his oft-repeated attempts to belittle the electoral process, described the democracy as practised prior to the revolution as a five-minute exercise every five years – a clear reference to going to the polls on election day and putting a mark against the candidate of one's choice. This he erroneously regarded as the limit of one's participation in the democratic process. No one dared challenge him on this spurious assertion. There could be no voice of dissent. Anyone courageous enough to openly raise objections to the pronouncements or programmes of the great leader would be branded as a counter revolutionary. Counter revolutionaries were hurriedly taken to Richmond Hill Prisons as common criminals, there to remain at the pleasure of the People's Revolutionary

Government without trial and without recourse to any form of judicial process. In an address known as the Line of March speech to a general meeting of the party on September 13, 1982, Bishop succinctly explained how people were detained in these words, "We don't go and call for no votes. You get detained when I sign an order after discussing it with the National Security Committee of the party or with a higher Party body. Once I sign it – like it or don't like it – it's up the hill for them." The hill is a reference to the Richmond Hill Prisons, though detainees were also kept at Hope Vale, a kind of concentration camp that accommodated Rastafarians and others who were carefully selected for humiliation. Some of the detainees were kept at Fort Rupert that has since gone back to its pre-revolutionary name, Fort George. Still others were detained for shorter periods at Mount Royal.

Of the three thousand Grenadians detained without trial during the revolutionary period, one case readily comes to mind. A most respected medical practitioner, Rupert Japal, had served with distinction not only in his native Grenada but also in the other Windward Islands. Dr. Japal was a great lover of cricket and had a knack of bringing people of all walks of life together by organizing cricket matches on the village green or by providing generous hospitality at his home or in the open air on his farm. His humility was no bar to his graciousness as a host. Just as he loved to entertain so he made himself available to see patients by day or night at their homes or in his clinic. He also was a great conversationalist. Apart from cricket he liked to discuss politics and world affairs generally. He cherished his right to freedom of speech that he thought was the ultimate in the liberation of man.

One of Dr. Japal's patients, Earle George, a bright young man of Hermitage, St. Patrick's, would use Dr. Japal as a conduit to send me written notes, most of them critical of the Revolution. George would hand Dr. Japal an envelope addressed to me every so often at the Government clinic in Hermitage where Dr. Japal attended weekly. At first I did not know the young man but I was very impressed by his style of writing and the contents of his notes that were so logically and clearly put together. After discreet enquiries I discovered that young George had been a very promising teacher who, like many of his colleagues, had joined the ranks of the revolutionaries. He soon became disillusioned and began to criticize the Revolution. He had also become a Rastafarian and, with his long and dishevelled locks of hair, was living in the bush. Out of the abundance of caution, I quietly advised Dr. Japal not to receive any further letters from George who might be viewed by the Government security agencies as a counter revolutionary. Instead, he should use the normal facilities of the post office.

I do not know whether Dr. Japal's tenuous involvement with Earle George was in any way responsible for Dr. Japal's subsequent incarceration. But in the early hours of the morning, he was literally dragged from bed at his home in the heart of the northern town of Sauteurs, beaten, put into a waiting vehicle in true terrorist-like fashion, and driven to St. George's where he was tortured and detained first at Fort Rupert, then at Richmond Hill. The High Command of the People's Revolutionary Army obviously chose that hour when no one could come to the doctor's rescue. Nor was there any chance of escape as the native Caribs successfully did over three hundred years before (and not far from Dr. Japal's home) when they jumped into the sea rather than surrender to the exploiting French intruders. Hence, the name of the town "Sauteurs" that was built around Leaper's Hill. Rupert Japal, a most patriotic, popular and generous Grenadian was never the same again as his arrest and subsequent detention for several months adversely affected his health. He had to be hospitalized during his detention. When I visited Dr. Japal at the General Hospital, I found him in a very sorry state. He told me of his experiences at Fort Rupert where his torturers pushed his head into a toilet bowl.

Bishop's much vaunted idea of democracy was based, as he claimed, on "people's participation." Zonal councils were established to give effect to the efficiently propagandized doctrine of people's participation. Through these councils, the people would express their views in the presence of members of the government and other high-ranking party officials. The councils had no voting rights and no legislative powers. What was significant about them was that they were a mere extension of the party apparatus. While in theory anyone was free to attend and purportedly anyone could express his views freely, in practice the councils were so well manipulated and so superbly orchestrated that the opinions expressed at meetings had to be in keeping with socialist thinking. Any expression to the contrary was looked upon with suspicion, and those with non-socialist views were regarded as incipient counter revolutionaries who were closely monitored by the Party. Indeed, the whole country was under surveillance with spies in the hotels, at social functions, in the banks, in the offices, and even in homes with children spying on their own parents and acting as channels for reporting anti-government sentiments expressed in the privacy of their homes. Whether one was vocal or silent, everyone was a potential counter revolutionary as far as the party activists were concerned. Young men and women acting on instructions from the Politburo would pace the public rooms of hotels unobtrusively finding out what guests thought about the Revolution or clandestinely listening to their conversations. One visitor was booted out of

Grenada following the bomb blast at Queen's Park on June 19, 1981, when three people were killed. His unpardonable sin was that he was heard that evening to make an overseas phone call in French from the hotel where he was staying. It was no secret that operators in the telephone company listened to overseas calls and frequently recorded them.

Keeping a close watch on the movement of currency and oblivious of the fiduciary relationship between bankers and customers, the Government took into their confidence certain bank clerks who dutifully reported excessive withdrawals of money from the bank. Those luckless people guilty of such practice were more often than not questioned and searched at the point of embarkation by zealous revolutionaries whose task it was to stem the flow of capital out of the country. At cocktail parties and receptions, part of the work of Government Ministers' bodyguards was to eavesdrop on conversations. I actually witnessed two of them assiduously writing notes while the Minister was in a group of six persons carrying on "small talk" at a cocktail party at my Residence. Similarly, I shall never forget the occasion when I delivered the graduation address at the Westmorland Secondary School. What I said was faithfully recorded *verbatim* by a Guyanese internationalist female worker and, as I learnt later, passed to the Central Committee. When I observed that she was struggling to write what I was saying, I obligingly and compassionately reduced my speed to dictation level in order to put her out of her misery.

Amid all these intimidatory tactics, the cry for parliamentary elections came from far and near – from the United Kingdom, from Canada, from the U.S.A. – through their respective envoys. Persistent and more vociferous calls came from regional heads of government particularly from Eugenia Charles of Dominica and Tom Adams of Barbados. On November 5, 1980, Prime Minister Adams called for General Elections in Grenada. Bishop was quick to reply to the distinguished Prime Minister of Barbados on the following day in a most caustic manner. The immediate withdrawal of VIP. facilities at Grantley Adams Airport in Barbados for Grenada government officials was added ammunition to the war of words which forthwith escalated. Unison Whiteman, Minister for Agriculture, was the first casualty of this Barbadian declaration. On November 8, 1980, he was thoroughly searched as he landed at Grantley Adams Airport.

The war of words continued unabated. On November 10, 1980, at a political rally in Barbados Prime Minister Adams and his Foreign Affairs Minister, Henry Forde, launched a verbal tirade highlighting the sordidness of the Grenada coup and Government. Prime Minister Eugenia Charles of Dominica, who completed her secondary education at St. Joseph's Convent in Grenada, did not escape the verbal wrath of her Grenadian counterpart. She, too, was called by all sorts of uncomplimentary names. Bishop was loud and clear in his message to his regional colleagues: "Keep your nose out of Grenada's business." While his message was clear, his manner of delivery was crude and savoured of gutter politics. He chose to make strong verbal attacks on his fellow Prime Ministers in language which was neither complimentary nor parliamentary. The only diversion in this war of words was the gunning down of four men in Plains, St. Patrick's, on the night of November 17, 1980, while being driven in a car.

In rejecting the democratic principle of one man one vote, Selwyn Strachan, Minister for Mobilisation, came up with the formula of "one man, one gun." He went on to explain that the gun had replaced the ballot box with the advent of the Revolution. Strachan brusquely reminded all and sundry that on the morning of March 13, 1979, the Revolution had the overwhelming support of the Grenadian people and the gun was central to that Revolution. One year after the coup, people were becoming so frustrated and disillusioned that they began to vote with their feet by using the simple device of migrating. There was a steady flow of emigration as support for the Government began to crumble even among some of the most fervent revolutionaries. The disillusionment gained momentum as the democratic freedoms which Grenadians had taken for granted over the years were aggressively and rapidly eroded. However much they tried, the increasing number of so called internationalist workers who were converging on Grenadian soil could not stop the slide in support. These internationalist workers, as was their aim, wreaked havoc on the minds of the Grenadian youth and subtly tried to introduce their communist ideology to innocent individuals under the guise of helping in the developmental process. In an effort to buttress the Revolution, Prime Minister Bishop decreed that political education was to be compulsory for workers, not least for civil servants. Classes were held for policemen, civil servants, workers in statutory boards and other government-inspired organizations. Little did Bishop and the upper echelons of the revolutionary movement realize how deep was the feeling of resentment among those who were forced to attend the classes in political education. These classes were held at different times of day. For example, the police had their classes at five o'clock in the morning while the civil servants had their offices closed one hour earlier on certain days of the week for similar lectures. Members of the public, particularly business sector individuals, were equally resentful of this new trend in the public service. The classes constituted a mere imparting of socialist ideology, and failure to attend resulted in the withholding of annual increments in salary.

Some political analysts assert that if Bishop had called elections within six months after the coup he would have won overwhelmingly. I doubt it. Indeed, if such elections had allowed for participation by political parties other than the New Jewel Movement, he certainly would not have won. I think Bishop knew it. Within six months the People's Revolutionary Government had already done enough to expose their true ideological colours as it had become easy to detect the political direction in which the Government was heading. Bishop had already effectively silenced the other parties. The key politicians were languishing in jail and when the Grenada National Party (GNP) attempted to hold a meeting on the grounds of the St. Patrick's Anglican School, a mere stone's throw from the Sauteurs Police Station, they had to run for cover from a barrage of unwelcome rocky missiles. Many believed that this was inspired by the New Jewel Movement and by inference the Government. In any case that was the first and last attempt by any political group to hold a public meeting in Grenada during the years of the Revolution. Grenada in fact was a one-party state and Bishop would not allow any alternative system.

Amid continuing calls for parliamentary elections in the face of declining popularity of the Revolution, Bishop was groping in the dark to find some formula to enable the holding of elections that would result in a victory for his New Jewel Movement. But this was not a serious attempt. In fact, it was another piece of deception. Bishop was already under pressure from his comrades who were not interested in elections even though any such elections would have been a one-party affair. To the People's Revolutionary Government, general elections were not a priority and Bishop himself clearly stated that the three priorities were more political education, more adult education and greater production to enhance economic development. With the increasing number of internationalist workers in Grenada including teachers from the Soviet Union for our secondary schools, all with a common ideology, it became clear that parliamentary elections were irrelevant and had no place on the agenda of the People's Revolutionary Government.

The parliamentary chamber, York House, was immediately bereft of all symbols of authority and all photographs and paintings which enhanced the graciousness and splendour of this magnificent building. Fortunately, the Clerk of Parliament, Curtis Strachan (now Sir Curtis), had the foresight to rescue both maces, the symbols of authority for the Senate and the House of Representatives respectively and put them securely away. The books in the parliamentary library also escaped the vandalism of the thoughtless comrades. The parliamentary chamber was quickly transformed into an open room without any attraction or embellishment. It was more like a barn; though it was not used for storage it became the venue for all kinds of insignificant low level meetings. Thus there was no respect for the Parliament building, just as there was none for the erstwhile parliament-arians themselves. The dress code for the Parliament building dropped to its lowest level.

From March, 1979 to October 25, 1983, Parliament, and, by extension, all democratic institutions in Grenada ceased to exist. This was consistent with the rapid decline in freedom of speech during that period. There was no forum for the expression of alternative views, no form of protest could be registered against decisions taken by Government. In the absence of Parliament, my responsibility for signing Bills to give the effect of law came to an end. Laws were styled "People's Laws." They were in fact proclam-ations by the People's Revolutionary Government and signed by the Prime Minister. This mode of proclaiming laws was perhaps appropriate within the context of the revolutionary period. It would have been extremely awkward for me to sign some of the more repressive laws. In any case it was never the intention of the People's Revolutionary Government to involve the Governor General in the law-making process. The Laws were merely signed and dated.

It was never clear to me whether these Proclamations originated in Cabinet or in the Central Committee of the Party, or perhaps as the outcome of discussions held in some other forum. From my own observations it appeared that some came about as a result of Cabinet conclusions – a view which gained credence from Bishop's famous Line of March speech, in September, 1982, in which he explained to his comrades how laws were made in these words: "Laws are made in this country when Cabinet agrees and when I sign a document on behalf of Cabinet. And that is what everybody in the country – like it or don't like it – has to follow." This would seem to suggest that Cabinet at least approved legislative measures prior to their submission for Bishop's signature.

Cabinet met weekly and I continued to receive Cabinet papers as was the case prior to the Revolution. However, it became quite clear to me that many important decisions of national interest were never reflected in the Cabinet papers. I can only conclude that there were other decision-making bodies equally powerful, if not more so than Cabinet. Indeed with the passage of time Cabinet's role seemed to have been limited to the taking of decisions that in the main can be described as administrative for the guidance of the Civil Service. And although Prime Minister Bishop maintained the principle of keeping the Governor General informed, in his visits to me, he never revealed everything that I should have been told. I was no longer responsible for the appointment of Cabinet Ministers nor for Junior Ministers who had dropped the term "Parliamentary" from their nomenclature. Quite understandably they were no longer named "Parliamentary Secretary" but simply Secretary. Nor were Ministers required to take the Oath of Allegiance or the Oath of Office.

With the withdrawal from the regional Court system and the subsequent establishment of the Grenada Court of Justice, Bishop was determined to maintain the independence of the judiciary. He therefore did all he could to separate the judiciary from the executive arm of Government. However, despite his best efforts the independence of the judiciary was severely shaken when on several occasions convicted persons were freed by the Government soon after the commencement of their prison sentences. Similarly, inmates were made to continue their sojourn in prison long after their sentences expired. Francis Jones, a former superintendent of prisons, after being detained for one year, was found not guilty by the court on a charge of larceny. The Government, however, ordered that he should be kept in prison despite his acquittal. Rowland Budhlall suffered similarly. Tried and acquitted, Budhlall was rearrested as he left the court and re-imprisoned. Teddy Victor was also kept in prison after his sentence had expired, even though he had been in preventive detention for twenty-three months prior to his trial. Victor was the main charter member of the JEWEL Movement (Joint Effort for Welfare, Education and Liberation) and was secretary of the party from its inception in 1971 to 1977 when he resigned. When JEWEL merged with the Movement for the Assemblies of People (MAP) to form the New Jewel Movement (NJM) , Victor and others felt supplanted by the more middle class and more educated members of MAP. Victor did not fail to voice his opinion against the extreme leftist leanings of Bishop and Coard particularly. After a failed attempt to ambush him and to gun him down as a counter revolutionary, Victor was eventually arrested on illegal possession of weapons, although no arms and ammunition were found in his possession.. Yet he was tried and convicted despite the absence of *prima facie* evidence.

The first Chief Justice appointed was Grenadian Archibald Nedd, who at the time of his appointment was a judge of the West Indies Associated States Supreme Court. An erudite judge and former Grenada Island scholar, Nedd had worked for many years in Nigeria before returning to the Caribbean to take up a judicial appointment. There was really nothing revolutionary about the new Court. It was business as usual and there were no discernible differences between the pre-revolutionary Court and the existing judicial arrangement. The Chief Justice and other Judges and indeed all the other law officers were appointed by me on the recommendation of the Prime Minister. I administered the appropriate oath, though slightly modified. Prime Minister Bishop succeeded in getting some of the finest legal minds in the Caribbean to be Justices of Appeal. The Court of Appeal consisted of judges who, though practising law in other jurisdictions, came to Grenada three times a year to hear appeals from the lower court. Meanwhile the functions of the Magistrate Courts were extended under People's Law No. 6 to include jurisdiction over all acts of violence against state property and essential services as well as breaches of the financial laws and regulations. The maximum penalty on conviction for each of these was put at five years' imprisonment.

One of the aims of the Revolution was to eradicate Gairyism completely. Thus Bishop had to curb whatever residual vestiges of enthusiasm that might have been lurking among the more ardent followers of Gairy. The latter were quickly rounded up and detained indefinitely. Later on the detention net was cast more widely to facilitate, in the name of national security, the incarceration of all those who by their actions or words have condemned the revolutionary movement. Regrettably, some innocent people were caught up in this extended net. Indeed, two of my staff were detained indefinitely. Captain Michael Campbell, my aide-de-camp, was the first to be arrested, and to this day, no one including Campbell himself can give me any reason for his arrest. Later on, Corporal Scott, one of my more conscientious orderlies, was apprehended while on duty and taken to Richmond Hill Prisons. The cause of his arrest was equally inexplicable, and he was shattered by his incarceration, no doubt out of concern for his wife and two young children. As I made my customary round of the wards one Christmas to greet patients at the General Hospital in St. George's, I was dismayed and saddened to find Scott as a patient with a self-inflicted wound on his left wrist. Suffice it to say that when I visited the hospital the following Christmas, all hospitalized detainees were in a ward that was out of bounds to visitors, including myself. Bishop, of course, had no hesitation in signing detention orders for individuals whom his comrades had labelled as counter revolutionaries.

People's Law No. 8 provided for the establishment of a Preventive Detention Tribunal consisting of not less than three persons whose task was to review cases of those placed in preventive detention. On April 18, 1979, the People's Revolutionary Government appointed the Tribunal with Adolf Biersynski, a medical practitioner and one time parliamentary Senator and junior minister in a former Gairy administration as Chairman. The other

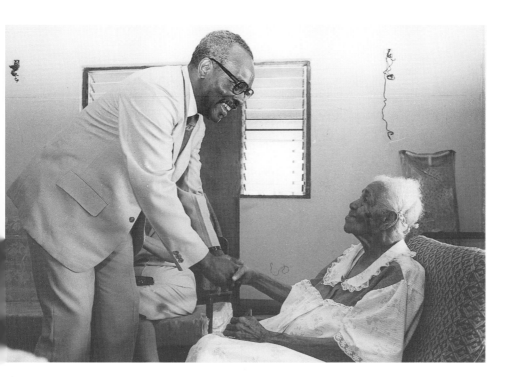

SERVICE AMONG GRENADIANS"

*bove*, The Governor General brings birthday greetings from Her Majesty to a centenarian

*elow*, Sir Paul's meeting of workers at the country's productive Boulogne Cocoa Station

"SERVICE AMONG GRENADIANS"

*Above*, Sir Paul visits Gouyave, his home town, during the Interim Administration

*Opposite, above*, Sir Paul presents a trophy to Deputy Police Commissioner Cosmos Raymond for the Annual Police Athletic Sports Competition

*Opposite, below*, The opening of Point Salines International Airport. To Sir Paul's left is Nicholas Bradwaithe, Chairman of the Advisory Council

"IN THE SERVICE OF GOD"

*Above*, Sir Paul and Lady Scoon are received by His Holiness Pope John Paul II

*Left*, Sir Paul receives Holy Communion from Bishop Sydney Charles

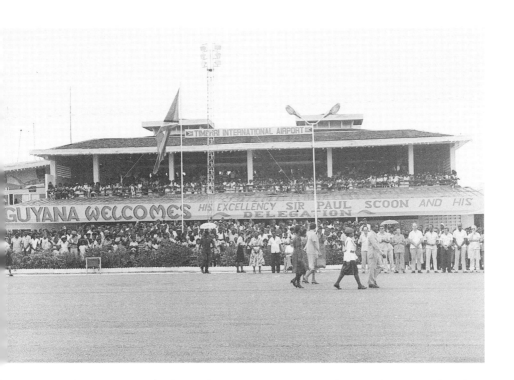

*bove*, An enthusiastic Guyanese crowd at Timehri International Airport greet the Governor General
*d* his wife

*elow*, State visit to Guyana; President Desmond Hoyte and Sir Paul take the salute

*Opposite, above*, Sir Paul inspects the Guyanese Guard of Honour

*Opposite, below*, Among those welcoming Sir Paul was the Secretary General of CARICOM

*Above*, Meeting the Mayor of Georgetown

"GUYANA ODYSSEY"

*Above*, Meeting Guyanese school children

*Below*, A visit to the world-famous bauxite works in Lynden, Guyana

members appointed were Bryce Woodroffe and Alice McIntyre. As enshrined in the Law, the Government was under no obligation to act in accordance with the recommendations of the Tribunal. A detainee might apply for a review of his or her case within fourteen days of detention and thereafter at two-monthly intervals. The work of the Tribunal proved quite futile. The Tribunal met four times. According to the chairman "charges against the detainees were often irrelevant, sometimes inapplicable and invariably deficient in material information." The Tribunal's recommendations were generally disregarded and Government took its own action, sometimes in contradiction to the recommendations. The Tribunal was never formally disbanded but simply faded into oblivion.

In the aftermath of the Revolution an additional flag was brought into use. This was the revolutionary flag which was flown alongside the national flag. On ceremonial occasions whenever I was present spectators were treated to the unusual spectacle of the Governor General's ensign fluttering in the breeze alongside the national flag and the new flag of the Revolution. This revolutionary flag consisted of a white background with a circle of massive red in the centre, similar to the Japanese flag. No wonder why on their first visit to Grenada during the Bishop regime the Japanese Ambassador and his wife could not help observing the generous exhibitions of these colours as they drove from Pearls Airport to their hotel in St. George's and mistakenly thought they were receiving a very special welcome through this ubiquitous display of the Japanese flag.

It had been the practice since Grenada became independent to greet the arrival of the Governor General at ceremonial occasions by playing the British National Anthem, while reserving the Grenadian National Anthem for the arrival of the Prime Minister. This was the practice when I took up my appointment as Governor General in 1978. Prime Minister Gairy, of course, liked his anthem. He regarded it as his own thing. It had been composed for him. He would not give it up. Anyway I had always felt that it was out of order to play the British Anthem in independent Grenada as a mark of recognizing the presence of the Governor General. After all, he represents the Queen of the Sovereign State of Grenada who also happens to be the Queen of the United Kingdom. Grenada has an equal place in the Commonwealth of Nations like any other member State. Similarly, I thought it was equally wrong to have the National Anthem played on the arrival of the Prime Minister when the Governor General was to be present at a ceremony. But one of the lessons I quickly learnt was that some Prime Ministers in the Caribbean take a delight in basking in the glory of the Anthem and the flag as if these were their own personal property. To them the symbolic paraphernalia associated with political independence were of paramount importance.

Within days of the Revolution I wrote to Maurice Bishop advising him to cease playing the British Anthem to mark the presence of the Governor General. Instead, it was proper to recognize the presence or arrival of the Governor General by playing the National Anthem. As for the Prime Minister a fanfare of some sort should be played on his arrival, if and when it was thought necessary. Bishop and his comrades were manifestly happy to cease the playing of the British Anthem, especially as the suggestion had emanated from the Queen's representative himself. But when it came to the National Anthem he only met me half way. He accepted my advice that the full National Anthem should be played on the arrival of the Governor General and the first half of the Anthem on the arrival of the Prime Minister. However much the revolutionaries criticized the trappings of independence, I became convinced that they, too, loved their anthem and flag, as if they were prized personal belongings.

While on a personal level the revolutionary Government extended the usual courtesies to me, I have to admit that for them the maintenance of Governor General's House was not a priority. The Governor General's Residence must be seen to be the symbol of respectability, stability, impartiality and integrity of the highest order. Its image cannot be otherwise. The interior of the Residence as well as the grounds should be a national show-piece. The Revolutionary Government evidently thought otherwise, since any request for improvement or refurbishment was met with polite rejection "due to lack of funds." Personal appeals to the Prime Minister himself fared no better. The gardeners had their working days reduced from ten to five per fortnight. It was difficult to face the reality of a decrease in their already meagre wages. Not surprisingly, about half their numbers resigned and looked for employment elsewhere. By 1982 no provision was made in the annual estimates of expenditure for the payment of the Head Gardener who up to then had been paid on a monthly basis by the Ministry of Agriculture. It was only after a sharp exchange of letters between my office and the Ministry of Agriculture that the matter was rectified. Further economic measures imposed upon my Household included a reduction in the number of security guards, the withdrawal of the maintenance man and a reduction in the number of domestic staff with no temporary replacement for staff on vacation.

The Governor General's bathhouse on Grand Anse beach was severely damaged, no doubt willfully, on the morning of the Revolution. All requests for its restoration, like those made frequently for the re-roofing of my residence and the upgrading of its interior, proved futile. The deliberate retrenchment of staff and appurtenances of the Governor General was intended to send a clear message to the rank and file of the revolutionary comrades that in a revolutionary situation the privileges of the Queen's representative must at least be seen to be reduced. While it was important to retain the Monarch as titular Head of State to preserve a veneer of respectability and acceptability, it was equally important in a revolutionary situation to lower the public profile of the Office of the monarchical representative.

The foregoing catalogue of ideologically motivated deprivation was further exacerbated by nuisance created by the Prime Minister's retinue whose acts of trespass and praedial larceny within the perimeter of my grounds were commonplace. These individuals tested my patience and tolerance to the fullest. Obviously believing they were a law unto themselves, the revolutionary soldiers on duty at the Prime Minister's Residence clearly thought they could enter the grounds of my Residence with impunity and, for example, help themselves to fruits and vegetables grown there, even in the presence of my gardeners. The Head Gardener was powerless to do anything, so also were the police officers attached to my Residence. They feared that they would be categorized as counter revolutionaries. But the nuisance level and the damage to the grounds were considerable.

Mt. Royal in the colonial days had been the official home of the Administrator. With independence it became the residence of the Prime Minster. For whatever reason Maurice Bishop declined to live there. The nearby Mt. Royal lands were used as an animal farm for the rearing of pigs and goats by the soldiers assigned to Prime Minister Bishop. This was in keeping with an order that the soldiers would engage in some form of agriculture, no doubt to reduce the mounting bill for their upkeep. However, it soon became clear that farm management was not one of the strengths of the People's Revolutionary Army. Nor were they versed in the art of animal husbandry. The pigs, constantly on the loose, caused much damage to the grounds of my Residence. Not only did they destroy the lawn but also devoured whatever crops were in their way. When I myself from my office window watched them mowing down the growing stools of corn, there was no longer any doubt in my mind that these animals were not properly and regularly fed.

The goats, too, were a source of nuisance giving rise to stunted growth of flowers. One or two goats intruding from time to time could have been overlooked. One day, as the evening shadows began to fall, my wife and I were sitting on the verandah overlooking the beautiful harbour of St. George's when suddenly we saw a great herd of goats invading our grounds. My wife sighed heavily at this dreadful and bizarre sight and thought aloud of the damage they could do to the plants, especially the crotons. I have never seen so many goats in the area – big goats, small goats, brown goats, black goats. Helplessly, we observed them as they moved, as if on a mission, from the tennis court area towards the Residence destroying whatever flowers were in the way. We were not aware then that goats were reared in the neighbourhood. However, I immediately reached for the telephone and made my displeasure known to the Prime Minister in unambiguous and emphatic terms. To the credit of Prime Minister Bishop, he immediately ordered his men to retrieve the animals and by the next day these unwelcome neighbours were removed from what had been transformed into the Mt. Royal animal farm. But the visitations by the pigs continued. So too were the acts of trespass and larceny by the Prime Minister's men who looked upon our grounds as the people's property.

The non-governmental organizations, especially those which had a branch relationship with Britain, came in for a good battering. The more traditional ones like Boy Scouts, Girl Guides, Red Cross, St. John Ambulance, Duke of Edinburgh Award Scheme were particularly at risk of becoming obsolete. In fact, they survived the revolutionary period partly because they had been deeply entrenched in the ethos of Grenada for a considerable length of time and partly because there were still some dedicated Grenadians who were determined to carry on their leadership role in these organizations even under very trying conditions.

The young people were specially targeted for systematic recruitment to the pioneer movement and to the militia and such other new-fangled youth groups as were to be found in other revolutionary socialist countries. The propaganda machinery was programmed to spread the doctrine that the young people were the property of the State, that organizations like the Scouts and Guides were for the bourgeoisie rather than for the children of the working class. When, for instance, a couple of conscientious comrades visited the Grand Anse Roman Catholic School with a view to starting a pioneer group there, they gave the school Principal a sharp rebuke when she told them that she first had to consult the children's parents. Further, they had the effrontery to suggest that the State had a prior claim over parents in the control of children. In contrast, they had little or no regard for the elderly who did not fit into the new scheme of things and who could not make any significant contribution towards the sustainability of the Revolution. In fact, one of the first acts of the revolutionary Government was to close down a newly established Home for the Aged which had been officially opened just three months previously in the village of La Borie and to use the building as a Day Care Centre for the children of working mothers. The revolutionary leaders never failed to refer to such children, and understandably so, as the flowers of the Revolution.

While many of the non-governmental organizations seemed destined to undergo a period of stunted growth, service clubs like Rotary, Lions and Soroptimists had to walk a tight-rope. Although these were non-political organizations, the political Directorate kept a close watch over them for fear of their involvement in counter-revolutionary activities. Amid all this distrust and because of the pressure brought to bear on non-governmental organizations there were more frequent calls on my Office and, by implication, on my time. These non-governmental organizations needed patronage, they needed support, they needed someone to speak on their behalf, and they needed some one to whom they could turn and with whom they could discuss their problems at the official level. Thus during the revolutionary period, both my wife and I had to devote a great deal of our time and energy to the needs of these organizations. I greatly admired and appreciated the untiring efforts of my wife in the work of the Red Cross, the Girl Guides, the Young Women's Christian Association and the Netball Association particularly during that difficult period.

Bishop and his colleagues in the Government and in the Party perfectly understood the power of the Church in Grenada, particularly the Roman Catholic Church, and its potential to destabilize the ideological structure of the People's Revolutionary Government. The Church was, therefore, a prime target, but the Government also knew that the Church would be a difficult and controversial nut to crack for there could be no dichotomy between Christianity and the Grenadian psyche. The Christian way of life was the solid foundation upon which our cultural and behavioural patterns had been developed. With that certain knowledge the Government had to devise strategies to loosen the firm grip that the Church had on its members. The measures adopted were subtle and purposive. Weekend manoeuvres took the young militiamen and women not only away from home but also, and more importantly, from their Sunday worship. Community work done on a voluntary basis was an important part of the Government's action programme. But such activity was always orchestrated to take place on Sundays starting at daybreak. Those doing community work fell into the habit of not going to Church on a Sunday. For the Government Sunday was like any other day of the week, while for most Grenadians it was a day of rest and worship.

At school many teachers sympathetic to the Revolution ceased to teach religious knowledge claiming suddenly that they were ill-equipped to do so. Furthermore, they became nonchalant about the morning act of worship which in some schools simply faded away. Some fifteen principals were removed from their schools ostensibly to form a research unit in the Ministry of Education. The truth of the matter was that these teachers were not of the socialist mould and would not allow their schools to be infiltrated with socialist ideology. At the same time the Government brought into the school system a number of Russian teachers who clearly lacked the necessary historical and cultural perspective to operate effectively as non-biased and non-ideological teachers. Meanwhile the internationalist workers who were for the most part pushers of communist propaganda, in their assessment of the state of education in Grenada, concluded that there was too high an element of religion in the schools.

Having carefully analyzed the effects of the ideological model on the minds of our youth, I came to the conclusion that the erosion of family values was accelerating and that certain activities of the revolution were rapidly gnawing away at the fabric of society. I also concluded that in order to sustain the revolutionary movement, the Government would take the young people under its wings.

I was deeply concerned about the youth, our country's future. They had to be saved from the new wave of atheism that was threatening the very foundation of our State. I took the bold and unusual step of devising my own programme of school visits in order to speak to the children and the teachers. I visited every school in Grenada including those in Carriacou and Petit Martinique. My message was simple – namely, that the pupils owed a duty to God, a duty to their family and a duty to the State in that order. I emphasized that God and their parents had priority over the State and, for the benefit of the teachers, I further emphasized that I differed vehemently from those who advocated the notion of state ownership of the youth. I enjoyed these visits. I was well received by staff and students. Although I was advised that many of our teachers were revolutionaries, I did not allow this to deter me. I said what I felt I should say. Indeed, when I visited the Corinth Government School I observed one teacher taking copious notes of what I was saying. In Crochu Roman Catholic School, there was a gentleman feverishly recording every word I uttered. I learnt later that he was not attached to the school at all but that he was an ardent supporter of the Government and a Party activist. It eventually came to light that I was reported to the Politburo whose members were unhappy about my visits to schools and about the speeches I made from time to time. More specifically my speech to open the annual conference of the Grenada Union of Teachers at the St. Andrew's Secondary School in April, 1983 seemed to ruffle the feathers of the Minister for Education, Comrade Jacqueline Creft. The result of all this was a decision by the Politburo that the Prime Minister should ask the Governor General to "toe the line." Following the demise of the Revolution, I was highly amused when I read this in the minutes of a meeting of the Politburo.

Bishop Sydney Charles, the head of the Roman Catholic Church in Grenada, was my closest ally and confidant during those difficult and uncertain years of Revolutionary Government. He is a deeply religious man who constantly preached love and forgiveness. His cautious optimism of the early days of the Revolution gave way to disillusionment and deep concern about the future of the Church. He, more than anyone else, knew that the Church was under attack, and he himself suffered great indignity when he was summoned by Prime Minister Bishop to his Mt. Wheldale residence to explain what he knew of a letter that had been smuggled out of the seminary in Trinidad. The contents of the letter, which the Prime Minister subsequently read out on radio, dealt with suggestions for strengthening the Church in Grenada to meet the growing challenges of communism. His Lordship was received in Mt. Wheldale not as the spiritual leader of the largest denomination in Grenada but as a less than ordinary man to whom the Prime Minister's staff was most uncivil. His departure from Mt. Wheldale was characterized by similar discourtesy. Such humiliation was the more galling since Maurice Bishop himself was a Catholic. Needless to say, Bishop Charles knew nothing about the letter which had been allegedly stolen from the seminary by a Grenadian trainee for the priesthood who, after this daring act, left the seminary to work for the People's Revolutionary Government. Communists do have a way of infiltrating places that are normally regarded as sacrosanct.

Bishop Charles visited me almost weekly and many a Saturday I invited him to stay on for lunch. He greatly inspired me and his constant prayers greatly fortified me. Our frequent discussions covered matters of topical interest, the role of the Church in our current situation, the excesses of the Government and the effect of the ideological indoctrination of the people of Grenada. On one occasion Bishop Charles expressed fears that my reception room might be bugged. I tried to convince him that I had no reason to believe that it was, adding that, even if it were bugged, I could not care less as I would not be muzzled in my own home. Further, I had a duty and a responsibility to the people of Grenada and I would continue to welcome into my residence people of all shades of opinion.

There was one thing Bishop Charles and I certainly had in common. We both believed in the power of prayer and we shared the vision that one day with God's help, we would be released from the unwelcome mind-boggling stranglehold on our country. In nearly all my addresses, especially those to the youth, I stressed the importance of the centrality of God in our lives and constantly reminded my audience that for us there was no alternative to our Christian way of life. Being cognizant of the fact that the Church was constantly undermined, I responded positively to invitations from the various religious denominations throughout Grenada. I was determined that my presence at their functions would leave no doubt in the minds of the Revolutionary Government and of the people about the high value I placed on religion as an instrument of hope.

Maurice Bishop's foreign policy led to an expansion of diplomatic relations. Having declared that his foreign policy was one of non-alignment, he quickly established diplomatic relations with communist and socialist countries, especially those whose leaders constantly bellowed anti-imperialist sentiments and slogans. Even the obscure Polisario Liberation Front was not to be left out of this diplomatic conglomerate. His aim, which he stated repeatedly, was to forge links with all peace-loving people of the world. In doing so he maintained relations with Grenada's traditional friends and former colonial powers whose Western style democracy we had zealously followed up to this point.

Bishop established a number of new diplomatic relationships without first seeking Her Majesty's approval or even discussing it with me, Her Representative. Some of these countries were not acquainted with the procedure for presenting Letters of Credence, and many of their Ambassadors did not quite understand how the country was governed with particular reference to the differing roles of Queen, Governor General and Prime Minister. Still others had a perception that Grenada was a republic and they seemed at first quite baffled on entering Governor General's House where the monarchical ambience remained constant.

Letters of Credence are addressed to the Queen as Head of State. The Governor General receives these letters on behalf of Her Majesty. He does not open the envelope but sends it direct to Buckingham Palace where the Letters are laid before the Queen. After reading them the Queen initials them and sends them back to the Governor General for his perusal and safekeeping. However, a number of these Letters were addressed to me rather than to Her Majesty. Nevertheless, as protocol demanded, I humbly and dutifully forwarded all Letters of Credence to Her Majesty without first opening them.

This expansion of diplomatic relations resulted in the appearance of two new Embassies in Grenada – those of Cuba and the Soviet Union, each with a resident Ambassador. Libya also established a diplomatic facility here with Abdullah Attir, Secretary of the People's Bureau of the Socialist People's Libyan Arab Jamahiriyia. The multiplicity of Ambassadors meant that much more of my time had to be set aside for receiving diplomats, many of whom were non-resident, as well as other delegations from abroad. This was particularly so in the month of March when a large number of Ambassadors and dignitaries converged on Grenada for the anniversary celebrations of the March 13 Revolution. A State Dinner at my Residence was always a highlight of the celebrations and at the height of the Cold War it was a most unusual spectacle for West and East to meet around the same festive table, sharing a common meal, invoking God's blessings before the meal and toasting the Queen at the end of dinner. On one occasion I had to untie a diplomatic knot of my own making. I purposely omitted printing a Toast List that is normally laid on the dinner table. Instead, I opted for my aide-de-camp to perform the duties of Toastmaster whose duty it was *inter alia* to announce the various speakers. It was not my wish to have the Cuban Ambassador, Julian Torres Rizo, reply to the toast to the guests. As Dean of the Diplomatic Corps he was the obvious choice to do the honours. But I had concluded by this time that this former intelligence director was becoming somewhat arrogant. Further, I was never convinced that he really understood the significance of the Governor General's House or the niceties of such a dinner. Over pre-dinner drinks I invited the non-resident French Ambassador who was the longest serving Ambassador to Grenada to reply on behalf of the guests. With some prodding from three other western diplomats, he agreed. On another occasion, the Foreign Minister of Nicaragua, a former Roman Catholic priest, arrived late for dinner. He was in army fatigues and accompanied by armed bodyguards who were also in uniform. What a funny sight for a State Dinner! We were all seated at table having completed the first course. I was too polite to notice the gentleman's late arrival, but my ADC seemed to have sorted him out.

It was always a pleasure to receive Ambassadors and High Commissioners and I rather enjoyed the preparatory work of briefing myself about the countries they represented. On my part this was essential in order to ensure intelligent conversation. Of course, some of these visits were not without their lighter moments. The resident Soviet Ambassador, Gennadiy Sazhenev, came in army uniform replete with medals to present his credentials. This was quite an experience for me as I had never seen so many medals on any one man, at any one time, and spread all over his body.

At the request of Prime Minister Bishop, I led the Grenada delegation to Moscow to attend the funeral of President Leonid Brezhnev. I left Grenada on Saturday, November 13, 1982, at crack of dawn, accompanied by Deputy Prime Minister Bernard Coard, and one of his aides, on an Air Cubana flight. Ambassador Richard Jacobs, our man in Moscow, was also a member of our delegation. This was to be my first ever visit to a fully fledged communist country and my first and only opportunity to meet Dr. Fidel Castro who, I must admit, was a very gracious host and treated me with the usual courtesies.

The six-hour flight to Havana, Cuba, was pleasant and uneventful, though the engine of the aircraft was very noisy. Our first stop was at the airport of Santiago, the second largest town in Cuba, where the aircraft refuelled. A further two hours of flying took us to Havana Airport where we were met by the Minister of Justice, the Deputy Minister of Foreign Affairs, the Grenadian Ambassador to Cuba and other officials. After some four hours, we returned to the airport where we boarded an executive jet for the fourteen-hour flight to Moscow.

On board were the Cuban, Nicaraguan and Laotian delegations apart from us. The President of Laos was on a visit to Nicaragua when the Soviet leader died. The Cuban delegation being the largest was headed by the President, Dr. Fidel Castro. We finally touched down at Moscow Airport at 2.00 p.m. on Sunday. We were met by Mr K. U. Chernenko of the Politburo, Mr M. A. Yasnov, the Deputy President of Supreme Soviet of the USSR, also by the Deputy Minister of Foreign Affairs and the Chief of Staff of the USSR Armed Forces, among others. Grenada's Ambassador, Mr Richard Jacobs, as well as his assistant Mr Bourne, were also on hand to greet us. We were then whisked to the Moscow Hotel where we were accommodated. The Moscow Hotel is situated in the square of the 50th Anniversary of the October Revolution. At four o'clock we went to the Hall of Columns, which is situated within the House of Trade Unions, and where the body of Mr Brezhnev was lying in State, to pay our respects. The floral arrangements were gorgeous as they were huge. There were hundreds of Soviet citizens still filing past the body, and various overseas delegations were visiting intermittently to pay their respects.

The funeral took place the following day, Monday, in Red Square. We left our hotel at approximately five minutes to eleven o'clock. When we arrived thousands of people were already in their positions. We stood waiting for about forty-five minutes before the start of the burial ceremony at mid-day. At exactly 11.45 a.m., the Armed Forces band started to play the funeral march, and soon the small procession arrived from the Hall of Columns with the body on a gun carriage. The procession comprised close relatives including the widow and the son and daughter and the main members of the Politburo. The lid of the coffin was removed and again the body was exposed and exactly at mid-day, the funeral orations began.

The speeches were delivered from the top of the Mausoleum; the first and main speaker was Mr Yuri V. Andropov, the man who had succeeded Mr Brezhnev as General Secretary of the Communist Party. Then the Minister of Defence, Marshal D. F. Ustinov, a worker from a Moscow factory, the President of the USSR Academy of Sciences, Mr A. P. Alexandrov, a representative from Mr Brezhnev's native town of Dneprodzenzhinsk, spoke in their turn. After the speeches, the coffin was again covered and taken to the back of the Mausoleum where it was committed to the ground. Mrs Brezhnev, followed by other top officials of the Party, threw some dust into the grave and then it was covered by the grave-diggers. Immediately the coffin was placed in the grave the National Anthem was played and following this sirens were sounded to signal a five-minute break from work throughout Russia. The dignitaries led by the new General Secretary then again took up their positions at the top of the Mausoleum to witness the March Past of the troops from the Air Force, the Navy and the Army.

This was a magnificent display of precision. After the March Past, the visiting dignitaries filed past the grave to pay their last respects, and then we all proceeded to the grand Kremlin Palace for a reception. It was not a Western style reception where one might expect light refreshments. It was simply to shake hands with the Vice President of the USSR, Mr V. V. Kuznetsov, the Foreign Secretary, Mr Gromyko, the Prime Minister, Mr N. A. Tikhonov, and the General Secretary, Mr Andropov.

One hundred thousand persons attended the funeral and among them were 130 overseas delegations from both West and East. Of these delegations, there were some 47 Heads of State / Heads of Government. The British Monarch was represented by the British Ambassador to Moscow, the British Government was represented by Mr Francis Pym, Secretary of State for Foreign and Commonwealth Affairs, the U.S.A. delegation was headed by Vice President Bush, Canada was represented by Mr Trudeau, India by Mrs Ghandi, Ireland by President Hillery, France by the Prime Minister and Minister for Foreign Affairs, among others. I had as my guide and interpreter during my stay, Mr Alexei Chervontsev, attaché for the Caribbean Section of the Russian Ministry of Foreign Affairs. Mr Chervontsev was no stranger to me, as he had visited Grenada with Mr Musin, the first Soviet Ambassador to Grenada, who was then resident in Jamaica. Mr Michael Yemelyanov also attended upon the Grenada delegation. He was the head of the Caribbean

Section of the Latin American Department of the Ministry of Foreign Affairs. As previously arranged, I left Moscow the following morning on the 8.45 flight on Swiss Air for Zurich where I embarked on a Trans World Airline for New York on my way back to Grenada. The other member of my delegation, Deputy Prime Minister Coard, stayed behind in Moscow on government business.

I failed to embrace the only other opportunity presented to me to visit Cuba when I declined an invitation to do so, much to the disappointment and surprise of the Cuban Ambassador, Rizo. This invitation dated December 16, 1982, came from Mr Oscar Fernandez Mell, President of the Executive Committee of the Provincial Assembly of People's Power in the city of Havana, on behalf of his Executive Committee. He invited my wife and me "to travel to Cuba for a visit of rest and relaxation." I felt unable in my capacity as Governor General to accept such an invitation.

# 6

## The Revolution in Decline

IN any computation of the factors that contributed to the decline of the Revolution, the worsening economic situation must rank high. The fragility of the Grenadian economy had never been in doubt. Agriculture, the corner stone of the economy, had been severely shaken in the recent past as a result of both natural and human causes. The vagaries of the weather, the rising cost of production and the falling commodity prices on the world market had adversely affected agricultural production from time to time. In addition, the injudicious division of large tracts of agricultural lands, in keeping with Gairy's "land for the landless" policy, dealt a heavy blow to the agricultural sector. This political measure turned out in so many instances to be purchase of lands for speculative rather than productive purposes.

Further, the shortage of agricultural labour partly because of a massive flight of workers through both emigration and movement from country to town, proved unhelpful to the growth of the rural economy. The reluctance, if not the refusal, of the young to cultivate the land was also an inhibiting factor in the advancement of the agricultural industry. Rising opportunities in an education system, which bore little relevance to the needs of the rural community, led younger people away from the land.

By 1979 when Bishop seized power, the future of the plantations looked dim. The writing was already on the wall for a downturn in the production and pricing of our main export crops of nutmegs, cocoa and bananas. Proprietors, large and small, were finding it increasingly difficult to meet their wage bills. Fertilizers, agricultural implements and other equipment were becoming more and more expensive. Attempts at diversification of crops for export had not proven successful. In the absence of a soundly-based agricultural policy, these half-hearted attempts hardly went beyond the talking stage. To give a boost to agriculture the People's Revolutionary Government did make a worthwhile effort in agro-industrial development by starting a modest enterprise for the production of guava and nutmeg preserves as well as fruit juices and banana chips. But, at best, such efforts elicited only lukewarm support from farmers who amid growing fear that their lands might be taken over by the State at any time were unwilling to put their scarce resources into their farms. In such a political atmosphere, the sustainability of agriculture remained uncertain.

The 1973 Manifesto of the New Jewel Movement had called for agrarian reform. After four years in office, the People's Revolutionary Government proved unable to bring about any significant improvement in the utilization of agricultural lands. Nor were they able to produce any effective plans for the transformation of the rural areas into vibrant and prosperous communities. Apart from the continuing flight of agricultural workers and the growing abandonment of cultivable land, there was little else to see on the agricultural scene. We were yet to witness the emergence of co-operative ventures such as producer co-operatives and peasant associations. In addition, because no serious effort was made to promote animal husbandry the country continued to depend on the importation of poultry and livestock products from abroad.

A modest attempt to start a people's co-operative farm at River Antoine Estate was thwarted by the Government, who apparently felt that the main participants in this initiative might, under the guise of farming, unfold their own hidden political agenda. Meanwhile the Government resorted to the use of slogans as a means of motivating people to greater production. At an emulation ceremony workers were made to repeat the slogan: "Work harder, produce more, build Grenada." As one observer put it, they sounded like children doing rote learning in a kindergarten class. What is of significance here is that agricultural workers had lost the will to work. They could not see any brighter prospects for themselves or for their families. As far as they were concerned, greater effort on their part was no guarantee for the enjoyment of maximum benefit. It was common practice for army personnel to enter people's property and generously help themselves to fruit and vegetables.

With the widespread abandonment of cultivatable land, and probably in desperation, the Government came up with a plan to bring back under cultivation lands which had been neglected or which had been allowed to lie fallow for a number of years. In addition, apparently without seeking adequate professional advice, they also proposed a grandiose scheme to clear forest lands for the purpose of planting food crops. This entailed the indiscriminate felling of trees that lowered the water table and adversely affected the domestic supply of water. Already numerous forest trees had been cut down to facilitate the building of roads for military purposes as the arsenal of arms continued to grow.

In flagrant disregard of the Acquisition Law, which had long preceded the Revolution, the Government and their agents continued to seize people's lands without any apparent intention to compensate the owners. In fact, these lands were not acquired under the Acquisition Law which had outlined the due process to be used and had guaranteed compensation to the owners. When asked about the unusual way of seizing property one would get a sharp retort – "This is a revolutionary situation." The slogan adopted for this new initiative was "idle lands plus idle hands equal an end to un-employment." The shortened version should be "idle lands for idle hands." This slogan in itself was illogical and it was difficult to discern how productive "idle hands" could be.

So the dream of agrarian reform was lost. Low wages continued to plague the lives of agricultural workers, most of whom actually experienced a reduction in the number of working days. As unemployment in the agricultural sector became more acute, the hopes of having any stake in the ownership of lands through co-operative ventures were dashed to the ground. The rural communities therefore remained dull and unattractive and saw no real progress during the revolutionary years. These rural communities were the stronghold of Sir Eric Gairy. By 1982 the people in rural Grenada could see no change for the better. While neglecting rural Grenada, Bishop concentrated on the urban proletariat as the first step towards socialism. This was an unpardonable miscalculation, given that Grenada was basically an agricultural community.

The People's Revolutionary Government established agricultural schools in some of the Plantation Houses or Great Houses where a limited number of young people went to learn the rudiments of agriculture. Apart from their classroom training they had to do practical work in the fields. I visited these schools. While the concept was a good one, their impact on the rural communities for agricultural production was minimal. They were severely lacking in organization and discipline. Staffing was poor and inadequate, and maintenance posed quite a financial burden for those who were entrusted with the task of running the schools.

The Grenada Revolution, which Bishop so often described as glorious, did little to buttress the country's weak economic foundation. Tourism, which prior to the Revolution was set to make a steady upward flight, had its wings virtually clipped, and it suffered a dramatic set back during the revolutionary years. Arrivals from the traditional source markets of North America and Europe fell dramatically. This was due in part to the unfavourable international coverage which sought to blacklist the island as a tourist destination. But more sadly, the anti-imperialist rhetoric not only kept prospective investors away but also effectively called a halt to the berthing of cruise liners at the St. George's harbour. One after another the cruise ships stopped calling at St. George's harbour, and stay-over visitors increasingly regarded Grenada as too risky a destination. The transparent communist doctrine adopted and manifested by the political leaders and their cadre of top supporters dulled the competitive edge and sapped the productive energy in both the private and public sector.

The business community was very cautious about expanding their commercial activities. One of the first draconian acts of the Revolutionary Government was the seizure of the Coca Cola Factory. By letter dated September 21, 1979, Selwyn Strachan, Minister for Communications, Works and Labour, directed the Commissioner of Police in these words:

"Please accept this as your authority to collect from the Manager of Messrs W. E. Julien and Company Ltd. the keys for the Coca Cola Factory at Tempe."

The Coca Cola Factory was owned and operated by the long standing and reputable firm of W. E. Julien and Company Ltd. whose Managing Director was Andrew D. R. Taylor, a kind and affable man. For his own personal safety Taylor gave up the keys, and the Government and its agents proceeded to operate the factory, though they did not have the franchise to produce Coca Cola. This was an eye opener for the business community whose leaders were no longer in doubt as to the efficacy of the political shift to the left. A dispute had arisen between the Coca Cola Bottling Company and its workers over the dismissal of two men who had threatened the life of the manager of the plant. The workers were represented by the Commercial and Industrial Workers Union whose president was Comrade Vincent Noel. At the same time this very man, Vincent Noel, was Minister for Home Affairs. The Company and the Union agreed to go to arbitration. It was further agreed that both parties should submit names of people considered suitable for the chairmanship of the Arbitration Tribunal. The Company submitted a list of six names including two retired judges. All six were rejected by the Union. The Union, in turn, proposed the Labour Commissioner (who, according to law, was debarred from sitting on such a tribunal) and a former President of the Trade Union Council whose impartiality was in doubt in so far as the Company was concerned. Thus the Company rejected both men.

Intimidatory tactics followed. The workers picketed the Company's premises, A maintenance man was threatened when he attempted to do some masonry work on the building, the night watchman was not allowed in by the striking workers on the picket line, and a crane was prevented from entering the compound of the Bottling Plant. The Company then had to resort to security guards, but they, too, could not cope as they had to shield themselves from the barrage of stones hurled unto the building and the grounds. On the morning of September 19, the two security guards were attacked by four men with stones. When the General Manager sought police protection, he was told by a member of the Criminal Investigating Department that he should seek such help from Comrade Noel, the Minister for Home Affairs, whose portfolio bore responsibility for the police.

In a letter to the Prime Minister, the Chamber of Commerce, through its President, flatly condemned Government's actions in this matter, with particular reference to the callous confiscation of private property and the Government's failure to adhere to the legal and established principles of settling industrial disputes. The President of the Chamber warned the Prime Minister that such actions could destroy public confidence and could have a serious negative effect on the overall economy of the country as a result of the loss of investor confidence. In my own view the Government's intervention in this industrial dispute was puerile, provocative and smacked of ideological dementia. Of course, the Government claimed that they were a Government for the working class. The upshot of all this was that Government handed back the Coca Cola Bottling Plant to W.E. Julien and Company Ltd. on March 1, 1982, almost three years after the factory was confiscated. During that period there was a reduction in production and a lowering of the quality of the product.

No amount of largesse from communist and other socialist countries could bring about the economic miracle which the leaders of the Revolution were anxiously hoping for. These leaders obviously failed to understand that economic development was inextricably bound with the noble concepts of personal liberty, peace, harmony and unity among a people who had grown over the years to enjoy the freedoms associated with a democratic society.

The work force continued to dwindle through emigration. Qualified Grenadians abroad refused to return home. Many feared they would be caught in the entangling communist net with its concomitant disregard for human rights plus the frightening prospect of denial of freedom of movement if and when they were ready to return from whence they came.

The finances of the administration came under increasing pressure. Bernard Coard, Minister for Finance, under whose general control the country's finances and fiscal policy lay, had embarked on a massive expenditure of public funds on high profile projects which were to a large extent unfunded. For example, many of the projects included in the 1983 budget were dependent on resources from Iraq, Algeria and Libya and other leftist militant regimes. The Iraq/Iran war completely eliminated Iraq's financial support for the capital budget which was further devastated by the dramatic drop in the price of oil in the summer of 1982 and spring of 1983. As Minister for Finance, Coard totally ignored the adverse effect of these economic developments on the 1983 Budget, and consequently plunged the country into the red, increasing the overdraft to $16,707,974 or 22% of Recurrent Revenue.

The Public Debt rose to $89,125,667 while Government Revenue dwindled helplessly in the face of a deteriorating economy which was squeezed by the anti-capitalist policies of the Bishop regime, relating to ownership of land, transfer of money, entrepreneurship, taxation and state control of the commanding heights of the economy which was already in shambles. As has already been pointed out, tourism was severely depressed with the precipitous fall in the number of visitors and cruise ships. Agriculture was not flourishing, with output reaching its lowest in recent economic history. The country found it difficult to find markets for rising stockpiles of nutmegs, the only significant contract sale being to the Soviet Union for political purposes. In retrospect it is difficult to avoid the conclusion that Grenada faced some form of economic embargo.

The timing of the internal Party crisis of mid-1983 was interesting. Why 1983? The serious criticisms of Bishop's leadership qualities and the doubts expressed about his ideological commitment, which precipitated the crisis, would have been just as valid in 1982. I think there were two reasons for the choice of 1983. Firstly, although Grenada's economic situation in 1982 was deteriorating rapidly, Coard, as Minister for Finance, was still able to manipulate the national figures to conceal the true position; but, by mid-1983, he had run out of financial options. Secondly, 1982 was rather too early for Coard to make a hostile move against Bishop and his faction. His position was not quite strong enough; he still had some work to do within the Party. He might even have wished to bide his time even longer than 1983, but, as I have already indicated, by then his gross mismanagement of the economy and the country's scarce financial resources could no longer be concealed. I suggest therefore that in mid-1983, an increasingly desperate Coard, under pressure to provide incentives to certain members of the PRA and eager to divert attention from his Ministerial shortcomings, was pushed into precipitating the 1983 Party crisis.

In such a tight economic environment, Bernard Coard felt cornered. He set about to save his face by staging the scene for the *coup d'état* and for the arrest of Prime Minister Bishop. Tactically, the Revolutionary Military Council (RMC), Coard's creation for the seizure and transition of power to himself, mounted a campaign of lies against their own people, putting the blame for the economic collapse of the Grenada Revolution on Bishop.

The situation described above was fairly predictable since the People's Revolutionary Government had inherited a fiscal imbalance as a result of the excess of Recurrent Expenditure over Recurrent Revenue. However, this fiscal imbalance was temporarily masked by the inflow during the early period of the Revolution of capital aid for general and specific projects from certain Arab countries. These monies apparently were routinely spent to deal with recurring budget deficits rather than on the projects for which they were earmarked. When the International Airport Project began to call for funds in 1983, the fragility of the Government's finances was graphically exposed as the Treasury was unable to produce the resources necessary to meet the demands made by the project. Prudence should have dictated that the capital aid, which was received during the early period of the Revolution, should have been set-aside in a separate fund for use when necessary.

The early period of construction on the International Airport Project involved mainly civil works which were provided virtually free of cost by the Cuban Government through direct labour of Cuban personnel and the use of Cuban equipment. Had such a mechanism not been put in place, the structural weakness in the Government's finances could not have been utilized for recurrent purposes. On the contrary, the misappropriation of Capital Funds deluded the People's Revolutionary Government into large-scale recruitment of staff and the general expansion of Government's services beyond the capacity of the Recurrent Revenue to sustain.

By January, 1983, notwithstanding the high-sounding and ostensibly positive rhetoric from the lips of the comrades, the economic failure of the Revolution was clearly evident. Mere words could not bring forth an economic miracle. The situation became more acute in this case where, in the absence of unity of purpose in the society, the grandiloquence of the revolutionary leaders became rootless and unreal. Grenada by then was a society of contradictions, mixed emotions and mixed reactions. It must not be taken for granted that unity is conformity, which is imposed from a central authority. In the existing Grenadian situation, the conditions for openly expressed divergence of opinion were absent. Moreover, with the hurt felt by so many Grenadians and the rift within so many families, conformity was never likely to be forthcoming. Nor was there a commitment to greater productivity.

All was well as long as there was financial and other support from the communist fraternity worldwide. This initial support was clearly demonstrated by the hard work done by the Cuban workers in the construction of the Point Salines International Airport – perhaps the largest single project undertaken by any Grenadian Government since Independence.

All praise should go to Maurice Bishop whose personal commitment to the building of the airport was inspirational. Sadly, he never saw the completion of the project. The Governments of the U.S.A. and Canada completed the airport, which I officially opened on Sunday, October 28, 1984.

In addition to the economic woes outlined above, another factor that contributed significantly to the dramatic collapse of the Revolution was the high level of deception at which Bishop and his cohorts were past masters and which was practised daily by the Party and the Government. But like other would-be masters of the art of deception they made the cardinal error in believing that they could fool all of the Grenadian people all of the time. With youthful vigour they artfully set out to convince the local populace and the international community that they were a group of dedicated Grenadians who were singular in their determination to change the existing order by transforming Grenada into a just and prosperous society after years of injustice and oppression. Their engaging rhetorical style persuaded many who would otherwise have doubted their sincerity of purpose. They were truly adept at substituting words like "revolution" and "socialism" for communism and Marxism. The cheering sections of the crowd at rallies were specially recruited and well-orchestrated to give thunderous and prolonged applause at intervals whenever the leader spoke. This was designed to send a powerful signal that the Revolution was enjoying a great measure of support.

To achieve their well-ventilated objectives, they frequently acted callously and at times actually resorted to brutality, which they unleashed on those who either refused to slavishly follow their dictates, or openly opposed them. They invariably claimed, unashamedly, some measure of justification for their acts of inhumanity in the name of the Revolution. The so-called "progressive" elements in the West accepted all this without question and gave the nod to the revolutionaries in their efforts to transform the mini-state of Grenada. These "progressives" were to be found in the media, among the professions, in the universities and even in democratically elected governments. How gullible can educated men and women be when reason gives way to emotion.

At home, still musing over the wild excesses of the regime of Eric Gairy, people were slow to detect the true colour of their new political masters. What was not known locally, regionally and internationally was that all along Bishop's public pronouncements were vastly different from what he was saying behind closed doors to his senior colleagues in the Party. In fact this piece of chicanery was confirmed in private documents that came to hand after the demise of the Revolution.

With the cunning use of the propaganda machinery, which was well oiled and carefully manned, Bishop and his supporters were able to conceal their true motives. Internationally they kept people guessing as to exactly what ideological card they were holding. When in the early 1970's Gairy in and out of Parliament repeatedly branded Bishop and his associates as a bunch of communists, he was scoffed at both at home and abroad. Many thought he was over reacting after the fashion of his ultra right wing "friends" like Somoza of Nicaragua, Duvalier of Haiti and Pinochet of Chile. But Gairy was right, as subsequent events showed and as secret documents later revealed.

As early as April, 1974, in a secret meeting of the New Jewel Movement, a decision was taken to build a Leninist Party in theory and in principle even though it might not be possible to implement such a decision immediately and openly. Yet when asked on several occasions before and during the Revolution what his political persuasion was, Bishop never gave a straightforward answer. Instead he would garble or mumble a few short sentences about freedom or workers' rights or the virtues of a just society. Even when the question as to whether he was a communist was put to him, he replied neither in the affirmative nor in the negative. Was it that he could not come to terms with what was turning over in his mind given his own erstwhile "petit bourgeois" life style and Christian upbringing, or was he a man of no conviction?

While socialism is not a clearly defined concept, it is generally accepted that in the socialist system the workers control the means of production and the distribution of goods. This, of course, varies from country to country. In the case of Grenada, a predominantly agricultural community with a high degree of peasant farmers who worked their own modest plot of land, it was difficult to envisage a system of collective farming. Grenadians take pride in their own property, however small, and guard it jealously. In such circumstances the imposition of radical socialism in Grenada would always be risky because of the invalidity of the premise on which it was launched. The social playing field was much more level in 1979 than it was in 1951 when the working class revolted. As long as one was prepared to be industrious, social mobility presented no problem. One could not detect any class struggle. The Grenadian society was an open one in which people mixed freely and had grown over the years to appreciate and enjoy the democratic freedoms. The problem in Grenada was basically one of political discontent. People could no longer trust their political masters.

Bishop understood only too well the pervasiveness of the Christian way of life in Grenada and the power of the Christian Churches, not least the

Roman Catholic Church of which his parents were devout members and where he himself had been spiritually nurtured. He had received a sound Catholic education from the Presentation Brothers College. In Grenada hardly a business meeting or social function begins without a word of prayer. So deep are the roots of Christianity that for the vast majority of Grenadians there can be no alternative to the Christian way of life.

Communism on the other hand was taboo in Grenada even among the least educated. The general perception was that communism was synonymous with atheism and oppression. To most Grenadians a communist was an individual who did not believe in God and who treated his fellow human beings brutally. Thus in no way could Bishop and his colleagues proclaim publicly that theirs was in fact a Communist Party. In his famous Line of March address Bishop reminded the party faithful that there were several token bourgeois and capitalist personalities in influential government positions in Grenada. He was obviously referring to individuals such as Dr. Bernard Gittens, a medical practitioner who was Secretary for Health. While Gittens might have been accurately classified as petit bourgeois, he was far removed from the party or the Central Committee. Norris Bain, a businessman from Grenville, was a Minister in the Government. He too did not belong to any of the party organs. But the classic example of a capitalist recruited into the Government was Lyden Ramdhanny, a young businessman from Grenville who was engaged in the family business. The Ramdhanny family, under the wise leadership of Mr L. L. Ramdhanny, Lyden's father, had been very successful in agriculture and business. By dint of hard work and astute financial management, L L. Ramdhanny made his way, not without difficulty, to the topmost rungs of the ladder of success. Lyden, the Junior Minister for Tourism and Civil Aviation, had no membership either in the Politburo or in the Central Committee. A fourth such member of Government was Miss Palme Buxo, retired civil servant who also worked in the administration of the ill-fated West Indian Federation. From all accounts she was a dedicated and efficient civil servant. She was the first to abandon the revolutionary ship. She left for St. Vincent in early 1980 to represent Grenada in Independence Celebrations and never returned. I was officially informed that she had proceeded to the U.S.A. for medical attention. Palme Buxo could not last long in the Revolutionary Government. By no stretch of my imagination could I see her as communist or even as revolutionary. A devout Anglican, she was very prayerful. She obviously became concerned when very early she observed the godless direction her colleagues were taking. She always gave the invocation at the beginning of public meetings held by the Government, but since her departure these prayers ceased. Apparently there was no understudy to Sister Buxo.

Bishop went on to explain that the inclusion of these capitalists and petit bourgeois in his Government was a deliberate ploy so that imperialism would not get too excited and would say: "Well they have some nice fellas in that thing; everything alright." And as a result they would not think about sending troops. If the political pundits in the West and the liberal progressives were gullible enough to give Bishop a chance to govern, the Grenadian people, some six months after the Revolution, had begun to send a clear message that while they admired Bishop they did not like what he was doing. Though many of them were silent and appeared to be supporting the Revolution, in private they condemned it sternly and unequivocally.

Prior to the Revolution the New Jewel Movement through its political leader, Maurice Bishop, posed as a great champion of human rights, of freedom of expression and of the rule of law. Bishop effectively used his legalistic skills in his thrust to ostensibly uphold these democratic principles. The London based Amnesty International was one of the darlings of Bishop and his New Jewel Movement. But after March, 1979, Bishop made a complete turn around with reference to these democratic principles. He proceeded to send over three thousand men to jail without trial, to silence the press, and deny decent and innocent citizens the right to express themselves freely. He placed under heavy surveillance anyone who was suspected of having the inclination to indulge in counter revolutionary acts and others who in the view of his colleagues were likely to do so. Jerry Romain, well known broadcaster and Government Information Officer in the Gairy administration, was incarcerated from the day of the coup and throughout the revolutionary period not for any crime he had committed but for what he was deemed capable of doing. Romain, who was a great supporter of Sir Eric Gairy, received this explanation from Bishop himself.

In this revolutionary state one was uncertain about one's rights and privileges. Typical perhaps was the case of a Trinidad national with Grenadian connections who once told me that he was keeping away from Grenada. His reason was that if he were to keep quiet while in Grenada he would be considered a counter revolutionary. He stood a chance of being arrested and detained. On the other hand if he expressed his views he would suffer the same embarrassment and humiliation. Therefore for his own safety and comfort he was keeping out of harm's way. Similarly, one of Bernard Coard's contemporaries at the Grenada Boys' Secondary School told me that he would not even pay a fleeting visit to Grenada for fear that Coard and his comrades would prevent him from leaving the island. This young man, an island scholar, who had done well in medicine, chose to work overseas rather than in his homeland.

West Indians never fail to evoke laughter in the midst of adversity. We are full of humour. We can laugh at ourselves. The story is told that a Grenadian went to Trinidad for dental care. The dentist said to him: "Are there no dentists in Grenada?" "Yes," replied the Grenadian. "We have many dentists, but I can't open my mouth in Grenada. If I do, I will be sent to jail."

The People's Revolutionary Government's efforts to gag the press and thus stifle criticism was well illustrated by the treatment the press received. People's Law No. 81 made provision for the publication of newspapers. Some twenty-six shareholders got together and formed themselves into a company called "Spice Island Printers Ltd." to publish a newspaper known as *The Grenadian Voice*. In compliance with the law, no shareholder held more than four per cent of the paid up share capital of the company. Indeed the company fulfilled all the legal requirements to the letter. In the editorial of the first edition of the paper Volume 1, No. 1, of the week ending June 13, 1981, the policy of the paper was set out as follows:

"The policy of this paper is to practise the highest standard of journalism; to encourage and promote freedom of expression in a free Grenada; to raise and ventilate issues which are important to the progress and development of our country, our nation and our people; to assist in creating an informed public opinion; to support those policies and programmes of Government which, in our opinion, are beneficial to the nation and the people as a whole – but to be ready to counsel caution or offer constructive criticism when we differ from Government."

Yet the well-intentioned individuals who attempted to re-establish freedom of the press through the publication of a newspaper soon experienced how shallow were Government's public pronouncements. Some shareholders, including the editor, were detained and never tried nor given the opportunity to defend themselves. Their detention seemed endless, and some were eventually released only after the Revolution had collapsed. Bishop ordered the closure of the newspaper, and apart from detaining the editor and some of the shareholders, kept a close and provocative watch on the others including leading businessmen and professionals. As Bishop himself would say, he placed them under "heavy manners." This piece of rough justice was mentally painful not only to the shareholders but also to their wives and children, many of whom were watched in the environs of their home, in their work places, and even as they worshipped in their respective churches. Among those placed under "heavy manners" was Alister Hughes, Grenada's foremost news commentator and journalist, who had been under constant pressure. Suffice it to say that Hughes had been a supporter of the revolutionary process during the early days of the Revolution. He later became critical of some of Government's policies and actions.

On enquiry about his unconscionable deeds, which varied conversely with his words of pre-revolutionary times, Bishop glibly replied to Amnesty International that he had changed his mind on these matters. It was precisely that kind of deceitful and untrustworthy behaviour that led to the complete and irreversible alienation of the Grenadian intelligentsia and leaders of the business community. Thus the Revolution continued to lose much needed domestic support.

Another group that withdrew its support was the Rastafarian brotherhood. The Rastafarian cult rapidly spread from Jamaica to the rest of the Caribbean, to the United States of America and across the Atlantic to England. The members of the cult look upon Haile Selassie as their Supreme Being. They keep their hair long, they generally look unkempt, they live close to nature and many of them take to the hills where they feed on herbs and vegetables. Some of them produce excellent craftwork. They understand freedom in terms of Negro survival. They feel deeply that the Negro can never be truly free unless all the African countries are free, for Africa is in their souls. The Rastafarians had not been slow in observing the Government's proposal of cultural pluralism. The brethren thought that their support for the New Jewel Movement, and by extension the Revolution, would bring them benefits and privileges that had not been forthcoming under the democratically elected former administration. The New Jewel Movement flirted with them and they in turn threw in their lot with Bishop and his colleagues. They were loyal supporters of the Revolution and they were determined to use their talents to further the cause of the revolutionary movement. They even expressed their elation in song as beautiful as it was impressive:

> "A long long time me never see natty dread so happy
> A long long time me never see natty dread so gay."

During the early months of the Revolution the song was featured with consistent regularity on Radio Free Grenada as the national radio station was then called.

Soon, realizing that they were in no better position than they had been in before, the Rastafarians felt that they were hypocritically used. From their standpoint they could no longer trust the revolutionary leaders who had allegedly made to them certain promises that were never fulfilled. As they withdrew their support, life thereafter became even more difficult for them. The withdrawal of their support was a virtual rejection of the Revolution, a development that did not go down well with the revolutionary comrades. Beginning to see the Rastafarians as a threat, the Revolutionary Government thereafter ensured that the armed forces keep a close watch on them. Needless to say, many of the Rastas were jailed and tortured.

I often wondered whether Maurice Bishop fully understood the implications of his foreign policy for Grenada, for the region, and for the international community. The verbal assault against the United States of America and its President, Ronald Reagan, was the one common thread running through his foreign policy. This was very much in evidence whenever and wherever he opened his mouth to make any foreign policy statement. The consistency and regularity with which he made these derogatory swipes at the United States could hardly be tolerated by any self-respecting nation however great or small.

Grenada was much more visible in the international arena than hitherto. We forged diplomatic relationships with all different shades of socialist countries including some of the most radical of the communist bloc countries, for example, North Korea. They became the most trusted friends of the Government of Grenada. Diplomatic relationships existing before the Revolution were never formally severed, although, in cases like Chile, South Korea and later on the United States, the respective non-resident Ambassadors ceased to call at St. George's. The coolness between Havana and Caracas had its impact on St. George's, as the resident Ambassador of Venezuela, and later the Charge d'Affaires, received scant courtesy at the hands of the Government. This particularly manifested itself in the Government's lukewarm attitude to receiving aid from Venezuela. An offer of a portable health clinic for use by the Ministry of Health was never taken up, and pre-fabricated houses from Venezuela remained on the docks for over two years waiting to be assembled in the countryside where people were in dire need of homes. In fact, those houses were put up only after Grenada reverted to democratic rule. Further, the revolutionary government refused to give the government of Venezuela permission to purchase a property in Sans Souci, St. George's, for use as their embassy as it was considered by Bishop to be dangerously close to the Prime Minister's residence.

Among distinguished visitors to Grenada during the four and one half years of the Revolution was Kenneth Kaunda, President of Zambia. His 1979 visit was the first State visit of any foreign dignitary during the revolutionary period. Generally his visit was well received by Grenadians – the adherents of the Revolution as well as those who were not supportive of it. Bishop had extended the invitation to Kaunda when they met at the Commonwealth Heads of Government meeting in Lusaka. Kaunda was evidently impressed by the charisma and charm of Bishop, not to mention the articulate manner in which he always expressed himself. Kaunda's visit to Grenada was a plus for the People's Revolutionary Government. A most respected Commonwealth leader, Kaunda was obviously seen by the people of Grenada as a benign statesman who genuinely cared about his people. He was my houseguest during the visit. The warmth of his personality and the discipline of the members of his entourage impressed me greatly. At a mammoth rally at Queen's Park, Kaunda admonished Grenadians to pray hard for he knew what revolutionary politics entailed. This timely and fatherly piece of advice went down well with all right thinking Grenadians. Sad to say, subsequent events showed that Kaunda's words were not heeded by the revolutionaries themselves.

Samora Machel, President of Mozambique, also visited Grenada. Our Prime Minister told me that it was not a State visit. His presence in Grenada would give him an opportunity to hold discussions with the Government. Machel stayed in the Government's protocol house, the great house of what used to be Mt. Parnassus Estate. When President Machel visited, cracks were already beginning to appear in the revolutionary structure. The reception party held for him at Butler House was poorly attended. There were many flaws in the arrangements for his visit and from what he saw and heard Machel himself was not convinced that the Revolution was born out of genuine social and economic discontent. I was invited to see Machel off at Pearls Airport. The afternoon before he was due to leave, my office was informed of the time of departure and the arrangements at the airport. To my surprise when I arrived at the airport I met Bishop and some of his colleagues in what appeared to be an informal conference. There was no airplane on the tarmac and Machel was nowhere around. Bishop, in pensive mood, informed me that President Machel left earlier than was planned. I returned to St. George's where school children with their teachers were still dutifully lining the route to say goodbye to President Machel. They too did not see the President as he made his way to the airport.

The anniversary of the Revolution was a hardy annual observed in fine style with all the pomp and ceremony befitting such an occasion. In this regard it superseded the Independence anniversary, which the government had relegated to a very low-key affair. Every year the non-resident diplomats from both East and West converged on Grenada, no doubt anxious to see how this "Glorious Revolution" (to use Bishop's own words) was developing in Grenada. The military parade at Queen's Park was an occasion to put on display not only the revolutionary army and militia but also their weaponry and other appurtenances of war, including armoured personnel carriers – first time to be seen in Grenada. Although the police and other uniformed groups were also there, it was obvious that they did not rank high in the order of priority.

Daniel Ortega, President of Nicaragua and a member of the same ideological fellowship as Bishop, was the guest of honour for the second revolutionary anniversary. At the military parade and rally he, like Bishop, made the usual fiery anti-imperialist speech. As usual the United States of America, which was not visibly represented at the rally, came in for a good tongue-lashing. My wife, who was with me on this occasion, was terribly upset when Ortega presented to Bishop a machine gun as his anniversary gift. When Bishop proudly showed her the gun, she firmly told him that she would not be attending any more of these rallies as she was not comfortable sitting in the VIP section near to him with so many guns around her. This was the last national rally she attended.

The distinguished Prime Minister of Jamaica, Michael Manley, who had his own period of flirtation with communist Cuba, was the official guest for the third anniversary. He and Bishop occupied centre stage at Queen's Park on March 13. Both men respected each other and there was also mutual admiration between them. In his own oratorical style Manley held the crowd spellbound. His visit to Grenada was most welcome – not least because he was held in high regard throughout the Caribbean.

In his very first foreign policy statement, Bishop guaranteed Grenada's continued membership in certain international organizations. One such organization was the Non-aligned Movement in which Grenada had gained membership during the Gairy administration. This body had held out to the world the hope of peaceful co-existence and meaningful friendship among nations. Envisioning the promotion of peace and justice, its membership was based on mutual respect and the non-interference with the internal politics of nations. Adherence to these articles of faith meant that the Non-aligned Movement was well poised to demonstrate to an imperfect world that neutrality and detente were possible notwithstanding differences in size, in political systems and in the level of economic development. The Non-aligned Movement stood out as a beacon of hope for the lessening of tension and the resolution of conflict in a troubled world. The principles of this great organization were clearly extolled by such leading statesmen as President Joseph Tito of Yugoslavia, President Kenneth Kaunda of Zambia and President Julius Nyerere of Tanzania.

Grenada's shift from neutrality came early in the Revolution. At the 1979 summit of non-aligned nations held in Cuba, Grenada decided to join hands with the USSR and its communist satellites who were all engaged in a bitter ideological war with Western imperialism. The main target for their attack was the United States of America. Quickly Grenada viewed the U.S.A. as its major foe. No doubt the Grenadian leader could not do otherwise in the awesome presence of his formidable mentor, Fidel Castro of Cuba, whom he loved so dearly. To adopt this course of action was no error as far as Bishop was concerned. It was well calculated and happily executed. It was the same Bishop who, defying all protocol and unmindful of security considerations, would rush to the podium at a session of the General Assembly of the United Nations to embrace Fidel Castro who had just completed a typical hard hitting speech against Western imperialism. What a bizarre sight it was!

Grenada then was clearly and faithfully aligned to the communist bloc. This was reflected not only in the enhanced intensity of anti-American rhetoric by our revolutionary leaders but also in the growing involvement of communist personnel in the internal affairs of Grenada. The latter development contributed much to the deep, though muted, disgust of an ever-growing number of the Grenadian populace. Many of them remembered fondly their sojourn in the United States of America where they had acquired higher education and had learnt useful skills. They felt very uneasy about this new wave of verbiage. In addition many Grenadians who were increasingly dependent for their livelihood on remittances from relatives in the United States of America, Britain and other so-called imperialist powers questioned the meaning and purpose of Government's growing hostility to these countries. Did the leaders not care about the livelihood and well being of the people? Ultimately, these shifts in Grenada's foreign policy enhanced the disaffection with the revolutionary cause of a number of potential supporters.

All of a sudden there was a steady flow of internationalist workers into Grenada. They came mainly from communist countries, but there were others who were adherents to the Marxist/Leninist teachings living in non-communist countries. These workers were obviously attracted by the new variety of ideological seeds that were taking root in the Isle of Spice. The majority of these workers came from Cuba. They worked very hard on the international airport project in Point Salines. They were also working in the fisheries training school, in agriculture, in hospitals and health clinics. Internationalist workers were also to be found in the field of education, in the legal profession, in the army and police, and in several areas of the civil service.

What was quite clear was that Cuba was gaining a firm foothold in Grenada. There was much speculation in the region as to the extent of Cuba's influence in Grenadian affairs. Some claimed that Ambassador Rizo attended Cabinet meetings. I doubt there was validity in that claim. I received all Cabinet papers and I could trace no evidence of Rizo's presence. Although I had no firm knowledge about his alleged participation in meetings of the Central Committee or the Politburo, I would not doubt that he attended some of them.

Whatever the level of his participation in the affairs of the party or in the business of government, Ambassador Rizo, so ably supported by his American wife, was not without influence in charting the revolutionary course. Given his own Marxist background and the confidence that Castro placed in him, he was well placed to assess the limitations or otherwise of the Grenadian comrades amid the political turmoil and machinations within the Party, particularly in the months leading up to October, 1983. As the official link between Havana and St. George's, Rizo could monitor and interpret the growing strength of the relationship between the two countries. As to his capability as an intelligence officer, which I understand was his primary role, I could neither commend nor condemn him, but, I thought little of him as a diplomat – a view that is supported by Rizo's apparent failure to inform Havana about the growing precariousness of Bishop's position in the third quarter of 1983.

In the context of West Indian politics, Cuban involvement in the revolutionary process placed Grenada in a most unique position. Technical assistance was all to the good, whether it was in the form of scholarships, in the provision of technical experts, or in the construction of the Point Salines Airport. No one could seriously object to these forms of assistance even though every Cuban worker on the airport, according to their own testimony, was first and foremost a revolutionary in the Marxist/Leninist mould. However, it was quite another matter when it came to projects like the adult education programme which was subtly used to inculcate the tenets of the communist doctrine. Meanwhile the placing of the internationalist workers in leadership positions in the public service was a grim signal that we were fast becoming a neo-colonial state, a mere appendage of Cuba. But what mostly worried our brothers and sisters in the English-speaking Caribbean was the accelerated erosion of freedom in Grenada coupled with the lack of opportunity for the people to exercise their freedom of choice in parliamentary elections.

There was a growing body of opinion in the Caribbean community (CARICOM) that only a victory in parliamentary elections could give true legitimacy to Bishop's regime. But within the New Jewel Movement itself opinion was divided on the necessity of holding elections. There was still much work to be done to bring to fulfilment the aims and objectives of the Revolution. In response to the numerous calls for elections Bishop emphasized that participatory democracy was of much more benefit to the people than parliamentary democracy. He relegated parliamentary democracy to a five-minute visit to a polling station every five years. That, he claimed, was the extent of the people's participation in the democratic process – a very arguable claim. What Bishop never grasped was that the Grenadian people were happier with their parliamentary democracy than with his new fangled brand of participatory democracy which was never clearly defined or institutionalized, and which restricted freedom of speech to mutterings in support of the Revolution. Anything to the contrary was classified as counter-revolutionary and anyone suspected of harbouring such thoughts was labelled a "Contra." Either of these categories might constitute eligibility for a prolonged stay in the Richmond Hill Prison.

By 1983 it was generally felt that Grenada was part of the Communist triangle in the Caribbean zone. Cuba and Nicaragua made up the other two sides of that triangle, thus embracing the north, south and west Caribbean. Further, with the embassies of Cuba and of the USSR so well entrenched in Grenada, there was no doubt that our nation was rapidly developing into an ideally suitable place from which to launch political propaganda and promote the communist cause. The incendiary nature of the political rhetoric together with the mounting arsenal of arms and ammunition unequivocally put both national and regional security at risk. The exclusion of free elections from Bishop's agenda, and the continuous erosion of personal liberty caused more than a ripple of anxiety in the rest of the English-speaking Caribbean whose Prime Ministers did not know exactly how to deal with Grenada. As regional support for Bishop and his comrades dwindled, the level of vigilance rose. Immigration authorities in our sister states became very suspicious of our nationals who, on entering their islands for holiday, business or even as transit passengers, were subjected to an unusual spate of questions and sometimes were thoroughly searched. And anyone bearing the surname of Bishop or Coard had to undergo a severe interrogation by alert and seemingly heartless immigration officers. Officials in neighbouring islands hoped to screen out political undesirables and insulate their country from Grenadian revolutionaries.

When the Revolution lost its popular appeal, the Grenadian society had already become very fragmented. The Revolution struck a severe blow at the noble institution of the family, and old family values rapidly disappeared. As teenage boys and girls were lured into joining the militia and participating in weekend manoeuvres which the revolutionary leaders claimed would never be over, sons and daughters turned against their fathers and mothers. Parents had to be careful how they spoke in their own homes for fear that what they said in the privacy of their sitting rooms or verandahs might be taken back to the revolutionary authorities by their own children or by those who designedly chose to visit their children on a regular basis. At church people were openly praying Sunday after Sunday for the children of our nation. Those who were members of the New Jewel Movement or one of the other revolutionary organizations had everything going their way. Others who were outside the ambit of these organizations could expect no favours or help in upward economic mobility. As the gap between the old and the young widened, the Government showed little or no interest in the elderly. For them, day care centres for young children had priority over homes for senior citizens.

Four years after the fall of the Gairy version of parliamentary democracy, cracks began to appear on the revolutionary terrain. As revolutionary fervour steadily waned, cries and prayers for deliverance were on the increase. In fact, there was a closely-knit network of prayer groups throughout the tri-island State of Grenada. The prayer leaders made good use of the telephone to announce the hour of prayer and asked others to pass the word around.

Meanwhile rumours abounded about dissension not only among the leaders themselves but also among the rank and file of supporters. Although the Minister for Finance and Deputy Prime Minister, Bernard Coard, took the unusual but urgent step to increase unilaterally the stipend of the men and women in uniform, that alone could not paper over the deep and widening fissures of discontent.

Rumours soon turned into reality. It was becoming increasingly clear that there were factions in both the army and government. Bishop's visit to Washington in an attempt to make peace with the U.S.A. did not and could not achieve anything of value. His bitter and prolonged anti-American rhetoric was too frequent and too caustic to be easily forgotten. What was more significant was that some of Bishop's colleagues were against such a visit and felt it was a display of weak leadership. Prior to his departure to the U.S.A., Bishop's public statements were more conciliatory in tone. Gail Reed, American wife of Cuban Ambassador Rizo, had advised Bishop on tactics to use with the American press during his tour. One of his aims was to whip up support among U.S. Congressmen and to gain the confidence of the American public particularly the black community. The most senior official he met was William Clark, National Security Adviser.

Some weeks before I was present at a cocktail reception at the Spice Island Inn. When I arrived at the reception Deputy Prime Minister, Bernard Coard, and three of his ministerial colleagues were milling around the guests. Then suddenly they all left the reception together. About ten minutes later Prime Minister Bishop arrived. When he did not see any of his ministers he rushed up to me to say that Coard and others should have been there and he could not understand their absence. When I told Bishop that they had left a few minutes before his arrival, he frowned. To assuage him I suggested that his comrades probably had certain pressing matters to attend to. But I myself wondered what could have gone wrong and I closely observed Bishop.

I discerned that he was a most worried man. On Friday, July 1, 1983, ten days prior to my own departure for the United Kingdom and Rome for audiences with the Queen and of the Pope respectively, I invited Bishop to lunch. After I said the grace before meals Bishop, in a moment of apparent conversion or reconciliation, devoutly made the sign of the cross. At the luncheon table that day, however, for the first time in four years he confided in me without going into specifics that he was under severe stress and that the Revolution was undergoing a very trying period. There was need to consolidate the gains of the Revolution and to forge ahead in unison with greater determination and discipline to achieve the goals.

Rising unemployment, the drop in financial resources, the non-fulfilment of promises, all too frequent caustic rhetoric, the mounting display of intolerance, the curtailment of freedom, and the ill discipline of certain elements in the army and in government – all these contributed to the continuing deterioration of the Revolution.

# 7

## The Revolution Collapses

ON that fateful morning of March 13, 1979, the successful action of a small, haphazardly-armed group of fledging political leaders was greeted, initially, with stunned disbelief in Grenada and beyond. The overthrow of the allegedly corrupt and widely unpopular Gairy regime was, in itself, sufficient reason for Grenadians to rejoice; but as the change quickly came to be perceived as the harbinger of a new era of freedom, social justice and political progress, a new dimension was added to their joy. Significantly, however, the euphoria of the moment was not combined with evidence of a popular demand for the kind of drastic socio/political change envisaged by the New Jewel Movement (NJM). Four years later the freedom, social justice, economic prosperity and political progress promised in the heady aftermath of March 13, 1979, and for which the people of Grenada yearned, had failed to materialize. Instead they had to watch helplessly while the nation's limited financial resources were squandered on vast quantities of arms and equipment for the People's Revolutionary Army and also while the young, self-appointed leaders engaged in internecine, ideological quarrelling as they sought to find scapegoats to blame for the fact that they no longer enjoyed the confidence of the people of Grenada – a situation which no amount of rhetoric could restore. The threat of arrest and subsequent imprisonment had lost much of its deterrent effect – especially for those loved ones who continued to languish in jail without trial, or those whose property had been confiscated. People took time off to pray while the Government looked to the weapons and Armoured Personnel Carriers of the PRA to sustain them in power. In the end, it was the power of prayer that prevailed.

The NJM seized power but whether due to arrogance, or inexperience, or a combination of both, they chose to interpret the undoubted broad support for their overthrow of the Gairy regime as providing them with *carte-blanche* (in political terms) to embark upon the arbitrary introduction of a Marxist-Leninist type regime. In doing so the new political leaders, like their Soviet/Cuban mentors before them, relied heavily on the power of the gun to gain acceptance for their alien dogmas. They never thought it necessary to formulate an acceptable, realistic, socio-political strategy that would meet at least some of the expectations of the people of Grenada. Further, they lacked the intellectual ability and associated discipline to sustain the momentum of their political initiative. Gun power begets gun power.

The absence of any analytical approach to the crucial problem of transforming a hitherto open society like Grenada into one moulded by an uncompromising, totalitarian Marxist/Leninist doctrine, proved to be one of the key inhibiting factors to the NJM's efforts to consolidate their Revolution. Moreover, when a new ideology and its implications are not fully understood by most of those seeking to impose them, this is tantamount to a regime sowing the seeds of its own eventual destruction. If radical change in the political environment of a society is to have any prospect of becoming established, it must have broadly based support at grass roots level; in other words, the process of change must reflect the will and aspirations of the people.

Consolidation of the NJM Revolution was based on the fundamentally flawed premise that Grenadians were a docile, rather submissive people, gullible enough to accept without question a new political and social order in their country. These new political masters had failed to do their homework. Students of Grenada's political history will be aware that in the past Grenadians have proved to be not all that submissive, for example, by being ready to challenge political directives which in any way infringed their established behavioural pattern and cherished lifestyle. They had adult suffrage for almost thirty years and had dutifully gone to the polls every five years to elect their parliamentary representatives. Through radio and television, they have kept abreast of world events and the widest possible range of matters of topical interest and they have long understood the potential of education as an instrument of upward social mobility and as a prerequisite for improved financial status. Such people would be most unlikely to sit idly by and condone the imprisonment of their kith and kin without trial. Nor would they be likely to turn a blind eye to the mounting incidence of curtailment of personal freedom.

All along the NJM and the PRG confused apparent conformity with unity and subservience. In reality the revolutionary government was never able to unite the Grenadian people. Indeed the only impediment to overt resistance and/or open revolt by the populace was the PRA. The inherent fragility of the Grenadian economy began to surface and this, together with clear evidence of growing popular discontent across the age spectrum, caused the NJM to examine themselves. It must be noted that there was a difference between the PRG and the NJM. Some members of the Government were not members of the Party, which, as in the former Soviet Union and its satellites, was the true source of political and executive power. The ascendancy of the Party grew by leaps and bounds and by 1983 there was no doubt that absolute power lay not in the Cabinet but in the NJM through its Central Committee and associated Party organs.

The self-analysis was characterized by panic and arrogance. Instead of soberly reflecting on their performance and planning for future action, on the one hand NJM went through a bitter and self destructive exercise of seeking scapegoats and apportioning blame; while on the other hand, still obsessed with ideology, they advocated and indeed introduced still more draconian measures to secure the people's compliance.

By mid-1983, amid growing discontent and fear reminiscent of the former Gairy regime, the majority of Grenadians had become alienated from the Party and Government. Similarly the chasm between the NJM and the PRG had widened to the extent that the already tenuous line of communication between these two entities had ceased to function. It was no wonder then that members of Government like Lyden Ramdhanny, Minister for Tourism, and Bernard Gittens, Secretary for Health, were unaware of the turbulence then current within the Central Committee of the Party. I too was equally ignorant of the bitter in-fighting taking place.

Bernard Coard, the chief proponent of the Marxist/Leninist ideology, was the first to resign from the Central Committee though not from his ministerial portfolio. This he did later. True to form, he expressed his displeasure that the Party was not run under strict Leninist principles and in a subtle swipe at the leadership of the Party complained that he had to work too hard to keep the Party afloat. Without doubt Coard was the most influential member of the Central Committee. He obviously thought his resignation would stimulate renewed enthusiasm among his comrades on the Central Committee who would then realize the importance and urgency of pursuing more rigidly the Leninist principles in order to accomplish greater output and a higher level of discipline. It has been mooted in some quarters that Coard was the hardline communist while Bishop was a social democrat *cum* nice guy whose mission was to create a classless society. I do not share this sympathetic view of Bishop. While it is true that, in ideological terms, Coard might have drunk more deeply than Bishop from the communist spring, there is no doubt in my mind that Bishop was equally ruthless. Responsibility for the human rights abuses, the torturing, the imprisonment without trial, and many other unseemly acts lay squarely with Bishop. On his own admission, in the famous Line of

March speech, it was he who sanctioned over and over again the injustice of sending people to jail without trial or the hope of one. Although Bishop pretended not to know about many of the injustices done in his name, I am convinced that he was privy to all of them. In most cases he personally gave orders that these injustices should be carried out. Bishop's residence was the venue for all kinds of discussions, both formal and informal. In any case, as leader of the Party and the Government, he was directly responsible for the governance of the country. This responsibility like any other could not be delegated. Coard might have spoken with greater authority than Bishop on ideological matters, but this was because he was an avid reader, a meticulous scholar, and better versed in the Marxist/Leninist ideology. With his own pretensions to leadership, and spurred by the subtle promptings of his ambitious wife, Phyllis, Coard was able to outflank Bishop and eventually gained the support of the senior army officers and the majority of the members of the Central Committee.

Between July and September, 1983, the Central Committee spent long hours behind closed doors examining themselves and evaluating the work of the Party and the Government. Bishop came in for the kind of severe and uncharitable criticism so reminiscent of that which used to precede the classic Soviet show trials. His leadership, it was argued, lacked ideological clarity; as Prime Minister he was undisciplined in his approach to dealing with the affairs of the nation. His failure to apply Marxist/Leninist principles in his Prime Ministerial role was the subject of unqualified opprobrium and heartless condemnation. If, indeed, Bishop was guilty of any ideological omission in his leadership role, he nevertheless demonstrated clearly that by accepting the criticisms levelled against him, he was strictly adhering to Marxist/Leninist principles. Or was he simply trying to save his job – indeed his future – even his life?

The meetings held in July, 1983, were inconclusive. A subsequent meeting held on August 24, 1983, was similarly unproductive. It was therefore decided to recall all Central Committee members from abroad for a crisis meeting in September. Clearly, even though they acknowledged his charisma and his popularity among the people generally, the Central Committee, while divided up to a point, was nevertheless heavily weighted against Bishop. The Committee again reiterated and emphasized Bishop's lack of ideological direction. It was at this meeting that Liam James, a serious and committed adherent of the Marxist/Leninist ideology, proposed joint leadership of the Party and of the Government. Whether or not James's proposal surprised the other Committee members or had been previously discussed in other forums is uncertain. In any event Coard was identified as the most suitable comrade to give ideological direction. He would also be responsible for re-organizing the Party and the Government while Bishop was to develop relationships with the masses, business leaders and professionals. A vote was taken on the proposal for joint leadership. Nine voted in favour, one opposed, and three including Bishop abstained. Bishop, visibly moved by the results, was not and could not be in favour of joint leadership. He abstained so as not to show outright opposition. To have opposed the proposal would have been tantamount to rejecting the sacred cow of self criticism – a serious flouting of Leninist principles.

The last meeting of the Central Committee took place on September 24, 1983, just before Bishop made what was to be his final overseas visit. This time he was heading for Eastern Europe. Bishop grudgingly accepted the joint leadership proposal. The assembled members of the Central Committee burst forth into singing the *Internationale* and warmly embraced both Coard and Bishop. This warm embrace did not prevent Bishop from becoming more and more suspicious and distrustful of the intentions of his colleagues.

A meeting of the People's Revolutionary Government called for October 12 proved abortive because of a rumour allegedly started and spread by Bishop that Coard was plotting to kill him. Immediately put under house arrest by the upper echelons of the armed forces, Bishop was joined voluntarily by one of his paramours, Jacqueline Creft, Minister for Education – already pregnant with his child. The news of Bishop's arrest sent shock waves throughout the length and breadth of Grenada. It was the people's turn to take action.

On Friday, October 14, I summoned Patrick MacLeish, Commissioner of Police, to my office so that he could brief me on the security of the State. His description of the widening schism in the ruling New Jewel Movement between what he termed the moderates and the hardliners confirmed my worst fears. With the Prime Minister under house arrest, the future of the Government hung in the balance. The rift in the party was now in the public domain following a meeting in front of the offices of the "Free West Indian" newspaper, at which Bernard Coard and Selwyn Strachan, Minister for Mobilisation, publicly denounced Prime Minister Bishop. They tried their utmost to whip up support for the removal of Bishop and the installation of Coard as Prime Minister, but to no avail. From the lukewarm reception they received from the crowd, it was quite clear that such support was unlikely to be forthcoming.

These events had already reached the media, regionally and worldwide. Chris DeRiggs, the Minister for Health, was sent abroad to explain the current situation to our diplomats and at the same time to solicit the support of Grenadian nationals for a change in the leadership of the Party and Government. However, his mission proved to be abortive due to events in Grenada.

Bernard Coard always had a passion for leadership. He was never content to play second fiddle. I discerned this peculiar trait in Coard when he was under my tutelage at the Grenada Boys' Secondary School. I taught him both in the lower school and in the sixth form and from the very outset was forcibly struck by his industriousness and diligence. I would never forget how he consistently questioned my marking of History assignments in the sixth form. More specifically he wanted to know why his classmate, Winston McIntosh, was always scoring higher grades than he, when he could see no substantial difference between his script and that of McIntosh. McIntosh, an exceptionally brilliant youngster, went on to annex the Island Scholarship with three distinctions in the Cambridge A level examinations – a feat which Coard could not attain.

Despite his inability to gain top marks in my class, Coard always seemed to consider me one of his favourite masters. When on leaving school he applied for a scholarship to Brandeis University in the United States of America, he insisted that I should give him a testimonial. I obliged and indeed I followed his subsequent career with interest.

Whenever Coard acted as Prime Minister, he made it his duty to call on me. Always punctual for his appointment he would bring me a pile of reading material as if to say: "Read on, old boy, keep yourself gainfully occupied and do not interfere with our business." He had an incisive brain and was very persuasive and logical in his arguments. He would proceed to bring me up to date on matters of State and outline the projects currently undertaken by Government. He usually concluded by giving me a mini-lecture on the world economic situation as it affected Grenada and the rest of the Caribbean. His visits were always instructive.

Selwyn Strachan, another of my former students, was nowhere near Coard in intellectual ability. His stand against Bishop surprised me greatly because of the longstanding closeness between the two men. But in the pursuit of power, friendships are often sacrificed.

Following the futile attempt to gain popular support for the sacking of the Prime Minister, Kenrick Radix, former Minister for Justice, got into the act. On Saturday, October 14, a public meeting was held in the St. George's Market Square in support of his very good friend, Bishop. This was not well attended, and Radix was rewarded for his effort by being arrested and put behind bars in Richmond Hill Prison allegedly for security reasons. Tension throughout the country increased – a situation exacerbated by growing uncertainty and fear.

Amid the tension the populace sought divine assistance. This was manifested by the reportedly massive congregations at church services throughout Grenada on the following day, Sunday, October 16. At the Blessed Sacrament Church in Grand Anse where my wife and I worshipped, we could not help observing the swollen congregation. After lunch on that day, my wife and I journeyed along the picturesque west coast to the town of Gouyave, some twelve miles from St. George's, to visit my mother. Along the route we could see and hear small pockets of people in discussions. As my car rolled along, they kept shouting, "Where is the Prime Minister? We want our Prime Minister."

On the following day with humble duty, I transmitted a despatch to the Queen apprising her of the deteriorating situation in Grenada. At eleven o'clock that morning, I received Bishop Sydney Charles. We held dialogue for about half an hour after which we prayed together. On Tuesday morning, October 18, I received John Kelly of the British High Commission, and in the afternoon I received the Commissioner of Police who briefed me on demonstrations held in St. Andrew's, St. David's and St. John's – all in support of Prime Minister Bishop. It was patently clear that the hardliners in the Party could depend only on gun power for their survival. They had lost the support of the masses.

On the evening of October 18, a Central Committee delegation proceeded to the Prime Minister's residence to present him with a proposal that he would remain Prime Minister but would be removed from the Central Committee and cease to be Commander-in-Chief of the Armed Forces. Bishop agreed to consider the proposal and to give an answer by the following morning. But on the morning of Tuesday, October 19, the atmosphere in St. George's was heavily charged with emotion. One had the eerie feeling that something horrendous was going to happen. While the comrades on the Central Committee eagerly awaited Bishop's reply to their latest proposal of joint leadership, the youth of the nation had other ideas that they rapidly translated into decisive action. A few days earlier, secondary school students had led a demonstration in the parish of St. Andrew's. They chose the tarmac at Pearls Airport to vent their feelings of disgust at the action of the Central Committee and to lay blame, unequivocally, on Bernard Coard who, as far as they were concerned, was the main architect of the house arrest of the Prime Minister.

After a peaceful and highly successful demonstration in St. Andrew's, the organizers decided to take their protest to the streets of St. George's where they joined forces with their counterparts in the secondary schools. Accordingly on that morning they assembled on the Tanteen playing field where their numbers were immediately augmented by students of the Grenada Boys' Secondary School and the Anglican High School. Later they were joined by their counterparts of the Presentation Boys' College and the St. Joseph's Convent at the other end of town. With youthful exuberance and in an unprecedented mood of defiance, they proceeded to Bishop's residence at Mt. Wheldale, firm in their resolve to free the Prime Minister. Without arms, the students marched to Mt. Wheldale chanting and displaying their placards. Along the route, they were joined by several adults. Those who were unable to join the march proffered every moral support and encouragement.

While all this was happening Norris Bain was in my office. He informed me that he had resigned as a Minister of Government. To whom the letter of resignation was addressed was immaterial at that point and I did not question him. Earlier in the morning, Lyden Ramdhanny, who had wisely remained at home with his gate securely locked, telephoned to inform me that he had resigned as a Minister of Government. Bain went on to tell me that for the past few days, Coard had been holding secret meetings in his residence which was just a stone's throw from where Bishop was under house arrest at the Prime Minister's residence. On behalf of the people of St. Andrew's, he urged me to intervene in an effort to affect some measure of reconciliation between the two factions in the Party, thus ensuring peace in the country. What I did not say to Bain was that it might be easier to dismantle the high wall between Bishop's residence and Coard's than to bridge the gap between the warring factions in the New Jewel Movement. I told Bain that there was nothing I could do except on the advice of the Prime Minister. Bain, an affable and successful businessman, had been an elected member of Parliament when the Revolution took place. He left my office perhaps with little comfort, but, at least, I had given him a listening ear. What was significant about Bain's visit was that in the current crisis, he felt that it was to the Governor General he should turn. But Bain was not alone in this, given the numerous phone calls to my office all in the same refrain. What is the Governor General doing about the chaotic situation in the country? All of a sudden, people seemed oblivious of the revolutionary situation which had gripped the tri-island State of Grenada since March, 1979. Or was it because they had a burning desire to return to democratic rule?

I was at my desk when cacophonous sounds that seemed to emanate from the western approaches to my premises warned me that the demonstration was on the final leg of its historic journey to the Prime Minister's official residence. Because the noise was coming through louder and louder, I hastened to my verandah to catch a glimpse of the crowd. From there I could see the mildly militant marchers purposively pacing their way along the western gate up the gentle incline to Mt.Wheldale where Prime Minister Bishop had been confined over the last six days. Soon I heard the gruesome sound of gun shots coming from Mt. Wheldale. For a moment, thoughts of a bloody confrontation were conjured up in my mind. However, from my vantage point, I could see no signs that the motley crowd had retreated or dispersed. I, therefore, came to the conclusion that the soldiers on duty at Mt. Wheldale had fired warning shots. This was subsequently confirmed by General Hudson Austin who informed me that the guards had been ordered not to turn their guns on the demonstrators, but to fire shots in the air. The melodrama continued. Eye witnesses later confirmed that there was no resistance by the guards when a small group of demonstrators led by Unison Whiteman, Minister for Agriculture, forced the door open and entered the building. Within minutes the human voices burst into a crescendo that could only be described as joyful. The demonstrators had accomplished their mission. They had freed their Prime Minister.

In a jubilant mood the demonstrators descended the little hill from Mt. Wheldale and made a right turn into Lucas Street towards the city centre. Returning to my office I began to ask myself all sorts of questions. What would be Bishop's next move? What would be the reaction of the Central Committee who had ordered his house arrest? Would they retaliate in some harsh and painful manner? Or would they at least temporarily put aside ideological considerations and re-assess the political situation objectively with a view to finding a peaceful solution to their current problems? Bearing in mind the deep chasm between the two opposing factions and the rigidity of their respective positions, I saw very little chance of any objective and common sense approach towards settling the leadership problem. Both sides were lacking in objectivity and maturity of thought and it would seem that both sides were determined to place ideological imperatives before the well-being of the Grenadian people who had clearly demonstrated that they were not in tune with the machinations of the Central Committee. Obviously not only was there a serious rift within the New Jewel Movement as manifested by the inability of the Central Committee to arrive at genuine consensus but also, and at this stage more significantly, the general populace continued to distance themselves more and more from the Party and the Government.

As I walked along the corridor from my office I had an uneasy feeling that business would not be as usual. My thoughts were interrupted by the ringing of the telephone when my secretary informed me that Mr Norris Bain was on the line. Mr Bain, whom I had received earlier that day, informed me that the Prime Minister was freed and the crowd went away with him to the Market Square where he would address them. "Your Excellency," he said, "you should see the bystanders cheering and waving as the procession moved triumphantly along the city streets. Maurice appeared to have lost weight but otherwise seemed to be in good spirits." The people in procession were chanting and displaying their banners. One banner read: "NO COARD, NO COMMUNISM." I told Mr Bain how very pleased I was to hear that the Prime Minister had been freed and I thanked him for keeping me informed.

Soon after this conversation, all the telephones at my residence ceased to work. Happily this was short lived, as within ten minutes the telephone service was restored. I learnt subsequently that the service had been disconnected throughout Grenada.

For some unknown reason, Prime Minister Bishop was not taken to the Market Square in St. George's where people had already started to assemble in anticipation of his arrival and to hear his address. Instead, the procession headed for the restricted area of Fort Rupert, the headquarters of the People's Revolutionary Army and a repository for guns, ammunition, explosives and other lethal accessories.

This fort stands majestically overlooking the picturesque land locked harbour of St. George's. Its ancient cannons are a quiet reminder of its eventful past. For decades it had been the headquarters of the Royal Grenada Police Force until the lawmen were edged out by the military. At the back of the fort and in close proximity stands the General Hospital occupying for the most part what used to be the military barracks. Built by the French in 1706, the fort was named Fort Royale. When the British finally wrested Grenada from the French by the Treaty of Versailles in 1783, they renamed the fort Fort George. After almost two centuries, Bishop renamed it Fort Rupert after his late father. Interestingly enough, in conversations about Fort Rupert, I was often cynically reminded that Prime Minister Bishop's middle name was also Rupert.

I anxiously awaited news about the unfolding of events with particular reference to the extent to which Bishop was able to re-assert his authority as Commander-in-Chief of the Armed Forces and as Prime Minister. Actions revolving around the Prime Minister wherever he might be would have without a shadow of a doubt implications for the country's future. Long shadows of fear and uncertainty seemed to have gripped the troubled landscape as it became well nigh impossible for me or my staff to get any official information. Even the local radio station seemed to have been silenced. From about nine o'clock that morning, the radio station was off the air. That did not ruffle my mental equilibrium in the least for in more recent times Radio Free Grenada was nothing more than a piece of propaganda machinery. From the vantage point of my verandah that overlooked the harbour and Fort Rupert, I observed the volume and the velocity of the vehicular traffic on the road below. There was nothing unusual except for military personnel carriers proceeding down the street supposedly towards the city centre. But suddenly there were sporadic columns of smoke ascending in the air. Hurriedly calling out to my wife, I said, "My God, something terrible seems to be happening at the Fort." In a split second I could see an enormous mass of human bodies trying to escape from Fort Rupert by jumping the walls. It was a dreadful sight. I at once concluded that the doctors and nurses at the nearby General Hospital would have an enormous job on their hands.

Such was the scene at Fort Rupert on that dreadful day when the People's Revolutionary Army, allegedly acting under orders from what was left of a truncated People's Revolutionary Government, turned their guns on the people. The people's response was to scamper for their lives. Unfortunately for Bishop's supporters, unarmed and unprotected, they were pretty much unable to get away from the scene by using the lone access road that was by then visibly blocked by an Armoured Personnel Carrier. They instinctively resorted to the flanks of the fort and jumped the walls. The spectre of Grenadians leaping from such heights in order to escape upset me greatly and I had to wait for some considerable time for any official or reliable information as to the outcome of what had appeared to be a bloody confrontation at Fort Rupert. All afternoon and into the evening, rumour was spreading its ugly wings, giving rise to conflicting reports of casualties. I was particularly interested in the fate of the Prime Minister. As evening approached, news of him was even more conflicting. No one could tell me what the true position was. There were no further calls from Norris Bain. I simply had to wait. Meanwhile the first bit of news I heard of the Prime Minister was that he had been arrested. I later heard that he had been injured and taken to the hospital weak and exhausted. Still later the more persistent rumour was that he was dead.

Any thought of a scenario of mayhem and carnage was far from the minds of those who had assembled on Fort Rupert to hear from the lips of their leader his part of the story of a Revolution that had turned sour. Without any resistance they had successfully released Bishop from house arrest and their main aim was to restore the integrity of his prime ministership. As the shots rang out over Fort Rupert, pandemonium broke loose and quickly spread throughout St. George's as everyone tried to get to the safety of his or her own home. In the process many were left stranded as the busmen themselves were so scared and so overcome by their eagerness to return to their home base that they left behind many of their passengers. In desperation and fright many had to walk home that night, in some instances as far as Grenville. By the time news of the Fort Rupert massacre reached the outer parishes, families became worried about their relatives whose arrival back home seemed ages away. There was no way of knowing whether any missing family members were dead, at the hospital with injuries, or stranded on the roadside under the cover of darkness.

Radio Free Grenada was back on the air in the evening with its normal programmes as if nothing grave had happened in St. George's during the day. I had to wait until 10 o'clock that night when General Hudson Austin, who had apparently assumed control of the country, went on radio to tell Grenadians about the events at Fort Rupert. All Grenada had waited with bated breath to hear from General Austin who, as announced by radio, was to make a national broadcast. I first met Hudson Austin when I served on the Prisons Visiting Committee in 1967/68. Austin was then a Prisons Officer. He later ran foul of the Gairy administration and was made redundant. Austin felt certain that it was political victimization. I recall his visiting my office at the Botanical Gardens seeking my assistance in the payment of some terminal benefit that he claimed was due to him. He was then a staunch supporter of the Grenada National Party that was in opposition to Gairy's Grenada United Labour Party. In his capacity as lay preacher, he regularly worshipped at the Bethel Methodist Church in St. Paul's. After leaving the Prisons Service, Austin got attached to a road building company where he acquired some knowledge of road construction. I remember him as a very jovial and polite individual who seemed to be able to get along with people. However, from all reports, his career in the army seemed to have brought to the forefront his rough edges. Those who knew him well thought that he had changed into a brutal man. To what extent the communist ideology clouded his better judgment it is difficult to tell, and I firmly believed that the likes of Austin were more concerned about removing Gairy from office than imposing a foreign ideology on the Grenadian people.

At last came the voice of General Hudson Austin. He was clearly nervous and it was obvious that he was reading a prepared text. According to an eye witness, who was an employee at Radio Free Grenada, two armed soldiers had accompanied the General. Their demeanour and the way they had their guns fixed on Austin made it unclear if they felt their task was to protect the General or to ensure that he faithfully recorded the contents of the paper from which he read. Indeed, as told by the same eye witness, one of the armed soldiers interrupted the General and admonished him not to look so sad as he made his first attempt at recording the statement which he nervously held in unsteady hands. The General tried hard to oblige, but he could not hide his emotions. In the end he mispronounced the word "curfew" by saying "cuffoo.'" For some time afterwards, people referred to him as the "cuffoo man." As I listened to the broadcast I felt certain that it was not Austin's composition.

Shivers ran through me when Austin rattled off the names of the dead – Maurice Bishop, Jacqueline Creft, Unison Whiteman, Norris Bain and Fitzroy Bain among others. His report that they were all victims of a cross fire was clearly intended to make us believe that they were in the wrong place at the wrong time. He informed the nation that there were eighteen dead including a soldier in an armoured car. Neither the figure nor the manner in which these eighteen reportedly met their death was accepted by the populace. However, no one as far as I know has ever come up with a list of missing persons or of other persons known to be killed at Fort Rupert on that dreadful Wednesday. Whether or not Austin's figure was accurate he could not have been far wrong. Austin further announced a twenty-four hour curfew with immediate effect and soldiers were empowered to shoot on sight anyone flouting this proclamation. He also informed his listeners that a Revolutionary Military Council was now in charge of the affairs of Grenada. Austin, of course, was head of the Military Council.

While news of Bishop's death shook me profoundly, I was particularly saddened by Norris Bain's passing. Only hours before his untimely death, Bain, an affable and non-violent man, had been in my office giving me useful information on the current divisiveness of the New Jewel Movement and the virtual collapse of the Government. Firmly entrenched in Bishop's camp, Bain claimed that all the shots were being called by Coard who, in his estimation, was the chief architect of the dismemberment of the People's Revolutionary Government. It was Bain who in a jubilant mood telephoned me to say that Prime Minister Bishop had been released from house arrest. With hindsight I should have kept Bain at my residence by inviting him to stay on for lunch. Or better still, I might have warned him to make a hasty retreat to his home in Grenville and not get involved in the protest demonstrations.

Bishop's assassination was the occasion of the demise of the People's Revolutionary Government. It was not the cause. To seek the causation of the collapse of the Government, one must examine deeply the growing disenchantment and discontent of the populace, the slender financial resources of the country, and the unacceptable arrogance of certain elements in the government and the army. Months before his death Bishop had lost control of the Party and by extension was powerless to lead the Government. He no longer had the support of key ministers and the senior cadre of the army. In the opinion of some of his own comrades, Maurice Bishop had to die the way he did.

Grenada had registered yet another first. The expiration of Bishop marked the very first execution of a Prime Minister, albeit a non-elected one, in the English-speaking Caribbean. This dastardly act completely traumatized the Grenadian people. The massacre at Fort Rupert was followed by six days of military rule. It was a period of unprecedented fear and terror. But what was especially frightening was a man-hunt for Bishop's key supporters, many of whom had gone into hiding. Members of what was left of the People's Revolutionary Army armed with AK47 rifles and submachine guns were assiduously searching for these supporters, some of whom remained in hiding about a fortnight long after it was safe enough to be out and about breathing a new air of freedom. One teacher, a Bishop supporter, told me that after the massacre at Fort Rupert, she abandoned her own home and went into hiding at her grandmother's residence some four miles away. After a futile visit to the teacher's home, the armed soldiers pounced on the grandmother's residence, but despite a grueling inter-rogation meted out to the grandmother, they failed to find the young lady who had securely hidden herself underneath the bed.

Similarly, a high-ranking official in the Ministry of External Affairs, another known supporter of Bishop, could not be found for days afterwards. The high command of the RMC was completely flabbergasted. Major Leon Cornwall, a young rising star in the ruling faction, asked me whether I knew anything about his whereabouts as his services were required to send an urgent message to London and other world capitals about the true situation in Grenada. No wonder that a telex which was intended for the Foreign and Commonwealth Office in London made its way to an office in Bruton Street.

The Richmond Hill Prisons became so overcrowded that the authorities had to resort to a goat pen in the Prisons compound in order to accom-modate some fourteen detainees who were herded together without the basic necessities. These recently arrived detainees – all men – included well known, decent, non-violent and upright citizens.

The abuse of human rights was at its peak. What came to be known as a concentration camp was established at Good Hope just outside the capital.

Potential trouble-makers who were known supporters of Bishop were taken to Good Hope for an unknown period of confinement. The economic life blood of the country ceased to flow and social interaction was almost at a standstill. Soldiers armed with AK47 rifles were on patrol to ensure that the curfew was strictly observed. Passes were given by the army to workers in the essential services, and pregnant mothers in labour and the critically ill were escorted by army personnel to maternity clinics and to the General Hospital. The staff at my Residence were issued with passes.

# 8

## The Six-day Rule of Terror

THE despicable atrocities perpetrated at Fort Rupert were completely out of character with the traditional way of life in Grenada. Homicidal acts are so rare in this normally tranquil country that it is not uncommon for a murder, whatever the circumstances, to be considered as a national tragedy. How much more the bloody events of October 19, 1983! These murders evoked not only anger and disgust but also widespread emotional shock. Yet if one were to examine critically the style of governance during the revolutionary regime, one would probably conclude that what occurred at Fort Rupert was inevitable. The new brand of freedom about which the Government and its agents so often boasted was negated by their innumerable acts in breach of human dignity.

With "gunocracy" as the order of the day during the revolutionary period, the tragic events of October 19 provided appropriate vindication for Christ's rebuke to one of his disciples – "for all they that take the sword shall perish with the sword." The formation of public opinion was inhibited by the ever-present threat of the gun. Thus it was farcical to say that Grenadians supported the arbitrary acts and unconscionable edicts of a Government that systematically restricted freedom of speech, subtly withdrew the right to dissent, and was all set to launch a blistering assault on freedom of conscience by uprooting the deep seated pillars of the Church. But Grenadians are too independent-minded to accept without question imposed communism or any other "ism" in which they did not believe.

When Bishop made what turned out to be his final journey to Fort Rupert, his purpose was neither to invoke God's blessing on his beleaguered nation nor to seek personal forgiveness. Rather, his main objective was to re-assert himself as Leader of the Revolution, as Prime Minister and, of course, Commander-in-Chief of the Armed Forces. This was by no means easy. For he could not accomplish this mission without the loyalty and ready support of the senior Army officers who had helped to elevate him and who were now firmly in control of Grenada's massive arsenal of arms and ammunition. Bishop belatedly discovered that he could no longer depend on his charisma and rhetoric to faceplate his last ditch effort to regain effective power.

The revolutionary regime could be aptly described as having ushered in a period of arbitrary arrest. From its early days the Revolution's so-called security forces had been apprehending people at will and putting them behind bars. In many cases the arrests were brutally carried out in the early hours of the morning. Soldiers and/or militiamen would knock on a door or simply burst it open and forcefully drag out their prey in the presence of loved ones who dared not utter a word of protest. The AK47 was the symbol of authority. Warrants of arrest had become obsolete.

The People's Revolutionary Army happily received an increase in pay when Bernard Coard, Minister for Finance, correctly read the potentially unsettling situation in the country and thought it prudent to be on the right side of the Army by singling them out for increased salaries. Cunning strategist that he was, Coard, who by then considered himself well versed in the ramifications of financial control and sufficiently knowledgeable about the role of the Treasury, instructed his chief Civil Servant in the Ministry of Finance, Lauriston Wilson Jr., to proceed on leave. In Coard's estimation Wilson seemed a tired man. This was conveyed to Wilson in a handwritten letter from Coard. In his typewritten reply to the Minister, Wilson denied that he was in any way suffering from debility, but he nevertheless, in strict accordance with Civil Service practice and procedure, sought permission from the Public Service Commission to proceed on leave and to take all the leave due to him with immediate effect. His leave was granted. An accountant by profession Wilson had advanced through the ranks of the Civil Service by dint of hard work, including a period of study at Leeds College of Commerce in the United Kingdom. He had ultimately reached the topmost rung of the ladder in the Ministry of Finance.

Coard obviously felt that he himself was up to the task of running the Treasury comfortably and competently without the input of this experienced and well qualified Permanent Secretary and Director of Finance who was devoid of the current revolutionary fervour and who was too prone to be guided by established financial rules and regulations. Notwithstanding a temporary replacement for Wilson, the Minister could now have his way without any bureaucratic impediment. He no longer needed Wilson's sage advice to deal with the International Monetary Fund or World Bank. Nor did he need any input from Prime Minister Bishop with whom relations had been strained.

Following the special increase in their remuneration, the Army, particularly the senior officers, warmed considerably to Coard whom they saw as their benefactor. Because of that increase and their newfound influence in the Central Committee, it was virtually impossible for anyone to call a halt to the excesses of the Security Forces. In the absence of civil or even political structures to curb human rights abuses, the Security Forces arrogated to themselves the right to treat the rest of the population as objects to be manipulated rather than citizens to be served and protected. In short, the Security Forces gave themselves licence to arrest on a whim and even to kill at will.

As early as June, 1981, Strachan Philip was mercilessly killed at his home for allegedly detonating a bomb during an official rally at Queen's Park just beneath the pavilion where the Prime Minister and I, among others, were sitting. Three persons were killed by the explosion. Despite Philip's violent end, three other persons were arrested, subsequently tried, and convicted for the same offence. On the night of that rally the quiet village of Mt. Airy about four miles from the capital was rocked by heavy gunfire in the pursuit of Strachan Philip who was relaxing at his home. This was a most degrading manifestation of the abuse of power and a shameful act of official violence. Strachan Philip had played a leading role in the assault on the True Blue barracks on the morning of March 13, 1979, but he soon became disillusioned with the direction the Revolution was taking. His disaffection was presumably regarded by the regime as sufficient justification to kill him, and the Queen's Park bomb incident provided a convenient opportunity to do so.

On Thursday, October 13, 1983, Vincent Noel, a committed comrade and by his own admission a communist, was arrested immediately after a meeting with Maurice Bishop. Members of the Security Forces accosted Noel as he left Bishop's residence. According to his own account, he was taken below a nearby mango tree and questioned by Chalkie Ventour and Ian St. Bernard, two senior officers in the Army. A former Junior Minister in the government, Noel was apprehended for alleged conspiracy, placed under house arrest and had all his firearms and ammunition taken away from him. He was among those killed at Fort Rupert on October 19.

The brutal massacre at Fort Rupert was spontaneously and immediately condemned throughout the Caribbean. The editorial columns in the regional press sharply rebuked the perpetrators of such a heinous crime. Newspaper headlines and commentaries on radio and television broadcast a storm of protest steadfastly deploring the vicious and senseless action of a group of power hungry, ideologically motivated thugs. In Grenada itself, with freedom of the press in abeyance, people intensified their prayer efforts within the confines of their homes and made highly effective use of the telephone to strengthen and lengthen the prayer chains, which had been in existence even before the horrendous action at Fort Rupert. Their brothers and sisters in other Caribbean islands remembered Grenadians constantly in prayer. From their various pulpits throughout the region ministers of religion profoundly deplored this unchristian event in a Christian society as they sought God's help for reconciliation and the early return to normalcy in the tri-island state of Grenada.

Only Radio Free Grenada seemed unmoved by the enormity of the macabre events at the Fort that day. For our national radio it was business as usual. Not one funereal note, not a word of prayer, nor the sound of sombre music was heard on our airwaves as the dead bodies were hurriedly and surreptitiously removed from the eighteenth-century fortifications. No official reference was made to the communist style executions until General Austin came on the air that evening to make the infamous broadcast in which he tried to hoodwink his listeners into believing that those who were dead had been killed accidentally.

The work rhythm of the populace was seriously interrupted by the imposition of the rigorously enforced 24-hour curfew. Industry and commerce were brought to a standstill in a country with a fragile economy and where financial resources were less than adequate in both the public and private sectors. It was in rural communities that the stringency of the curfew was most acutely felt. Farmers could not go to their fields early in the morning, as they were accustomed to do, to tend their animals and to harvest fruit and vegetables for the sustenance of their families. It took individuals like Grenadian born Archbishop Cuthbert Woodroffe, Anglican Archbishop of the West Indies, to point out the particular difficulties being encountered by people in the rural areas.

Speaking from his Cathedral chair in neighbouring St. Vincent, he pleaded with the Grenadian authorities to spare some thought for the acute suffering of the people generally. It was not clear whether the subsequent temporary lifting of the curfew was attributable to the Archbishop's intervention, but Grenadians were given a whiff of freedom for three hours on Friday, October 21, during which they rushed to their fields and to the shops to replenish their stocks of food. People without pipe borne water at home were able to collect drinking water from the nearest standpipes. But the greatest number of people converged on the banks. Long queues developed outside all the banks as customers tried to get in before the curfew deadline. In an atmosphere of fear and uncertainty many customers were busily engaged in withdrawing most, if not all, of their savings. They were afraid that the Revolutionary Military Council might seize whatever money they had in their accounts. Thus the drain on the funds of the Government owned National Commercial Bank was particularly severe.

Sunday, October 23, 1983, must go down in the annals of Grenada's history as a painful day for our overwhelmingly Christian community. For the first time Grenadians were denied the right to attend Holy Mass or other religious services on the Lord's Day. The 24-hour curfew was still in effect. True to form, the RMC did not consider Christian worship a priority but an irrelevance and were not prepared to lift the curfew to facilitate religious obligations.

Moreover, the enforced closure of all places of worship could be construed as a further hostile attempt to weaken the power of the Church. In this sense the curfew provided the kind of opportunity which the ruling authorities so desperately wished and so happily embraced an opportunity to muzzle the Church even for a day. It cannot be over-emphasized that the Church was always a thorn in the flesh of the People's Revolutionary Government, which swiftly exploited every opportunity to embarrass and belittle the clergymen. The treatment meted out to Rev. Keith Ledson, Head of the Methodist Church in Grenada, was a case in point. That Reverend gentleman was expelled from the country because he had refused to hold a funeral service on a Sunday for McGodden Grant, a political activist and member of the hierarchy of the People's Revolutionary Government. Refusal to bury the dead on a Sunday was in keeping with an agreement among the members of the Grenada Conference of Churches. As a member of the Conference the Methodist Church was naturally party to that agreement. Thus in this regard Rev. Ledson had committed no wrong. He had not broken any law of the land. He had simply taken a principled stand notwithstanding the fact that Grant had come from a most devout Methodist family. According to repeated radio announcements Grant was to receive a State funeral as decreed by the Government. I thought this was farcical. Further, my office was not informed. Therefore, I took no notice of the radio announcement. I did not attend the funeral. Nor did I send a representative.

The Anglican bishops in the Caribbean were not exempt from receiving scant courtesy from the Government. As part of the centenary celebrations of the Anglican Province of the West Indies the bishops assembled in Grenada for eight days, September 25 to October 2, 1983. They preached and officiated at services throughout the country, and the Grenada celebrations culminated in a procession and public mass at Queen's Park in St. George's. The Government distanced itself as much as possible from the celebrations. A previously arranged appointment with the Prime Minister proved abortive and the bishops could not even make contact with the Deputy Prime Minister. This was very embarrassing for me as the Archbishop of the West Indies, Cuthbert Woodroffe, was my houseguest. Being treated in this way in the land of his birth, too, embarrassed him.

The six-day rule of the Revolutionary Military Council was a period of unprecedented trepidation and uncertainty. This was a situation exacerbated by the ensuing atmosphere of hatred and division that devastated the customary tranquility of an island of naturally friendly people whose hopes and aspirations for a better quality of life had been suddenly shattered. The average Grenadian could not come to terms with the harsh reality of his Prime Minister being killed by his own colleagues in broad daylight and in the presence of hundreds of citizens. Could this dastardly act have been premeditated? Could it have been a ghastly mistake? Could it have been accidental? To attempt to find answers to these questions it is necessary to examine closely the flirtation with violence which characterized the activities of the New Jewel Movement from its inception and which became an essential part of its ideological strategy during the four-year regime in Grenada. Indeed, I think it conceivable that if, on October 19, Bishop had succeeded in re-establishing himself as Prime Minister and Leader of the New Jewel Movement, Grenada would have veered off on a political course rather different from the parliamentary democracy (freedom of speech and press freedom included at no extra charge) we have enjoyed since October, 1983. Coard and others, now imprisoned, would presumably have met the full force of his vengeance – perhaps tragically – leaving Bishop to pursue his revolutionary course, unhindered by hostile, factional opposition to his policies from within the Party.

The rapid growth of fanaticism within the New Jewel Movement was most evident in its communist style Central Committee, of which Bishop had been the senior member. This was the body that had deliberately precipitated the Party leadership crisis (which eventually toppled Bishop) and later ordered his execution at Fort Rupert. The interim outcome of the internal Party crisis involved Bishop having to accept the humiliation of becoming merely joint leader – in tandem with Coard, who would take over as *de facto* leader. When, on his return from a visit to Eastern Europe – with a brief stop-over in Havana for a word with Castro, his guru, Bishop announced that he had changed his mind, that is reneged on a Central Committee decision about Joint Leadership, his house arrest followed immediately. Similarly, by proceeding to Fort Rupert on October 19 (after having been freed by an enthusiastic crowd) and proclaiming himself once again Prime Minister and Commander-in-Chief of the Armed Forces, Bishop committed a further grave breach of Party discipline. This was anathema to, and could not be tolerated by, the local adherents of Leninism, the chief among whom were the members of the Central Committee. To them the infallibility of Lenin was supreme, and as such had to be respected – any challenge to this doctrine being met with brute force, even by death. The mass of the Grenadian people never really understood this. When the people reacted to put an end to Bishop's house arrest they were motivated by the norms and usages of Western style democracy. Contrastingly, the Central Committee clearly believed that such behaviour should, if necessary, be punishable by death in order to maintain their chosen path of democratic centralism.

Nevertheless, the ensuing trauma was so great that many people after more than four years of having to look over their shoulders before expressing themselves now trembled to open their front doors. The insidious malign effect of the "shoot to kill" curfew was to place the entire nation under virtual house arrest. In view of the hunt for known supporters of Bishop, no one could feel safe in his own home. In this atmosphere of fear and uncertainty the Revolutionary Military Council unabashedly utilized the radio to vilify Maurice Bishop whom they labeled bourgeoisie. He was castigated for the lack of proper roads and other infrastructure in the country. He was discredited for under-achieving as Prime Minister and for even squandering the gains of the Revolution. His reportedly "vulgar" behaviour at Fort Rupert where he attempted to give orders to Army personnel was intolerable. Indeed the RMC tried their utmost to paint their former beloved Commander-in-Chief and Prime Minister as a devil whose death was entirely justifiable.

Meanwhile what was uppermost in my own mind was the extent to which normalcy could be restored in the shortest possible time. This was a most difficult time as I feared there might be further bloodshed. The clamp down on free expression was intensified. It became clear that the local radio had reached the nadir of absurdity and I could not depend on what emanated from that source. As I tried to make an objective assessment of the political morass into which the country had been suddenly plunged, thoughts of an official Enquiry came to my mind as a first reassuring step towards the restoration of law and order. As to whether these twin pillars of civilized society could be restored without outside help I was doubtful. The void created by Bishop's death could not be filled without difficulty and pain. Despite the pronouncements of the RMC, I felt that I was without a Government. Even more worrying was the fact that I had grave doubts about the RMC's ability and moral authority to form a Government that would be acceptable to the majority of Grenadians.

At 10 o'clock on the morning of October 21, I received General Austin who was accompanied by a smartly dressed soldier. The General had sought an appointment in order to inform me about the current situation in the country. My personal assistant later expressed her surprise that I had agreed to see Austin who might well have come to execute me. My curt reply to her was, "To live in fear is to be dead." Obviously the moment had come when it was in the interest of all to put aside fear and face the problem with an emboldened spirit. General Austin looked tired and forlorn. I told him how deeply shocked I had been by the tragic and unprecedented happenings at the Fort and that, in my view, it would not be easy to restore normalcy to the country. Nor would it be easy to gain respectability from outside. According to radio reports the overwhelming majority of our regional brothers and sisters were outraged and angered and remained deeply concerned. The General did not demur. He went on to explain that Bishop's death could only be attributed to his own folly. Bishop and others who were killed at Fort Rupert were caught in crossfire. His attempt to take over the arms and ammunition and hand them over to civilians had been fraught with danger. Had he not failed in that attempt he could have caused a holocaust. The nearby hospital and other buildings could have been blown up and many more people would have died. Bishop seemed to have been insensitive to the potency of the arsenal of arms at Fort Rupert. I listened carefully to what the General had to say on this subject.

We then discussed burial of the eighteen persons, including the Prime Minister, who, according to Austin, had lost their lives. I emphasized that Grenada was a Christian country and that it was important that the victims of the Fort should be accorded Christian burial. Quite understandably Austin pointed out to me that these funerals could end in chaos, if not civil disorder, as people were too emotionally charged. I then suggested that perhaps private funerals could be held, with attendance being restricted to the closest family members. Later on, when hopefully normalcy had been restored, memorial services could be held if families so desired. Austin accepted these proposals and I offered to discuss the matter with religious leaders. I attached such importance and urgency to this matter that, in the presence of Austin, I immediately instructed my ADC to invite the Roman Catholic Bishop, the Most Reverend Sydney Charles, and the Anglican Archdeacon, the Venerable Hoskins Huggins, to come in to see me at 11.15 o'clock that same morning.

Resuming our conversation Austin then informed me that the intention of the RMC was to form a Government consisting of civilian as well as military personnel with the minimum delay. Both the Prime Minister and the Minister for Foreign Affairs would be civilians. The RMC, he declared, was already in touch with possible candidates for these posts including Earle (Mario) Bullen and Richard Jacobs, our Ambassadors in Brussels and Moscow respectively. I impressed upon Austin that it was important to get the country working again and to have the schools re-opened for classes. He gave me an assurance that the curfew hours would be adjusted as from Monday, October 24, to enable the work force to resume normal duties and children to return to school. Senior civil servants would be called to a meeting at Butler House, the Prime Minister's Office, for a briefing by the RMC.

Since under no circumstances could I regard the events at Fort Rupert as being closed, I persuaded Austin that a high powered Commission of Enquiry should be established without delay to investigate the tragic events of October 19 at Fort Rupert. Austin readily agreed and sought my assistance in identifying persons who could sit on such a body. Clearly it would be best to look outside Grenada for candidates. Austin appeared deeply concerned to achieve a quick return to normalcy and he implored me to obtain whatever assistance I could whether it be regionally, from the Commonwealth, or otherwise internationally not only for an Enquiry but in order to assist in restoring law and order in Grenada. He admitted to the enormity of the task that lay ahead.

At that point I divulged to him that it was my intention to demit office soon after the fifth anniversary of the Revolution due on March 13, 1984. He quickly said that he hoped I would change my mind as he and his colleague would need every assistance from me especially in the changed circumstances. Austin, still looking exhausted as though having lost much sleep, then took leave of me. His next task was to re-assure Vice Chancellor Geoffrey Bourne that all would be well with staff and students at the St. George's University School of Medicine – a matter of deep concern in Washington.

In the months preceding the tragic events at Fort Rupert my wife and I had been giving much thought to my stepping down from Office. Having already resolved that the timing had to be right, we decided that perhaps the most suitable time would be around the fifth anniversary of the Revolution. I happened to know that great plans were being made for the occasion, which was supposed to be the biggest and best ever. Anniversaries of the Revolution had previously attracted Daniel Ortega, President of Nicaragua, and Michael Manley, Prime Minister of Jamaica, as well as Heads of friendly diplomatic missions from both East and West and vast numbers of international comrades who were in solidarity with the People's Revolutionary Government. Speculation was rife in certain quarters that Fidel Castro, President of Cuba and personal mentor of Maurice Bishop, would be in Grenada for the occasion. The new airport at Point Salines would be opened then and the Prime Minister would make certain pronouncements, which would have far reaching consequences for the future of Grenada. My deep suspicion was that Grenada would be declared a Socialist Republic. I had just completed five difficult and unusual years in Office and my wife and I felt it was time we started packing our bags.

In prompt response to my invitation Bishop Sydney Charles and Archdeacon Hoskins Huggins followed closely on the heels of Austin. I apprised them of my conversation with Austin about burial of the Prime Minister and the others killed at the Fort on October 19. After a brief discussion and having regard to the problems that might arise at an open funeral, they agreed that a simple private funeral service followed by interment was the best way to proceed. They also agreed to organize between them that such services would be held on a special day.

Although I was doubtful about Austin's ability to govern, I must confess that after my discussions with him at least I felt I had something on which to work. Thoughts about in-fighting among the members of the RMC temporarily receded from my mind and for the next few hours I saw Austin as an almost reasonable man, apparently receptive to constructive ideas and anxious to restore peace and order. However, any trace of the optimism I had begun to feel about the future quickly vanished after I had received Mr Patrick MacLeish at 4 o'clock in the afternoon. Mr MacLeish in his dual role as Commissioner of Police and Superintendent of Prisons came to me as an emissary from General Austin. The message from the General was that the bodies of Prime Minister Bishop and others would not be available for another two years. "Two years!" I exclaimed. "Yes, two years," came the confirmation. Therefore, plans for private funerals would have to be abandoned as it was felt that even a private funeral could end in disorder. But in a softer voice, as if passing the word to a brother in a secret society, he whispered that the bodies had been removed from Fort Rupert, burnt and buried. What he had whispered to me was in confidence and not part of General Austin's message. He could not inform me where the remains were buried. Nor could he tell whether they were all buried in the same place.

This horrifying revelation put a different light on the situation. MacLeish seemed both worried and sad. He was a man under great stress. He had also been commissioned to pass on a similar message to Mrs Alimenta Bishop, mother of Maurice Bishop, but he could not face Mrs Bishop with such news. Patrick MacLeish, an upright gentleman, was well known as a devoted, loyal and industrious officer and public servant: he had been recalled from retirement to head the Prison Services soon after the Revolution. In the twilight stages of the Revolution MacLeish was made to double up as Commissioner of Police and Superintendent of Prisons.

When MacLeish left my office I began to wonder why Austin had not come clean when I received him earlier that day. Was it because he was unaware of the disposal of the dead bodies or was it a further piece of cruel deception so characteristic of the revolutionaries? Could the bodies have been disposed of after Austin's meeting with me? It was more likely than not that such an operation had taken place under the cover of darkness. Two further questions came to my mind. To what extent could I trust the new regime? Should I sit back and do nothing in a seemingly deteriorating situation where more violence could flare up at any time? It was becoming increasingly obvious to me that I was without a Government. Leon Cornwall, former Ambassador to Cuba, seemed to be emerging as the key figure in the RMC. I never saw Austin again though I had two telephone calls from him. Cornwall was the one who kept in touch with me. I had taught Cornwall at the Grenada Boys' Secondary School where he showed great promise in his academic work.

Amid the escalating tension I thought it prudent not to take telephone calls. My staff was under orders to use their utmost discretion in passing calls to me. Further, they were not to answer any enquiries about Bishop's death. In any case whatever information they might have gathered would have been hearsay or rumour and as such less than authentic. None of them had been anywhere near Fort Rupert when Prime Minister Bishop was murdered. My Orderlies followed the instructions faithfully and, as always, displayed a high level of loyalty and professionalism. Of the numerous calls to my Residence very few were diverted to me, and these the Orderlies considered essential. Free from the hassle of the telephone I was able in the quiet of my room to think deeply and pray fervently about this unnerving and potentially explosive state of affairs.

John Kelly, a member of the staff of the British High Commission, Barbados and resident British diplomat in Grenada called on me on three consecutive days, on one occasion with his wife, Jennifer. Kelly was most concerned about my personal welfare. At my request he was instrumental in putting me in touch with London. I knew only too well that all telephone calls originating in Grenada had to go through an operator in the Telephone Company. These calls were carefully recorded and subsequently analyzed for any trace of counter revolutionary activity. The Telephone Company, which appeared to have been taken over by Bishop temporarily on the morning of Wednesday 19, was a veritable revolutionary den fully equipped with arms and ammunition. The Company was now firmly under the control of the Revolutionary Military Council.

On the morning of Saturday, October 22, I received telephone calls from Robert Fellowes, Assistant Private Secretary to Her Majesty the Queen, from Shridath Ramphal, Secretary General of the Commonwealth and from Ellis Clarke, President of Trinidad and Tobago. I should like to emphasize that these telephone conversations had nothing to do with subsequent events in Grenada that were to take place within three days or so. It was my desire to talk to all three men because I wanted to bring them up to date about the death of Prime Minister Bishop and, in the case of the Palace, about the situation in Grenada generally and my personal safety. I did not solicit advice from these individuals, nor did they proffer any. Whatever the turn of events I realized that at some point I would have to seek help from the Commonwealth and from the sister islands of the Caribbean, not least from Trinidad where there was a large number of our kith and kin. I knew Ramphal well and Clarke even better. Although the situation was becoming more and more desperate, I nonetheless confided in Ellis Clarke that I would prefer not to have a military solution even though in the back of my mind I thought this was perhaps the best option.

At 1.30 p.m. on that same day I received Major Cornwall who had come on behalf of General Austin. This was less than twenty-four hours after MacLeish had passed on what I thought was a bitterly disappointing and heartless message from Austin. Cornwall confirmed that the bodies would not be delivered for any private funeral service and advised that any form of memorial service for Maurice Bishop be postponed. In the light of what I knew I considered it pointless to discuss the matter further with Cornwall. It was a "no win" situation. Cornwall showed me the draft text of a message that the Revolutionary Military Council, under the guise of Government, was about to send abroad. He sought my advice and comments. The message that purported to inform friendly governments about the "true" situation in Grenada before and after Prime Minister Bishop's death was couched in terms that implied an expectation of business as usual. I read it carefully but made no comment on the contents, nor did I offer any advice. I wanted no part in that exercise. A copy of the message intended for the British Foreign and Commonwealth Office in London was erroneously sent to a private office in Bruton Street, London. Unhappily, but possibly providentially, the officer in Foreign Affairs in Grenada who dealt with these matters could not be found. I learnt later that he had been in hiding. As the hours passed I reflected on the extent of the pain and distress generated by the wanton massacre of October 19. The widespread emotional wounds would be deep and enduring. Thoughts of a peaceful solution receded further and further from my mind.

Regional Heads of Governments were strong in their condemnation of the execution of Prime Minister Bishop – some more vocal than others. Michael Manley, Leader of the Opposition in Jamaica, and other political leaders in both English-speaking and non-English-speaking Caribbean countries, not least of whom was Fidel Castro in Cuba, roundly condemned the senseless murders. Castro called for exemplary punishment for those responsible. Michael Manley described the event as "a squalid betrayal of the hopes of the ordinary people of our region." Eugenia Charles, Prime Minister of Dominica and current Chairman of the Organisation of East Caribbean States (OECS) would have nothing to do with the so-called authorities in Grenada. For her, mere expression of her displeasure was not enough. She felt that something more tangible had to be done with the greatest measure of urgency, and she needed no prompting from anyone to consider moving into Grenada to restore law and order and re-instate the democratic freedoms. Prime Minister Charles had always had a special fondness for Grenada where she had received part of her secondary education at the St. Joseph's Convent in St. George's, and where she had come to know many people very well. Similarly, no one had to convince John Compton, Prime Minister of St. Lucia, about the necessity and urgency of intervening militarily. In 1979 Compton had spoken out forcefully against the Revolution, which he had always seen as posing a potential threat to the security and stability of other states in the Caribbean, particularly the smaller ones.

But it was the late Tom Adams, Prime Minister of Barbados, who was the first to grasp the significance and the implications of the executions of October 19 and the turmoil into which Grenada had been plunged. In the ensuing days of feverish, high-powered political activity, culminating in the United States-led military intervention on October 25, 1983, Adams played a pivotal role. As might have been expected from someone of his political and intellectual stature, it was he who inspired the people and most Eastern Caribbean and other influential governments in the region (notably Jamaica, led by Prime Minister Seaga) to take the swift, decisive action needed to restore the situation in Grenada. Seaga, who had always been an antagonist of the Cuban/Nicaraguan/Grenadian communist troika, readily agreed to be part of that effort.

Widespread public outrage of the kind displayed at the height of the crisis in Grenada is a highly potent force. If, however, it is to be deployed to optimal advantage it needs a talented coordinator, someone who understands its potency and who has a natural flair for political leadership plus the associated ability to articulate outraged feelings. Adams filled that role effortlessly, without fanfare and with drive, energy and imagination. Moreover, he quite unashamedly used that ability to advantage in his efforts to cajole the United States into joining with the Organisation of East Caribbean States and others in mounting a military operation to restore normality in Grenada. Sadly, a few Caribbean Governments raised a (fairly predictable) dissenting voice about the need for military action but this was simply ignored by Adams and the more enlightened Heads of Government like Prime Minister Eugenia Charles in Dominica, Prime Minister John Compton in St.Lucia and their staunch ally in Jamaica Prime Minister Edward Seaga.

In any case there was an overwhelming feeling throughout the Caribbean that "something had to be done." Adams was the man who was largely responsible for ensuring that something was done – and above all that it was done in days, rather than weeks or months. He enjoyed the fullest support of his Cabinet colleagues who more or less gave him *carte-blanche* to take whatever action seemed appropriate. Barbados was not a member of the OECS but Adams nevertheless agreed, without hesitation or reservation, to participate in any initiative by OECS Governments designed to restore peace and democracy in a land where people's hopes and aspirations had been suddenly and severely shattered. Barbados was to be used as the launching pad for any military action, which meant commandeering a substantial part of the facilities of its excellent airport.

Tom Adams had grown up in a domestic environment which exuded great hopes for West Indian unity – politically, economically, and socially. His father, the late Sir Grantley Adams, was the first and only Prime Minister of the ill-fated Federation of the West Indies, his West Indies Federal Labour Party having emerged the winner following Federal Parliamentary Elections contested on March 25, 1958 The Federation suffered an untimely demise in 1962 after only four years in existence.

On Friday, October 21, the political Leaders of the OECS assembled in Barbados under the Chairmanship of Eugenia Charles. With unanimity of purpose they set about the task of considering how best they could help the people of Grenada in the wake of the unprecedented murders at Fort

Rupert. Uppermost in their minds was how to bring an end to the existing chaos and restore law and order and political stability – two cornerstones of democracy. They had no time for intellectual posturing or academic propositions as they deliberated on this grave, and for them, unprecedented problem. These relative newcomers to independent statehood, more than any other group of people, understood that something had to be done quickly to save Grenada from the prospect of serious civil unrest, or worse. They also knew only too well that to turn a blind eye on what was happening in Grenada would be tantamount to inviting similar problems in their own countries. The OECS as a sub-grouping of the larger English-speaking Caribbean had the maintenance of security in the sub-region as an integral part of their charter. Thus it was agreed to establish a peacekeeping force which would move into Grenada. However, conscious of their limitations in terms of the resources that would be needed for such a mission, they resolved to seek help from friendly, non-OECS countries, and if need be, from non-regional countries. Within the region the only non-OECS countries on which they could depend were Barbados and Jamaica.

Fortunately, the OECS Heads of Government remained steadfast in their resolve to restore the situation in Grenada by what they perceived as the only realistic course i.e. military action. With Prime Ministers Adams and Seaga on board, the OECS – spearheaded by Prime Ministers Eugenia Charles and John Compton – was a formidable grouping-in Caribbean terms.

Giles (later Sir Giles) Bullard arrived in Barbados in August, 1983, to take up his appointment as British High Commissioner with additional accreditations as High Commissioner to several other Eastern Caribbean States – giving him an area of responsibility extending from St. Kitts and Nevis in the north to Grenada in the south. He had no previous career experience of the Eastern Caribbean and spent the months of August and September settling in and presenting his Letters of Appointment in the various States to which he had been accredited. Having done so he left Barbados for some long overdue leave at the beginning of October, 1983, leaving David Montgomery, the experienced and able Deputy High Commissioner, in charge. Bullard returned to Barbados on October 16 to find a rapidly deteriorating situation in Grenada. His lack of hesitation in proceeding on leave clearly illustrates that not the least remarkable aspect of the serious crisis that developed within the New Jewel Movement in the summer of 1983, was the secrecy in which it remained shrouded (even from many members of the Party). In a small island state like Grenada this was an amazing achievement. For example, it was not until October 9 that the first tentative rumours of trouble began to circulate.

On Saturday, October 22, Bullard was summoned by Prime Minister Adams who presented him with a request for Britain's participation in a military intervention in Grenada. Bullard could not really relish the thought of his country's participation in such a venture involving an independent Commonwealth country of which The Queen was Head of State. This was unlikely to be viewed favourably in London. Bullard's advice to London was that the Caribbean leaders making the request were serious, democratic politicians who were the best judges of how to deal with the situation in Grenada. He went on to recommend that if the United States agreed to participate then Britain should give its support or, at the very least, should refrain from doing anything that might weaken or jeopardize the Caribbean initiative in any way. Bullard's advice was not accepted in London.

The Grenada crisis presented the British Government with an extremely difficult constitutional dilemma. Better informed about the mounting crisis than other Governments (via the reporting of British diplomats in Grenada and Barbados), London was in no doubt about the need for something to be done about the alarming situation following the tragic events of October 19; but Grenada was an independent State within the Commonwealth with The Queen as Head of State and Her Governor General was still in place. In a Commonwealth context these were matters of constitutional importance that could not simply be brushed aside to facilitate military intervention in Grenada. But even if that imponderable had not existed the United Kingdom was in no position to provide the necessary military resources for a successful operation – especially as time was of the essence; only the United States had that level of capability.

Against that background it was hardly surprising that once President Reagan (in the early hours of October 22) had authorized planning for U.S. military participation to begin, the United Kingdom, still grappling with the constitutional aspects of the problem, was increasingly sidelined – in terms of consultation about (and detailed planning for) such intervention. It was not until late evening on October 24 that the British Prime Minister, Mrs Thatcher, learned that a U.S. led military intervention would be launched at dawn the following morning. In a personal telephone call to President Reagan she made a last minute, but unavailing, effort to persuade him to cancel the operation. The Grenada crisis was an unhappy time for Britain and for Anglo/United States relations.

Washington had no diplomatic presence in Grenada. Milan Bish, the United States Ambassador resident in Barbados, had never visited Grenada to present his Letters of Credence. This, no doubt, was America's way of registering their displeasure over the distasteful verbal attacks which were repeatedly levelled against the American Government and people by the Revolutionary Government. Yet diplomatic relations between the two countries continued to subsist. The hiatus in communications at diplomatic level was sometimes construed as the United States having abandoned Grenada, but the lack of interest in Grenada was more apparent rather than real.

By the effective use of modern technology Washington kept a very watchful eye on Grenada. Additionally, there was much intelligence gathering on behalf of the United States by people resident in Grenada. No matter how hard they tried, the People's Revolutionary Government failed to identify the informers either individually or collectively.

Milan Bish quite properly stayed out of Grenada during the crisis period. He remained in Barbados where, following the OECS decision to intervene militarily, he was deeply involved in the intense diplomatic activity, which eventually led to America's participation. Tony Gillespie, an Assistant Under Secretary of State at the State Department in Washington, had already arrived in Barbados where, accompanied by Bish, he was engaged in meetings with Prime Minister Adams, Prime Minister Charles and Prime Minister Seaga. Frank McNeil, President Reagan's Special Envoy, who had been commissioned to see, to meet and to assess, soon joined Gillespie. My information was that it was not easy to persuade the United States to participate in the military operation envisaged by the OECS.

While these negotiations were taking place and as a precautionary measure, a U.S. naval Task Force which included the aircraft-carrier *U.S.S. Independence* originally heading for the Mediterranean, had been diverted to the Eastern Caribbean to protect and, if necessary, evacuate the 1000 plus United States citizens living in Grenada. The majority of these citizens were students and faculty members at the American owned St. George's University School of Medicine. It was about this time that rumours began to circulate in Grenada that American troops would be landing to restore order and democracy. This gave an immediate boost to the hopes and expectations of the overwhelming majority of people in Grenada. Meanwhile, my office continued to receive calls from prospective evacuees, many of whom were Grenadians. They were all seeking seats on whatever carrier – ship or airplane – was taking the non-nationals away.

Maurice Bishop had been killed by his erstwhile colleagues, not by "imperialist" or other foreign agents. Some might be tempted to say that he had been devoured by the system which he had been instrumental in creating. The six-day rule of terror that followed seemed like years and we now know that apprehension mounted among those who had been arbitrarily imprisoned by the PRG regime. They feared that their lives would be at risk should there be any attempt at intervention by foreign forces. Such at least was the impression of their relatives and close friends

As to how the Revolutionary Military Council would cope with a military assault by outside forces was a matter of conjecture. For their part the RMC mistakenly believed that their arsenal of arms and ammunition was adequate and sufficiently sophisticated to repel any invading force, most of whom, it was assumed, would be left dead on our beaches. They seemed oblivious of their total inability to respond effectively to airpower. They could only envisage sea-borne landings with subsequent engagements on land.

Radio Free Grenada intensified its efforts to generate patriotic fervour among the citizenry, encouraging all and sundry to take up arms in defence of their homeland. Such calls went unheeded. There was no likelihood of a positive response. The general public was still in shock following the horrendous events at Fort Rupert on October 19. For many of the young soldiers and militiamen, the execution of Maurice Bishop was the final blow. For them the Revolution died with Bishop. Indeed, they would have welcomed some form of deliverance from what remained of the Central Committee rather than provide support to prop it up.

One of the first acts of the Revolutionary Military Council was to dissolve the People's Revolutionary Government and dismiss all members of the Cabinet. This largely cosmetic action was clearly taken as a first step toward justifying and legitimizing their assumption of power. But they had no plan of action for governing the country and there was no evidence of firm leadership. The intellectual and administrative inadequacies of Hudson Austin became more obvious by the hour, and while I fully expected him to collapse at any time under the increasing strain of his new responsibilities, speculation was rife that Coard was in fact masterminding the actions and pronouncements of the RMC. Coard's voice was conspicuous by its silence, as was that of his wife, Phyllis, during this dreadful period.

It often happens following the violent overthrow of a government that the victors are ill equipped and ill-prepared to form an administration with credible policies to govern and to motivate government officials and associated professionals and technocrats. And so it was with the RMC who concentrated their energies on rounding up known supporters of Bishop, as part of their strategy to ensure their own survival. However, these activities were increasingly inhibited by the need to devote attention to the serious business of governance. For this they required the expertise and cooperation of a loyal Civil Service as well as the goodwill and support of the general public. The RMC enjoyed neither, thus adding to their growing confusion and bewilderment.

On Saturday, October 22, the larger grouping known as the Caribbean Community (CARICOM) met at the Hilton Hotel in Trinidad. CARICOM is an association of the English-speaking countries in the Caribbean (former British colonies). Heads of Government of CARICOM meet at regular intervals to discuss and take decisions on issues affecting the region. Sadly, experience has shown that many of these decisions are binding more in the breach than in the implementation. The leaders meet, they speak at length, they socialize and they return to their respective countries at which point national and territorial interests take over. Regional matters are quietly shelved until the time of the next Heads of Government meeting. A survey of the voluminous reports and communiqués over the years would reveal the repetitiveness of issues discussed and decisions taken.

Notwithstanding the difficulties imposed by geography and the inequalities created by significant differences in economic strength between the smaller and the larger states, the telling point is that leaders do not wish to give up the benefits of sovereign power, which some of them apparently believe to be theirs in perpetuity. Deep in their hearts they continue to act as insular politicians, not as West Indian patriots, not as regional statesmen. For years they have been unable to bring freedom of movement, either of people or goods, to fruition and we still have no regional air-carrier of international standing and no common currency.

The Grenada situation provided an ideal opportunity for West Indian leaders to show solidarity, to demonstrate that they were mature enough to resolve the crisis that had befallen a sister state by restoring peace and freedom. Instead, they emerged from their meeting in Trinidad (which went on late into the night) having failed to reach a consensus. The following day, George Chambers, Prime Minister of Trinidad and Tobago and Chairman of the meeting, announced on radio and television that agreement had been reached on imposing sanctions against Grenada but that there had been disagreement among members about foreign intervention. Thus the larger grouping of CARICOM had, in reality, agreed to put even more pressure on the Grenadian people who were living in fear; whereas the OECS sub-grouping had resolved to take decisive action and intervene militarily to rescue our people from an appalling and deteriorating situation.

On the afternoon of October 22, David Montgomery, British Deputy High Commissioner, accompanied by two diplomatic colleagues from the United States Embassy in Barbados, Ken Kurze and Linda Flohr, arrived in Grenada by charter plane, their visit having been agreed with the

Revolutionary Military Council. For Montgomery the main purpose of his visit was to make personal contact with, and to receive a first hand report from John Kelly (resident British diplomat in Grenada) and his wife, about the well-being of British subjects; to call on me and hopefully to meet Coard, General Austin or some other senior member of the RMC. Ken Kurze and Linda Flohr were primarily concerned with checking on the situation of United States citizens and in particular, the American students at the St. George's University. My office turned down repeated requests from Linda Flohr to see me. She was relentless in her efforts to obtain this appointment as she was under strict instructions from Ambassador Milan Bish to call on me. I felt unable to see a junior officer at the request of an ambassador who had not presented his credentials. Even in adversity I thought I should get the protocol right. However, having learnt of the difficulties she was having with the Revolutionary Military Council and mindful of the number of American citizens living in Grenada, I finally decided to receive Miss Flohr who felt a sense of relief that she did meet me. She told me of her ambassador's instructions to call on me as a matter of priority. It was not easy for her to arrange a meeting with General Austin and his colleagues, and when a meeting was finally arranged discussions on the possible evacuation of U.S. citizens proved a nightmare. Our meeting was quite brief. She heard nothing from me about the events which were unfolding in Grenada, nor did she get my personal assessment on the state of affairs in Grenada.

I received Montgomery on the morning of October 23. As a precaution I arranged that he should not sign the Visitors Book. Furthermore, I received him much more informally than on his previous visits to Grenada. We conducted most of our conversation sitting on a bench in the garden. After passing on a number of messages Montgomery gave me a detailed briefing on the high-powered diplomatic activity taking place in Barbados and elsewhere and also brought me up to date on the already substantial and rapidly growing United States military build-up in Barbados. In reply to a question Montgomery said that he was unaware of any imminent military action to restore the situation in Grenada, but it could not be ruled out that the outcome of the high level discussions currently taking place between Prime Minister Adams, Prime Minister Seaga and OECS Heads of Government on the one hand and the United States Government on the other might be agreement to take joint military action. He went on to say that, in the context of these discussions, I was now widely acknowledged (in the Eastern Caribbean and elsewhere) as the sole representative of constitutional authority in Grenada. In a calm, reassuring voice

Montgomery suggested that, in these circumstances, I should perhaps give urgent consideration to the role I would be expected to assume if a military operation were to be mounted against the Revolutionary Military Council adding that clearly my views on military action as an option to restore my country to normality, would be crucial to any decision on that score. The awesome significance of these disturbing words caused me to ponder for some time before commenting that while military intervention into one's territory was not the sort of thing I would normally advocate, the current, potentially explosive situation in Grenada was such that it was difficult to avoid the conclusion that only the presence of friendly, foreign troops could rescue Grenadians from the abyss into which they had fallen and bring stability and law and order back into our daily lives. Therefore, if a military operation to achieve that were to be undertaken by our sister states – if necessary with assistance from the United States, I would give such an initiative my fullest support.

Montgomery then enquired whether, if requested to do so, I would be prepared to express these sentiments in writing. I temporized by suggesting that since, self evidently, such an undertaking would have to be cloaked in the utmost secrecy, this vital factor could not be guaranteed if I were to put such thoughts in writing. The Revolutionary Military Council was still in control of Grenada and would stop at nothing to save their necks. That said, I recognized immediately that Montgomery was trying to indicate that while Caribbean political leaders like Tom Adams, Eugenia Charles, Compton and Seaga might just possibly regard an oral request from me, conveyed via Montgomery, as sufficient justification to initiate military action, it was in the highest degree unlikely that the United States Government would even consider being associated with such action in the absence of an unequivocal, written request from me. The position of the United States on the world stage was rather different from that of the member countries of the Organisation of East Caribbean States or the wider CARICOM.

Sitting in my garden on that Sunday morning, listening to the first reliable report of what was happening outside Grenada and also having my attention drawn, however discreetly, to what could be about to happen, I began to have the uneasy feeling that the fate of my country and my fellow Grenadians might well depend on the relatively simple act of my signing a piece of paper. Alarming thoughts like these were turning over in my mind when Montgomery, who agreed with my concerns about the risk attached to the sending of a written request on that day and who was due to return to Barbados that afternoon, suggested that I could perhaps authorize him to pass on the gist of my views to, say, Prime Minister Adams, adding that I would not wish military action by friendly states to be inhibited by the absence of a formal request from me. That being so and having regard to the paramount need for secrecy, I would be content for the message being conveyed (by Montgomery) to be regarded *pro tem*, as such a request with a formal written request from me to follow as soon as a secure, practicable means of communication became available.

Once again I found myself in the uncomfortable position of having to make a decision of the highest importance with no time for sober reflection. On this occasion I considered only three factors: firstly, the situation in Grenada on that Sunday, October 23, was grim, with a shoot to kill 24-hour curfew still being rigorously enforced; secondly, I could not rely on the word of Hudson Austin that the curfew would be eased and that life would return to normal with a new RMC/Civilian Government in prospect; thirdly what Montgomery had proposed seemed an entirely sensible and justifiable compromise. I therefore authorized him to speak to Prime Minister Adams along the lines we had discussed.

The Central Committee, or what remained of it, continued to meet daily at their new headquarters at Fort Frederick. They were planning strategy, issuing bulletins and directives, ordering the arrest of suspected, or known dissidents and also discussing ways and means of governing the country. All radio pronouncements emanating from Fort Frederick and Radio Free Grenada continued to appear oblivious to the mounting concern being expressed by our brothers and sisters in neighbouring countries. No apparent heed was paid to the regional meetings taking place to discuss the situation in Grenada. Instead RFG pressed on with its vilification of Bishop, who though he was dead, remained the principal propaganda target for a torrent of invective. According to RFG, Bishop's death was attributable to his own bourgeoisie stupidity. As a petit bourgeois, he had allowed the bourgeoisie friends who had taken him to Fort Rupert to lull him into a sense of false security. His ill-disciplined action on that day in acquiring arms and ammunition for distribution to his bourgeoisie associates who would have used them against the Central Committee and other heroic comrades, had left the Central Committee with no choice but to act quickly to prevent what could have been a holocaust. The soldiers who had met their death in the process of liberating Fort Rupert on October 19 were hailed as heroes. A period of national mourning was ordered in their memory.

Some two months after the fall of the RMC, Dr. Jensen Otway, a Medical Practitioner, called on me to confess that he had been ordered by General Austin to write false death certificates for bodies that had already been buried.

# 9

## The Rescue Mission

I T was Tuesday, October 25, 1983, six days after Maurice Bishop and a number of his Cabinet colleagues had been savagely murdered at Fort Rupert. The vulnerability of our small state was increasingly obvious and painfully worrying. The previous evening, General Austin had called me to say that he and his colleagues had sighted American ships on the horizon just outside Point Salines at the southernmost tip of the island and that an invasion seemed imminent. He also disclosed that President Forbes Burnham of Guyana, a close ally of the Revolution, had given him prior warning that the Americans were going to invade Grenada.

By the time morning had broken, I thought I was hearing continuously the zooming sound of an aircraft when suddenly my telephone rang. My aide-de-camp, Denzil Lord, was at the other end of the line: "Your Excellency," he said, "the action has begun." I knew exactly what that meant. From the day Bishop was killed, I ordered the aide-de-camp to spend all his time on the premises and to be very sparing with time off for the Orderlies and other security officers under him.

My wife and I not knowing what the day had in store for us got out of bed immediately. I could see from my balcony an aircraft hovering over St. George's. I could also see shots being fired at the aircraft though they fell far short of their intended target. It was not difficult to imagine where these volleys were coming from. Then my private telephone rang. I at once thought it was a member of our family as this number was very restricted. In fact, I had not even given it to General Austin. The phone call was from my stepson who informed me that friends from Grenville had just called his wife to say that armed forces had landed at Pearls and had taken over Pearls Airport much to the delight and relief of the people in Grenville.

By then the Orderlies had already opened the house as they normally did at 6 o'clock every morning and the drivers had embarked on their daily chore of cleaning the vehicles. They were all aware that there was some sort of foreign intervention given the rumblings in the skies above and the sound of artillery below. The lone guard at the main entrance was so frightened that he abandoned his post and joined the men at the house complete with his AK47. I then instructed the ADC to have everyone on the premises repair to the basement at once. My wife and I would join them there.

And so to the basement we all went. After about five minutes, we could hear what seemed to be a helicopter flying over the driveway and making a clean sweep of any light objects in its path. Indeed it was a helicopter trying to land in front of the house but because of difficulties the men had to disembark with the assistance of a rope in the sloping front garden. Almost instantaneously I could hear footsteps above us in the main reception room and I could also hear strange voices shouting with a great deal of urgency: "Is anyone here? Mr Scoon, Mr Scoon."

Well knowing that one of the main objectives of their mission was to protect me, I told the men that we had to show ourselves. My wife, a very meticulous person, said to me, "Suppose they are Russians." I had to assuage her fears by assuring her that the visitors were Americans by their accent, and in any case it was well nigh impossible for Russian soldiers to get to us so quickly. These Americans had come to rescue us.

Sergeant Lincoln Williams, my senior driver, opened the door of the basement and was confronted by a soldier pointing a gun directly at him. The soldier quickly put him at ease by telling him that they had come to protect the Governor General and not to harm anyone. When my wife and I emerged from the basement, these visiting American Seals had no difficulty in recognizing me as they had my photograph in their possession. They were naturally very cautious and wanted me to tell them the status of all in my party. There were eleven of us. Sergeant McIntyre had with him his wife who had joined him in his quarters the same day Bishop was murdered and his son who since Bishop's death elected to be with his father and mother. Ironically, McIntyre's son, an intelligent young policeman, was regarded as a spy by my police staff at the house and they never trusted him. He was very close to the top brass of the People's Revolutionary Army and the Government and it would appear that his duty was to gather intelligence for the party hierarchy. Even his father was well aware that he could not be trusted.

Another stranger in our party was the guard at the main entrance. He was a member of the PRA turned police officer and he was not well known by my household staff. Guards were sent daily by the Central Police Division of the Royal Grenada Police Force to keep duty at the main entrance. When asked by the Americans to hand over his gun, he quickly responded that the PRA would punish him for giving up his gun, whereupon Corporal Hypolite, a plain blunt officer with a deep and sonorous voice, snapped at him, "Don't be stupid boy, give the people the gun." Then we all went to the dining room that turned out to be our resting place for the next twenty-six hours.

Under instruction the Seals came to ensure my safety until the arrival of a contingent of Commonwealth Caribbean Forces who would be stationed at Governor General's House to give me more permanent protection. But this was not a mission so easily accomplished. Years of military training in the USSR, Eastern Europe and Cuba together with the possession of some very sophisticated weapons had fortified the People's Revolutionary Army to offer some measure of resistance to the military might of the U.S.A. Little did we know that we would experience some anxious moments during the next few hours.

No sooner had the Seals arrived than Governor General's House and its environs became a target for the bullets of the PRA. There has been some speculation that the Cubans had joined the Grenadian soldiers in the assault on my residence, but I have no proof of this. We were constantly under attack from the arsenal of arms and ammunition in the backyard of the Prime Minister's residence as well as from the gunnery set up on nearby private property on the Tempe road. One American soldier had already been seriously wounded as his helicopter tried to land on the tennis courts that were perilously close to the Prime Minister's official residence. In fact, it later came to my attention that some of the PRA members were perched on trees with loaded guns ready for any reinforcement that dared to land to approach Governor General's House from the tennis courts.

For the next twenty-six hours, the dining room was our dormitory without food, without water, and without the necessaries for a comfortable rest. In fact, there was no sleep during the long and perilous night that followed the dismal and dreadful day. As the sounds of gunfire resounded in our ears, the portraits of members of the Royal Family – past and present – looked down solemnly upon us as we quietly and humbly lay on the bare hard wooden floor. The Seals thought, and quite rightly so, that the dining room was the safest part of the house as the PRA even with their sophisticated instruments could not see any movements in the dining room.

I had with me a portable radio tuned to the Barbados Radio Station from which came all the news on Grenada. My wife and I occupied one corner of the dining room. While we lay on the floor for the most part, we were able to sit on the mahogany couch occasionally whenever the shooting subsided. The Seals told us that every time there was movement in the house, shots were fired towards the house, so we were advised to remain quiet and not venture even to the adjoining reception room. When it was announced on radio out of Barbados that the Governor General, the only remaining official with any constitutional authority, would be expected to appoint a government to run the country until democratic elections were held, the shelling towards Governor General's House was intensified. Three times an Armoured Personnel Carrier drove up the driveway. Three times the Seals turned it back. Its persistency and audacity led to its destruction from a direct hit from the air after the Seals had reported to their superiors on the U.S.S. *Guam* the imminent danger they faced from the ever advancing Armoured Personnel Carrier.

But the Seals had other problems. Their ammunition was running low, they had temporarily lost radio contact with headquarters, and there was no sight of the Marines who themselves had been ill-equipped in terms of maps and so could not make their way to Governor General's House before daybreak the following day. The Seals were becoming so desperate that they were looking into the possibility of moving me from my residence during the night. This of course was a frightening prospect, and when they asked me about possible roads to Queen's Park, I told them that I felt much safer in my residence and I would rather do any journey on foot during the daytime. By then we could feel the full force of mortar hitting the building and for the first time we could hear the shattering of glass from the windows of the dining room and the adjoining reception room. Another helicopter landing on the tennis court was just not on. It would be too risky to take me out by helicopter especially under the cover of darkness.

The Commander of the Seals performed superbly throughout the siege. He was never too far from my wife and me and his ever-watchful eye over us helped to embolden our spirit. He appeared not to be ruffled. From time to time he would enquire about our health, always reassuring us that all would be well. He also kept us informed as much as he was willing to tell as to what progress the Americans were making in this challenging warlike encounter. My wife bombarded him with all kinds of questions and she wanted to know how much longer we had to stay on the floor of the dining room. At one point he explained to us how dangerous it would be if we were to retire to the comfort of our bedroom upstairs which was too exposed and was in the direct line of fire. He had to try his best to avoid accidents of any kind and particularly accidents in which I might be involved. One of his men was on sentry duty on the platform that projected off the bedroom next to ours. It must have been very uncomfortable for this soldier as shots were flying from every direction. In fact, the row of white cedar trees that flanked the eastern side of the house acted as a repellant to the shots which were coming from the Tempe direction. But even so the house was hit and damage caused to the walls and windows.

As the battle for the Governor General's House grew in intensity, my wife broke down and wept. At about the same time just before midnight the telephone rang. This was the only call to me since we were under protection. The Commander answered the phone and hastily came to ascertain whether I knew anyone by the name of Bishop Charles. "Yes," I told him, "he is the Bishop of the Roman Catholic Church in Grenada." I would gladly speak to him. The Commander led me to the phone advising me not to be too long as that part of the building was in full view of anyone outside. In fact, the telephone was on a table near one of the windows and I was reminded that our movements could be seen by those who were shooting at the house.

I was relieved to be able to talk to my friend and spiritual leader, Bishop Sydney Charles, who was speaking from the St. Joseph's Convent not far away. On the advice, if not the insistence, of the religious in St. George's, Bishop Charles had reluctantly left his residence at Morne Jaloux for the Convent following the tension occasioned by the death of Maurice Bishop. With the advent of the American and Caribbean Forces, all the priests, religious brothers and sisters in St. George's occupied the safe Roman Catholic enclave on upper Church Street. It was only fitting that the Shepherd of the flock should be with them rather than left alone in his residence with no guarantee of safety.

Bishop Charles told me that on hearing the constant gunfire in the vicinity of my residence, he thought that my wife and I might be in some danger. He assured me that they were all praying for us and with some kind and soothing words he boosted my courage. Then Sister Francis Xavier, Superior of the Convent, came to the telephone and expressed similar sentiments and said that they were solidly behind me in prayer. I was most grateful for the telephone conversation at the end of which some tears of joy rolled down my cheeks. I suddenly felt happy to know that amid our unprecedented trials and tribulations on a ghastly night we were not alone.

When I told my wife the contents of the telephone conversation, she too felt a sense of relief and this, I thought, beefed up her courage. "Suppose we were to die," she said to me, "is it really worth it?" I told her that if it was the Lord's will that we should die, then I truly believed that we would be dying for the sake of our country in which common humanity, love and freedom would hopefully prevail thereafter. But it was Corporal Hypolite who eased the tension and caused a ripple of laughter when he declared, "I don't care if I die now. I am happy that these people have come to our rescue. They should have come long before now." His words were greeted by a blast that hit one of the bay windows in the adjoining room. It was the same Hypolite who by the end of that week would boldly recover his brother-in-law's car that had been confiscated by the People's Revolutionary Government during the Revolution and used by an active supporter.

After a sleepless and altogether dismal night, morning came upon us as evidenced by a faint glimmer of light peeping through the bay windows of the adjoining reception room. But it was a different kind of morning. The birds seemed to have gone into hiding for we were deprived of their melodious chirping. There was not a sound of vehicular traffic on the street below. The whole atmosphere was sombre and sad as if a company of satanic ghosts had just passed by and had thrown a damper on all the usual morning activities. It was only the bleating of a young goat in the backyard that disturbed the stillness of the morning. Two years later one of the American soldiers, accompanied by his wife, returned to visit Grenada and took a photograph of the goat that he had remembered so well.

But despite the unusual quietude around Governor General's House, we were soon reminded that military action was not over as all of a sudden we began to hear sporadic gunfire from the distance. This was an indication that the Grenadian soldiers were prepared to fight to the bitter end making full use of their armoury and equipment the quality of which, perhaps, no other national army in the English-speaking Caribbean possessed. Also, any thoughts the Americans might have had about mopping up the operations within a few hours were dramatically dispelled. They obviously had to rethink their strategy as their military intelligence on the preparedness of the People's Revolutionary Army for combat seemed woefully inadequate. So, too, was their knowledge of the Grenadian terrain.

Back in the dining room, the trek to the washrooms had begun. No time was to be wasted. The nearest washrooms were a few yards away, and each of us had to be escorted by a soldier to ensure safe passage between the dining room and the washroom. At the end of this ritual, one member of my staff cried hunger. Bearing in mind that none of us had anything to eat for the past twenty-four hours, my wife who felt much better in the brightness of the morning asked one of the soldiers to fetch a tin of biscuits which was in the pantry upstairs. The soldier quickly obliged and some of the staff delved into this with relish; others could not eat. My wife and I could give no thought to food and for us it was more important that our staff should have some morsel, however small, in their stomachs. We ourselves could prolong our enforced fast. Quite naturally no domestic staff had come out to work and the kitchen was securely locked.

The Seals were still firm in their resolve to get my wife and me out of Governor General's House. This departure from their original plan stemmed from their own assessment that it was not yet safe for me to remain in residence, notwithstanding their success in keeping me alive up to that point in time. They had a rude awakening by the stubborn resistance, if not aggression, of the People's Revolutionary Army over the last twenty-four hours. From that initial experience they could not afford to take unnecessary risks. Also it was manifestly premature and equally risky for the Caribbean Forces to install themselves at the Governor General's House.

At long last a contingent of Marines arrived on the grounds and it was time for us to evacuate. At our request, my wife and I gingerly made our way upstairs under the piercing eyes of an accompanying soldier. We went to our bedroom where within five minutes my wife was able to put into a small bag the barest necessities for both of us. Everything had to be done quickly. I took nothing except my portable radio and my wrist watch. In this state of uncertainty, I gave no thought to putting away valuables or even having the main doors of the building securely locked. For me these material things were less important than the security of the State and in the circumstances this included first and foremost our personal safety.

When we returned to the dining room, the Commander of the Seals announced that it had become necessary for the Governor General and his wife to leave the house immediately. He explained that their mission was to secure and safeguard the Governor General and his wife. They had no instructions pertaining to the Governor General's staff. However, if any of the staff wanted to go with them, they should feel free to do so; whereupon with one voice they chose to go "wherever the Governor General was going." This was a clear victory for loyalty.

The Seals with a reinforcement of about sixty Marines took what I considered to be the shortest possible route to Queen's Park where a helicopter was awaiting us. Evidently some reconnoitering had been done. If we had used any other route, it would have been too dangerous and too long. So in single file with Marines interspersed we walked along the back of our residence to the dirt road that separates our grounds from Mt. Royal. Turning to the left we proceeded along the road for about one hundred yards before moving to the right to a pathway which led to Sans Souci. Just before taking the right turn to the Sans Souci road, we could not help seeing a lorry fully laden with ammunition in the vicinity of the Prime Minister's residence at Mt. Wheldale. By then the Seals had punctured all the tyres of that lorry and had flushed out the warring faction that had positioned itself at Mt. Wheldale. On reaching Sans Souci, we did not take the Mortley Hill road. Instead we turned left, and after about fifty yards we turned right, and descended some steps into the River Road area. Along those steps we were fired at and it sounded as if our assailants were dangerously close at hand, but no one was hit. Just then I slipped and fell.

I sustained some slight almost painless bruises on my left arm and my spectacles that fell to the ground were not broken. I got up quickly without any help and continued the journey.

Soon we were on a narrow pathway that skirted a number of small houses where people here and there were clustered in small groups talking, no doubt, about the current military impasse in the country. Normally, these people would be on their way to work and their children would be getting ready for school. But as on the previous day, both workplaces and classrooms were closed. On entering the main road, we turned left for the final part of our journey to Queen's Park. Grenadians remain indoors only when it is raining. With the slightest shower of rain, they dash for shelter. But nothing else prevents them from making their presence felt in the open air, not even the thundering sounds of guns. The people of River Road did not conceal their curiosity when they came out in their numbers along the road to see the unusual spectacle of their Governor General and his wife taking what looked like a morning stroll under the direction and protection of army personnel, and accompanied by their staff on a road which is known for its heavy vehicular traffic on a working day.

But I felt fortified and spiritually renewed by the comforting, encouraging and supportive remarks coming from the onlookers all along the road. "Sir Paul," they shouted, "we are solidly behind you, God bless you, Sir." I was not at all surprised when I learnt about a week later that the people of River Road were supplying breakfast and local fruits daily to the U.S. soldiers who were encamped at the nearby Queen's Park pavilion. This was their way of saying "thank you" for their liberation.

When we arrived at Queen's Park, a middle-aged man informed us that we should check the Darbeau Hills as there was a PRA camp there. Darbeau Hills overlook Queen's Park. Just outside the fenced cricket field were two helicopters to take me and my party away – a direct target for any gunfire from the Darbeau Hills. To the hills the U.S. soldiers speedily went and rapidly disbanded the camp. They met with no resistance whatsoever as the local PRA men dropped their guns and ran away. Out of the abundance of caution, a helicopter scoured the area to be satisfied that it was safe for us to be lifted up for the journey to the *U.S.S. Guam* which was at anchor way outside Point Salines.

My wife and I embarked on the open helicopter for the journey to the *U.S.S. Guam*. Meanwhile my retinue was flown direct to Point Salines. On the *U.S.S. Guam*, I had a shower while the clothes that had been soiled when I fell were laundered. Then, dressed in borrowed navy overalls, I sat down to a very hearty breakfast. The senior naval officers showed interest in my personal well-being. This was their main conversation piece and they chatted with my wife and me in a very friendly and cordial manner. We had no discussions on the military exercise then in progress. After putting on my freshly laundered clothing, I gratefully received a small bag with much needed toiletries. Then we were ready to start the final stage of our journey to Point Salines. But before we left the *U.S.S. Guam*, a message was passed to the British warship, *H.M.S. Antrim*, which was anchored some distance away but in our territorial waters, requesting that Her Majesty the Queen be informed that my wife and I were safe.

When we landed on the Point Salines airstrip, we said goodbye to the Seals who had protected us during the battle for Governor General's House. Their mission was accomplished and we expressed our gratitude to them for our safety. This had not been an easy task and one that had proven to be much more difficult than they had envisaged. As we made our way to the Point Salines Great House, I could see some Grenadian faces as well as Cubans who were obviously held in captivity. They were cordoned off in the open air, some of them shirtless. Although the guns seemed to have been silenced, the area around the unfinished terminal building was humming with activity particularly among the armed U.S. soldiers. The sun was shining brightly and at least we felt safe.

It was a great relief to enter the Great House where I at once recognized some familiar faces and for the first time since the start of the military action I came face to face with Caribbean personnel. Notably among the persons I knew was Brigadier Rudyard Lewis, the Barbadian who headed the Regional Security System. I also met Major Mike Hartland, an affable former British Army man, who had retired in Grenada for many years and one of the men I had consulted at the time Gairy was about to establish the local army. Major Hartland was now serving with the Barbados regiment having left Grenada during the revolutionary period. He knew the Grenadian terrain well and he knew the Grenadian people equally well. The Great House was the headquarters for the Caribbean troops. It was here that Brigadier Lewis handed me the draft letters which I should have received from Prime Minister Tom Adams two days earlier. Lewis apologized for the late delivery but explained that it was not practicable to get them to me earlier in view of the delicate nature of the preparedness for the military exercise. In fact, an attempt was made to get the letters to me at Governor General's House on the morning of October 25 with the arrival of the Seals but the risk was too great. I perused the letters carefully and made one alteration before signing them. These letters were addressed to Tom Adams, Edward Seaga, Eugenia Charles and Ronald Reagan.

No sooner had I signed the letters than an American functionary came brandishing a draft press release in front of me for my signature. I did not know the man but he was obviously a civil service type. I read the contents carefully and told him that I did not feel able to append my signature as he requested. Quite frankly, I did not think the time was opportune to put out press releases. Nor was the text of the release appropriate especially as hostilities had not yet come to an end. In any case I was not going to comply with such a request from this individual. Yet despite all his stridency that I considered typical, he was taken aback. Perhaps he thought that in the current circumstances, he and others like him could get me to do whatever they required of me. Quite mistakenly the gentleman did not realize that Caribbean public figures were less gullible and more alert and self-confident than hitherto. The information explosion, technological advances and travel had equipped the Caribbean man to be more analytic, more critical and more constructive in thought and in action. But more pointedly I was always mindful that Grenada was a sovereign state and I was representative of Her Majesty the Queen as Head of State. It was my duty, therefore, to uphold my honour and dignity even in times of adversity. Indeed when some two hours later the doctor from the Jamaica Defence Force examined me, he gave me a clean bill of health. My blood pressure was surprisingly normal and I was ready to work.

On leaving the Great House, my wife and I were escorted to the nearby home of Professor and Mrs Geoffrey Wagner where we were re-united with our staff for the next three days. The staff had been flown by helicopter from Queen's Park to Point Salines. The Wagners' home had been vacant. The owners were away as they were wont to do every year for about four to six months. They had been resident on the island for a number of years. I first met Geoffrey Wagner when I served as Cabinet Secretary. A retired Professor of English, Wagner has published a number of books and scholarly papers.

Sir Deighton Ward, Governor General of Barbados, whom I had got to know well over the last four years, kindly sent me a crate of foodstuff which was most welcome and timely. This we used for the next three days to feed not only my wife and me but also the staff who accompanied us. Sergeant McIntyre's wife, who as reported earlier had left their home in the somewhat remote village of Bylands to be with her husband, cooked for us. My wife and I were comfortable in the Wagners' home and we felt safe. We had a good view of the air raids as the bombers zoomed their way from the U.S.S. *Guam* to the mainland. There was nothing that Austin and his comrades could do to resist the action from the air. Perhaps they never anticipated being faced with such overwhelming air power. The PRA was never equipped with air power. The only aircraft to which they could lay claim was a small plane parked desolately on Pearls Airport. This was a gift from the USSR on one of Bishop's visit to Moscow and ostensibly it was to be used for spraying bananas. Of course, it was never used for that purpose. The plane was so well equipped with paraphernalia for launching paratroops that it seemed admirably suited for landing adventurers in remote areas in any of the smaller Caribbean islands. Where we sat in our temporary home, we could see clearly aircraft making their way to the Richmond Hill area and almost in seconds we could witness the heavy bombing taking place there, and the resultant thick columns of black smoke. While their target was obviously the PRA Headquarters at Fort Frederick, nevertheless it appeared to us that the houses in the vicinity were in the centre of the danger zone. For us this was of great concern as we had relatives and friends living near Fort Frederick.

Larry Rossin, a young American diplomat, was one of the first to make contact with me at the Wagners' home. He had been quietly and unofficially visiting Grenada during the revolutionary years and had obviously accumulated useful information on Grenada. But he had also kept in close touch with Grenadians living abroad. Brimming with confidence he handed me a list of names that he thought might be of help to me when appointing an Interim Government to run the affairs of Grenada pending parliamentary elections. Rossin had obviously done some homework. Further, he gave me a verbal synopsis on each member of the team he proposed for appointment. I simply looked at the list, remained impassive, made no comments and put it aside. I suppressed any form of body language that might convey any message to the enthusiastic diplomat. Far too many people look upon a national crisis as an opportunity for their own self-aggrandizement and advance. In this particular case, so many of them claim that they played an important part in solving Grenada's political problem. Some are bold enough to say that the Americans intervened because of their relentless efforts in lobbying and writing directly to the White House. Others would keep close to such diplomats as Rossin for intelligence gathering and hope to be rewarded later with some prestigious job. Further, these gentlemen whose names were listed to form the government were obviously lulled into a false sense of security or were under the impression that the Americans would either appoint an Interim Government or would have great influence in the composition of such a government. Neither happened.

But the real purpose of Rossin's early visit was to get me to do a broadcast that Jean Kirkpatrick could use with advantage in the United Nations.

Ambassador Jean Kirkpatrick was the American representative in the United Nations. I told him that I was not ready to make any broadcast. He tried his utmost to persuade me that this was the proper course to follow, but to no avail. He left somewhat disappointed, if not dejected.

A frequent visitor was Dr. Vaughan Lewis, Secretary General of the Organisation of Eastern Caribbean States (OECS), whose headquarters were located in Castries, St. Lucia. Dr. Lewis was well versed in Caribbean affairs having served as Director of the Institute of Social and Economic Research in the University of the West Indies prior to his appointment as head of the OECS Secretariat. We had several fruitful discussions on the way forward. His scholarly but pragmatic approach to our problems was both soothing and sobering. Lewis briefed me on the meetings that the OECS leaders held in Barbados and the agreements reached between the OECS, Barbados, and Jamaica with the U.S.A. to mount a rescue mission to Grenada. He was thoughtful enough to bring me a copy of the Grenada Constitution and we agreed that out of sheer necessity and being the only person left with any constitutional authority, I would have to take over and direct the affairs of the country in accordance with Section 57 of the Constitution.

It was after speaking to Vaughan Lewis that I began to think seriously as to how I should proceed in the governance of the country once the fighting ceased. By then certain key installations were either taken over or destroyed. Radio Free Grenada was bombed. The Prime Minister's office, the former Islander Hotel built on a promontory with a most commanding and magnificent view of St. George's town, was destroyed. The Central Police Station was set on fire allegedly by the locals. The military camp at Calivigny was completely destroyed. So too were all the other military camps. The Richmond Hill Prison was taken and all the political prisoners walked out to their freedom. In the process many of the convicted criminals escaped. They were seen all over St. George's and were heard to tell their friends that they were enjoying a short vacation from behind bars. Amusingly, they all reported back to the Prison after three days without any coercion on the part of anyone. I was told that some of them were very helpful in the release of the political prisoners and saw them to freedom safely. The Headquarters of the People's Revolutionary Army at Fort Frederick was also bombed, and sadly in error the nearby Mental Hospital on Fort Matthew was partly destroyed with a number of casualties among the patients. Fort Matthew was separated from Fort Frederick by a narrow archway and the Grenadian military authorities had hoisted their flag on the grounds of the Mental Hospital and had actually issued guns to some of the patients.

David Montgomery, Deputy British High Commissioner, called on me and with him was Tony Gillespie, U.S. Special Envoy to Grenada. Montgomery had already briefed Gillespie about the role of the Governor General. Americans, and not least American officials, have some difficulty in understanding the position of the Queen in an independent country and even greater difficulty in grappling with the role of the Governor General *vis-a-vis* the Prime Minister. They still talk of the British Commonwealth rather than the Commonwealth. Grenada is an independent state with Her Majesty Queen Elizabeth II as Head of State. The Governor General is her representative and performs tasks on behalf of the Queen – all enshrined in the Constitution. The Governor General must be impartial and he is expected to be above politics. Grenada is also a member of the Commonwealth which is made up of monarchical states headed by the Queen (or in some cases by a local monarch), republics headed by Presidents (executive or ceremonial), and from time to time some of these republics are controlled by the army. The Queen is recognized as Head of the Commonwealth by all the Commonwealth countries but she has no real authority either by proxy or directly over the affairs of these Commonwealth countries. For the next few months, I would have to explain all this to foreign media people who never understood the Commonwealth concept, and they usually started by posing the question: "How long have you been in politics?" They seemed amazed when I replied that I was never in politics. And to the Americans whose State Governor is a politician, they seemed even more astonished when I tell them that the Governor General is appointed by the Queen on the recommendation of the Prime Minister and in the exercise of his functions he must be non partisan as far as politics is concerned.

Montgomery presented Tony Gillespie to me. From the very outset, I thought Gillespie was the right man at the right time to be America's Special Envoy in Grenada. His warmth, his friendliness and his cool manner impressed me greatly. He seemed committed to do everything he possibly could to help us restore normalcy and repair the damage done to our democratic principles and institutions. He pledged every support to me and looked forward very much to working in Grenada in the months ahead. My early impressions of Gillespie were not misplaced, and he turned out to be a great ally with a listening ear and a helping hand. He also kept me fully informed on all matters as we moved towards normalcy and the restoration of democracy. I learnt later that Gillespie thought also that I was the right man at the right time.

One of the things that concerned me most was the state of the country's finances. The government's accounts were then with Barclays Bank and when Montgomery visited a second time, I sent by him a note to the banker, Geoffrey Comissiong, asking him to freeze the Government account until further notice. Montgomery himself was extremely kind. Apart from offering any help he could to smooth my path, he was lavish, and I think sincere, in his words of support and encouragement. Montgomery, who was a frequent visitor, monitored closely the progress towards the restoration of democracy with particular reference to our democratic institutions.

A temporary radio station was set up in a vehicle in Point Salines. This was operated by Leslie Seon, veteran and well known broadcaster and commentator. Grenadian-born Leslie Seon was resident in Barbados when the American and Caribbean troops intervened. Seon was persuaded by Prime Minister Adams to go to Grenada and help with the information services particularly with radio broadcasting. The advent of Seon who had a wealth of experience in the field of broadcasting was most welcome. With Radio Free Grenada bombed there was no means of communication between me and the populace in general. Grenadians needed to hear my voice and to know about my whereabouts. Whenever the Governor General is in Grenada, his flag is flown at his residence. But on this occasion notwithstanding the flag many people, as I learnt later, thought that I had been recklessly removed from the country. Thus one of my main tasks was to make a national broadcast on the makeshift Spice Isle Radio. In this broadcast, I called for reconciliation and resumption of work and of school. I sought the return of guns and ammunition and I gave some insight into the kind of people I would be inviting to form an Advisory Council. The text of my broadcast ran this way.

"I speak to you today as your Governor General and as one who has great faith in the Grenadian people. I am confident that you will find the courage to put these tragic events of the past two weeks behind you and join with me in the task of restoring our country to its normal peaceful way of life. At this trying period of our country's history we must be guided by thoughts of reconciliation, forgiveness and reconstruction. Our energies must be devoted to restoring the process of democratic life, true freedom and human dignity to all our people. At the same time we must insist on high standards of morality in public life.

There is no need here for me to enumerate the tragic and un-Grenadian events which led to the death of Prime Minister Maurice Bishop and three of his Cabinet colleagues. Innocent men, women and children were also killed or injured. To say the least I was deeply saddened and I should like to extend my heartfelt sympathy to the bereaved families.

The killing of Prime Minister Bishop and the subsequent control of our country by the People's Revolutionary Army so horrified not only Grenadians but the entire Caribbean, the Commonwealth and beyond that certain Caribbean states with the support of the U.S.A. decided to come to our aid in the restoration of peace and order. Of course intervention by foreign troops is the last thing one would want for one's country but in this case it has happened in deteriorating circumstances repugnant to the vast majority of the people of Grenada – people who live and work in Grenada – who I am well advised have welcomed the presence of these troops as a positive and decisive step forward in the restoration not only of peace and order but also of full sovereignty, thus enabling our democratic institutions to function according to the expressed wishes of the Grenadian people at the earliest possible time.

Sad to say, it is now known that the People's Revolutionary Army (PRA) had in its possession an incredible amount of foreign sophisticated weapons. I wish to thank the countries involved for coming to our assistance and I call upon you the people of Grenada to give your fullest cooperation to the Peace Keeping Force in our country. Colonel Barnes of Jamaica has been appointed Commander of the Peace Keeping Force. In these difficult times I would endeavour to do my best as I have done in other circumstances since my appointment as Governor General on September 30, 1978.

It is my intention in the next few days to appoint in my own deliberate judgment a representative body of Grenadians to assist as an interim measure in administering the affairs of our country. This administration will comprise persons of integrity and ability. Let it be clearly understood that this will not be an administration of politicians. This Interim Administration will provide us with the necessary breathing space to enable arrangements to be made for an early return to full constitutional government by way of General Elections.

All Government employees must report to work on Monday, October 31, and I hereby ask the business community to re-open their doors to the public as from today. Schools will re-open on Monday morning, October 31. Meanwhile in order to facilitate the work of the Peace Keeping Force who will be on patrol at nights and for your own safety and protection I urge you to stay indoors from 8 o'clock in the evening to five o'clock in the morning until further notice.

In conclusion I hereby direct the members of the People's Revolutionary Army and the Militia to lay down their arms. You will be told shortly when and where you should hand in those arms prior to the formal disbandment of the Army. I wish to assure you that every precaution will be taken for your personal safety like any other Grenadian citizen.

Ladies and Gentlemen, the task ahead is difficult, but I know that with your cooperation and God's help we shall succeed.

May God bless you all."

We returned to our official residence on Friday evening. It was still not safe to make the journey by road as snipers continued to operate in the Grand Anse area. So we had a helicopter flight to Queen's Park, then we journeyed by car to Governor General's House only to meet a ransacked house with some of our personal belongings looted. Much of the food and drink we had left behind also disappeared. Apparently they had been using my private car to transport the booty from the house to the Western Gate, as the car was found at that gate. It would appear that our residence was occupied by the household staff of late Prime Minister Bishop from the evidence the men left behind such as the official diary of the Prime Minister's residence, personal bank books and other personal belongings. They obviously fled when a contingent of the Caribbean Forces under Major Robin Keaney went to the house the day before we arrived primarily to satisfy themselves that it was safe for our return. There was so much to be done to get the country moving again that I could not be bothered about investigating this looting as the material things stolen were worthless compared with our lives.

October, 1983, will go down in history as the month in which Grenada, the Spice Isle of the Caribbean, took up the central spot on the world stage. It is in Grenada that the fall of communism began. Since then the world saw the dramatic dismantling of the Berlin Wall and the gale force wind of change which knocked down the prevailing political system in the Soviet Union and opened up the way for democracy and personal liberty. After four and one half years, the communist imposed Central Committee of Grenada quarrelled bitterly among themselves and then savagely and fatally reduced their comrade leader to nothingness. The final blow came when the American and Caribbean Forces demilitarized Grenada, captured the alleged killers of Prime Minister Bishop, and decisively wiped out the vestiges of that alien ideology. Grenada could justifiably claim to be the first country to have escaped from communist domination and immediately revert to democracy and freedom. In less than a week after the fighting ceased, I started to prepare the groundwork for the holding of free and fair elections thus ensuring that Grenadians would go to the polls and freely elect a government of their choice. This transformation from communism to democratic freedom was a remarkable feat for a tiny island.

By Thursday, October 27, the fighting was all over except for a few snipers hiding in the bushes. Key targets including the prisons and the various bases of the local People's Revolutionary Army – not least their headquarters at Fort Frederick – had been taken. The Cubans who perhaps for the first time engaged in combat against the Americans held out to the end in self defence as ordered by their President Fidel Castro. They too finally surrendered at "Little Havana," a built up settlement quite close to the airport. Austin, James, and Layne tried hard to leave Grenada but their efforts proved unsuccessful. General Austin, exhausted and dejected, had got no favourable response to his request for help. Fidel Castro who had categorically condemned the killing of Bishop made it abundantly clear that no help would be forthcoming from Cuba. However, when an aircraft from Cubana Airlines touched down at Pearls Airport on the east of the island around midday on Monday, October 24, General Austin headed a welcoming party to greet Colonel Pedro Tortolo Comas, Chief of Staff of the Army of the Centre and his accompanying small staff including Carlos Andres Diaz, the Caribbean Section Chief in the American Department of the Central Committee of the Party. They came to take an interest in the seven hundred Cuban workers on the Point Salines Airport who had been issued with small arms and many of whom had some form of military training. Diaz died in the fighting in Little Havana. Military advisers from the Soviet Union and the communist countries of Eastern Europe took no part in the conflict. Throughout the combat and beyond, the Soviet Embassy acted with rectitude. They corresponded with me during that period, even complaining about shots that were fired at their Embassy. Their diplomatic notes were sent to me, not to the Americans. The Cuban Embassy, on the other hand, either through arrogance or ignorance, chose not to deal with me. On one occasion during the conflict, the Cuban Ambassador tried desperately to call John Kelly, the senior British diplomat on the island, but to no avail. He had the wrong telephone number. But I long knew that Rizo, the Cuban Ambassador, never understood our Constitution and he was totally confused about the role of the Governor General.

Troops and paramilitary police from Jamaica, Barbados, Antigua/ Barbuda, Dominica, St. Kitts/Nevis, St. Lucia and St. Vincent joined the U.S.A. in the mopping up exercise, and the Caribbean personnel were to stay in Grenada specifically to maintain law and order. This was vital as we could not depend on our drastically reduced police force which was disorganized and lacking in loyalty and commitment. Some of the American troops were to stay on for a while to consolidate the success of the rescue mission. It is to be noted that the Bahamas, Belize, Guyana, and Trinidad and Tobago – all CARICOM Countries – did not take part in the rescue mission. CARICOM missed a rare opportunity to act decisively and in concert. But not only did they not unite over the Grenada issue but they thought it more important to take up their own posturing while their brothers and sisters were suffering in Grenada. The politicians did not have the will nor could they use their imagination to come up with some sensible and practical initiative which would redound to their own integrity and maturity and mitigate the hardships of their kith and kin in Grenada. Perhaps they never understood what was happening in Grenada during the revolutionary period or they did not care to know. They took no account of the sensitivity of the Grenadians and they were oblivious of their desires, their fears – and their tears. What is worse after the fighting was over, they stood aloof. Instead of coming forward and offering assistance on humanitarian grounds or otherwise, they spent their time in some cases spouting out a great deal of intellectual nonsense about the correctness of the military intervention. This was clearly a time for these righteous and legalistic men to be pragmatic in their approach to the Grenada affair and to seek together to rebuild democracy in one of their sister territories. Grenada's problem struck at the very roots of the CARICOM ideals and aspirations. To remain aloof was to be careless about the future of their own countries, for current local difficulties in Grenada might be a future disaster in some other part of CARICOM. Their posturing at the United Nations, at the Commonwealth Heads of Government and other international gatherings could not change the U.S.A. policy, could not undo the military events in Grenada and certainly could not and did not thwart my own efforts at reconciliation and rebuilding.

Guyana, a CARICOM State, joined with Nicaragua in sponsoring a resolution in the Security Council of the United Nations condemning the military action – an endeavour initiated by the OECS, Barbados and Jamaica who together sit around the table year after year talking regional integration and functional co-operation. But the attitude of the Government of Trinidad and Tobago and their Prime Minister, George Chambers, was incredible. Their non-participation in the rescue mission was their sovereign right and no one could quarrel with them for that. But when it came to slapping a visa requirement on Grenadians for entry into Trinidad and Tobago, that was hard to take, given the close ties of kinship between the people of Trinidad and the people of Grenada, and needless to mention the contribution of Grenadian nationals over the years in the general developmental process in Trinidad. At first Grenadians had to get their visas from the Trinidad and Tobago High Commission in Barbados, but later an officer visited Grenada weekly to issue these visas. The hardship experienced by Grenadian traffickers who went frequently to Trinidad was exceptional. It was shameful to see the long queues outside the office week after week in quest of visas. I sought help from the Government of Trinidad and Tobago but without success. I did not ask for financial assistance; I simply asked for the loan of personnel to help us in certain areas of the public service. With that kind of attitude it is no wonder then that integration of any kind continues to elude us. While Britain and other countries came to offer assistance once the fighting ceased, our CARICOM partner sought ways of putting more pressure on an already traumatized people. I was highly amused when some months later the same Government of Trinidad and Tobago sent a fact-finding mission to Grenada under the leadership of a retired jurist who was against the military intervention. His problem, not mine! What the mission discovered I do not know up to this day. At any rate I was not interested because I thought it was a waste of time. What was even more amusing was this fact-finding mission visited Grenada only after delegations from the Opposition Parties in Trinidad had called on me to wish me well, to express sentiments of solidarity with our efforts at restoring democracy and freedom. They lamented that the Government in Trinidad could not see its way to comply with our request for help. One such delegation was headed by Mr Basdeo Panday and the other was led by Grenadian-born Karl Hudson-Phillips whose father, also a Grenadian by birth, had played a significant role in the development of local government in Trinidad and Tobago.

International reaction to the military intervention varied from total support to downright condemnation. Those who had taken the trouble to follow the murky course of events in Grenada during the revolutionary period and had clearly witnessed the erosion of personal liberty voiced their fullest support for the rescue mission. While Margaret Thatcher, British Prime Minister, seemed not happy about Ronald Reagan sending troops to Grenada without her full knowledge, it must be admitted to her great credit that the British Government did not condemn the intervention and they were the first non-participant to offer assistance in the reconstruction programme. In the Security Council of the United Nations Britain along with Zaire and Togo abstained when a resolution condemning the military action was vetoed by the U.S.A. On the day after the intervention Thatcher in responding to a question in Parliament had this to say: "We understand that what weighed heavily and conclusively with the United States was the view taken by a number of Caribbean States who see things in a different perspective from that which we do. They are very much closer."

For several days the British press freely referred to me as the British Governor General. This only went to show that imperial habits die hard. I was born in Grenada and I grew up in Grenada. Even a cursory glance at me would tell that by no stretch of imagination could I have Anglo-Saxon blood in my veins. Mr Denis Healey's impudent and widely publicized charge that Eugenia Charles had either invented or much exaggerated the appeal for help which the authorities in Grenada had made was met with sharp rebuke by the lady herself. Eugenia Charles retorted that Mr Healey had dared to speak like that about her because her country is poor, small and black. The stunned Mr Healey (Labour member of Parliament) appeared to have been silenced instantaneously and would make no comment on Eugenia's retort.

Sir Geoffrey Howe, the British Foreign Secretary, in an interview tried to explain how wrong the Americans were to intervene militarily in Grenada and how in that regard the principles of international law had been violated. He, of course, completely ignored my own role in all this, appeared to be oblivious of the hardships Grenadians had to endure during the Revolution and paid no heed to the overwhelming support the Grenadians showed for the intervention when they welcomed the Forces as liberators. Perhaps he was not properly briefed as to what was happening in Grenada or he failed to grasp the true import of the hopes and fears of the natives. For sure Sir Geoffrey's ramblings could score no credit with the Americans. As for me I knew that I was under no obligation to consult the British Government either before, during or after the military intervention. When a British warship anchored in St. George's harbour in February, 1984, some young lads who were enjoying a swim seriously told the sailors that they had arrived in Grenada four months too late. In interviews with the foreign press it became quite clear to me that there was a great deal of misunderstanding even among British journalists about the constitutional status of Grenada and more particularly about my role as representative of Her Majesty the Queen. Some British journalists seemed peeved that the Americans, and not the British, led the military action and they asked me whether I had to seek permission from the Queen or the British Government before the Forces could land in Grenada. My reply was obviously in the negative, Grenada being a sovereign independent State. For all practical purposes it was far better to seek the aid of Americans if only because of proximity. The breakdown of law and order bordering on civil war required swift and decisive action. One senior British reporter disgustingly and condescendingly put it to me that the Americans were running the country and not the Governor General. I pitied his ignorance and simply told him that I did not agree with him.

At home the support for the military action was overwhelming. The Conference of Churches in Grenada supported the intervention without any reservation and promised any help which they were in a position to give at any time. The Chamber of Industry and Commerce called a special meeting on November 1, 1983, to express support for and gratitude to the liberation forces. In a news release put out by the Chamber afterwards the following sentiments were expressed: "Not often are people afforded the opportunity to escape from tyranny. The people of Grenada have been given this opportunity It is seldom that a nation is given a second chance for a new beginning. Let us hope that all our people will use this opportunity wisely and well."

The Grenada Hotel Association was not to be left behind. The Association issued a statement that was approved at a special meeting held on November 9, 1983. The statement after pointing to the total disregard for the lives, rights and freedom of the Grenadian people, went on to record the level of militarization as well as the presence of military advisers from Cuba, East Germany and the Soviet Union. The statement concluded: "Without external assistance we would have been condemned to rule by a military dictatorship which had vividly demonstrated its capacity for ruthlessness."

Within five days of my return to Governor General's Office, I called in all the active non-governmental organizations including the Trade Union Council for consultation, and to explain to them my own thoughts for the future. What was significant about these meetings was that the participants felt a new sense of involvement in the decision making process. They pledged their loyalty and support. I invited them to send suggestions to me for the composition of an Interim Government bearing in mind my own parameters for the establishment of such a government.

# 10

## The Exercise of Executive Authority

THE fighting ceased. The blasts of war faded away. The Revolutionary Military Council expired. In response to my request, members of the People's Revolutionary Army and the militia ambled nonchalantly to the Queen's Park pavilion daily to turn in their arms. The comrades of the Central Committee including Bernard Coard and his Jamaican-born wife, Phyllis, had abandoned their headquarters at Fort Frederick three days after the commencement of hostilities. They were soon brought together again, but this time in lawful custody. Without arms, without ammunition, without an army, they were assisting the police with investigations into the murder of Prime Minister Bishop and others at Fort Rupert on October 19. Scores of internationalist workers were busily packing their bags for home. I took the bold and unprecedented step to sever diplomatic ties with the Soviet Union, Libya, East Germany, North Korea and other communist countries with the exception of Cuba. Some self-appointed constitutional purists considered my action unlawful. But this was not the time for intellectual niceties; it was a time for action. I was motivated by what I thought to be best for Grenada and I had the overwhelming support of my fellow citizens. I politely asked the Soviet and Libyan diplomats to leave the country. At the Point Salines Airport, two cases of arms and ammunition were seized from the Soviets as they were about to embark.

Contrary to widespread reports I did not break diplomatic relations with Cuba. In my carefully worded note to the Cuban authorities, I pointed out that I had declared their Ambassador *persona non grata* and his presence in Grenada was no longer welcome. By mutual agreement the two countries could name Ambassadors on a non-resident basis. In effect Grenada would no longer maintain an embassy in Havana and at the same time would not welcome a Cuban embassy in St. George's. One might be tempted to ask why Cuba was treated differently when it had been generally perceived that Cuba was the driving force in Grenada's march towards full-fledged communism. Some emphatically blamed Cuba for the progressive erosion of personal liberty, although they were quick to acknowledge Cuba's paternalistic assistance to Grenada in various spheres of endeavour. Others felt that whatever help we might have received from Cuba we got it at too high a price, namely, the deprivation of democratic freedom. In making my decision I took into account the close affinity which historically existed between the peoples of both countries, dating back to the late nineteenth century at least when large numbers of Grenadians had migrated to Cuba in search of employment on the sugar estates and railroad lines that were being built. I was also cognizant of the number of Grenadian students who were currently in Cuba, and of the extreme generosity of the Cuban government and people. Having considered all these factors, I felt it was not prudent to sever diplomatic ties with Cuba.

Without question and without delay, the Soviet diplomats complied with my request and left. So did the Libyans. Not so the Cuban diplomats who, presumably acting on instructions from their homeland, were defiant and exhibited a pattern of behaviour which struck at the integrity of Grenada's sovereignty. Perhaps Havana was making a final attempt to remind all and sundry that Cuba was the *quasi* colonial power in Grenada. When Ambassador Rizo and his colleagues eventually left Grenada, a sizeable cache of arms was found concealed in their Embassy at Morne Jaloux. There were no East German or North Korean diplomats resident in Grenada.

The time for reconciliation, forgiveness and reconstruction had come. Clearly the rebuilding process must include the manner in which we face the psychological challenge of healing the broken hearts and disturbed minds of our people. The young man who had been stripped of his army uniform and his AK47 suffered a serious deflation of his ego and had to readjust to a new way of life. The young pioneer who was taught that there was no God had to be carefully de-briefed, and this posed a special challenge to parents, teachers and ministers of religion. New employment opportunities had to be created for the hundreds of young men and women who would be out of work as a result of the disbandment of the army. This also had implications for education and training. In addition the reinforcement of our democratic structures and the rekindling of our democratic institutions called for tolerance, equanimity and unremitting effort.

With the cessation of hostilities, I assumed control of the affairs of Grenada. Without a government I exercised executive authority up to November 15 when I appointed an Advisory Council to perform the functions of an Interim Government. I was in the unusual and novel position, where as representative of the Monarch, I was using my own deliberate judgement in taking far-reaching political decisions. There could be no denying that I was the sole constitutional authority left in the country.

The *de facto* Prime Minister had been executed. General Austin's Revolutionary Military Council failed to gain acceptance either locally or externally. He and his political and military cohorts were disarmed, arrested and detained. It fell upon my shoulders to keep the country afloat. I, therefore, invoked the doctrine of necessity and made use of the powers of Section 57 of the Grenada Constitution Order which is as follows:

"1. The executive authority of Grenada is vested in Her Majesty.

2. Subject to the provisions of this Constitution the executive authority of Grenada may be exercised on behalf of Her Majesty by the Governor General either directly or through officers subordinate to him.

3. Nothing in this section shall prevent Parliament from conferring functions on persons or authorities other than the Governor General."

This section is quite clear as to where executive authority lies. In practice such authority is exercised by the Prime Minister and his Cabinet colleagues. By October 27, we had neither Prime Minister nor Cabinet. Of course, we were without Parliament since March 13, 1979. But life in Grenada had to go on, and as Governor General I could not allow any hiatus in the governance of the country. Hence the reason I took full control in order to exercise executive authority on behalf of Her Majesty.

In my broadcast shortly after the intervention I had made it quite clear that I would not include politicians in any Government which I subsequently appointed. For four and one half years, Prime Minister Gairy had been unable to give advice to me as Governor General, and in any case his five-year term of office would have been long expired. Given his insatiable appetite for power, I was not surprised to learn that Gairy was advocating that he should be invited to head the Interim Government as he had been the last elected Prime Minister. In my view this claim was without merit.

In order to carry on my work, I had the protection of the Caribbean Peacekeeping Force and the American military. Most importantly, within a few days after the fighting, I grew in confidence by the astounding messages of goodwill and affirmation of support I received from the Grenadian people – a people who had spent over four years looking over their shoulders before they opened their mouths, who had silently stood by and observed private property confiscated without compensation, who were totally upset about the communist indoctrination meted out to their children, and the systematic dissolution of their Christian values. Grenadians wanted change and they now saw the opportunity for revival of their cherished way of life.

Four businessmen, led by Fred Toppin, Managing Director of the leading firm of Jonas Browne & Hubbard Ltd., were the first to call on me after I had returned to my official residence. With anxious expectation they stood at the eastern entrance almost at the crack of dawn pleading with the guard to let them in. Because of the chaotic situation in the business sector, I readily agreed to see them. After pledging unreserved loyalty and support, they reported that the business community had suffered tremendously at the hands of looters. Shops were broken into, and people unabashedly walked in and helped themselves to items large and small. In some cases vehicles were parked outside business places to collect the more cumbersome merchandise. Amid all this criminal activity, law enforcing officers could not be found on the streets of St. George's. The businessmen saw the re-organization of the Police Force as a top priority. As a short term measure they urged me unambiguously and forcefully to get the police back on the streets of St. George's without delay as a first step towards the restoration of law and order.

The paucity of law enforcement officers was immediately apparent. The Commissioner of Police had advised me that there were only one hundred and eighty-one policemen and women left in the Force. This decline in numbers was due mainly to government's deliberate policy of downsizing and downgrading the Police Force. As far as the People's Revolutionary Government was concerned, the army and the militia took precedence over the police. Whether this policy was based on ideological considerations was not quite clear, but Bishop's claim that he and his colleagues had been constant targets for police harassment before he seized power in 1979 must have been a compelling factor.

Our already depleted Police Force was further reduced when at the commencement of the military intervention many officers deserted their posts either through fear or because of ill-discipline. But prior to this and particularly during the revolutionary regime, the rate of attrition was high while the level of recruitment was low. Adequate replacement for those who left the Force had never materialized and this was in accordance with Government's policy. Some of the best policemen left the Force and actually fled from their homeland. The common practice was to join the traffickers on one of the schooners that plied weekly with fruit and vegetables for the Trinidad market. The policeman would travel to Trinidad purportedly to see a relative who had fallen ill, or to visit with an uncle or aunt. Once he arrived in Trinidad, he would then make his international flight connections either in Trinidad or Barbados. There were a few who used St. Vincent as the gateway. Whichever way, it was goodbye to the Royal Grenada Police Force. A dwindling Force with low morale could not satisfactorily maintain law and order. Because of this soldiers, both American and Caribbean, had perforce to do some policing work. Their presence on the streets brought back some semblance of order as well as renewed confidence particularly among the business community.

Within the first week I had a stream of visitors, both local and foreign, all supportive of the intervention and many of them offering to be of service in whatever way they could. Prime Ministers Edward Seaga, Tom Adams and John Compton of Jamaica, Barbados and St. Lucia respectively came to see for themselves how the intervention was holding. What was remarkable about all three men was that they never attempted to suggest to me how the country should be governed. They fully understood that Grenada was a sovereign independent state with a Governor General at the helm exercising executive authority in accordance with the Constitution. Instead the visiting Prime Ministers were more concerned about my personal welfare and they listened with intense interest when I told them of my personal experiences during the military intervention. They each promised to provide any assistance I thought they could offer as Grenada moved towards the restoration of democracy. Meanwhile after all the American bashing in the United Nations, not unexpected of course, the Secretary General sent down a one-man fact-finding mission. His task was easy, and I did everything possible to make his path clear as he proceeded with his assignment. He came. He saw for himself. He left.

The Civil Service was in total disarray. The high esteem in which the Grenada Civil Service had been held was a thing of the past. It became increasingly difficult to tell where policy directives ended and implement-ation began. What is more policy directives were diluted into ministerial advice as to the manner in which the Permanent Secretary should deal with matters that were purely administrative. For fear of reprisals Permanent Secretaries either did not tender advice to their Ministers, or if they did, their advice would constitute just what they thought the Minister would want to hear. Ministers in the People's Revolutionary Government were taking matters in their hands signing letters which should normally be done by the Permanent Secretaries, bending the time-honoured financial rules and regulations, becoming impatient of Civil Service procedures, and sometimes ignoring them as being too colonial or too bourgeoisie. Ideological exuberance completely overshadowed tried and tested administrative practices.

During the Revolution it was mandatory for Civil Servants to attend lectures in Marxism. Some like the police started as early as 5.30 a.m. while others like the Post Office staff attended from 3 p.m. It was not uncommon for Permanent Secretaries to go on paramilitary manoeuvres

"... THE HURLY-BURLY OF GRENADIAN POLITICS"

*...ove*, Sir Paul arriving in the courtyard of Grenada's Parliament for his inauguration of ...tober 4, 1978

*...ow*, Sir Paul with Opposition Parliamentarians Maurice Bishop and Bernard Coard outside ...rliament after his inauguration

*osite*, Sir Paul poses with other Parliamentarians for a group portrait after the ceremony

*ve*, Sir Paul takes the Oath of Allegiance and Office

*w*, A less fraught moment in the Governor General's 14-year career: the investiture of Mr Hugh
*on* Baptiste with the insignia of Her Majesty's OBE

"IN THE HURLY-BURLY OF GRENADIAN POLITICS"

*Above*, Sir Paul with his nine-member Advisory Council during the Interim Administration pledged t restore democratic elections

*Opposite*, Democracy restored: Parliament reassembles after a lapse of five years as Sir Paul reads the traditional Throne Speech

*Opposite, above,* Lady Scoon signing the visitors' book in Jamaica as her husband and Sir Florizel Glasspole look on

*Opposite, below,* The Governor General in Moscow viewing the body of the late USSR President Brehznev

*Above,* More "aboard" than "abroad": Sir Paul and Lady Scoon on the Royal Yacht Britannia during the Royal couple's historic visit to Grenada

"MORE WORLD TRAVELS"

*Above*, Governor General Sir Paul and Governor General Sir Lambert Eustace of St. Vincent and the Grenadines are welcomed in Kingstown Cathedral

*Below*, Sir Paul and Lady Scoon at lunch at Broome Community College in the U.S.A. Broome Count and Grenada are partners under the Partners of the Americas Programme

clad in army uniform and proudly swinging their arms under the weight of the AK47. During one of the week-end manoeuvres, the Permanent Secretary in the Ministry of Health, all dressed in battle array, made her way to the Princess Alice Hospital in St. Andrew's and asked for a glass of water. When the nurse on duty showed a little hesitancy, this formidable female snapped at her, "Do you know who I am?" At that point the nurse nervously obliged.

There were many internationalist workers holding senior administrative and managerial positions in the public service. By the end of October, I had given them all marching orders, and they sadly packed their bags for home. This, of course, created a void and at once I took what I thought to be the most appropriate action, namely, to recall to service some competent persons who had recently retired.

Within days my mail started to pile up. The numerous messages of goodwill, the unsolicited advice from some of the most unlikely sources, the offers of help – voluntary or otherwise – constituted a massive pile of mail which could not be handled by my normal staff. Additionally, and prior to the establishment of an official Interim Government, official mail addressed to the Prime Minister was forwarded to my office. The destruction of the Prime Minister's Office during the military action was not helpful and, as if this was not enough, the Cabinet Secretary, a career Civil Servant, tendered her resignation on October 31 with immediate effect. There was no difficulty in transferring staff from the Prime Minister's Office to my office, but I was wary of doing this because I had reservations about the loyalty of these potential transferees. What is more, I never believed that the way to improve efficiency and effectiveness was merely to increase the size of staff. This has been the *bête noir* of the Grenada Civil Service for years and the practice of creating new posts degenerated into the recruitment of incompetent political lackeys into the public service, much to the resentment of qualified hardworking civil servants.

However, there was a felt need for additional staff in my office. I wanted trustworthy people who had a track record of loyalty and devotion as civil servants. I, therefore, called Mavis Fletcher out of retirement. She was of immeasurable help to me amid the temporary added responsibilities in my office. On the recommendation of the retiring Cabinet Secretary, I transferred only one officer from the Prime Minister's Office to mine.

I also called out of retirement Norbert Fletcher whom I asked to perform the duties of Information Officer. Otto George, a well known disciplinarian, was another retired civil servant whom I recalled. His loyalty and devotion was second to none.

I also took out of retirement two selfless, loyal and devoted former Permanent Secretaries in the persons of Elma Thorne and Ruth Rahim. All these persons were brought back to head the ministries and their business was to inject order into the Civil Service and restore the pristine qualities of loyalty, devotion, confidentiality and industry which had once characterized the Grenada Civil Service.

But in order to bring about orderliness in the public service, I first had to do something about the Public Service Commission. By Executive Order dated October 31, 1983, I dissolved the Public Service Commission and replaced it by more reputable and capable men and women under the chairmanship of Godwin Brathwaite, a retired Cabinet Secretary. The wisdom of my action is reflected in the fact that Brathwaite served in this post with distinction for another nine years afterwards during the regime of two different governments.

During the Revolution, classrooms throughout the nation were in a state of confusion as the struggle for supremacy between the Christian doctrine and the Marxist ideology intensified. This was manifested in many ways. The reluctance of teachers to observe the morning act of worship and their non-compliance with the teaching of religious knowledge even in denominational schools, where religious instruction had been the norm. The concomitant debasement of religious and moral values in our schools led to a lack of respect for authority, helped to produce a blurred distinction between right and wrong and funnelled a worrying disrespect for other people's property. Children were told they should believe in people they could see, not in those they could not see – a clear admonition to those who were adherents to the Christian faith. It was not uncommon for secondary school boys who were enlisted in the militia to attend school with guns in their school bags referring to them as their "little things." From a very tender age the children had the revolutionary fervour instilled into them. Depending on which side of the fence they stood school principals were rapidly surrendering their authority. Student Councils grew in numbers and became more vocal and more demanding. One Minister for Education told me during the revolutionary period that if there were a problem in the school involving either teacher or student, or both, she would just send in some armed soldiers of the People's Revolutionary Army. I simply told her that she would do no such thing. She stared at me and probably thought that I was a slow learner who did not understand what a revolution meant. While some teachers were still teaching from a Christian perspective, others were motivated by the Marxist ideology. With some fifteen Soviet teachers let loose on our schools there was additional cause for concern.

Now that the revolutionary period was ended, urgent corrective action was necessary. One of my first acts was to instruct the acting Chief Education Officer, Jerome McBarnette, to re-instate immediately a number of head teachers whom the People's Revolutionary Government had without warning removed from the schools and transferred to the Ministry of Education ostensibly to form a research unit. The truth of the matter was that the government felt that these head teachers were not sufficiently proactive in espousing the Marxist/Leninist cause. In fact the revolutionary authorities firmly believed that they had been too reactionary, too church oriented. I also invited Valentine Francis, another retiree, to resume the office of Principal of the Institute of Further Education, a tertiary institution preparing students for the University of Cambridge A level studies.

Financial propriety is the hallmark of any good government. Given the machinations of the Treasury during the PRG regime I thought strong leadership was needed at the administrative level in the Ministry of Finance. Bearing in mind that October salaries were due for payment I called in the two most senior officers in the Ministry of Finance to ascertain the state of the country's finances. The behaviour of the more senior officer puzzled me. He seemed not his usual self. Admitting that he was close to Bernard Coard, he was very negative throughout our conversation and advised me that there was no money to pay salaries for October. I put all this down to the emotional shocks which he and countless other Grenadians had experienced over the previous few days. I soon discovered that I was wrong. It was a great surprise to me when soon after he left my office I learnt from a very reliable source that this individual had been actively engaged in battle against the Americans in the Grand Anse/Morne Rouge area during the military intervention and that during the course of action his car was destroyed. Hence the reason for his strange behaviour during our meeting. Armed with this bit of intelligence, I immediately sent for Lauriston Wilson Jr. whom Bernard Coard, then Minister for Finance, had earlier advised to take his leave. At any rate, the recall of Wilson was one of my priorities. It would appear also that Wilson was well prepared to answer my call as he seemed to have wasted no time in getting to my residence.

Wilson resumed immediate control of the Ministry of Finance. He was not only the administrative head of the Ministry of Finance but he also played the role of my chief administrative adviser. He had at his fingertips the names and conditions of service of all the main internationalist workers, some of whom had been receiving lucrative salaries, especially those whose paymasters were some of the aid-giving international organizations. An indefatigable worker who stretched his working day, Wilson reported to me at the end of every working day usually around 7 p.m. to brief me on financial matters generally and on the daily state of the finances in particular. He was my chief adviser up to November 15 when I appointed an Advisory Council giving them full authority to act as if they were ministers of government and urging them to take decisions as if they were duly elected by the people. Of course, I reserved the right to veto any measure approved by them.

In October, 1983, Richard Hart was the Attorney General. Suave and polite, Hart had come to Grenada presumably on the invitation of Prime Minister Bishop to help in the Legal Department. From the outset he adopted a friendly posture. Little did he know how aware I was of his political incursions in his native Jamaica before he was expelled from the People's National Party. After the execution of Prime Minister Bishop I felt the need to talk to the Attorney General who was the chief law officer of the Crown. Accordingly I summoned Hart to Governor General's House to brief me and advise me. He never turned up for the appointment. He vacated his post and left the country. Two years later following our parliamentary elections Hart planned to revisit Grenada. He wrote from the United Kingdom to seek an appointment with me. I did not feel able to comply and without any difficulty persuaded the Prime Minister to deny him entry into Grenada.

With Hart and other internationalist lawyers out of the way a void was created in the Legal Department. Circumstances demanded that this void be filled immediately. Fortunately the old stalwart, Edwin Heyliger, was available. He threw his weight of experience and knowledge solidly behind me. He pledged his loyalty unreservedly and promised to give me any help I needed in the legal field. Heyliger was an active player in Grenada's constitutional drama over the last forty years – from colony to statehood, to independence to *coup d'état* to military intervention. Heyliger was always on spot serving any government who required his expertise. Guyanese by birth, he spent most of his working life in Grenada first as a young Magistrate. He served for many years as Attorney General and once administered the Government of Grenada for three months. He retired as a Judge in the Supreme Court of the Windward and Leeward Islands. After retirement his services were in demand and he filled in as Legal Adviser. He was a member of the Government delegation to the independence talks held in London in 1973.

Without formally appointing Heyliger as Attorney General I asked him to take charge of the Legal Department until I could make arrangements to appoint a new Attorney General. It was Heyliger who adroitly drafted the earlier Proclamations and Ordinances. His sage legal advice was of immense value.

For the most part our Embassies and High Commission offices abroad were staffed by people with strong socialist, if not communist, commitments. Heads of Mission either did not understand what was going on in Grenada or refused to subdue their revolutionary fervour. Some of them actually made public statements against the military intervention. Others thought they could continue to represent Grenada abroad against my wishes, and foolishly behaved as if the People's Revolutionary Government was still in office. By Proclamation dated October 31, 1983, I recalled all the Heads of Mission and ordered that the Embassies and High Commission offices be closed immediately. I also ordered all members of staff who were recruited in Grenada to return to the country. My view was that the Embassies should remain closed until a democratically elected government assumed office. I strongly felt that our resources should be utilized in rebuilding the appropriate structures at home rather than continuing to pay these oversea officers who in our special circumstances might be sending wrong signals to the outside world. Further, I thought a case could be made for streamlining our Missions abroad. We could save money and at the same time have more effective and efficient representation. The Tourist Offices remained open for business. I did not wish to give any impression that the day-to-day operation of our Tourist Offices was politically inspired.

The law enforcing arm of government was always a worrisome concern. The morale of the Royal Grenada Police Force was at its lowest ebb. So was that of the Richmond Hill Prisons. Leadership in the Police and Prisons was critical. I obtained the services of three senior policemen from the Royal Barbados Police Force. One of them, Mervyn Holder, I made Commissioner of Police. The Government of Barbados was also generous in releasing Lionel Maloney – a no-nonsense prison officer – to assume duties as Grenada's Commissioner of Prisons.

Parliamentary democracy had always been near and dear to me and its restoration was of great significance. Historic York House was in a state of disrepair having lost the awe and majesty it had previously enjoyed. During the revolutionary period, all sorts of ordinary meetings had been held there. Photographs had been taken down, books were removed, the horseshoe table around which the parliamentarians deliberated was dismantled, windows were broken. Thanks to the instinct of Curtis Strachan, the Clerk of Parliament, the mace of the House of Representatives and that of the Senate were securely hidden.

On Monday, November 1, I called Curtis Strachan to my office and gave him instructions to have York House prepared for Parliament without delay.

As this entailed extensive refurbishment I later the same day called in the top officials of the Ministry of Works and instructed them to make the refurbishing of York House a priority and work should start at once. Strachan set out to work immediately in restoring the parliamentary chamber and the offices, and the Ministry of Works with due deference complied diligently with my request and gave York House a new look.

The selection of members of the Advisory Council was not easy. But I was never daunted by the negative attitudes of those who expressed the view that it would be impossible to find an adequate number of Grenadians who could satisfy the criteria which I had laid down for membership. Some felt that the country was too polarized politically for anyone to be able to select non-partisan people to form an Interim Government. Others were of the view that the trauma of October, 1983, would be an inhibiting factor in getting suitable candidates to serve on such a body. The Revolution had turned out to be an extraordinarily divisive rather than an unifying force. Because of this, it was the generally accepted view in some quarters that one could not contemplate the equanimity, fair play and justice which would be required of every member of the Advisory Council.

But while this scepticism was not entirely baseless, I felt it was not an impossible task to find nine to twelve Grenadian men and women whether they resided in or outside of Grenada to constitute the Council. As I kept thinking daily about the establishment of the Advisory Council, my confidence grew in the certain knowledge that I would present to our nation a slate of patriotic men and women with integrity, knowledge and commitment. Should I head the Advisory Council or should I not? That was the question which was uppermost in my mind when I began the process of selection from a short list I had drawn up after taking into account the recommendations submitted to me by non-governmental organizations. I had to decide whether it would be in the best interest of the country for me to place myself at the head of the Advisory Council. Opinion varied. There were those who thought that the Governor General as the only remaining constitutional authority in the country should not only exercise executive power but should be seen to be doing so actively. With the Governor General at the helm of the Council more far reaching decisions could be taken, and implementation of those decisions would be more speedily done in the Governor General's Office where a secretariat would be set up with a very senior Civil Servant as Secretary to the Council and head of the secretariat. Alternatively, the secretariat could be headed by a member of the Advisory Council who would be the principal adviser to the Governor General. There were others who were of the opinion that the Governor General should stick to his ceremonial role as much as circumstances would permit and depend on the advice of the Advisory Council for his various actions.

Having carefully weighed the two options, I came to the conclusion that it would be a retrograde step to have the Governor General actually sitting in Council. It would smack of the colonial days when the Administrator or the Governor presided over the Executive Council. I took cognizance of the fact that Grenada was an independent sovereign state and thought it might be injudicious to go back in time and establish what could be construed as an Executive Council in the colonial mould. I therefore opted for a Council which looked more like a Cabinet of Ministers and which would be presided over by a named Chairman. The Council would be collectively responsible to the Governor General for the conduct of the Government of Grenada, as a caretaker administration, until fair and free elections were held and an elected government in place. Responsibility for particular departments of the government would be assigned to the Chairman and other members of the Council in accordance with the recommendations of the Chairman. The Council, or the Chairman or other individual members acting with the authority of the Council, would give directions of policy to the departments of Government.

When I analyzed the recommendations submitted to me by non-governmental organizations I found that the majority of them did not meet the requirements for serious consideration. I first had to jot down on paper the conditions I wanted for such appointments. It went without saying that the Council should consist of Grenadian nationals only. To avoid inbreeding I needed to seek some Grenadians living abroad who had done well in their chosen careers. Administrative experience would be an asset. Prospective Council members should be well known to me and I should be able to trust them. An all male Council was undesirable.

One of Grenada's celebrated sons, Alister McIntyre, was strongly recommended to me both on the home front and abroad. A noted Caribbean economist, McIntyre had had wide and varied experience regionally and internationally. I thought McIntyre would make an admirable Chairman and bring to that office a wealth of scholarship and experience. Nicholas Brathwaite was from the outset my natural choice to direct and stimulate educational development. Brathwaite had been Chief Education Officer in Grenada before he was recruited by the Commonwealth Secretariat to take charge of the Commonwealth Youth Training Programme based in Guyana. Always mindful of Commonwealth principles the Commonwealth Secretary General, Shridath Ramphal, offered to do whatever he could to assist Grenada, one of the smallest member states of the Commonwealth, to regain democratic freedom. Ramphal readily agreed to second Brathwaite to the Advisory Council with no cost to the Government of Grenada. He had also agreed to provide funds for the services of Alister McIntyre once the latter was released from his assignment with United Nations Conference on Trade and Development.

Once I settled on McIntyre and Brathwaite, I then had to look back to my school days to think of my own contemporaries and those who were just ahead of me or just after me. I also looked at the alumni of the other Boys' School, the Presentation Boys' College. The ladies were not to be left out and I perused carefully a list of former students of the St. Joseph's Convent and the Anglican Girls High School. I jotted down a number of names and then checked each one against my list of criteria. By a process of elimination I arrived at a short list. Genderwise, I was determined that the Council should be mixed and I greatly expected that at least two women would agree to serve. Unhappily my hopes were slightly dashed when only one acquiesced and that was after some deep persuasion on my part. In my interviews with prospective women candidates I found them either timid or disinterested to take up that kind of responsibility. That was November, 1983.

In the realm of national service at any level it would be foolhardy to underestimate or ignore the worth of men and women who by their daily acts reflect the mores of their society and are capable of bringing to their jobs values which can keep a nation together by enhancing national development for peace, harmony and prosperity. Thus, in order to get a proper mix on the composition of the Council, my roving mind took me to rural Grenada where I hoped to find not necessarily professionals or technocrats but rather civic minded and patriotic men and women who had a good track record in community work and were widely respected.

It was never my intention to make the Advisory Council a representative body. No member was to represent any particular interest. Each member was to be chosen on his or her own merit and in a private capacity. I paid no heed to those who were sending signals that there should be mainly lawyers or businessmen on the Council. Not that I purposely left out these categories. But in my estimation the best of those represented in those professions did not quite fit into the body of criteria that I had laid down. The myth that businessmen can manage better than anybody else has never hypnotized me. Nor have I ever subscribed to that other myth that attorneys-at-law make the best politicians.

One of my objectives was to reduce the cost of government. Throughout my public life in Grenada I had seen a colossal and unnecessary growth of government that stemmed from the fact that the party in government found jobs for all the elected representatives and for many of those who were unsuccessful in their bid to capture electoral seats. As a first step towards reducing the cost of government I restricted the numbers on Council by appointing nine rather than twelve members. Thus without shouting to the roof tops, I effectively got rid of a number of ministries and government departments. Indeed, there were two permanent secretaries who had not held letters of appointment from the Public Service Commission. They, therefore, were not civil servants. Sadly they were counted among the civil service casualties, and there was nothing I could usefully do for them.

Before appointing the Advisory Council I first had to approach the Prime Minister of Jamaica, the President of the Caribbean Development Bank, the Pro-Vice Chancellor of the Cave Hill campus of the University of the West Indies and, as stated earlier, the Secretary General of the Commonwealth to obtain release of individuals in their employ. I could not ask for more genuine support from these men who promptly agreed to let me have the services of four Grenadians who worked for them. These four, Allan Kirton, Arnold Cruickshank, Patrick Emmanuel and Nicholas Brathwaite, were to be named members of the Advisory Council.

At 10 o'clock in the forenoon of November 8, I went downstairs to announce the names of the members of the Advisory Council. Standing on the steps of the verandah which overlooked the circular lawn I read the names from a sheet of paper to an audience comprising mainly of international and regional press and other media personalities who had been anxiously awaiting the announcement. With a whetted appetite for news some of them had assembled on the lawn about an hour before. The drizzly rain which greeted my arrival neither dampened their enthusiasm nor diluted their interest. The news of the appointment of the Advisory Council was immediately flashed on the local radio. The Council comprised the following:-

Mr Alister McIntyre – Deputy Secretary General of UNCTAD
Mr Nicholas Brathwaite – Well known Grenadian educator and currently Director of the Commonwealth Youth Centre, Based in Guyana.
Mr Arnold M Cruickshank – Senior Manager, Agricultural Division of the Caribbean Development Bank.
Dr. James DeVere Pitt – Director of the Grenada Science Council.
Dr. Patrick Emmanuel – Senior Research Fellow, Institute of Social and Economic Research, University of the West Indies.
Dr. Allan Kirton – Permanent Secretary in the Jamaica Civil Service.
Mrs Joan Purcell – Local Director of the Canadian Save the Children Fund.

Mr Raymond Smith – Former Manager of the Windward Islands Broadcasting
  Service and Advisor on Telecommunications to the Grenada Government.
Mr Christopher Williams – Former Head Teacher and currently Welfare and Youth
  Worker.

In an impressive ceremony the Council members were sworn in on the
morning of November 15. Seated in the main reception room to witness the
ceremony were dignitaries of Church and State, members of the Judiciary,
members of the Diplomatic Corps, Commanding Officers of the Caribbean
and American forces, and a number of prominent citizens. The oath taken in
my presence was administered by the Honourable Chief Justice , Archibald
Nedd. Absent from the ceremony was Alister McIntyre who was unable to
be in Grenada because of illness. I therefore appointed Nicholas Brathwaite
to be acting Chairman of the Council, Curtis Strachan was named Secretary
to the Council.

Two weeks after appointing the Council I began to entertain in my
mind some degree of uncertainty about McIntyre's membership, apart
from his protracted illness. Commonwealth Heads of Government
meeting in India gave the Americans the not unexpected bashing for their
continued presence in Grenada. Mrs Indira Ghandi and others of her
colleagues felt they should not have been in Grenada in the first place. In
an emotional outburst they condemned flatly what they called the
invasion, but what over ninety per cent of Grenadians called a rescue
mission. Our local difficulties gave the Commonwealth leaders an
opportunity to discuss the vulnerability of small states. But Grenadians
were not moved by the intellectual outpourings of these distinguished
leaders. Our people had gladly welcomed the American and Caribbean
Forces and felt that their presence in Grenada would undoubtedly in the
shortest possible time restore peace and democracy. Grenadians liked it
that way and they were the ones who really mattered. Perhaps the debate
on Grenada would not have been so lopsided if the Commonwealth
governments had sent out a fact-finding mission to Grenada immediately
after the 1983 debacle to assess the damage, to meet the people, to
ascertain their hopes and fears and to see for themselves how greatly the
people welcomed the American and Caribbean Forces. Secretary General
Ramphal visited Grenada, but after the New Delhi meeting. Even some of
the Caribbean Prime Ministers did not understand what was happening in
Grenada and so they could not speak on the Grenada affairs with any
degree of authority. Indeed, if you spoke to any of the CARICOM leaders
who did not participate in the intervention each would give you a different
version on the Grenada affairs.

After assessing the mood of the Commonwealth leaders I thought Ramphal would find it extremely difficult to commit Commonwealth funds to pay for McIntyre's secondment to Grenada as he had earlier promised. In terms of Chairmanship of the Council my mind began to shift from McIntyre to Nicholas Brathwaite. I had been in constant touch with McIntyre who had earlier given me some useful hints as to how the Advisory Council should proceed. I called McIntyre, who was in Switzerland, to let him know that because of the uncertainty of his taking up the position I was inclined to name Brathwaite as Chairman of the Council. Two days later I revoked McIntyre's appointment and named Nicholas Brathwaite as Chairman of the Advisory Council. This appointment met with popular approval. The Council then was reduced by one. In my search for a replacement I fell upon Randolph Mark, a man with great experience in farming and community work. On the Chairman's recommendation I appointed Mr Randolph Mark of the parish of Saint Andrew as a member of the Advisory Council. But McIntyre's removal from the Council left the body bereft of a sound economist. I contacted William Demas, the President of the Caribbean Development Bank, and asked him to be our Economic Consultant. Demas agreed and we worked out the modalities over the telephone. While it was not convenient for Demas to be physically present in Grenada, he assigned responsibility for Grenada Affairs to Mr Marius St. Rose, Director of the Economic Department, who would regularly report to him. That officer visited Grenada periodically and the Council referred any economic matter to Mr Demas for advice. This area of government was crucial to our future development. The composition of the Advisory Council received popular acclaim. The only note of caution reached me by post three days after the Council was named. I was warned that there were two members with "leftist tendencies" who were supportive of the Revolution. This did not bother me. In fact I thought this accusation, if true, added strength to the collective wisdom of the Advisory Council. I never envisaged a Council which would be monolithic in thought and I expected well informed discussions embracing differing points of view before decisions were taken. Members of Council were not elected by the people and they knew full well they were not Ministers of Government although in their *modus operandi* they might be fairly perceived as *quasi* Ministers. They also knew that I could remove them from Council at any time without question, without explanation. Further they ought to have known that I would keep a watchful eye on their behavioural pattern as well as on their performance.

In my Proclamation of October 31 I clearly stated that I would exercise executive authority on behalf of Her Majesty in consultation with an Advisory Council. But this was followed by an important *caveat* namely "except when the matter to be decided is too important to require consultation or too urgent to admit of consultation by the time within which it may be necessary for me to act in respect of any such matter." Also embodied in the Proclamation was my right to summon any person as an extraordinary member of the Advisory Council if on any special occasion I thought it desirable to obtain the advice of any such person relating to the affairs of state.

# 11

## The Interim Administration

THE Advisory Council began its work on November 15, 1983. This *quasi* Cabinet was an experiment in government the likes of which had never been tried in Grenada before. I did not think that any member of Council knew exactly what the observable outcome of that experiment would be. But they had a fixity of purpose that bound them together. Despite their differing disciplines and the novelty of being responsible for blocks of departments in a government, they were all bent on giving the best of their skills and talents to rebuild a shattered democracy and a battered economy. From their very first sitting, they seemed anxious to forge a partnership between themselves and the community at large. In particular they set out to build bridges between themselves and senior civil servants who could influence policy, between themselves and the private sector who could generate employment, between themselves and the trade unions who could make their members understand the efficacy of a fair day's work for a fair day's pay, and especially at this time the importance of putting in an extra effort for the common good.

From my vantage point at Governor General's House I, too, knew that the success of the Interim Government would have to depend primarily on the co-operation and good sense of Grenadians everywhere, not least those resident at home. However, I was fortified by the large number of congratulatory and supportive letters and telegrams that reached me. I believed I read the mood of the people well. Fortunately the vast majority of them were in tune with me, and I could readily discern mutual trust and affection. They were anxious to live in an atmosphere of peace and harmony, and they felt committed to bring back normalcy to the country.

One of the experts who rushed to Grenada in the wake of the military intervention was Anthony Rushford, a British constitutional lawyer. He was no stranger to officialdom in the Eastern Caribbean and had been the principal author of the constitutions of most of the islands. In fact he was a member of the British delegation at the independence conference on Grenada held in Marlborough House, London in May, 1973. I had known

Rushford for a number of years, and when Shridath Ramphal recommended him as a person who might be helpful to me I unhesitatingly agreed to have him. What was more, he was coming to Grenada under the auspices of the Commonwealth Secretariat.

Quickly Rushford came. Quickly he left, but never too soon. On arrival in Grenada some six days after the cessation of hostilities, Rushford reported forthwith to Governor General's House where he was accommodated until his wife joined him some two weeks later. He then moved to St. James Hotel in the heart of St. George's. It would seem that Rushford was utterly disappointed that no government official met him at the airport. What he failed to appreciate was that in those early days in the aftermath of the intervention our Ministry of External Affairs was practically non-functional and could not extend the usual courtesies.

The only useful piece of work Rushford did in Grenada was to take the 1973 Constitution Order and fashion it into a practical working paper embodying the role of the Advisory Council. He wasted no time in doing this. This working paper could be aptly described as a temporary "constitution" designed to give authority to the Advisory Council. I had had sufficient experience in public life to be able to spot, with a fair measure of accuracy, the propensities of men and women who would grasp any opportunity for personal self-aggrandizement. If Rushford thought he could come to Grenada and run roughshod over me or the Advisory Council, he needed to revise his thinking. Rushford came to Grenada as my Legal Adviser and nothing more. It was not for him to dictate policy or give directives, however subtly. It did not take me long to detect that he had an agenda of his own. He probably was lulled into believing that Grenadians could not extricate themselves from their chaotic position without the guiding and patronizing hand of people like himself. If so, he obviously miscalculated the capability of the Grenadian people.

Against my better judgement, and contrary to advice from the Foreign and Commonwealth Office in London, I appointed Rushford Attorney General. He asked for it and I courteously obliged. He further requested to be made a Justice of the Peace. That also he received. But when he sought a Knighthood, I informed him that I had no authority to make such a recommendation. Honours would have to wait until after general elections were held and a democratically elected government was in place. He seemed disappointed. When I learnt that he had taken upon himself to send dispatches to Buckingham Palace, ostensibly on my behalf, I rebuked him sharply, and could not hide my annoyance when I asked him to cease that practice immediately. Perhaps that was the only occasion when Rushford could truthfully say that I was visibly annoyed with him.

The members of the Advisory Council had warned me that they were not enthusiastic about Rushford's attendance at their meetings. Hence the reason why it was provided in Proclamation No. 5 of 1983 "that the legal adviser may take part in the proceedings of the Advisory Council whenever the chairman requests or authorizes him to do so but shall not vote therein" – a remarkable compromise. As it turned out the chairman never invited Rushford to any of the Council meetings. The nightly sessions with his media friends at the bar in St. James Hotel greatly infuriated Council members, one of whom inquired of me whether the legal adviser was ever given the responsibility to speak on behalf of the Government. But what mostly upset members was that Rushford, having arrogated unto himself the role of Government spokesman, made public statements before they were authorized.

The Legal Adviser, a retired civil servant in the British civil service with a wealth of experience, abandoned his post and left the island without informing me and without submitting his resignation. I was absolutely astonished, though not unhappy, when David Montgomery, the British Deputy High Commissioner, rang me from Barbados to say that Rushford had left Grenada and was on radio purporting to have left because of a rift between himself and the Governor General. If there was a rift between us, my own instinct would have been to pick up the telephone and tell the Commonwealth Secretary General that I no longer required the services of Rushford and I would like him withdrawn immediately. The last time I saw Rushford was the Friday afternoon in my office, three days before he left the island. Our conversation was cordial and we had no disagreements.

Having left Grenada Rushford tried his utmost to discredit me by his constant vituperations on the international news media. But I remained unmoved and undisturbed. On learning of his sudden flight from Grenada, I immediately revoked his appointments as Attorney General and Justice of the Peace. The Advisory Council took no notice of his premature departure from Grenada. Some six months later Rushford proceeded to make overtures to our High Commissioner in London, Oswald Gibbs, in order to re-ingratiate himself by offering to send me a set of insignias (large and miniature) of the Officer of the Most Excellent Order of the British Empire as replacements for those which had been stolen during my temporary evacuation of my residence. Our man in London politely refused to accept those insignias and was pleased to inform Rushford that they had been replaced already. Rushford's unwarranted and disrespectful verbal attack on one of Her Majesty's representatives was, to say the least, a matter of deep regret. By then he must have abandoned all hope of ever receiving the honour of knighthood.

The security of the State was of paramount importance. The whole process of development, the implementation of well intentioned policies, and the repositioning of structures befitting a democracy could only move forward if the country was secure and safe. One could never be too sure that under the amnesty all the guns and ammunition had been given up or collected. In fact they were not, as evidenced by the number of appeals that were made up to the end of 1984 for the return of guns which might still have been in the possession of former members of the People's Revolutionary Army. Bombs had to be detonated, one of which was perched uncomfortably close to my garage. There was need also for increased vigilance in order to deter the small core of dedicated revolutionaries who would want to turn back the clock to the days of the Revolution.

Equally, we had to be watchful for socialist sympathizers who might slip into Grenada to assist in the regrouping of the revolutionary cells or to give them advice on how to destabilize the country. Possibility of sabotage at the Electricity Company, disruption at public offices, molestation by those still intoxicated with the murky waters of the Revolution, normal crime prevention, trial of those accused of killing Prime Minister Bishop and others at Fort George were all matters of a security nature which had to be addressed seriously and swiftly. Fortunately the Caribbean and American forces were well deployed to ward off any symptoms of an uprising.

Scores of young Grenadians were at training institutes, colleges, and universities in communist countries. Some were receiving military training, others were pursuing academic and professional studies. The majority of them were on scholarships to Cuba. With the closure of our embassy in Havana, and in the face of growing anxiety as exhibited by parents whose children were studying in Cuba, the Interim Government wisely chartered an aircraft to bring the students home. However, those who wished to stay for whatever reason were free to do so. The majority of them availed themselves of the opportunity to return home. Donald McPhail, our former Deputy Chief of Mission in Havana, did a commendable job in coordinating the homeward bound trek of these students. In other communist countries we sought and obtained the assistance of the British embassies to safeguard the welfare of our students and to facilitate their repatriation. The returning students posed no threat to the security of the state.

For me the maintenance of peace and order was a matter of top priority. I became actively involved in matters pertaining to security. I had direct linkages with the heads of the Caribbean and the American forces, with the Commissioner of Police and the Commissioner of Prisons. I quickly formed a security committee comprising the Commanding Officers of the American force, the Caribbean force, the police and the prisons. This security committee met with me every morning Monday to Friday in the main reception hall and briefed me for at least one hour. Later the briefing days were reduced to three, and still later, because of the growing confidence on the part of both the security personnel and the people generally, the briefing took place once weekly. These meetings continued up to December 4 when the elected Prime Minister was sworn in. During that year I was initiated into the art of intelligence gathering and I learnt a great deal about the way security personnel operates. The assuring light in all this was the zeal with which Grenadians and other residents volunteered information of a security nature. Many of them channelled their information directly to me. Quickly I grew accustomed to receiving those unsigned hand written notes. Perhaps I shall never know who these informers were, but what they had to report proved very useful to me and the security forces. I took no chances with matters of security, and sometimes I had to act quickly in my own deliberate judgement to frustrate the plans of those whose agenda were not in accordance with the gallant efforts calculated to restore democracy. One such instance arose when I deemed it necessary to order the Commissioner of Police to get an Englishman off the island immediately. It had been brought to my attention that the gentleman, who was living at a guest house on Tyrrel Street, had been holding meetings with known revolutionaries and had been visiting with members of the New Jewel Movement in certain areas of St. George's. This information was given to me by another visitor living at the same guest house and one whom I knew quite well. No sooner than the Commissioner of Police carried out my orders than the alarm bells began to ring in the United Kingdom, not least in the corridors of the House of Commons. Almost immediately the Chairman of the Advisory Council began to receive telephone calls from London. But none of these could either disturb or deter us. Nor could they cause us to deviate from our mission of peace and prosperity.

I also denied Ramsey Clark permission to visit the alleged murderers of Bishop and others. I was advised that Clark, a former Attorney General of the United States of America, did not hold a licence to practise law in Grenada or in any other East Caribbean State. He was so determined to speak to those prisoners who were on remand at Richmond Hill Prisons that I became suspicious of his motives. In any case he could not claim the right to see these prisoners as he was not qualified to practise in Grenada. This might have been humiliating to the learned attorney, but as far as I was concerned his time could be better spent lazing on one of the beautiful beaches or enjoying the warmth and friendliness of our people as he toured our picturesque countryside.

The return of Sir Eric Gairy to Grenada in January, 1984, was potentially a security nightmare. Having heard from good authority that one of the objectives of the New Jewel Movement was to exterminate Sir Eric, I was worried about his personal safety. Prior to the Revolution his movements, especially at nights, were well monitored by his youthful adversaries. For his own part Gairy was always security conscious, and, especially when out at nights, constantly devised ways and means of thwarting any potential attempts on his life. The fact that the New Jewel Movement failed to achieve their morbid objective bears testimony to the astuteness of the man no less than to the timidity of the members of the New Jewel Movement. Nor could they find someone skilful enough to do the job without fear of apprehension. Gairy had travelled from the U.S.A. with a bodyguard in the person of former Inspector of Police Denis Duncan of the Royal Grenada Police Force who was then resident in the U.S.A. It was pathetic to observe the disrespect meted out to Sir Eric particularly by the younger folk as he moved around St. George's. They jeered at him, insulted him and called him by ugly names. Gairy, realizing that he was not made to feel welcome by certain sections of the community, decided to remain indoors and operate from inside.

I received Sir Eric on Tuesday, January 31, 1984, ten days after his return from the United States of America where he had been in exile for almost five years. He was accompanied by Herbert Squires, his one time Attorney General and close friend. My aide-de-camp, Major Courtenay McConney, was in attendance during the fifty-minute-long meeting. This was my first encounter with Sir Eric in five years. He was not the dashing debonair figure he used to be. I had been briefed on the elaborate preparations his party faithful had been making for his arrival. Gairy saw himself standing in a roofless car in the middle of a long motorcade from the airport to St. George's with school children on both sides of the road proudly waving little flags. He could feel the presence of the American and Caribbean forces who would give adequate and appropriate protection all along the way to St. George's. He could see himself entering St. George's as a hero. Of course none of this happened. From all reports hardly more than sixty of his followers were at the airport to welcome him. The day before Sir Eric was due to arrive, I brought together the Chairman and the Deputy

Chairman of the Advisory Council, the Commissioner of Police, and the Head of the Caribbean Peace Keeping Force. We met at my residence to discuss the impending arrival of Sir Eric and to devise a strategy for his own personal safety. It was agreed that the security forces should maintain a low-keyed presence at the airport, no mention should be made on radio about his return to the island, and his supporters should be advised to call off any rally or procession they might have been planning. Security men at the airport reported that Sir Eric seemed disappointed with what turned out to be a low-keyed reception. While still in the United States of America, Gairy had spoken in gleeful anticipation about his return to Grenada where his people would joyfully receive him. Six times he had tried to reach me by telephone, but without success.

It was no surprise that Gairy came to me full of complaint about the manner in which he was received when he disembarked at Pearls Airport. There was not even one government official to meet him. After all he was the last elected Prime Minister of Grenada, and as a Queen's knight and privy councillor he was *ipso facto* entitled to VIP privileges. Sir Eric resented the discourteous treatment meted out to him and asserted that it was a mistake of which the Governor General and the Advisory Council were not aware. I was less than diplomatic when I looked Sir Eric straight in the eyes and told him bluntly that he had entered Grenada as an ordinary citizen and the Advisory Council was under no obligation to extend any special courtesies to him.

The word "ordinary" which I used advisedly seemed to have struck a raw nerve. He never forgot this. Months later he was to tell his party executive as well as the media that he would have me removed from office the day after his party's victory at the forthcoming parliamentary elections. Shades of pre-revolutionary Gairy! What I did not tell this great Knight was that scores of Grenadians had made representations to me that he should be prevented from returning to Grenada. Others had petitioned that if he did return, he should be arrested to answer charges of brutality and abuse of human rights as outlined in the findings of the Duffus Report. This was in reference to a three-man Commission of Enquiry set up by the Gairy administration in 1973 to investigate civil discontent and matters incidental thereto. The Commission was headed by the distinguished Jamaican jurist, Herbert Duffus.

I saw no merit in those requests. I could not deny a Grenadian admission into his own country. As for the Duffus Report, the people through the electioneering process had given Gairy and his party a clear mandate to govern after the findings of Duffus had been made public. This was manifestly so in the parliamentary elections of 1976 when the Grenada United Labour Party gained the majority of seats. What is more, I was advised that there was nothing in the Duffus Report that directly incriminated Sir Eric. My own feeling was that anyone who wanted him charged for any offence should produce the evidence to the Commissioner of Police.

Back to our meeting, Sir Eric found no comfort in the preliminary item on his agenda. He must have been utterly disappointed to observe that hardly more than fifty of his supporters had turned up to welcome him. This was the figure quoted by both security personnel and other eye witnesses who were at the airport when Sir Eric disembarked. But it was the absence of any official reception at the airport that upset him. He got no apologies from me. I had no explanations to offer him. In fact he was clearly not satisfied with my response to his complaint, and he made it quite clear that if he were in charge he would have acted differently. Speaking about the real purpose of his call he told me that among the matters which he had come to discuss was the return to him of his property – a three and one half acre of land in True Blue on which stood a wooden house. He needed desperately a house in which to live as he was staying with friends. I advised him to put that request to the Advisory Council.

Sir Eric mentioned two other matters with which he was greatly concerned. He said that several persons who had acquired property by means of bank loans had been forced to leave the country during the Bishop regime, and as a result had defaulted in their repayments to the banks. The banks were in the process of foreclosing on some of these properties and he suggested that the banks should be asked to place a moratorium of about six months on those cases in order that any of these persons who wished to rectify their positions with the banks could have a chance to do so. The other matter concerned persons who had been summarily dismissed from their substantive jobs, and who had been in some cases imprisoned. He mentioned specifically the case of Osbert James, former Commissioner of Police. Sir Eric suggested that all these persons should be compensated. I shared Sir Eric's concern for these matters and assured him that I would personally take them up with the Chairman of the Council.

His denunciation of the current administrative arrangements was emphatic. Sir Eric was not in favour of the Interim Government . He felt strongly that elections should have been held immediately after the intervention. Nevertheless, he intimated that as the last elected Prime Minister of Grenada he had no intention of offering any open or hostile opposition to the Interim Government. Nor did he intend to face the polls at the forthcoming elections, but would be a consultant for his party. Between us there was a divergence of opinion on the composition, role and status of the Interim Government. I tried my utmost to impress upon him that the Interim Government was best for the country. The mood of the majority of Grenadians indicated that they had been badly misled by their politicians over the past decade. The people had lost confidence in their politicians and appeared hesitant to entrust them with the government at that point in time. Moreover, I had to take cognizance of the unusual and lingering trauma with which the populace was afflicted , and sufficient time was needed to prepare for the holding of fair and free elections. I also reminded the goodly gentleman that among the criteria I had set for appointment to the Interim Administration was that no politicians were to be considered.

On a more general note Sir Eric could not agree that Bishop's popularity at any time during the latter's regime was as extensive as some people were trying to make out. The veteran politician was adamant that Bishop never reached his level of popularity, even his current level. He went on to decry the state of the roads and the attitude and brusqueness of young people who had evidently lost respect for the older folk. He could not come to grips with my view that the younger people were now more politically mature, more critical of their environment and no longer accepted without question the pronouncements of their elders. Their attitude should not be so blandly defined as a lack of respect for elders but rather as a growing awareness of and willingness to participate in the affairs of the country. These traits in the young had been definitely developed during the Bishop regime. Of course, Sir Eric did not appear to agree with my opinion and instead went on to criticize the education policy of the Bishop administration which he thought was all based on communist indoctrination.

On a more personal note Sir Eric admitted that he was "no saint," but that God was his forte. He claimed that the People's Revolutionary Government portrayed him to the people of Grenada and to the world as a prince of the devil. They used his love for religion and his many robes, crosses, rosaries and crucifixes as well as the numerous gifts he had received from people on his many tours (including his 293 local meet the people tours) in such a manner as to discredit him as a Christian. Sir Eric claimed that several valuable gifts together with large amounts of gold and jewelery were stolen from his residence by the People's Revolutionary Government. He had been in the habit of buying gold, then US$36.00 per ounce, through a source in New York.

Before Sir Eric left he requested a guarantee from persecution and harassment by people and police. He also asked for protection and security from the police. I gave him every assurance that in common with all citizens of the country he would be free from harassment and persecution, and that he would be entitled to the same protection and security as are provided for all citizens. Reiterating that he was not in agreement with the method of appointment of members of the Advisory Council Sir Eric, however, promised to co-operate with, and not oppose, the Council.

For years Grenada and the other Commonwealth Caribbean countries shared the same parliamentary traditions which were rooted in the Westminster model. An essential ingredient of this transplant from Britain, the colonizing power, was that people should be given the opportunity at regular intervals to select their own representatives who would speak on their behalf in Parliament where various measures affecting their daily lives are debated and sanctioned before becoming law. The levying of taxation, decisions pertaining to the upkeep and integrity of our institutions, to the protection of our environment and to social and economic advancement are all matters where people's voices should be heard through their elected representatives.

It was of paramount importance that the people be given a chance to choose their parliamentary representatives as soon as possible. Being well aware of the value of Parliament in the democratic process, I made up my mind early that elections would be held before the end of 1984, and although I listened to many arguments which sought the prolongation of the Interim Government I was nevertheless firm in my resolve about the timing of elections. Moreover, our Constitution, which was vulgarly suspended on March 13, 1979, could not be fully restored until we had in place machinery for parliamentary elections and subsequently a parliament in operation.

High on the agenda of the Advisory Council were preparations for general elections. In order to accelerate the process I took personal control of those preparations. With the minimum of delay I appointed Roy Chasteau, Registrar of the High Court, as Supervisor of Elections, and gave orders for the setting up of a Parliamentary Electoral Office with adequate and appropriate staff. Alan Kirton, a member of the Advisory Council who showed great enthusiasm for early elections, was assigned by Chairman Braithwaite to do everything possible to ensure that the work of the Electoral Office was right on target for the holding of elections before the end of 1984.

The last parliamentary elections in Grenada had been held in December, 1976, when Gairy's Grenada United Labour Party annexed nine of the fifteen seats at stake. The remaining six seats went to the combined opposition consisting of the Grenada National Party and the New Jewel Movement.

Bishop was named Leader of the Opposition. What was significant about these results was that Gairy's popularity was on the decline given that in the 1972 elections he had swept the polls by winning a 13-2 majority. In fact Gairy himself told me that the 1976 elections were the most difficult he had fought in his political career. He privately admitted that with the entry of young articulate university graduates into front line politics, he had to rethink his strategy with a view to wooing some better educated young men and women into his own party. It was achingly clear that he recognized the potential of Maurice Bishop, Bernard Coard, Unison Whiteman and others who had offered themselves as candidates in the 1976 elections.

While Gairy remained an astute politician I did not think that he had anything new or stimulating to bring to Grenadian politics. Nor did he have any substantial blue-print for the economic development of Grenada. He seemed to have lost his visionary perspectives of earlier years. He had reached the point where he was not only directing policies but also was trying to dispense administrative solutions and pretentiously dictating technical know-how. In his speeches he never failed to enumerate his past achievements as he harangued his listeners, as of yesteryear, in believing that he was their saviour. With the exception of his dwindling die-hard followers, the adult population was tired of hearing this kind of rhetoric, while the young, who had greater access to both formal and informal education, did not take kindly to Gairy's political pronouncements. The people wanted change and this was revealed in the final counting of the votes in the 1976 elections.

Grenadians were denied their right to vote in free and fair elections when the Constitution was suspended in March, 1979. By 1983 the normal election date had elapsed by two years. Bishop had always taken pleasure in holding the electoral process to ridicule. He often described it as "sham democracy." He claimed that the Westminster style democracy took voters to the polls every five years for five minutes to put an "X" against the name of a man who had no political conviction of his own but who followed blindly the dictates of an autocratic leader. This, according to Bishop, was the extent to which democracy was practised in Grenada – once in every five years with no people's participation in the formulation of policies. As one of the objectives of the Revolution was to efface Gairyism completely from the hearts and minds of Grenadians, Bishop unceasingly pointed an accusing finger at Gairy for rigging elections over the years. Gairy had won the most parliamentary elections since the introduction of adult suffrage into Grenada. I have never been convinced that these accusations of rigging were justified. Nor can I find any concrete evidence of corrupt practices in our general elections. It is my belief that Gairy had the support of the majority and he truly won those elections. Further, it is my view that with the passage of time Gairy would have lost that majority. The slide had already begun. If Bishop and his colleagues had been prepared to exercise some patience and restraint the revolutionary pangs which Grenadians were made to bear could have been avoided.

If, indeed, elections had been rigged, the matter could have been taken to court to be determined. It is an unhealthy practice among some of our political leaders in the Caribbean and elsewhere to cry foul when they lose elections. They accuse the winning side either of rigging or bribery. In fact some of them, out of sheer desperation and quite cognizant of their inability to be victorious, claim from very early that the incumbent party in office would rig the election. All through the electioneering campaign they affix the label of corruption on their opponents instead of presenting a viable programme to the electorate. Although this kind of accusation seldom gains acceptance from the voters, nevertheless it is a serious slur on our self-esteem as a people and projects an unwholesome image of the country.

Preparations for elections were different from what Grenadians had grown accustomed to. The essential difference was that the enumerator had to interface with the prospective voter during registration. For the first time it was required that a photograph of each voter be taken as part of the registration process. It was my strongly held view that the compilation of the electoral list should be above suspicion. Every eligible voter should find his or her name on the voters' list. Therefore I made abundantly clear to all concerned that the registration exercise should be as transparent as it should be thorough. From the outset I gave orders that under no circumstances should the existing list be used in whole or in part. This was to obliterate any concerns, real or imagined, as to the accuracy of the new list which was about to be compiled.

I believed deeply that there was virtue in starting afresh. But first I had to approve a new elections ordinance which was formulated with the help of the attorney attached to the Parliamentary Office in Barbados. Mr Errol Chase came to Grenada and worked assiduously to give legal effect to the new features in the registration process. The Right Hon. Tom Adams, Prime Minister of Barbados, had pledged his Government's support to put in place the machinery for free and fair elections in Grenada. The Barbadian Government delivered that support with dispatch. Not only did they provide the necessary legal services but also made their own electoral office accessible to the Grenadian counterpart for any technical assistance which the latter might need. Nothing was too much for the Government and people of Barbados to do in order to ensure that structures be put in place for an early poll. Just as the Barbadians were at one with their Grenadian brothers and sisters in their time of peril, so too were they manifestly concerned about the restoration of parliamentary democracy in our tri-island State. This demonstration of togetherness is what I believe to be the true essence of the CARICOM spirit.

The Jamaican Government and people were equally committed to the restoration of parliamentary democracy in Grenada. The Right Hon. Edward Seaga was overly generous in providing technical assistance to Grenada for the holding of free and fair elections at the earliest possible time. Jamaica provided on a loan basis the cameras for taking the photographs of the prospective voters, and also seconded electoral officers to Grenada to help in the use of the cameras and in the production of the voters' identification cards which were to be used in Grenada for the first time. The East Caribbean countries which took part in the rescue mission of October, 1983, continued to supply policemen and military personnel to maintain law and order as Grenada moved towards elections. These countries gave every support and encouragement in this most difficult period.

Many people seemed to forget that the holding of elections calls for budgetary provision. Given the stark impecuniosity in which Grenada found itself in the twilight days of the People's Revolutionary Government it would have been extremely difficult for any succeeding Government to find sufficient revenue to provide for even the basic services. The Interim Government was no exception and was naturally hard pressed to find the financial resources not just to ensure the holding of elections in 1984 but also to provide the basic services and good governance for the people of Grenada, Carriacou and Petit Martinique. In response to a request from me the Government of Australia gave a grant in the sum of fifty thousand Australian dollars to be used for the purposes of the elections. The ballot boxes were a gift from the Government of Canada.

Enumeration of voters began on Monday, April 12. Each enumerator was bound to visit every dwelling house in his or her polling division and to interview every individual who was eligible to be registered as a voter. The enumerator would ascertain from the prospective voter his or her name, age, address and occupation. He would further enquire whether he was a Grenadian citizen, or whether he was a citizen of another Commonwealth country with residency in Grenada for a period of at least twelve months immediately before the date of registration When satisfied with the particulars the enumerator would record them on the Master Registration

Record Card. Only after a photograph of the elector was taken was the registration complete. On completion of the registration the enumerator would issue a Certificate of Enumeration to the person registered. Despite the scepticism in some quarters surrounding the new style registration of voters, people generally co-operated with the enumerators. On the one hand there were those who felt that the whole exercise was a ploy designed to compile a new tax list. On the other hand an overwhelming majority welcomed the new features in the voters' registration, and agreed that they would enhance the prospects of free and fair elections. They particularly welcomed the ID card which would be used not only for identification on polling day but also as an easy reference in daily business transactions.

In times of crisis or societal dislocation there are always those who would be lurking in the wings ready to exploit such situations for their own personal gains. Others grasp every opportunity to amass a fortune having found themselves in the right place at the right time. Grenada after October, 1983, was an attractive base for an unusually wide circulation of American dollars. Rental of living quarters suddenly soared, an unprecedented and steady flow of technical and professional personnel settled temporarily, new economic activities started, projects funded by Governments and international agencies brought with them increasing employment opportunities at least on a short term basis. Things seem to be looking up after a gloomy period of economic stagnation under the People's Revolutionary Government. Individuals, especially those with entrepreneurial skills, came into their own again. It was not surprising, therefore, that those who made exceptional gains were opposed to early elections.

The captains of the tourism industry displayed their usual nervousness when they suggested to me that one stone-throwing incident during the election campaign could ruin the fragile industry which was then being resuscitated. I had to remind them that Grenada did not have a history of violence at election time, and it was my gut feeling that the electorate would be on their best behaviour and would turn out at the polls in large numbers. I also received a delegation from the Chamber of Commerce. Because I thought they would raise the matter of the forthcoming elections I pre-empted them by saying that the elections would take place as announced earlier, that is, before the end of the year. The holding of elections during 1984 was not a matter for discussion. I then apprised them of the progress made by way of preparations for elections. They left seemingly contented.

Every Tuesday afternoon beginning at 3 o'clock I had a briefing session in my office when the Supervisor of Elections accompanied by appropriate personnel from the Electoral Office apprised me of matters pertaining to the upcoming elections. Also present was Dr. Alan Kirton of the Advisory Council. These briefing meetings were serious working sessions. The main objective was not merely to pass information on the preparedness of the Electoral Office to supervise the elections but more importantly to seek to ensure that the best possible structures were put in place within the limits of our resources for an orderly, fair and free election. These weekly meetings lasted for about an hour, though sometimes much longer. The Supervisor of Elections was subjected to some rigorous questioning, and quite often had to consult his office by telephone for further information or clarification. On no account was I going to allow the Supervisor to brief me by telling me just what he wanted to tell me. For example, when I was told that all the polling stations had been identified I sought a list of them with their exact locations. Although I had been given assurances both by the Supervisor of Elections and his field officer that all the polling stations had been visited, and consent given for their use wherever applicable I nevertheless caused a survey to be done of all the polling stations throughout Grenada, Carriacou and Petit Martinique in the interest of security. This assignment I gave to the police. To my surprise it was discovered that one of the polling stations no longer existed. Obviously, the field officer was not as meticulous as he claimed to be. What in fact happened was that the field officer simply reproduced the list of polling stations used in the 1976 elections, without physically inspecting them.

As the months rolled by I became increasingly concerned about the security as well as the quality of supervision in the Electoral Office. By then I had got a note from a friendly Government about the background of Roy Chasteau who incidentally was born in Cuba. Locally, and in particular in Civil Service circles, questions were being raised about the suitability and competence of his secretary. The Supervisor somewhat allayed my fears when he told me that he had every confidence in her. He was fully satisfied with her work, and her loyalty and devotion to duty were second to none. However, I was baffled to learn that there were lights inside the Electoral Office late at nights and sometimes before dawn. We were never sparing in the provision of staff for that office, and I just could not imagine what excessive work-load the Supervisor and his secretary were trying to tackle at these unusual hours. I immediately put a nightly surveillance on that office, and I asked the Commissioner of Police to place guards around the building. This latter measure seemed to have caused a diminution in the workload and the subsequent cessation of the nightly activities. After receiving reports about the misuse of the office vehicles, I gave instructions that they be parked on the grounds of Governor General's House everyday after working hours, and the keys handed to the orderly on duty who would make an appropriate entry in the diary. It was never the intention that the vehicles be used for fun and frolic.

In October Chasteau fell ill with angina and had to be hospitalized. On strict medical advice I relieved him of his duties as Supervisor of Elections. I further revoked his appointment of Justice of the Peace which went with his electoral assignment. I replaced him with Alphonsus Redhead, a senior civil servant, a man of unquestionable character. Chasteau would revert to his definitive appointment in the civil service after a period of leave. Instead of resting at home he chose to be a frequent visitor to the Electoral Office. Early in the morning of Friday, October 26, I received intelligence of a degree of unrest among the staff at the Electoral Office and the possibility of strike action. I was quick to move. Within half an hour I was at the Electoral Office which was about two minutes drive from my residence. I was shocked to find Chasteau in the building. He was casually dressed. It was immediately apparent to me that little or no work was being done. I assembled the workers and explained to them why I replaced Chasteau . I admonished them to get on with their work and I ordered Chasteau to leave the premises and advised him not to return. Mine was little more than a fleeting visit as I was due to receive the Governor of Florida, Bob Graham, that same morning. After I had left the Electoral Office someone from the media went in and interviewed the workers. Oh, what a field day they had. Six o'clock that evening I heard it all on Radio Antilles, and I carefully noted their strident remarks. It did not take me long to conclude that the continued presence of these workers could be prejudicial to the smooth running of the election. I had to draw on my own civil service experience to deal with them. Most of the workers were temporary workers and they were the trouble makers.

On the morning of Sunday, October 28, Nicholas Brathwaite , Chairman of the Advisory Council, came to see me. We discussed at length matters pertaining to the Electoral Office and the state of preparedness for the holding of elections. Registration of voters had come to an end, the preliminary voters' list had been prepared, returning officers had been named, the ballot boxes had been received and, generally speaking, preparations were well in train for nomination day and polling day. I called a meeting for 8 o'clock that evening in my office to deal with the unease in the Electoral Office. But prior to that meeting I had a more pleasant and satisfying duty to perform at Point Salines.

Grenadians from all walks of life and from all parts of Grenada, Carriacou and Petit Martinique journeyed to Point Salines on that bright and beautiful

Sunday afternoon to witness the official opening of the newly constructed airport. It was a grand and colourful affair in the presence of numerous friends and well wishers from the Caribbean and further afield, thus giving the proceedings an international flavour. Dignitaries from abroad who included Prime Ministers, Ministers of Government, diplomats, representatives of regional and international organizations put up a brilliant show of solidarity with the Grenadian people on this happy occasion. The main religious bodies were represented and they invoked God's blessing in true ecumenical fashion. There was also a cultural component that received loud and appreciative applause. I was there to deliver the key-note address.

But for me the day was not ended. I was determined to straighten out matters in the Electoral Office before midnight. The meeting scheduled for my office started promptly at eight o'clock. Present were the Chairman and two other members of the Advisory Council, the Attorney General, the new Supervisor of Elections, the Commissioner of Police, the Chairman of the Public service Commission, and my Personal Assistant. My secretary was on call at her office in case she was needed to do any typing. The upshot of the meeting was that I was advised to dismiss immediately all the temporary workers. That was in line with my own thinking. Letters to that effect were typed and signed and handed to the Commissioner of Police for delivery to the workers the following morning. The Commissioner volunteered to be at the Electoral Office at 8 a.m. to deliver the letters himself, and to see to it that the workers in question vacated the building. He was to warn them that they should not return except on legitimate business. The building would be properly guarded twenty-four hours per day, and the Supervisor of Elections would recruit staff on a loan or secondment basis as he deemed fit and necessary. In this regard the Chairman of the Public Service Commission pledged his fullest support and co-operation.

It was a rainy Monday morning. Despite the inclement weather Mervyn Holder, Commissioner of Police, undeterred and unmolested, made his way through the main door of the Electoral Office, quietly distributed the dismissal letters, and advised the recipients to leave the premises. They acceded without any show of resistance. Surprisingly, some of them went to put their case to Sir Eric Gairy. Unhappily, for them, they could find no comfort from that quarter. But there was a curious twist to all this. Of all persons, Rev. Alan Kirton, the Secretary General of the Caribbean Conference of Churches, questioned my actions. He was not related to the other Alan Kirton who was a member of the Advisory Council. Whether or not the reverend gentleman was possessed of some divine right to question my authority I would never know. But mark the audacity of the man! From his headquarters in Barbados he sent a hurried note to the Council of Churches in Grenada asking them to meet with the Governor General with a view to ascertaining the reasons for his actions with particular reference to the stripping of Chasteau as electoral chief and as Justice of the Peace. When Eileen Byer, secretary of the local Council of Churches, sought an appointment she was told in no uncertain manner that the Governor General would be pleased to receive a delegation from the Council of Churches not out of deference to Rev. Kirton or his Conference but because of the high sense of loyalty and patriotism our local churches continued to demonstrate.

It was always a pleasure to meet representatives of the local churches. They have been solidly behind me and their moral support and encouragement have always motivated me. At that meeting I availed myself of the opportunity to bring the churches up to date on matters pertaining to the governance of the country, and to let them know about the state of preparedness for the forthcoming elections. I pointed out that I had made Chasteau a Justice of the Peace only by virtue of his position as Supervisor of Elections. It had been expedient to do so then. Now that he was relieved of his position as Supervisor of Elections, I used my discretion and revoked his appointment as Justice of the Peace. I purposely brushed Rev Kirton's enquiries aside and informed the delegation that I had no covenant with either the Reverend gentleman or his Caribbean Conference of Churches.

While preparations were well advanced in terms of the actual conduct of the polls, the organization of political parties was still embryonic and without appeal. In fact some of the newer parties were slow to get off the ground. Their inaction and apparent inability to win the hearts and minds of the electorate caused many from overseas and at home to conclude that the Grenadian people were not yet ready for elections. Others thought that in the circumstances Gairy would romp home gleefully and his party returned to power with a comfortable majority. In fact Gairy was beginning to feel that way, and he was growing in confidence. The alarm bells began to ring in the corridors of power in Washington and in the Caribbean cities which had mounted and supported the military intervention. It would be the irony of the century if Gairy's party were to be returned to power after the relentless efforts of so many in restoring peace and democracy in Grenada. Yet the only sign of solidarity in terms of party politics was to be found in the ranks of the Grenada United Labour Party (GULP). Party leader Eric Gairy, though scared (and quite rightly so) to appear on political platforms, was nevertheless still a strong voice in the political arena. His tactics were to lead the GULP campaign from home. When his voice came over in the form of a recorded speech it was with a certain degree of authority reminiscent of the time when he was all persuasive.

Francis Alexis, a scholarly young man and text book writer, resigned from his post as law lecturer at the Cave Hill campus of the University of the West Indies immediately after the intervention to embark upon a political career. He was founder and leader of the Grenada Democratic Movement. It was most difficult for a newcomer as Alexis to get a solid nation wide following. He had as his chief lieutenant another brilliant young man, Keith Mitchell, who, in similar fashion, abandoned his academic posting at Howard University in the United States of America to seek political honours in his homeland. Alexis and Mitchell, one a Ph.D. in law, the other a Ph.D. in mathematics and statistics seemed a formidable pair. Mitchell was no stranger to politics. In the 1972 elections this brave and industrious youngster had contested the North West St. George seat as the Grenada National Party candidate. He was flatly beaten by the incumbent, George Hosten, of the GULP. George Brizan, another intellectual type, also resigned from the Government service, where he had held the post of Chief Education Officer, to enter the political fray. He was named leader of a new party, the National Democratic Party. I was somewhat surprised when I learnt that Brizan had decided to enter politics. When I was constituting the Advisory Council I thought Brizan might be a suitable person to be a member. Indeed I offered him a place on Council, but he declined. At that time he responded that to accept would not be in keeping with the wishes of his family who wanted him to have nothing to do with politics. He would not be drawn even though I was at pains to explain to him that it was not a political position, and that the Council would be made up essentially of technocrats. Winston White, an eloquent and articulate young man, first entered politics as a GULP senator in 1970. He now headed a party, the Christian Democratic Labour Party, which was by no means broad-based and did not have a ghost of a chance of forming the Government.

Last but by no means least was the Grenada National Party under the leadership of veteran politician, Herbert Augustus Blaize, a solicitor by profession. The GNP was essentially the party of the middle class, while the GULP was the party of the working class. Ever since the introduction of adult suffrage in the 1950's these were the two main political parties in Grenada. All these parties and more were eager to contest the December elections. But there was still a mighty chasm between the parties and the electorate. This was particularly so with the newer parties. Time was running out. Rightly or wrongly the political leaders were beginning to feel that Gairy had a good chance of winning the elections if they entered the contest as separate parties. Vote splitting would give Gairy's party a decisive advantage. Party leaders were growing convinced that in order to keep out Gairy they had to enter the electoral contest as a united force. It was out of this concern that Blaize, Alexis, Brizan and Whyte agreed to meet in Union Island, one of the St. Vincent Grenadines, on August 26,1984, to see whether they could reach consensus on contesting the next elections as one entity. Whether or not the meeting was convened at the instigation of the OECS leaders it nevertheless had their wholehearted support. James Mitchell, Prime Minister of St. Vincent and the Grenadines, arranged the logistics of the meeting which was reportedly held in a relaxed and cordial atmosphere and in the presence of the Prime Ministers of Barbados, St. Lucia and St. Vincent and the Grenadines who were not silent observers.

The Union Island accord was a brief hand-written document duly signed by the four party leaders who had convened the meeting. The Prime Ministers present signed as witnesses. The party leaders admitted that there was a felt need to make a new beginning in Grenada, Carriacou and Petit Martinique and agreed to recommend to their party Executives the formation of a single political party to be known as the New National Party. They further agreed to the appointment of Herbert Blaize as Leader and Chairman of the new party, and the establishment of a joint steering committee to formulate a Constitution and party programmes. "The Leaders have agreed to carry out these steps with the greatest despatch to provide Grenada with the forward thrust that is now so necessary to ensure peace, stability and good government." So ended the communique.

On Thursday, September 20, in a broadcast to the nation I announced the date of elections as Monday, December 3, 1984. It would appear that this announcement roused the prospective candidates out of their slumber. For no sooner the date was named than they began in earnest to prepare for elections and wasted no further time hitting the campaign trail. Meanwhile, Herbert Blaize, George Brizan and Francis Alexis got together and in accordance with the terms of the Union Island agreement formed the New National Party and were ready to face the electorate as a united front. Winston Whyte and his Christian Democratic Labour Party withdrew from the alliance. Whyte subsequently told me that the reason for his withdrawal was what he discerned as an absence of any genuine intention to start a new party well managed along disciplinary lines and with an imaginative and robust national programme. He saw the obsession of his colleague leaders to keep Gairy and the GULP out of power as the mainspring of their political actions. Whyte came to the conclusion that they had their priorities wrong if they were really serious about forming a strong and lasting political party.

Matters of security and the forthcoming general elections were at the heart of my functions as Governor General from October, 1983 to December, 1984. Notwithstanding the relentless efforts of the Interim Government , I had to make sure that the security of the State was not at risk and that the elections were flawless. There could be no letting up in the security at the Elections Office itself, and I thought it necessary to maintain a high level of vigilance. A room in my office was reconditioned for the safe keeping of the ballot boxes and the ballot papers. Governor General's House and its environs were more than adequately guarded, and these election paraphernalia were better secured there than in the Electoral Office. Over the years there had been too many stories, imaginary or real, with reference to extra ballot papers being given to people who were either not registered at all or who might attempt to vote more than once.

Although I had my doubts about these assertions, nevertheless I was not prepared to take chances. Therefore, I directed that two sets of ballot papers be printed, one in the Government Printery and the other in the United States of America. Both set of papers were stored away safely in that specially prepared room. The American paper was of a better quality with a well-defined watermark. In the end, the Supervisor of Elections decided to use the ballot paper which was printed in America. The chances of reproducing this paper in Grenada were rather remote. This was not the first time that material for elections was printed in the United States of America. The voters' list for the 1972 elections was printed in the United States as the then Head of Government, Premier Gairy, did not have the fullest confidence in some of the senior officers in the Government printing office.

As the election fever intensified many prophets of doom, not least among them foreign journalists, waited for an outburst of violence as they expectantly perched themselves on Grenadian soil to report first hand to the outside world. Only bad news from small and economically weak developing countries hit the headlines in the so-called world press, all calculated to show that the natives cannot govern themselves. Although I was at pains to explain to the visiting media that there would be no violence during the election period, they seemed not to have trusted my judgement. I proved to be right. There was no instance of violence either on election day or on the days and weeks leading up to elections. The harbingers of bad news must have been disappointed when the trouble they had anticipated did not occur. The Interim Government had issued an open invitation to governments and international organizations to observe the elections. Only the Organisation of American States accepted the invitation, although I have reason to believe that there were some clandestine and unofficial election watchers as well. The three-man team from the Organisation of American States was absolutely satisfied with the preparations for, and conduct of, the elections and reported in glowing terms.

An aura of serenity encircled Grenada, Carriacou and Petit Martinique on election day. All day long there was peace and quiet as the electorate joyfully entered the polling stations to do their civic duty. Many of them had formed long queues long before the regulation time for the commencement of the poll. Although I was a registered voter, I elected not to vote because my conscience told me that to do so would be compromising the non partisan nature of my job. The police very carefully and very efficiently monitored the situation throughout the country on election day. There was radio connection between the Police Headquarters on Fort George and the various police stations, and the police gave me hourly reports on developments in the various constituencies. But this was not enough for me. Accompanied by my ADC, I went for a short drive through St. George's town stopping briefly at the polling station where I would normally have voted and then to the Police Headquarters to visit the radio room.

The election results clearly endorsed the enthusiasm of the people to get back to the democratic path through their parliamentary representatives. The people's participation in the elections was a victory for those who believed in democracy, and their behaviour at the polls was a source of joy for people like me who have a deep and abiding faith in the good sense of my fellow citizens. A record number of voters cast their ballots, 85.3% of the electorate, a percentage much higher than in the United States of America. Five political parties contested the elections. The New National Party, which only four months earlier was conceived in Union Island, won overwhelmingly with fourteen parliamentary seats to its credit out of a total of fifteen. This party got 58.48% of the popular vote. The one remaining seat went to the Grenada United Labour Party which was able to annex 36.06% of the votes cast. The power of persuasion of the other three parties appeared to have carried no weight among the electorate. The Maurice Bishop Patriotic Movement, named after the slain Prime Minister, could only muster 4.93% of the votes. The Christian Democratic Labour Party which had withdrawn from the Union Island accord could find favour only with .26% of those who cast their votes. The Grenada Federated Labour Party did even worse. They brought up the rear with .02%. The independent candidates got .25%.

The elections were free and fair. No one cried foul except Gairy who postulated that there was a chemical on the ballot paper which had the effect of changing GULP votes into NNP votes. By some chemical reaction the

"X"s registered against the names of the GULP candidates were shifted to those of the NNP. This was Sir Eric's theory that was greeted with the scorn and derision it deserved. The elections firmly rejected communism and signalled to the world that Grenada was ready to rejoin the fold of democracies. Before polling day, by proclamation I had brought back into operation all the sections of the Constitution dealing with Parliament. By December 3, election day, the Constitution was fully restored except for the sections pertaining to the judicial courts. The other East Caribbean States indicated that they would not accept Grenada back into the judicial system until the trial of those who were accused of murdering Maurice Bishop and others was determined. Following the elections I dissolved the Advisory Council, thereby bringing to an end the Interim Government. I also invited Herbert Blaize to form a new government. I subsequently called Marcelle Peters, the representative of St. Andrew's North East and the only successful GULP candidate, and made him Leader of the Opposition. Within half an hour Peters was again at my doorsteps, this time to inform me that he could not accept the leadership of the Opposition. He added honestly that he had just held discussions with the leader of the GULP, Sir Eric Gairy. Knowing the latter as I did I was not entirely surprised to hear of the delayed refusal of Peters. Nor did his quick retreat to my residence surprise me as Sir Eric, whom Peters had consulted, lived a stone's throw away. I later learnt from Peters that Sir Eric felt I should have consulted him as leader of the party before making such appointment. This, of course, would not have been in keeping with constitutional propriety, as such an appointment was to be made in my own deliberate judgement. The matter of the leadership of the opposition was resolved when two weeks later Peters returned to me to say that he was then willing and ready to take up the appointment. According to him, he was persuaded by his family and certain leading supporters in his constituency at the expense of incurring the wrath of his political leader. Peters apologized for any inconvenience his action might have caused. Without hesitation I gave him a new instrument of appointment and forthwith administered the oaths of allegiance and of office. I was fully prepared for all this, as I had anticipated the purpose of his visit.

The year 1984 started off with a flurry of visitors who came to see for themselves how Grenada was faring after the horrendous events of October, 1983. Many of them were Grenadians living abroad. Some of them came with preconceived ideas and were astonished to find the progress made so far on the road to normalcy. Others who came with open minds were impressed that the physical damage attributed to the military intervention was so minimal. Indeed, there was the bombing of the Radio Station which seemed bent on holding out to the bitter end while announcers were busy advising Grenadians to defend their country against the American and Caribbean forces. The Mental Hospital at Fort Matthew was accidentally bombed. Other casualties included Butler House which had accommodated the Office of the late Prime Minister. The Central Police Station was allegedly burnt down. The American and Caribbean forces had no hand in that. Damage to civilian property was minimal. The United States authorities established a claims office and compensated generously all those who suffered damage to property. They also built a new hospital for mental patients.

But more significantly some very important visitors came to Grenada in 1984. On the morning of January 5, yet again I received Shridath Ramphal, Commonwealth Secretary General, the same man who had predicted at my luncheon table some five years previously that the second coup would be worse than the first in that there would be more bloodshed in any succeeding coup. He was accompanied by Carl Dundas, Head of the Legal Division of the Commonwealth Secretariat and Patsy Robertson, Head of the Information Division. Ramphal showed every willingness to help in the restoration of normalcy to Grenada. It was he who agreed to second Nicholas Brathwaite with pay to serve on the Advisory Council. Brathwaite had then been in charge of the Commonwealth Youth Programme in Guyana. Ramphal also recruited Anthony Rushford for his assignment as Legal Adviser and he had promised Commonwealth Secretariat funding for Alister McIntyre who was my first choice as Chairman of the Advisory Council. Always an integrationist, Ramphal had a passion for West Indian togetherness. As chief servant of the Commonwealth he never failed to show deep concern for the less developed Commonwealth countries, especially the smaller and more vulnerable States. I first got to know him when he was Foreign Minister in his homeland, Guyana. Later, I was happy to see a fellow West Indian succeeding Arnold Smith, the first Commonwealth Secretary General who himself had Grenadian family connections and had never failed to remind Caribbean people about this.

While Ramphal was pleased with the progress made towards the restoration of normalcy in our battered country, he strongly felt that the American troops should take their exit and be replaced by a Commonwealth Police Force to maintain law and order. Before receiving Ramphal I had intelligence that he had been pushing this line of thought from his Marlborough House office in London since the military intervention. I listened to him intently and politely. He informed me that already he had taken soundings of certain Commonwealth governments, and they proved to be positive. I shared neither his enthusiasm nor conviction, and I failed to see any cogent reason why the Americans should leave prematurely. In fact I always felt that those who were pressing for the removal of the Americans were either taking an ideological stance or were acting more out of emotion rather than objective reasoning. The people of Grenada overwhelmingly welcomed the Americans and wanted them to stay as long as possible. Despite the anti-American sentiments emanating from some quarters, in the final analysis what mattered most were the wishes of the Grenadian people, many of whom thought of the American and Caribbean forces as their rescuers. Indeed, thousands of them in a fit of frenzy signed a petition asking President Reagan to accept Grenada as an additional State of the United States of America.

Ramphal tried to impress upon me and the Advisory Council whom he had seen separately that financial support for a Commonwealth Police Force was not a problem. He knew for a fact that certain Commonwealth countries would generously provide funds for this venture, and indeed for other projects. I was not moved by this disclosure given my own civil service experience and the recalcitrance of Ministries of Finance in making money available even after promises are made by ministers and heads of government. During my six-year sojourn at Marlborough House I learnt how difficult it was for some countries to pay their contributions to the Secretariat, to the Foundation and to the Commonwealth Fund for Technical Co-operation. Further, after all their traumatic experiences it was easier for Grenadians to deal with the Americans and their West Indian brothers and sisters rather than with a multi-faceted and multi-cultural force from the widespread Commonwealth even though English was the common language. For my own part I felt confident that the American and Caribbean Forces were capable of ensuring peace and stability in the country. Neither group interfered with the operations of the Interim Government. Nor did they in any way try to influence the Government's policy. Their remit was quite clear, and they stuck to their allotted task of maintaining law and order in the cause of the security of the State. But the most telling point was that the people of Grenada wanted the Americans with whom they had close ties and shared a common historical past. Over the years thousands of Grenadians had settled in the United States of America in order to make a living and had kept in close touch with their relatives at home.

While my meeting with the Secretary General was frank and cordial I am afraid that I was less than diplomatic when a British reporter from *The Guardian* newspaper came to me on the heels of Ramphal's departure to verify whether or not there would be a Commonwealth Police Force in Grenada. I was very blunt and told him that this was just not on. In fact the proposal was not on our agenda. Apparently, Ramphal on reading the report in the English newspaper was very upset and immediately telephoned Nicholas Brathwaite, the Chairman of the Advisory Council. Brathwaite could not provide him with any comfort.

This unpopular Commonwealth proposal as far as Grenada was concerned soon fizzled out into nothingness. Had it been a proposal that aimed at the creation of job opportunities, it would have received popular acclaim. The money for the upkeep of the proposed Commonwealth Police Force could be better utilized on more productive undertakings such as projects pertaining to education and skills training which would serve to enhance upward mobility in living standards. Young Grenadians had had more than their fair share of military training at home and abroad. They had been exposed to the appurtenances of war. Never before had they seen in their own country such a huge arsenal of arms and ammunition. They had heard rumours of war. They had been constantly lectured on threats of war. In the end they saw war itself, all of this in their homeland generally known for its peace and tranquility.

Replacement of the American service men and women by a Commonwealth Police Force would do nothing to temper the exuberance of our young or to help them find some directional purpose in life. What they wanted was gainful employment. What is more, while Ramphal was vigorously advocating a Commonwealth Police Force, the British Government would only agree to send us a Police Advisor, rather than a police officer to take charge of the Royal Grenada Police Force. The Canadian Government would not even agree to send an Advisor. Clearly it was the official view in London and Ottawa that Grenadian citizens under the guidance of their local authorities should take the initiative, and rightly so, in any plan of action for the restoration of their cherished way of life. These Governments did not wish in any way to appear to be interfering in the internal affairs of a sovereign State. They obviously recognized Grenadians as capable of running their own affairs.

Baroness Young, Minister of State in the British Foreign and Commonwealth Office, came by in early January, 1984. Her engaging personality no less than her humane qualities impressed me greatly. Very supportive of the work of the Interim Government she expressed pleasure at what had been achieved in so short a time in terms of rebuilding our democratic structures. In my talks with her she was evidently less concerned about the pros and cons of the American intervention, or about the fact that the British had not taken part in the action. Indeed, she was more excited to learn about the plans for a more secure and more prosperous future. She exuded confidence and hope and was altogether very positive and encouraging. On the evening of Thursday, January 5, a reception was held in her honour at the residence of the senior British diplomat on the island, John Kelly. There Baroness Young was able to meet and converse with a wide cross section of people. The British Government had already announced that they would make available the sum of EC$5m which was part of a delayed Independence grant to Grenada.

The British emphasis on law and order was reflected in the kind of assistance they so readily and willingly gave to Grenada in terms of human resource development and in terms of remodelling physical structures. The Police Headquarters on Melville Street had been set ablaze during the intervention. Thus as a matter of urgency alternative premises had to be found. Fort George, which had been previously used for that purpose, was the natural choice. It was Her Majesty's Government in Britain which provided the necessary finance for the rehabilitation of Police Headquarters on Fort George and for the refurbishing of a number of police stations throughout Grenada, some of which had ceased to operate in accordance with a policy measure during the Bishop administration. Soon after the intervention and before the appointment of the Advisory Council, I quietly ordered an investigation into the work and conduct of the upper echelons of the Force. The findings were embodied in a secret report which was submitted to me. It was not a happy picture. This report confirmed my worst fears that the restoration of public confidence in the Royal Grenada Police Force would be a gigantic task. By arrangement Mervyn Holder, a senior Police Officer from the Royal Barbados Police Force, was seconded to Grenada to take charge of a rather weakened and frustrated force. Holder's main objective was to build an efficient Police Force in whom the public would have confidence. Holder entered upon his new and challenging assignment with superb vigour, but there were certain elements in the force who still thought that they were in the employ of the People's Revolutionary Government, and upon whom the new Commissioner had to depend for information and advice. The recruitment drive did not produce the quality of men and women we were looking for. One of the first persons Holder enquired of was Cosmos Raymond, and expressed the wish that he would have liked a man of his calibre to assist him. I immediately summoned Raymond who was then resident in the United States, asking him to leave whatever he was doing and return home without delay. His country needed him. He responded to my call and came back home to be made Deputy

Commissioner of Police. Raymond was a most loyal and devoted policeman. As an Assistant Superintendent of Police he was well loved and respected by the rank and file. He had first come to my notice when I was Permanent Secretary in the Office of the Premier in pre-independence times. He later became my ADC. I could not desire a more knowledgeable, loyal and committed aide. I was sorry to see him go, but he reasoned that under the People's Revolutionary Government his future in Grenada would not be bright.

Structural rehabilitation at Her Majesty's Prisons in Richmond Hill was also undertaken with financial support from the British Government. Extensive refurbishment at the Prisons made it more comfortable and habitable for both prisoners and prison officers. I was appalled to see the physical state of the prisons when I visited soon after the intervention. Certain parts of the prisons were not fit for human habitation, and the work of sprucing up the buildings and their environs should be a matter of priority. In any assessment of the Prisons during the post-intervention period the name Lionel Maloney must stand high. We were very fortunate to get the services of Maloney, who was seconded from the Barbados Prisons Service to do a stint in Grenada under very trying circumstances. From all reports, Maloney has always been a no-nonsense man, a strict disciplinarian and a great believer in body fitness. If he presided over the Prisons with an iron hand, as his detractors alleged, he certainly won the admiration and respect of the business community who generously showered upon him various items of equipment which were desperately needed in the Prisons. Maloney had the knack of taking bureaucratic hurdles in his stride. The men and women who wielded their pens in the Ministry of Finance could not deter him in his commitment and in his resolve to build a prison service of quality. If they could not comply with his request for funds to purchase a refrigerator he would seek to find one elsewhere, and invariably he would get one as a gift to the Prisons through the kind generosity of the business sector. He vigorously revived the prison industries. Production immediately soared in the agricultural crops and in the arts and crafts. In-service training was an important component of the prison administration and it was this, more than anything else, which helped the prison officers to recapture their self-esteem and dignity. Once again prisoners respected prison officers. While many people expressed fears about the inability of the prison officers to keep the alleged murderers of Prime Minister Bishop under strict supervision in accordance with prison rules, I had every confidence in Maloney, and I knew for certain that these prisoners on remand would not be allowed to get away with any nonsense. With the passage of time that confidence mushroomed into the community and people felt less and less anxious about the possibility of any disturbance in the Prisons as long as Maloney was at the helm. Notwithstanding the fact that not long before some of the prisoners were the bosses of the prison officers.

The prison was a major security area. Its perimeter was well guarded by members of the Caribbean Forces day and night. Maloney made short shrift of those who thought they could visit the Prisons at anytime to talk to Bernard Coard and others who were on remand for the murder of Maurice Bishop. He incurred the wrath of a newspaper editor who tried to eke out information for his paper. He had to remind the goodly scribe that in the existing situation in the country it would be most imprudent for him to divulge anything which he as Commissioner deemed too sensitive to disclose. The editor was not satisfied and he did not hide his displeasure, whereupon Maloney asked him to leave his office. The editor left, but proceeded to use his newspaper to vilify the Commissioner on a weekly basis. But Maloney got on with his job unflinchingly. Even ministers of religion came under scrutiny when they visited the Prisons. No one was exempt. In fact clergymen who appeared recalcitrant by not wanting to observe the prison regulations while on visits to inmates had their passes withdrawn. Maloney kept me informed of all these matters, and he had my fullest support.

Since the downfall of the People's Revolutionary Government there had been no political prisoners at Richmond Hill. The claim by some that those in custody for the murder of Bishop and others were political prisoners was either shrouded with dishonesty or enveloped in ideological inebriety. Every right thinking and reasonable Grenadian knew that in keeping with the law of the land those accused had their preliminary hearing in the Magistrate court and the matter was subsequently sent to the High Court for trial. The trial judge was Justice Denis Byron of the OECS court who later became Chief Justice of the East Caribbean Supreme Court. The then Grenada Court of Appeal which was the final court of jurisdiction was established by the People's Revolutionary Government when Bishop severed connection with the British Privy Council and disdainfully withdrew from the East Caribbean Judiciary.

As Commissioner of Prisons Maloney had a keen sense of the importance of the security of the country as a whole. He so often assured me that as long as he was in Grenada I should have nothing to worry about in terms of my own personal safety and in terms of the security of the country. He felt that his responsibility in the area of security extended beyond the Prisons compound, and so it was his duty to be vigilant at all times and in all places.

He would visit my office at regular intervals to report on the state of the prisons and he would telephone me day or night to apprise me of any unusual activity in the country. Maloney's work at Her Majesty's Prisons was exemplary, and he made a tremendous contribution towards the growth of public confidence in the security and safety of Grenada.

Some misguided Grenada watchers who perhaps had never experienced such magnitude of local difficulties remained in their far away ivory towers and freely criticized almost every action of the Interim Government . One such area of criticism was the establishment of a law court on the prison compound in Richmond Hill. "Why not try the Bishop alleged killers in the courthouse in St. George's?" they asked. In fact they deduced all sorts of sinister motives as to why these prisoners were tried in Richmond Hill and by inference argued that they would not have a fair trial. Nothing could be further from the truth. When the accused were first taken to the St. George's courthouse for the preliminary hearing all hell broke loose. A barrage of stones was hurled at the bus in which they were travelling and one prisoner was hit. They were subjected to all kinds of insults and a large number of people were able to break the security cordon and make their way to the courthouse yard for what became a potentially dangerous confrontation as the accused attempted to alight from the bus. It was an unexpected and incredible nightmare for the security planners, and needless to say the security personnel who were so generously distributed in the environs of the court and along the bus route suffered monumental stress and strain. Grenadians were still angry over the summary and senseless execution of their Prime Minister and others. The sudden upwelling of that anger on that eventful morning only went to show that the people were prepared to take the law into their own hands and were anxious to carry out their own sentence. The Advisory Council, security advisors and I could not fail to take note and we had to nip this security problem in the bud so that such an occurrence would not happen again.

We acted expeditiously. The Lions Club had built an attractive and spacious den at Richmond Hill on grounds which had once belonged to the Prisons. During the revolutionary period Bishop and his Government confiscated the property on the grounds that it was too near the Prisons and it constituted a security risk. Ironically, Bishop's father was a prominent member of the Lions Club when the proposal to build a den at Richmond Hill was first mooted. On the timely advice of the Advisory Council and our security advisors I quickly established that building as a law court and had it duly gazetted in the Government Gazette as stipulated in law. It was in this courthouse that the preliminary hearing took place before the magistrate, and later the trial before judge and jury. This arrangement effectively ensured the safety and security of the accused. The courthouse was always full of listeners and on-lookers during both the preliminary investigation and the trial, but there was a reduction in the stress and strain earlier experienced by the security men and women on duty.

Other visitors to Grenada during the interim period included George Shultz, United States Secretary of State and Mrs Shultz. They came for our Independence celebrations on February 7. I received a steady flow of visitors particularly in the first four months of 1984. The visit of the Archbishop of Canterbury evoked much national interest and inspired much hope. Anglicans and non-Anglicans alike were touched by his visit which enhanced the cause of reconciliation as we moved steadily to regain normality and stability. Accompanied by a young chaplain and a layman Terry Waite, Archbishop Runcie came out to the Caribbean primarily to join the Anglican community in celebration of the centennial anniversary of the Anglican Province of the West Indies. On his arrival at Pearls Airport on March 26, he received a rousing welcome from dignitaries of Church and State as well as from the hundreds of faithful who were there to greet him. As his motorcade approached the St. Andrew's Anglican Church the Archbishop alighted from his car and did a walk-about mingling with the young people, their parents and teachers who flanked both sides of the roadway to greet this eminent spiritual leader. The school children were beautifully attired in their school uniform. The motorcade then slowly made its way to the St. Andrew's Anglican Church where the Archbishop stopped briefly for a short service. Continuing his journey to St. George's through the winding roads which skirt the picturesque forest of the Grand Etang, Archbishop Runcie was warmly greeted in the villages along the route. On his way to St. George's he had a helicopter escort, apart from the security provided in the police cars which were part of the motorcade. He had an equally rousing welcome as he approached the precincts of the St. George's Anglican Rectory where an official luncheon was laid for him. It was not entirely easy for Terry Waite to whisk the Archbishop away given the conviviality and warmth which pervaded the atmosphere at this luncheon. However, he was able to prevail upon the host, Archdeacon Hoskins Huggins, that it was necessary for the Archbishop to have a rest before his next engagement at the St. George's Anglican Church where he was to be the chief celebrant and preacher at a special eucharistic service that evening.

The Archbishop then repaired to Governor General's House where he was our guest during his two-day visit. Apart from meeting with Anglican Church officials, he also held discussions with the Chairman of the Advisory Council and with me. Characteristically he was mindful of those in prison and visited Her Majesty's Prisons at Richmond Hill where he saw, among others, the prisoners who were being held for the murder of Prime Minister Bishop and others on that dreadful October day in 1983. The Archbishop, in a press statement before his departure, described his visit to Grenada as undoubtedly one of the highlights of his visit to the Anglican Province of the West Indies.

As visitors continued to come from far and near I happily received those who wished to see me. This meant almost all of them. A Canadian technical team which included two members of the Royal Canadian Mounted Police came in early February. Canada has been a traditional ally and trading partner of Grenada, and over the years has poured much needed technical aid into Grenada to boost the quality of our human resources and to assist in our infrastructural development. Individual members of the Canadian Parliament came to make their own assessments. I well remember a Canadian parliamentarian pointedly asking me whether I had had any personal contact with American politicians or high-ranking officials in the U.S. State Department during the Bishop administration. I believed I read his mind correctly, as I quickly deciphered what prompted such a question. However, I could only answer truthfully in the negative.

From the U.S.A. came members of Congress and a number of high-ranking officials. From Europe I received members of the European Parliament as well as British Parliamentarians from both sides of the Houses of Parliament including members of a Select Committee who came on a fact-finding tour. Business leaders, professionals, prospective investors, religious leaders, high ranking army officials from the U.S.A. and the Caribbean, and diplomats from friendly countries all visited to get the feel of things. They travelled freely all over the country and met a cross section of Grenadians, not least the ordinary men and women who then went about their daily tasks much more relieved and with a great measure of confidence. Vaughn Lewis, Secretary General of the Organisation of East Caribbean States, was always a strong, reliable and committed ally to the cause of security and stability. His visits were frequent. So too were the visits of Brigadier Rudyard Lewis, the head of the Regional Security Service of which Grenada was the newest member. Media personnel were not to be left out of the Grenada-bound trek. Not surprisingly, they came from every region of the world. All these visits helped to restore the confidence of the Grenadian people and brought with them a groundswell of goodwill and, in some cases, offers of help to rebuild the country.

Project Hope, a U.S.-based organization, under the sound and experienced leadership of Dr. William Walsh, did a marvellous short term transformation of the health services and carved the way for a brighter future in health care delivery. First Project Hope was able to recruit rather rapidly a number of health professionals who came down to serve on a voluntary basis thus filling the gap created by the return of physicians and other health personnel to their communist lands. After this initial thrust the best available physicians were drafted into the Grenada Health Service under the auspices of Project Hope. These officers were on contract, and in order to attract them they had to be paid inflated salaries which the Government of Grenada and Project Hope jointly provided.

Unsolicited advice came from far and near, some from the most unexpected quarters. Everyone who proffered advice seemed to have had the panacea for all of Grenada's ills. Post-intervention visitors all spoke of the need for economic development. Potential investors came to ascertain for themselves whether Grenada was a safe enough risk for investment, and whether there was a trained labour force capable of propelling the profitability of an enterprise. Investors will only spend money in a country if they could comfortably predict that there was a reasonable chance of making profit.

The expectations of Grenadians soared high. They could see a great influx of American investors. They dreamt of intense economic activity with a number of small scale industries, increasing employment opportunities and a buoyant economy. Needless to say, they failed to see the transformation of their dreams into reality. People tend to talk glibly about investment opportunities, but investment does not come as manna from Heaven. A serious investor first looks for a proper investment climate which constitutes stability, good work ethics, infrastructural development and a skilled labour force. In the case of Grenada potential investors would rather wait for the outcome of the impending elections before committing themselves, especially when there was a widespread baseless assertion that Gairy's party was the most likely one to win the elections. Thus apart from the packaging of the exotic nutmeg and its by-products in one new enterprise and the manufacture of wooden toys in another, there was no other investment from the American side during 1984. What is more these two projects were short lived.

The only saving grace was that there was an unprecedented amount of money in circulation as a result of the temporary residence of diplomats, technocrats and professional men and women, not to mention the American and Caribbean Forces. All these people had to be housed and fed. There was a great demand for housing, and house rentals, particularly in the St. George's area, increased considerably. It would seem that American personnel were prepared to pay these astronomical rentals, and they were the ones who really set the pace for the rent hike. Resulting from all this many job opportunities, even though transient in nature, became available to Grenadians.

The intervention dust had hardly settled when I received Bishop Charles and Fr. Gerry Pantin, a brother of the Archbishop of Port-of-Spain in Trinidad and also a brother of Sister Rosa, a nun who had given years of devoted and distinguished service at the St. Joseph's Convent High School in St. George's. Fr. Pantin was the founder of SERVOL, an institution catering to the needs of youngsters who were without hope, without dignity, without self- esteem and who for some reason or other had failed to make optimum use, if any at all, of the educational opportunities offered to them at the school level. Fr. Pantin got his inspiration for the establishment of such an institution during the Black Power uprising of the early 1970's in Trinidad and Tobago, when he observed a number of aimless, desperate young people with no skills and no assured future who, having dropped out of school, were courting disaster for themselves and creating complex social problems for their communities. SERVOL was undoubtedly a success story.

I could not hide my joy when Fr. Pantin told me that in his view an institution as SERVOL would be appropriate for Grenada at that point in time thus giving another opportunity to our young men and women to acquire a skill, and to rediscover themselves as esteemed human beings. Fr. Pantin came with an offer of help to get such an institution started. He was willing and ready to put at Grenada's disposal the expertise and the accumulated experience of SERVOL. This was a godsend, and an opportunity not to be missed. The Interim Government had an almost insuperable problem on their hands. Hundreds of young men and women had suddenly lost their gun power, and in one fell swoop their egos were deflated. With the return of democracy it became urgently necessary to empower them with a skill. Bishop Sydney Charles had previously shared with me his deep concern about the young men and women who had been toting guns everywhere in the name of the People's Revolutionary Army and with the blessing of the People's Revolutionary Government. He felt that these young people should be taught skills which would make them employable. It was against this backdrop that New Life Organisation (NEWLO) was born. Situated in Palmiste on the west coast, NEWLO occupies property belonging to the Roman Catholic Church. On that property lay Pope Paul's camp which was built some years ago by the church as a centre for both recreation and skills training. During the revolutionary period the Government confiscated the property. The property reverted to the church with the demise of the revolution.

In the true spirit of ecumenism the four main churches – Roman Catholic, Anglican, Methodist and Presbyterian – combined their efforts to establish NEWLO. While the leaders of these churches were motivated by the apparent plight of the young people who suffered disengagement from the army and militia, their wider vision was to give a second chance to the many boys and girls who had dropped out of school and had not developed any particular skill for the world of work. Their aim was not merely to provide youngsters with employable skills, but also, and very importantly, to help them to become more responsible, more caring and more loving citizens. So apart from receiving training in particular skills, it was obligatory for all students to take specially tailor-made courses for their spiritual and social growth. At the end of their two-year stint at NEWLO it was expected that they would have an appreciation of the best traditions of the values of the Grenadian society, and that their behavioural pattern would embrace consideration and respect for their fellow citizens.

In July, 1984, NEWLO opened its doors to the first group of students under the leadership of Sister Reina Loe, a former principal of St. Joseph's Convent in Grenville. She was ably assisted by Teddy Victor, a former teacher, who had been considered a counter revolutionary by the Marxist regime and as a result was incarcerated for some time. There were also tutors in masonry, carpentry, plumbing and electrical wiring. In keeping with Fr. Pantin's promise of help, Victor did some short term training at SERVOL, and staff from Trinidad visited from time to time to help in setting up organizational systems and programmes. On my visits to NEWLO, I could not help but observe the orderliness and alertness of the students. The pragmatic approach to teaching impressed me greatly. NEWLO's programme of education and training is purposive. It prepares students to earn a living and to become responsible and caring citizens with a sound spiritual foundation.

During these critical times all sorts of people were proffering advice. I listened with bated amusement. My civil service experience had taught me that many people approach ministers under the guise of giving advice, when indeed and in fact they are acting under selfish motives with the hope that ministers would be so gullible, as to act on their advice. I would not be caught in that trap.

Some people wanted to see me just to be able to say, "I saw the Governor General today and I gave him some advice." That type I can spot at a distance. A group of old boys of the Grenada Boys' Secondary School paid a courtesy call on me and I gladly received them. I thought these goodly gentlemen had come to discuss something of substance, or at least to pledge their loyalty and support. Surprise, surprise they came to ask me to get rid of the headmaster of my "alma mater." I could find no fault in the man, and I would not comply with their request. From another quarter I received a request to deport a lady who had been living in Grenada for several years and who was engaged in the travel business. I quickly sensed that those making the request were getting stiff competition from the lady in the travel trade. I also had a persistent request to have a Guyanese sent back to her native land. There was no good reason why this lady should be asked to leave. This lady remained in Grenada and proved a great asset to the cultural life of the Grenadian society.

But what took the cake was a request for water. A St. Paul's resident rang my ADC frantically to complain that she went home to find no water coming through her taps and so she could not clean her fish which she had just bought in town. She insisted that the Governor General should do something about it. Then there was the gentleman, an old pensioner, from Mardi Gras who sent me a monthly handwritten letter. He always made sure that the writing pad was fully subscribed. Prolific writer he was. Another source of communication was the lady from Sauteurs, a so-called spiritual type, a perpetual dreamer who claimed to have seen me often in dreams. More often than not she informed my office that she had a message from God for me. An aftermath of Grenada's imbroglio was the sudden appearance of local "prophets" and other spiritual claimants who believed that they had divine power. I had no end of requests from individuals and groups who wanted to pray with me and for me.

One day three women dressed in white appeared at the main gate anxiously seeking admission. They had an urgent message for the Governor General, and they were determined to see him. After about thirty minutes the guard at the gate, no doubt overwhelmed by the persistence of the ladies in white, thought it prudent to telephone the ADC who in turn went down to the gate to face them. In his genial manner he explained that I was not able to see them but he would be happy to deliver their message. The message was that the Russians were back in Grenada and many more were on their way. In an effort to allay their fears the ADC went out of his way to assure them that the Russians would not be able to come through the gate, and in any case they would be deported forthwith. The intervention by the ADC seemed to have appeased them. They left immediately, but probably disappointed that they could not see me. Of course, no Russian had returned to Grenada.

A character about town who carried the sobriquet, Fuchong, took upon himself to write letters to Her Majesty the Queen as his pastime. The Post

Office always forwarded his letters to me as indeed they would in the case of any letter addressed to Her Majesty. If any such letter slipped through and got to Buckingham Palace, the Queen's Private Secretary would immediately forward it to me, in my capacity as Her Majesty's Representative in Grenada, for any appropriate action.

Another letter writer to the Queen was a young lady from Mt. Moritz who had spent some years in the United Kingdom. Lately she had been strolling the streets of St. George's and visiting offices and Government departments complaining about one thing or the other – some real, some imaginary. Her letters to the Queen had always been intercepted and sent to my office. But one day she wrote a lengthy letter to the Queen complaining that the Government owed her some money and the Police Department refused to pay her despite numerous requests. I never understood why she involved the police, except that it was brought to my notice that she was a frequent visitor to police headquarters always complaining about this and that or criticizing the police. But in that letter she reported me to the Queen. She paraded on me. Among other things she reported that I was allowing Sir Eric Gairy, who lived not far from my residence, to practise witchcraft. To the best of my knowledge this accusation was false and without foundation. The letter was posted in London and was received in the Palace. The letter was then passed to me in the usual manner. I took time off to reply. The lady must have been shocked when she received my reply. I availed myself of the opportunity to advise her that in future any communication to the Queen must first be sent to me. I well remember this lady as a brilliant, quiet Anglican High School student who attended my Saturday morning continuation class in Geography some years previously.

It is fair to say that the Interim Government had the country on an even keel notwithstanding the monumental challenges they had to face. These challenges were punctuated by the difficulties of democratic adjustment endured by a people who were still working under unusual stress and strain. But while most Grenadians gave top marks to the Government for the increasing stability of the country and for the peace and freedom which they once again enjoyed, nevertheless the Government was not without its detractors. These detractors, without restraint, were severely critical. It was felt that the Interim Government was sluggish in their efforts at promoting economic growth. They lacked dynamism and in some quarters were considered spineless and visionless. They allowed many investment opportunities to elude their grasp, and they were not sufficiently aggressive in their quest for aid from friendly countries, particularly the United States of America, at a time when there was tremendous international goodwill towards Grenada. Harsh criticisms indeed! But one must remember that following the demise of Marxism in Grenada, the Government had the most awesome task of finding skilled men and women to do certain jobs which were vitally important for the economic advancement of the country. The human capital inherited by the Government was both inadequate and deficient. Nor did the Government finances present a rosy picture. The total outstanding public debt as at November 30, 1983, was $136,497,093. The Government had to clear up the massive overdrafts of our diplomatic missions abroad, and they had to make good the fiscal arrears of contributions to regional and international organizations. It is to their great credit that with proper fiscal management and control they were able before their term of office expired to increase civil servants salaries retroactively.

The Interim Government created a climate not only for democratic growth but also for economic and social advance. Undoubtedly the Government brought back confidence and hope within the Civil Service. Senior civil servants were once again given the opportunity to use their initiative and to give professional advice without fear of any reprisals. Civil servants had a greater peace of mind as they were free from political interference and harassment. Industrial relations were good during the interim period. Union workers and managers displayed good commonsense and restraint. The most important ongoing project was the construction of the Point Salines International Airport. Generous grants by the United States of America and Canada ensured the completion of the airport.

Neither in the militia nor in the army was the development of human resources a top priority for the People's Revolutionary Government. The rank and file among the military and para-military were skilfully indoctrinated in Marxism. For the rest they spent their time harassing the populace, spying on innocent people and trying to split families by alienating sons and daughters. Hundreds of militia and army men had left school without any academic qualification, without any skills. Herein lay the difficulty for the Interim Government.

The Interim Government did not devise any programme to debrief our youth who had been fully exposed to communist propaganda. However, the Government was courageous enough to remove from schools and other public places all vestiges of communism. Meanwhile, I received bags and bags of communist literature addressed to the Prime Minister. I ordered all to be destroyed. The communist inspired pioneer movement was abolished, while organizations like the Boy Scout and Girl Guide were able to breathe a new lease of life. The latter were so often described as bourgeois groups by enthusiasts of the New Jewel Movement who made every effort to decry and destroy these well tried and tested organizations. Communist infiltration in any form or fashion was curbed. With all these measures and more it was hoped that some semblance of sanity and sanctity would return to our schools, to our youth clubs and to our backyards.

Some of the accomplishments of the Interim Government included the rebuilding of the Sauteurs market, reorganizing the Civil Service, and the abolition of Estate Duties commonly known as death dues. A new terminal building was constructed at Lauriston Airport in Carriacou, and pensioners were exempt from income tax. Despite the burden of impecuniosity which weighed heavily on its shoulders, Government was still able to increase the salaries of civil servants. The establishment of a rehabilitation centre for alcoholics was a bold and worthwhile initiative. In the area of farming a number of feeder roads received Government's attention, and these roads were again made comfortably motorable, thus enhancing the transportation of crops, especially bananas.

In the absence of an elected Government it devolved upon me as the only constitutional authority to keep as closely as possible to the general populace. This I did by increasing my visibility throughout Grenada, Carriacou and Petit Martinique, by making myself more available to listen to individuals and organizations and above all by making frequent national broadcasts. Whatever the critics might say no one could deny that the Advisory Council, in whose hands I had entrusted the governance of the country, successfully held fair and free elections, saw to the completion of the international airport and created a climate of peace and tranquility in which the democratic freedoms could flourish once again.

# 12

## The Blaize Administration

B Y December 3, 1984, the groundwork for the return of parliamentary democracy had been well and truly laid. After months of meticulous refurbishment the parliament building was again in top shape to welcome the new incumbents. The walls were redecorated, the floors re-carpeted, the furniture, or what was left of it, was re-polished and new items bought, and a new sound system was installed. The mace, the symbol of authority of the House of Representatives, emerged from its hiding place none the worse for its forced four-year period of hibernation and was shining resplendently. So too was the mace of the Senate. Seven days earlier I had signed a proclamation dissolving the Advisory Council with effect from December 4, the day after the general elections. Acting in my own deliberate judgment I had previously made an Order dated November 9, 1984, and entitled the Constitution of Grenada Order, restoring all sections of the 1973 Constitution which were still suspended except those pertaining to the judiciary. The results of the elections were decisive and, given the high percentage of voters (85% of the electorate), it was beyond the shadow of a doubt that the people of Grenada voted overwhelmingly for the return of democracy. In the process they firmly rejected both Gairyism and Bishopism. Even a cursory glance of the results would reveal that in many polling stations candidates for the Maurice Bishop Patriotic Front ended the day with a low scoring rate having been summarily dismissed with an impressive succession of ducks.

Herbert Augustus Blaize, the winner of the Carriacou and Petit Martinique constituency, returned to St. George's in a blaze of glory. I had invited him to form a government. When he disembarked at Point Salines Airport he was greeted by hundreds of Grenadians and immediately made his way to the St. George's Anglican Church for a short service to give thanks to God before coming to me to receive his instrument of appointment as Prime Minister and to take the prescribed oaths of allegiance and of office. Blaize, an exemplary Christian gentleman and devout Anglican, had arranged for this Te Deum prior to his departure from Carriacou. Although throughout his life he remained steadfastly faithful to Anglicanism, yet he was a great believer in the ecumenical movement. At his request, one week after he was sworn in as Prime Minister the churches held an open-air thanksgiving ecumenical service at Queen's Park in St. George's. This service drew a large congregation from our tri-island State. His idea was to bring back the people to God. At the end of the service and on the Prime Minister's advice in the presence of the congregation, I administered the oaths of allegiance and of office to the newly appointed ministers and senators. This was an historic act as these oaths had always been administered at Governor General's House.

I first met Blaize in 1955 when I accepted an invitation from Lieutenant Bertie Callender to accompany the cadet corps of the Grenada Boys' Secondary School on a camping expedition to Carriacou. The other non-uniformed master on that expedition was Desmond Hoyte who later became President of Guyana. Also in attendance was war veteran Ben Roberts, drill master of the corps. We were encamped in the Hillsborough Government School in August of that year, a month before the unusual visitation of hurricane Janet which completely ravished the building. When I subsequently saw the devastation meted out to that school I could only say thank God it had not happened a month earlier. Herbert Blaize gave an inspiring lecture to the boys of his alma mater. He held them in rapt attention for some forty minutes, and we were all very impressed by his clarity of thought, his general delivery and the content of his speech. The records indicate that Blaize was a model boy at the Grenada Boys' Secondary School and a student whose academic excellence in the classroom was equally matched by his athletic prowess on the playing field.

On leaving school Blaize's first appointment was a clerkship at the Revenue Office in the northern town of Sauteurs. From a bicycle spill at La Fortune junction early one morning while hurrying to work he suffered a massive spinal injury. Death seemed to have been near, but after months in the hospital he recovered sufficiently to enable him to return to work, but this time in his native Carriacou. Shortly afterwards, with determination and grit he migrated to Aruba at a time when the Lago Oil Company was recruiting workers from the British colonies in the West Indies. Like Prime Ministers Gairy, Bishop and Ben Jones, he, too, had an Aruba connection. Bishop was born in Aruba of Grenadian parentage, while the others migrated to work. In Aruba, Blaize's ability was quickly recognized and so he had swift and rapid promotion to a managerial position. While in Aruba he married Venetia Davidson, a native of Carriacou. But sadly the old spinal injury flared up and he returned home to Carriacou in 1953 after exhausting all medical probability of recovery. With patience and resignation Blaize bore his pain and discomfort with no complaint. He placed himself into the hands of God.

Service was the mainspring of Blaize's actions. He always had a burning desire to serve his people, not for wealth, not for recognition, but with honour. After limited recovery and much persuasion he entered the slippery field of politics. He was persuaded to do so by a dashing young dentist, John Watts, who had recently returned from the United States of America where he qualified. Watts was the prime mover in establishing the Grenada National Party in 1955. This alternative party was formed to check the steady advance of Gairy's Grenada United Labour Party. John Watts was good at rhetoric, plain spoken and fearless. But for some unknown reason he never presented himself to the electorate at an election. Watts would say that unlike other party leaders in the Caribbean he did not start a party for personal electoral honours. It was felt in some knowledgeable quarters, however, that he knew he personally was not a drawer of votes. Thus he had to find a potential leader, and so he turned to Herbert Blaize for whom he had great admiration. Watts continued as party leader for some ten years even though Blaize and others had won seats in the legislature. This anomalous state of affairs in which the party leader stayed shy of the electorate could not continue for much longer, and Blaize eventually became party leader.

The Grenada National Party was mainly a party of the middle class. It attracted primarily the professionals, white collar workers, businessmen and landowners. It was essentially a party of the townsfolk while Gairy was almost in complete control of the rural areas. The Grenada United Labour Party was a party of the masses whom the GNP hierarchy to their peril slated both overtly and covertly as a pack of asses. This obviously did not help the cause of the GNP. Rather, it strengthened the fraternal bonds of the GULP. What is more, Gairy shrewdly began very early to make inroads into the business community, the professionals in particularly the legal profession, and certain categories of white collar workers. The GNP found it very difficult to halt Gairy's advance. While Gairy embraced the masses and pulled them up from their degradation and poverty, the GNP's philosophy was that it was *infra dig* to go down to the masses. Instead the masses by their own efforts should come up to the standards of the middle class. This veiled aloofness was a grave political error.

While Gairy was able to make himself at home in the company of the so-called "little man," Blaize and the GNP hierarchy remained aloof, and more often than not they failed to identify themselves with the lesser mortals

THE BLAZE ADMINISTRATION                                      217

among their own supporters. Blaize himself was able to win his seat in Carriacou and Petit Martinique, a classical classless community, in successive elections. Generally speaking the people of Carriacou and Petit Martinique never liked Gairy's style of politics anyway: more importantly, the political manoeuvrings in Grenada were of little interest to them. They would go to the polls and vote for the best available Carriacouan or Petit Martiniquan candidate.

Blaize's earlier successes in politics led to his being appointed Chief Minister of Grenada in 1962. Later he became the first Premier. That was on March 3, 1967, when by a significant constitutional change Grenada, like the other East Caribbean States, entered upon a Statehood relationship with the United Kingdom. By this relationship Grenada was responsible for all internal affairs, while Britain kept the portfolios of defence and external relations. After the demise of the People's Revolutionary Government there were only two proven political leaders with the necessary experience to take Grenada back into the democratic fold, namely Herbert Blaize and Eric Gairy. Blaize as head of Government had led the delegation to London for talks on Statehood, and later as leader of the Opposition delegation went to London for talks leading to Independence.

Despite his lingering illness and his incursion into politics Blaize was able to find time to read Law. While in opposition he completed his law studies and qualified as a solicitor. This was the nature of the man whom I appointed Prime Minister and invited to form a Government following the elections of December 3, 1984.

Blaize had always been a tough politician. Some say he was obstinate. He was certainly not a gullible individual, and it was difficult to penetrate his mindset. This was manifest during his earlier premiership almost two decades previously. In full measure he had brought with him into public office his own peculiar brand of frugality, and the parsimonious attitude he had adopted as Minister for Finance was unique. But coming just after the "squandermania" period when the British Government had suspended the Grenada constitution and assumed direct financial control from Whitehall, Blaize's premiership was decidedly significant and was doubtlessly under heavy and constant surveillance. In January, 1960, Grenada, like the other Windward and Leeward islands, attained a fair measure of internal self-government. Gairy had the majority in the Legislative Council (the precursor of Parliament) and he was the Minister for Finance. It soon became evident that there was a certain degree of turbulence in the civil service which was brought on by excessive and unauthorized spending of public funds and a blatant disregard for the financial rules and regulations.

The society at large could not tolerate this abuse of power and looked askance at what they considered to be a wanton waste of taxpayers' money. It came as no surprise, therefore, when in 1961 Administrator James Lloyd appointed a Commission of Enquiry "to enquire into the control of public expenditure in the territory during the financial year commencing January 1, 1961, having regard to the financial provisions in the constitution of Grenada and other relative provisions." As was to be expected the Executive Council, which was dominated by Gairy and his colleagues, bluntly refused to sanction the appointment of the Commission. This was over-ruled by Administrator Lloyd whose action was endorsed by the Secretary of State in London.

The Commission, under the Chairmanship of Barbadian jurist, Frank Field, came down heavily on the Minister for Finance, Eric Gairy, accusing him of mismanagement and wasteful expenditure. The civil service did not escape the wrath of the Commission. Certain senior civil servants came in for severe criticism for condoning irregularities in the disbursement of public funds. Once the findings of the Commission were known, Her Majesty's Government in Britain passed an Order-in-Council which effectively dissolved the Executive and Legislative Councils and gave the Administrator executive authority and limited legislative powers until new elections were held. These elections took place on September 3, 1962, when Blaize's GNP won six out of the ten elected seats. The Constitution was restored, and Blaize became Chief Minister.

As Head of Government Blaize had left behind a legacy of orderliness in public life, transparency in financial dealings, financial propriety in the treasury, and a country almost free of debt. Generally speaking, law and order had prevailed in what looked like a very settled and peaceful country. In the 1962 elections Blaize uncharacteristically took a miscalculated foray into the realms of constitutional reform and foreign affairs by having as his main election plank a proposal to merge Grenada with Trinidad and Tobago into a unitary state. It was a gamble that perhaps helped him to win the elections, but which subsequently dented his political career.

This unitary proposal attracted many of the traditional GULP voters who thought that they could pack their bags the day after elections and travel to Trinidad without facing any form of immigration restriction in order to take up residence. After winning the elections Blaize feverishly pursued the proposed initiative of unitary statehood. But he was only able to get the Government of Trinidad and Tobago to mount a series of studies as to how the unitary statehood machinery might work with particular reference to public institutions and senior civil servants in Grenada. For example, one of the teams of wise men from Trinidad and Tobago recommended that Government House, the traditional home of the Monarch's representative, should be turned into a secondary school. However, the unitary statehood idea never materialized partly because of growing opposition to it in both Trinidad and Grenada. One could well imagine the resulting disappointment and, in some cases, the anger of those Grenadians who had been looking forward to their new place of abode. While Blaize was vigorously pursuing the unitary initiative with Trinidad and Tobago, there was an alternative proposal floating around the Caribbean. This proposal to establish an East Caribbean Federation between the Windward and Leeward Islands and Barbados, commonly known as the Little Eight, never appealed to Blaize. The Grenada Government never participated in the discussions of the Regional Council of Ministers who were assiduously trying to put together the pieces of what was left of the West Indies Federation after Jamaica and Trinidad had opted out. In true West Indian fashion, the Little Eight proposal also failed to materialize.

The failure of the unitary statehood initiative to come off the ground marked the beginning of the end of Blaize's sojourn in office. Gairy craftily used this dismal failure to help him win the 1967 elections handsomely. Thus after seventeen years out of office, Blaize regained political ascendancy in 1984 with a clear and decisive mandate. He brought back with him all his personal qualities, not least his penchant for parsimony. Whether these would be all acceptable to his cabinet colleagues, the civil service and the general populace was left to be seen especially after Grenada's serious flirtation with the communist block countries. From the very outset Blaize showed his concern for propriety and rectitude in public life, by making it clear to all that accountability at all levels was of paramount importance in effecting good governance. One of his first actions was to issue a directive to Cabinet ministers to deposit with the Governor General a list of their individual assets before embarking on their ministerial assignments. He himself led the way in this regard.

The Prime Minister was very conscious of the limitations of his parliamentary colleagues in terms of parliamentary practice and procedure. It must be remembered that Grenada had been without a parliament for almost five years. Over ninety per cent of the members of both Houses of Parliament had had no parliamentary experience. In his anxiety to ensure that the new lawmaking body be placed on a sound footing in accordance with the norms and usages of Parliament, Blaize set about to organize some training for all members of Parliament. The objective was to improve the standard of debate and decorum in Parliament. The guidelines written by

Curtis Strachan, the experienced and knowledgeable Clerk of Parliament, were not enough. Blaize felt that the parliamentarians should be brought together in a learning atmosphere alongside people who were well versed in the acceptable behavioral patterns of the legislature. Thus with the support of the Commonwealth Parliamentary Association, a seminar in parliamentary practice and procedure was held in Grenada in September, 1985, with resource personnel from the British, Canadian and St. Lucian Parliaments. The visitors included Hon. St. Clair Daniel, Speaker of the St. Lucian House of Assembly, Sir Paul Dean, Member of Parliament in Britain, Mr Michael Ryle of the British House of Commons, Clerk's Department, Hon. Arthur Danahoe, Speaker of the House of Assembly in Nova Scotia, Canada and Mr Philip Laundy, Clerk Assistant to the Canadian House of Commons. For me it was also a joy to see so many of our former parliamentarians, members of Government and members of the Opposition mingling so freely in an atmosphere of conviviality. Under the aegis of the Commonwealth Parliamentary Association, a similar seminar was held almost eighteen months later. This seminar was opened at York House on February 23, 1987, by Sir Hudson Scipio, Speaker of the Grenada House of Representatives. Although this seminar was essentially for the Grenadian parliamentarians, there were representatives from Britain, Canada, Zambia and Barbados. Among the visiting parliamentarians were the Rt. Hon. John Silkin and Sir Anthony Kershaw of Britain, Hon. L. Crouse of Canada, Hon. L. Mulimba of Zambia and Hon. Billie Miller of Barbados.

Blaize would not accept gifts. He had hardly assumed duties as Prime Minister when a businessman deposited a gift of a refrigerator into his office. As soon as this was brought to his attention, Blaize ordered that the refrigerator be sent back forthwith. Similarly, when a Grenadian offered his car to facilitate official transportation during the visit of Her Majesty, Blaize flatly refused it as he had already received credible intelligence that the owner of the car was allegedly a drug dealer.

Though a patient listener, Blaize was a difficult nut to crack. Endowed with a good intellect he would quickly grasp the matter in hand. He usually had an answer to show why one's suggestions could not be entertained. More often than not he would reply by asking a question, thus bringing the dialogue to a premature end. Once one's point of view coincided with his, he would readily accept it, and this led to a certain degree of divisiveness in his cabinet.

It was not easy for any elected Prime Minister to push post-revolutionary Grenada forward bearing in mind the social dismemberment and economic degradation which had severely scarred the country. Blaize had certain advantages. He was well respected and was a man of integrity in both public and private life. More importantly, he had experience in Government. Apart from the resounding mandate from the electorate, he was the recipient of tremendous goodwill both regionally and internationally. Many powerful and influential people in business, in politics and the professions made their way to Grenada primarily to meet with the Prime Minister. So, too, did government officials and representatives of regional and international organizations. The American presence in Grenada was still of a high profile as they continued to supply funding to help specifically in infrastructural development and more generally to strengthen the economic base of the country. The British were always with us. We could still count on the generosity of the Canadian Government who in good times and in bad never deserted us. Other Western countries, for example France and Germany and indeed the European Union as a whole showed renewed interest in Grenada as we set out to rebuild our democracy. Blaize was, therefore, in a truly unique position to seek diverse resources for developmental purposes.

Small states like Grenada with a weak economic base cannot depend on domestic savings or export earnings to stimulate or sustain any significant economic growth. More specifically, Grenada is mainly dependent on the export of primary agricultural products to satisfy its economic needs. With the downward trend in world commodity prices aggravated by fierce competition from larger producing countries and the likelihood of losing preferential treatment for certain commodities such as bananas, agriculture becomes less and less attractive to the young especially. The flight from agriculture to tourism may bring quick dollars. However, countries with inappropriate or insufficient human capital and inadequate infrastrutural development find it a tremendous burden to plan for and sustain a tourism industry which is undeniably fickle and which faces severe competition worldwide. Whatever economic course Herbert Blaize might chart he would either need resources from outside through grants and soft loans, or he would have to set up the necessary machinery to woo foreign investors without in any way compromising the integrity of the country's sovereignty. Most importantly, amid the growing complexity of patterns of world trade he should have on call at least one technocrat who was versed in the politics of international trade. In 1985 Grenada was still on the world stage, though not occupying the central spot as in the recent past and it would have been judicious on the part of a democratically elected government to capitalize on this. Many people had been waiting for the return of western style democracy before venturing to do business in Grenada.

The establishment of the National Economic Council was a step in the right direction. This was the brainchild of the Prime Minister who had a penchant for putting structures in place. The Council was under the chairmanship of the Prime Minister himself and other members included three Cabinet ministers, the Director General of Finance, the Economic Advisor, and leading persons from the private sector, one of whom was the President of the Chamber of Industry and Commerce. By forming such a body, the Prime Minister at once brought into being a social contract between the public and private sectors. It also showed a willingness on the part of Government to work with private sector organizations and to take them into its confidence. The private sector organizations welcomed this development and the Council began to work assiduously. In its National Development Strategy 1986–1990 the NEC pinpointed unemployment, which they put at twenty-five per cent, for special mention. Commenting on national unemployment the Council wrote thus: "Unemployment remains high and constitutes the most pressing problem to be addressed within the development strategy." In this regard Government had its work clearly cut out. The reduction of the unemployment rate was of paramount urgency, and in its developmental plans Government would have to focus on job creation as a top priority. In fact in the Elections Manifesto of the ruling New National Party it was clearly stated that "the opportunity of every Grenadian to have a job must be Government's first priority." I attended several graduations at the secondary school level during my term of office, and my heart always went out to the hundreds of school leavers who were about to begin their search for jobs in a severely limited market. Government was cognizant of the need to create jobs for the hundreds of children leaving school year after year.

As part of his economic strategy Blaize set up yet another para-statal organization, the Grenada Industrial Development Corporation (GIDC). This was established in 1985 as a focal point for investment in Grenada. Its first Chairman was retired Judge Samuel Graham. The GIDC was mandated to deal with all issues of investment. Therefore, it was expected that prospective investors would make one stop at the GIDC and get all their business done rather than having to go to various government ministries and departments. Generous concessions were offered to residents as well as non-residents who wanted to establish some form of productive activity which would provide employment opportunities. With the return of democracy it was believed that tourism would undergo swift and dramatic growth. It was with this in mind that Government encouraged Grenadians to invest in small hotels in order to avert the shortage of hotel rooms. A number of mini-hotels were built without any thought given to skilled management or appropriate marketing. Only time would tell whether these properties would survive amid world-wide changes in tourism marketing and in the face of increasingly fierce competition.

The fostering of small businesses naturally led to self-employment. But the conduct of small businesses would not have a sufficiently significant impact on rising unemployment. The GIDC would have to be more proactive in their *modus operandi*. They would need to go out aggressively to attract substantial investors rather than wait for investors to come to them. If GIDC were to live up faithfully to their mandate they would have to bring into Grenada some good investment projects with the capacity to sustain development, and at the same time, create gainful employment opportunities. An integrative approach to economic development in terms of education and training, tourism, communication and informatics should be the way forward and this should be central to whatever strategy upon which GIDC might embark.

But Blaize had certain disadvantages which impeded his progress. His deteriorating health was increasingly becoming a cause for concern, and for this reason his wife accompanied him on every trip overseas. Of all the Prime Ministers during my tenure of office, Blaize was the only one who strictly observed the time honoured convention of coming to see me once a week. From the very outset his car drove to the back of the building where it was easier for him to alight. By so doing, he also avoided the steps at the front entrance. He long suffered from arthritis as well as a prostate gland disorder. In his final year as Prime Minister he set up office in his official residence at Mt. Royal. Because of his failing health I volunteered to go to see him whenever he was ready for his weekly audience. A dirt roadway separated our two residences, and it was very easy for me to walk across. With his own peculiar sense of humour he would telephone and say, "Your Excellency, do you feel for a walk today?" I knew exactly what that meant, and we would arrange a mutually convenient time. Blaize faithfully observed the provisions of the Constitution and kept me fully informed on matters of state.

Blaize's other difficulty lay in the youthful exuberance of his inexperienced cabinet ministers, some of whom obviously had their own agenda and had hoped that the Prime Minister would step down within the first six months to give a younger individual a chance at the helm. As far as Blaize was concerned, this was merely wishful thinking. Very early in his tenure of office he confided in me that he had a very hard time trying to cope with the impetuosity of his Cabinet members. He never had these problems during his earlier tenure as Head of Government. Although his earlier colleagues were also green horns in government, their loyalty and devotion were unquestionable and their maturity was never in doubt.

Blaize always selected his loyal and trusted friend, Ben Jones, to perform the duties of Prime Minister in his absence. This often gave rise to ripples of dissatisfaction among cabinet colleagues as it was strongly felt that both George Brizan and Francis Alexis should be given an opportunity to act for the Prime Minister from time to time especially as they came into the New National Party as leaders of their own parties. Blaize would not budge, and continued to do it his way. The chemical mix which gelled the political parties together at the famous Union Island meeting the previous year seemed no longer effective. Cracks began to appear, with the New National Party looking more and more as an alliance of separate entities rather than as a single unified political party. Brizan and Alexis seemed to be warming towards each other, while Keith Mitchell was beginning to distance himself from his old party leader, Alexis.

In keeping with his 1984 election promise, Blaize wasted no time in setting up a Commission to review the Grenada Constitution and to make recommendations. Under the chairmanship of Sir Fred Phillips, former Governor of St. Kitts, the five-man Commission was made up entirely of lawyers with Bernard Gibbs, a former Assistant Administrator of Grenada, as secretary. The Commissioners were appointed on February 14, 1985. Professor Randolph McIntosh, Grenadian-born Professor of Law, Howard University, was later named as an Associate Commissioner. He joined the Commission in the summer of 1985 and again in early October when the Commission was working on its report which was presented to me on November 5, 1985. Blaize evidently fulfilled his promise. However, I thought that the appointment of a Constitutional Review Commission should not have been given top priority. In fact, I saw it as a waste of time and of scarce resources. If my opinion was far-fetched, perhaps it was not without merit. Some fourteen years have elapsed since the Commission's report was submitted, and no action has been taken on it. From all available evidence it was quite clear that the man on the Gouyave bus or the farm worker in Moyah in St. Andrew's had no interest in constitutional reform. Constitutional reform could not boil their pot, nor could it pay for school books for their children. There was no popular demand for constitutional reform. Following the downfall of the People's Revolutionary Government I had received correspondence from some individuals calling for changes in the Grenada Constitution. They all seemed to think that our recent local difficulties had come about as a result of certain weaknesses in the

Constitution. A politician who subsequently became Head of Government in his own territory had written to me passionately advising that it was most timely to have our Constitution changed, and urged me to do whatever I could towards that end. Incidentally after many years in office, he has not done anything about his country's Constitution which is similar to ours.

The one common thread running through all these proposals for constitutional reform was that no one person should be Prime Minister for more than two terms. Another proposal was that there should be a system of recall so that elected parliamentarians who, in the view of their constituents, were not performing satisfactorily should lose their seats in Parliament. I have always regarded the Grenada Constitution as sacrosanct, and one which should not be tampered with at will. I felt that the quest for constitutional reform was shrouded in emotionalism and intellectual arrogance. I could see nothing fundamentally wrong with the Constitution *per se*, and I was never convinced that the recent political upheaval had anything to do with a constitution which, as some erroneously claimed, was either inappropriate or riddled with inconsistencies. Rather it seemed to me that our recent political problems had stemmed from uncontrollable human behaviour, and had to do with the weaknesses, gullibility, greed for power and impropriety as displayed by those who were chosen by the people to govern and those who seized power by the gun. Perhaps one could point to the vulnerability of small states as Grenada, but it is difficult to fathom why blame should be apportioned to the Constitution. Whatever constitution Grenada might have, as long as we elect people who are cunning enough to manipulate a constitution for their own self-aggrandizement, economic downturn and social discontent must surely follow. The smaller the country the greater the likelihood that such a chaotic state of affairs would arise.

Once parliamentary democracy was restored, expectations of better living standards ran high. Most Grenadians expected to witness the creation of more employment opportunities. I was disappointed that the Government did not have an immediate plan for economic reconstruction which I thought had to take priority over constitutional reform. In this regard I thought the Government lacked vision. What was needed, as a matter of priority, was a bold and imaginative programme aimed at increasing production at all levels, creating additional employment opportunities, and improving the quality of the work force. One of the main objectives of such a programme should be the maximization of the use of agricultural products by actively promoting and encouraging the establishment of agro-industries, by organizing packaging and marketing facilities, and by demonstrating the importance of utilizing home grown food in the daily diet in the cause of better health and in order to reduce the excessive import bill. All this would first require serious and detailed planning by a small team of technocrats. For example, there is no reason why Grenada cannot be self-sufficient in the production of chicken and eggs. Mere lip service is not enough. During my career in the public service I have heard with deafening monotony year after year policy statements on the diversification of our agricultural industry. As Governor General I was made to repeat these statements whenever I made the annual visitation to the Houses of Parliament to read the Throne Speech. But nothing changed. It was business as usual.

In order to foster greater production at the work place there would have to be a deliberate emphasis on the improvement of human resources or what some economists call human capital, a most important element in production. This would entail a pragmatic approach to education and training that would include on-the-job training. A system of adult education would be put in place not merely to improve literacy, but more importantly to provide relevant skills for the new agricultural thrust and also for secondary industries based on agriculture, inclusive of horticulture and animal husbandry. Further it would be the business of the education and training programme to provide the necessary skills for the development of small scale industries including the service industries.

★   ★   ★

Prime Minister Blaize was very anti-communist. He would not accept anything that smacked of communism. He once publicly accused the People's Revolutionary Government of turning Grenada into "a stinking Communist hole." Meanwhile, the Cuban delegations continued to challenge the presence of Grenadian representatives of a duly democratically elected Government at various international fora. What stupidity! Not unexpectedly, then, Blaize would neither adopt nor adapt any programme started by the People's Revolutionary Government. However, he might have done well to take a hard look at their adult education programme with a view at least of adapting the salient features which would find accommodation in a democratic state. While the adult education programmes aimed mainly at propagating the communist beliefs, there was no doubt in my mind that it did achieve some measure of success in improving adult literacy and numeracy. I had followed the programme closely. True, the text books were doctrinaire, and the methodology was based on the Cuban model. But in the absence of an alternative programme,

Blaize could have adapted the PRG's adult education programme and clothed it in a new dress so as to make it effective as a catalyst for economic growth.

Blaize chose as his Executive Advisor Nicholas Brathwaite who had served as Chairman of the Interim Government. He could hardly have made a better choice. But Brathwaite soon became disillusioned. Frustration crept in as his advice often went unheeded, and he resigned after two years. According to his own account, he was deeply disturbed by the infighting of ministers, and particularly by the treachery of one of the ministers. This was the main reason for his resignation, but he was also disturbed by the disproportionate amount of influence exerted by the old and loyal brigade of Blaize's "defunct" Grenada National Party (GNP). There seemed to be collusion on the part of the old GNP hierarchy to place the other two parties who had signed the Union Island Accord in a subordinate position. For example, in the 1985 party convention much to Blaize's delight, Francis Alexis was elected Deputy Political Leader over George Brizan, but he was never asked to perform the role of Prime Minister during Blaize's absence from the State. Blaize never fully trusted Brizan because of his earlier association with the New Jewel Movement. One year later Alexis declined nomination for the post of Deputy Political Leader at the party convention. Ben Jones and George Brizan were the two contestants, and Jones won handsomely. This pleased Blaize tremendously.

As Blaize's health deteriorated, a small but influential group in Carriacou started to work in search of a possible successor as parliamentary representative for the constituency of Carriacou and Petit Martinique. This was based on the presumption that Blaize would not seek parliamentary honours at the next general elections. I knew better. The goodly gentleman had no such intention. Anyway, it was felt that Brathwaite, with his wealth of experience in public life, would fit the bill admirably. The possible choice of Brathwaite as a candidate for Carriacou and Petit Martnique began to gain momentum. Whether or not he had by then made up his mind to contest the elections, Brathwaite realized that it would become more and more untenable to continue as Executive Advisor to the Prime Minister. Brathwaite's quiet departure did not cause any stir either in Government or among the populace in general.

One of the highlights of my tenure of office was the visit to Grenada on October 31, 1985 of Her Majesty Queen Elizabeth II, our Head of State. Her visit was one of inspiration and hope, and as a people we felt reassured of the importance and efficacy of the democratic path that we had long chosen to follow. Moreover, her timely presence in Grenada brought renewed confidence in the monarchical system of government. The Queen's previous visit was in 1966 when the current Prime Minister Herbert Blaize was styled Chief Minister in keeping with the constitutional status of the country at that time. Accompanied by His Royal Highness Prince Philip, the Queen disembarked from the Royal Yacht Britannia to a twenty-one-gun salute. The Britannia had anchored designedly in the outer harbour just after 9 a.m. to enable the Queen to come ashore on the Royal Barge as she had wished. Thus Her Majesty was able to enjoy the exquisite beauty of the harbour and the unique scenery of the surrounding hills which encircled the quaint St. George's city with its Georgian red roof tops. It was a very thrilling spectacle as the Royal Barge slowly and majestically with the Queen in full view glided along the placid and sheltered waters of the Carenage, and almost effortlessly berthed alongside the wooden jetty which was specially constructed for the Queen's visit. After greeting the Queen and Prince Philip I presented my wife, and then the Prime Minister and Mrs Blaize to them. A contingent from the Royal Grenada Police Force formed a guard of honour which Her Majesty inspected. The Prime Minister then presented members of Cabinet and their spouses. The hundreds of people who had braved the inclement weather to turn out to welcome the Queen had an opportunity to see the royal visitors at close range and in some cases to talk to them as the Queen and Prince Philip went on a walk about before leaving for a scenic drive in the district of Southern St. George's.

With the Queen's presence in Grenada, her representative, the Governor General, ceased to have any constitutional authority as long as the visit lasted. After all the Queen of Grenada was at home. Therefore, I was virtually stripped of any symbols of authority. The flag at my official residence was pulled down from its pole and replaced by the Royal Standard. My car flag was also removed for the day. At 10.45 a.m. Her Majesty, accompanied by His Royal Highness the Duke of Edinburgh, and attended by the Grenadian Equerry to the Queen, Inspector Daniel Searles, arrived in Parliament courtyard. Upon alighting from the State Car, Her Majesty and His Royal Highness were greeted by my wife and me, after which The Royal Grenada Police Band played the Grenada National Anthem. I then presented Senator the Hon. Lawrence Joseph, President of the Senate, The Hon. Hudson Scipio, Speaker of the House of Representatives and Curtis V. Strachan, Clerk of Parliament. Her Majesty and His Royal Highness were then escorted into the Parliament building by the President of the Senate and the Speaker of the House of Representatives. Amid the pomp and ceremony associated with such an occasion Her Majesty ascended the steps of the Throne to read the Throne speech which was handed to her by the

Prime Minister. Her Majesty began the speech in these words: "I share my Government's desire to uphold and strengthen parliamentary democracy in Grenada and I am delighted to be here today to inaugurate this special session of the Third Parliament." These were powerful words coming from the Queen. They were an endorsement of the return to parliamentary democracy and were of great significance for the future growth of the democratic process. The Queen in the presence of her ministers and other members of the legislature placed her stamp of approval on the people's freedom to choose their own parliamentary representatives and all it entailed.

Following the parliamentary session at York House the Royal party left for Governor General's House where, after a brief rest, the Queen in an impressive investiture ceremony invested with the respective insignias five Grenadians who had been awarded honours on Queen's Birthday 1985. At the same time in another room His Royal Highness presented medals to a number of young Grenadians who had qualified under the Duke of Edinburgh Award Scheme. These two ceremonies were followed by a reception where the Queen and His Royal Highness had yet another opportunity to meet and speak to a number of Grenadians, particularly the honourees and medalists and their relatives. At approximately 12.10 p.m. the Queen and her entourage left Governor General's House for the Royal Yacht Britannia which by then was berthed alongside the pier in the inner harbour.

On board the Queen hosted a luncheon for fifty-six guests. Among them were the upper echelons of the State, the Church and the business community. One couple almost missed their lunch. With the exception of that couple every one had assembled awaiting the presence of Her Majesty, the men in their lounge suits and the ladies in short day dresses in strict compliance with the dress code on the invitation. Time was running out. The Master of the Queen's household appeared to be somewhat anxious when he approached me to find out whether these missing guests had accepted the invitation. When I replied in the affirmative he very seriously said to me that they would not be allowed in after the Queen's arrival. As luck had it, this very senior Government officer and his wife entered the room exactly one minute before Her Majesty arrived, but over half an hour later than the time stated on the invitation, both smartly attired in full evening wear. Whereupon, with typical West Indian humour one of the guests quipped that they were not late, they were too early for dinner. After lunch the Prime Minister and I and our spouses posed with the Queen and His Royal Highness for a photograph. I then had a private audience of Her Majesty.

The next event, a grand rally, was held at Queen's Park, the normal venue for all major sporting events. Long before the start of the rally, and despite the ominous rain bearing clouds above, the public had been assembling to cheer their Queen. At precisely 3.30 p.m. the Queen arrived in an open jeep accompanied by His Royal Highness. The jeep drove through the ranks of uniformed groups and school children before the Royal visitors alighted to be met by the Prime Minister and Mrs Blaize. The Prime Minister then presented members of Parliament and their spouses, other than Cabinet ministers who had met the royal personages earlier in the day. A number of Grenadians in different walks of life, including the oldest Grenadian war veteran, were then presented before the Prime Minister made an address of welcome on behalf of the people of Grenada. Gracelyn Mitchell, a pupil from the School for the Handicapped, presented the Queen with a basket of spices. A cultural performance by school children and big drum dancers from Carriacou followed. In her address, the Queen expressed her deep appreciation and said how delighted she was to be visiting Grenada. She spoke as follows:

"Prime Minister,

Thank you for the kind things you have said and for the basket of spices for which this island is famous. Prince Philip and I greatly appreciate the happy and friendly welcome given to us by the people of Grenada since our arrival this morning. Today has brought back many happy memories of our first visit nearly twenty years ago and I am glad to see that Grenada has lost none of its charm and natural beauty, nor has your welcome lost any of its exuberance and warmth.

In the last few years Grenada has been through momentous events and you have emerged with tremendous credit. As your Queen I want to take this opportunity of congratulating the people of Grenada on the way you have prepared for and carried through the recent parliamentary elections which underlined your commitment to democracy. It has been a notable achievement and the world has watched with admiration. More remains to be done and your friends in the Commonwealth and beyond will help you in the process of reconstruction. You are rightly proud of your country and there is no greater legacy which a people can leave to their children than the stability which you are striving so hard to establish in Grenada.

I congratulate the Grenada Boys' Secondary School on celebrating their centenary. The young people are playing an active part in reconstruction and this should be encouraged. They have unlimited energy and they are not afraid to query the actions of their elders in their march for peace and justice. Adults have a responsibility to recognise the good in the young and to help them to build on it. By the example of decent conduct, honest advice and responsible guidance, adults can ensure that the natural exuberance and fine qualities of young people are channelled in the right direction so that they, the leaders of tomorrow, may be well equipped to enhance the legacy of stability and to maintain the best traditions of their country. The future of your country will be what you make it.

We shall long cherish happy memories of this gathering in Queen's Park of the people of Grenada, Carriacou and Petit Martinique. Our best wishes go with you and I am confident that if you show zeal, industry and patriotism in all you undertake, then this beautiful country can only prosper and grow from strength to strength. May God bless you all."

The Queen and her entourage left Queen's Park for Governor General's House where a garden party was held on the grounds. On Her Majesty's arrival at the party some more Grenadians were presented to her. She then mingled freely with the guests before leaving for the Carenage to witness the beating of the retreat by the men from the Royal Yacht. But as the Royal visitors approached their waiting cars it was discovered that one of the Ladies-in-Waiting was missing. This caused a bit of a bother, and the Queen's Equerry Major Lindsay, was left behind with a command to find her. The Lady-in-Waiting was so engrossed in conversation that she did not observe when the Queen was leaving. However, without any difficulty she was found.

Meanwhile on the Carenage hundreds of people turned out to see the beating of the retreat. I thought it was a fitting spectacle to bring down the curtain on a very busy and hectic day for Her Majesty. After the ceremony the Queen elected to walk rather than to be driven to the nearby pier where the Royal Yacht was berthed. It was the final opportunity for the day for her Grenadian subjects to see her at close range. They waved enthusiastically and exhorted her to come back soon. On board the Royal Yacht the Queen honoured me with the award of Knight Grand Cross of the Royal Victorian Order (GCVO).

Another very important visitor to Grenada was the President Ronald Reagan of the United States of America. A number of high-ranking American officials had dropped by before the President's visit not least of whom was George Bush, the Vice President, who assured us that America would never abandon us in our pursuit of rebuilding our democracy.

Air Force One with the President of the United States of America on board touched down at Point Salines International Airport at 1.10 p.m. on Thursday, February 20, 1986. The President was accorded a 21-gun-salute. Having been apprised of the welcome that awaited him by Florence Rapier, Head of the Grenadian Foreign Service and Roy Haverkamp, the resident American Charge d'Affaires, the President descended the steps of the aircraft to a warm and enthusiastic welcome from the highest officers of State, Cabinet Ministers, the Leader of the Opposition and Chairman of the

Grenada Council of Churches. The Royal Grenada Police Band was at its best when it played the American National Anthem and the Grenada National Anthem. For security and logistic reasons people were asked to stay away from the airport area on the President's arrival. Instead they could line the presidential route or attend the public welcome at Queen's Park where the President was due to make an address later in the day. One could discern that the President was greatly moved by the warmth of the welcome

Before leaving the airport the President unveiled a plaque in honour of the Forces from the United States of America and the Caribbean, especially those who sacrificed their lives in liberating Grenada on October 25, 1983. I accompanied the President to the Grand Anse campus of the St. George's University School of Medicine. At the campus he laid a wreath at the foot of the monument that carried the names of the nineteen American men who had died in combat here in 1983. There were people waiting to see and greet the President all along the route to Governor General's House. The President had a tumultuous welcome as he approached the residence. The vigorous waving of flags and the thunderous applause from the assembled crowd must have pleased him greatly.

At my residence the President retired for a short while before having discussions with me. Then it was the Prime Minister's turn to hold private discussions. After these one-to-one discussions the President held a meeting with the CARICOM Heads of Government who had assembled in Grenada for this purpose. The dining room was transformed into a virtual conference room. This was a closed session and the media personnel had to withdraw after the initial photographs were taken. They repaired to a specially constructed tent on the circular lawn that had been reserved for the Press. The large crowd who had assembled outside the eastern entrance to greet the President had earlier welcomed enthusiastically the Prime Ministers from the other territories as they approached the precincts of Governor General's House. Most of them had supported the October, 1983 initiative, and despite their limited resources had supplied soldiers and policemen to help in the restoration of law and order in Grenada. But there was one discordant note. The Prime Minister of Trinidad and Tobago, George Chambers, did not receive the enthusiastic and cordial welcome meted out to his counterparts. Instead he was severely booed as his car approached Governor General's House. The people obviously remembered his non-committal stance to the efforts of restoring law and order after our troubles here in 1983, and the hardships they had to undergo to obtain a visa in order to enter Trinidad. Immediately after the meeting at Governor General's House, Mr Chambers left for his return journey home. Unlike his colleagues, he absented himself from the Public Welcome at Queen's Park. Whether or not his precipitous departure was pre-planned was open to conjecture.

According to a head count some forty two thousand people entered Queen's Park to see and hear President Reagan. Fortunately, it was a bright and sunny day and the majority of people sat or stood before the temporary pavilion that was specially erected for the dignitaries. After a welcome address by Prime Minister Blaize, the President of the U.S.A. was invited to the microphone amid tremendous applause. As he spoke, that great communicator held the attention of the massive crowd from start to finish. In a speech punctuated by loud applause, he was at times jovial, at times filled with emotion. In a reference to the Caribbean leaders who were sharing the platform with him he told his audience, "We stand before you as friends who share a fundamental belief in democracy. Our commitment to humane and representative government is stronger than any tyrant's chain." He recalled the circumstances in which he responded to the call for help in October, 1983. He admitted that he was completely overwhelmed by the warmth of the welcome he had received in Grenada. He spoke of the beauty of Grenada and the charm and friendliness of its people. He pledged continued support in the rebuilding and strengthening of the democratic process, and he announced a three-year scholarship programme to train 1500 students from the islands each year. This programme would be particularly beneficial to those whose studies in Cuban universities had been prematurely brought to an end. He further announced a five-year $5.5 million programme to help support the judicial systems of the English-speaking Caribbean. President Reagan then enjoyed a cultural performance which was laid on for him. As the President's motorcade left Queen's Park, people were applauding and shouting, "Thank you, Mr President." At the airport the usual compliments were paid to the President before he embarked for his return journey to Washington. Before all this, my wife and I were pleased to be greeted by four of the Seals who had rescued us at our residence on October 25,1983. They had travelled with the President on his five-hour visit.

Very important visitors continued to grace our shores in 1987. His Royal Highness The Prince Edward who had been visiting Barbados in connection with the Duke of Edinburgh Award Scheme availed himself of the opportunity of coming over to Grenada to see how the Scheme was doing here after its dormancy during the revolutionary period between 1979 and 1983. This was not an official visit. When the normal LIAT Flight 301 touched down at Point Salines Airport, The Prince along with his bodyguard and the

Barbadian co-ordinator of the Scheme in the Caribbean emerged from the aircraft ahead of the other passengers. I was there to greet him, and he was our guest for the day. It was Prince Edward's first visit to Grenada.

After breakfast I accompanied the Prince via the Grand Etang route to the St. Andrew's Anglican Secondary School on the east coast where he met participants and leaders of the Duke of Edinburgh Award Scheme from St. Andrew's parish. We took the alternative east coast road on our return journey to St. George's. This was to give our royal visitor an opportunity to see as much as possible of Grenada. At a special fund raising luncheon at my residence for the benefit of the Scheme in Grenada, the Prince met all the guests as they entered the House and later briefly addressed them on the Duke of Edinburgh Award Scheme. After lunch the Prince went to the Grenada Boys' Secondary School for a meeting similar to the one held in St. Andrew's earlier. Here he met participants and leaders of the Scheme from the St. George's area. The Prince then had an hour of sight seeing around St. George's with brief stops at Fort George and Fort Frederick before his return flight to Barbados.

His Excellency Dr. Jaime Lusinchi, President of the Republic of Venezuela, landed at Point Salines International Airport at approximately 12.45 p.m. on Friday July 17, 1987. His was not a State visit. It was more or less a familiarization tour and public relations exercise. However, he was accorded the courtesies befitting a visiting President. I received the President at Governor General's House for a brief discussion, and he stayed on for a luncheon which I gave in his honour. Covers were laid for forty-five guests consisting of Venezuelans and Grenadians. The President then journeyed to the Prime Minister's Office in the Botannical Gardens to hold wide- ranging discussions with Prime Minister Blaize, during which time they signed an agreement on narcotics.

In September of that year my wife and I went on a State Visit to the Co-operative Republic of Guyana at the kind invitation of President Desmond Hoyte. We were accompanied by Mrs Abigail Sandy, my Personal Assistant, Adrian Hayes, Protocol Officer and Guyanese-born Lennox Halley, my ADC. The excellent relationship which once existed between Georgetown and St. George's had suffered a severe decline since the military intervention of 1983. Forbes Burnham, the then President, had distanced himself from the military operations and, in fact, was openly against them. He saw the intervention as an unnecessary and merciless onslaught on the sovereignty of a small and vulnerable island State. When Burnham died in August 1985, Hoyte was elevated to the Presidency, and at best relationship between our two countries could be rightly described as lukewarm.

President Hoyte had flown into Grenada on Wednesday, May 6, to attend the funeral of Mrs Audrey Palmer Hawks who had made an enormous contribution to the development of Caribbean tourism. It was over a private luncheon at my residence that Hoyte first invited me to visit Guyana officially. It was quite obvious to me that the President wanted to see a strengthening of the ties of friendship between Guyana and Grenada.

Thus my visit to Guyana was of great significance in terms of diplomacy and public relations. The programme for my visit was so well structured that I was able to meet the largest possible cross section of Guyanese, from dignitaries to market vendors, from professionals and university lecturers to farm workers, from school children to senior citizens. At the State Dinner held in my honour the President himself summarized the purpose of my visit in these words: "We in Guyana regard your visit as a very important step for further development of the friendly relations that have traditionally existed between the peoples of our countries."

I had a most colourful and enthusiastic welcome. I was met by the Director of Protocol who escorted my party and me from the aircraft and introduced us to His Excellency the President and other members of the official welcoming party, the Chief of Staff, Guyana Defence Force, the Commissioner of Police and the Director General, Guyana National Service. While all this was going on I received a twenty-one-gun salute. After inspecting the Guard of Honour and having completed the ceremonial niceties associated with such a visit I met the assembled dignitaries among whom were Ministers of Government, senior Government officials, and members of the diplomatic corps from both east and west of the ideological divide. The notable absentee was the Cuban Ambassador who declared, as I learnt later, that he would not breathe the same air I breathed. In fact I understood that he was out of the country for the duration of my visit.

At the Civic Ceremony which was held at the Botanic Gardens, Georgetown, in an area quite close to the beautiful hump-backed kissing bridge, the Mayor of Georgetown in a stirring address welcomed me warmly and presented me with the keys of the city. I replied suitably, conveying greetings from the Government and people of Grenada and recalling the contributions Guyanese nationals had made and were still making in areas of Grenadian life, not least in the fields of Education, Law and Administration. Once the more formal part of the ceremony was over we were able to chat informally with members of the City Council and others who had come out to welcome us. My wife and I ended the day by attending a State Dinner hosted by President Hoyte at State House.

There was so much to see in this vast 83,000 square-mile country that during the next six days we were taken to a different area every day, and even then this constituted only a small portion of the country. On every occasion we were accompanied by a senior Minister of Government. I laid a floral tribute at the 1763 Monument in Georgetown. This bronze monument conceived by Guyanese artist, Phillip Moore, was built to honour the heroes of the 1763 Revolution which took place in Berbice. Under the leadership of Cuffy, a house slave, the Revolution sought to put an end to forced labour and the plantation system then existing in Guyana. It was the first blow struck by Guyanese for their freedom and Cuffy became Guyana's first National Hero.

One of the areas that greatly interested me was the Rupununi region. The flight from Timehri to Lethem exposed me to the varied hinterland of grasslands and tropical forests traversed by rivers the size of which we were not used to in the islands. We then visited Karanambo Ranch where we had lunch in the main ranch house, the only original pioneer home still standing in the Rupununi. The combination of savannah and rain forest in an area that boasts outstanding tropical fresh-water fishing makes Karanambo very attractive. Perched on the Rupununi River with its brick and palm thatched buildings in a gravelled compound beside a private air strip, this settlement had the flavour of an Amerindian village. We also visited Dadanawa Ranch, the largest ranch in the country where we saw an exhibition of bull fighting. Our helicopter then zoomed its way south of the Kanuku Mountain Range and touched down at Sand Creek, some sixteen miles away on the right bank of the Sand River, a tributary of the Rupununi River. There we visited an Amerindian village and school. We spoke to many of the villagers whose main occupations are cultivation of bitter cassava, corn and ground provision at the foot of the mountain, cattle rearing in the savannah and balata bleeding in the forest. Their health needs are supplied by a resident Medex, community Health worker and Malaria personnel. We were accompanied on our visit to the Rupununi area by Hamilton Green, Prime Minister and First Vice-President, who enlightened me on much of the history and culture of Guyana.

Carl Greenidge, Senior Minister for Finance, escorted us to the Kimbia National Service Training Centre situated on the left bank of the Bukuruma Creek, approximately ninety-five miles south from New Amsterdam, up the Berbice River. There we were able to observe the young residents at work in their skills training classes. We had lunch with them and afterwards thoroughly enjoyed a cultural performance put on by them. On leaving Kimbia we made our way to the majestic Kaieteur Falls with its sheer drop of 822 feet.

The following day, accompanied by the President, we went to Linden, the bauxite town. A very special programme was arranged for us by the people of Linden. We were driven to the Mackenzie Sports Club for a civic welcome. Among the crowd was a Grenadian, then resident in Linden, who more or less insisted that he should say a few words. He had come to the rally with a prepared speech. Although we were pressed for time, the Mayor complied and Mr Gairy, a relative of Sir Eric Gairy, proudly went up to the rostrum and made his presentation. I signed the Visitor's Book and then left for Watooka Day School where we happily met the staff and students who greeted us in song. We then proceeded to the East Montgomery Mine where the General Manager and the Acting Mines Manager explained to us the mining operations before visiting the Bauxite Plant. A most sumptuous lunch in a most convivial and relaxed atmosphere at Watooka House Annex brought an end to our Linden visit.

On Friday, September 18, under the guidance of Dr. Patrick Mckenzie, Senior Minister for Agriculture, we visited the Mahaica/Mahaicony/Abary Agriculture Development Authority (MMA-ADA). This covers a large irrigation project for the enhancement of agriculture over a very wide area. Then on we went to the Institute of Applied Science and Technology where we observed the way forward in the manufacture of local products and afterwards visited the Ruimzight Rice Mill. In the evening my wife and I hosted a reception at the National Cultural Centre. We were pleased to meet so many Grenadians resident in Guyana as well as Guyanese nationals.

Our Saturday morning was taken up with visits to the La Bonne Intention Estate and the dairy farm at Liliendaal. The former, comprising an area of over 12,000 acres of land, is situated on the East Coast of Demerara and owned and operated by the Guyana Sugar Corporation . In the presence of the Minister for Agriculture we were given an overview of the productive efforts of this estate which has an approximate annual production of 20,000 tons of sugar. We were given a conducted tour of the sugar factory. At Liliendaal we were shown the steps taken in the production of milk and the use of modern technology in that process.

Sunday morning market is a grand affair in Georgetown. So, accompanied by Mrs Yvonne Harewood-Benn, Minister for Information and the Public Service, we paid a visit to Bourda Market. We mingled with the vendors and the shoppers, we got a greater insight into the Guyanese wit and humour, and we had a greater appreciation of the industrious nature of the people. Later in the morning, the President called on me at Herdmanston House when we held discussions on matters of topical interest in both the Caribbean and the international community. Among other things, I told the

President how impressed I was by the strides being made in import substitution in Guyana and to observe how the people were making such good use of locally grown and locally made products. I was also forcibly struck by the Government's Housing Programme. The President and I agreed that my presence in Guyana would have augured well for the future strengthening of the bonds of friendship and understanding between our countries. President Hoyte returned to Herdmanston House in mid afternoon to accompany us to the airport where we had a ceremonial departure.

Guyana was not the only Commonwealth country which had given Grenada a cold shoulder. Since the military intervention of October, 1983, the relationship between New Delhi and St. George's was strained. At the 1983 Commonwealth Heads of Government meeting held in India, Indira Gandhi, Prime Minister of India, led an onslaught on the American Government for sending troops to Grenada. From her vituperations and notwithstanding her socialist tendencies it was clear that she did not understand the true import of Bishop's revolution in terms of the sufferings of a large segment of the Grenadian community, the loss of democratic freedom, the social dislocation, the outward migratory wave of some of our best skilled compatriots. Her attitude towards Grenada fell short of severing diplomatic relations. She had ordered her High Commissioner to stay out of Grenada since 1983. Therefore, when His Excellency Shiv Kumar on Wednesday, February 3, 1988, presented his letters of Commission to me it was an act of renewal of active diplomatic relationship between our two countries. Prime Minister Blaize had attended the 1985 Commonwealth Heads of Government Meeting in the Bahamas. At that meeting he was at pains to enlighten his Commonwealth colleagues as to what really happened in Grenada during the communist inspired revolution. Blaize reported to me that after speaking to his counterparts many of them said: "Now I know."

On Wednesday, February 10, 1988, my wife and I journeyed to New York to participate in the belated celebration of Grenada's independence anniversary. We were the principal guests of the Celebrations Committee who were gracious enough to postpone their celebrations for one week in order to facilitate our presence. I could not be in New York on February 7, the actual date of our independence anniversary, because of the many pressing duties at home associated with our local celebrations. What is more the observance of Independence Anniversary was too important an occasion to miss. On arrival at Kennedy Airport we were met by Ambassador Lamuel Stanislaus, our representative at the United Nations, and a representative from the State Department. On that bitterly cold February evening we were quickly whisked off to The Sheraton Centre at 7$^{th}$ Avenue on 52$^{nd}$ Street in Manhattan which would be our home for the next five days. The following morning in the absence of the Secretary General who was out of town I called on Ambassador Reid at the United Nations. Reid was the Under Secretary General with responsibility for the General Assembly and for political affairs. We then had a conducted tour of the United Nations building. Afterwards, we made our way to the nearby church of the Holy Family where a thanksgiving mass was said for Grenada. The congregation was made up mainly of diplomats and Grenadian nationals living in the New York area. I read the first lesson at the mass, delivered a short address, and my wife and I received Holy Communion. At the end of the mass, refreshment was served at the presbytery where I embraced the opportunity to meet the Grenadian nationals and to talk to the ambassadors and other diplomats who were gracious enough to attend the mass.

In the evening of Friday, February 12, the big event took place at the Sheraton Center in one of its ballrooms. This event took the form of a dinner/dance which was well organized and well attended. Our Charge d'Affaires from Washington, Harry Ogilvie and Mrs Ogilvie were present. So, too, was our United Nations Ambassador. Friends of Grenada from all walks of life and Grenadian nationals all mingled together to enrich the conviviality that was so evident in the ballroom. The press and radio were there to record the proceedings. I gave an address and later received a citation from Partners of America. The Caribbean-American Chamber of Commerce presented me with an enlarged photograph of Martin Luther King. In turn, at the instance of the organizing committee, I presented awards to the St. George's Medical School, *The Everybody's Magazine*, and the *Carib News*.

On Sunday, February 14, we attended a special service at the St. Augustine Episcopal Church in Brooklyn. Ambassador Stanislaus accompanied us. The officiating pastor was Fr. Henry, a West Indian. The service was a most lively one with clapping, bodily movements, and frequent bouts of emotion. Here again I read a lesson and addressed the congregation. The homily was preached by Pastor Oden of the Seventh Day Adventist Church. He delivered a most stirring sermon on black history. Later we were luncheon guests of Ambassador and Mrs Stanislaus at their home on Rutland Avenue. On the following day it was good-bye to New York.

One of the main features of the Blaze administration was the frequency with which the Prime Minister's parliamentary colleagues deserted him.

The rate of defection was high, and during the closing stages of his term of office he found himself at the head of a minority Government. A majority of 14 to 1 in December, 1984, was reduced to a minority of 6 to 9 in the latter part of 1989. Yet the Prime Minister showed no signs of wanting to step down. In June, 1989, one of his fellow Prime Ministers speaking on behalf of others suggested to Blaize, in the privacy of his official residence, that it might be appropriate for him to relinquish office immediately after the CARICOM Heads of Government summit which was to take place in Grenada within a matter of days. He went on to say that the upcoming meeting would provide a good opportunity for Heads of Government assembled in Grenada to pay tribute to their Grenadian counterpart. Blaize in his usual manner listened intently. When no comment was forthcoming from him, his fellow Prime Minister sought a reply to take back to those on whose behalf he had come. Blaize simply said to him, "Tell them you spoke to me and I listened to you."

Fortunately for Blaize, not all his parliamentary defectors were speaking the same political language. So he could still depend on the votes of some of his erstwhile colleagues to get certain measures passed in Parliament. He was shrewd and experienced enough not to introduce any controversial measure in the House of Representatives. Kenny Lalsingh, the representative of St. Patrick's West and Parliamentary Secretary in the Ministry of Works, was relieved of his ministerial responsibilities because of alleged impropriety in the conduct of his duties. He was the first to withdraw his support. He was soon followed by Phinsley St. Louis who had won the South St. George seat in the general elections. This constituency had been the stronghold of Sir Eric Gairy who personally held it from the time he entered frontline politics in the 1950's. However, for some unknown reason Gairy did not offer himself as a candidate in the 1984 elections. Despite Gairy's open boast that his party, the GULP, would win the elections, I think he deeply felt that neither he nor his party could be victorious in the elections. Also, he had real concerns about his personal safety. Hence the reason he kept away from the electioneering meetings.

By virtue of his victory at the polls and having won such an important seat, St. Louis had expected a ministerial position, and thus a seat in Cabinet. Blaize obviously thought that St. Louis was not ministerial material. In discussing ministerial appointments Blaize always impressed upon me how very careful he was in selecting people to sit in Cabinet. He always chose from among the best available. Drawing on my experience as Governor General I have found that many parliamentarians have certain misconceptions about Government, about the role of the Prime Minister, about the role of Cabinet, and indeed about their own role as elected representatives of the people. One persistent misconception is that an elected member must be made a minister or at least a parliamentary secretary, and in this regard they should be given preference over members of the Senate. They seem not to understand that the people elected them as their representatives in Parliament, not as Ministers of Government. The latter is within the prerogative of the Prime Minister and the Prime Minister only. Many of them do not realize that the Prime Minister can fire any of his Ministers without giving reasons to anyone for so doing. Parliamentarians are servants of the people. They were not elected in order to find lucrative jobs in Government. Service, not personal gain, should chart their expectations and should be the driving force behind their every action.

The greatest blow of all to Blaize was the resignation of two senior Cabinet ministers, Hon. George Brizan, Minister for Education and Hon. Francis Alexis, Attorney General and Minister for Legal Affairs. They had been signatories of the Union Island accord that brought into being the New National Party. When they made their contribution to the budget debate in the House of Representatives on Friday, April 10, 1987, they were both highly critical of the budget for fiscal year 1987. They spoke in similar vein but George Brizan, in particular, made some very caustic remarks in Parliament about the budget, and stressed that he had been issuing warnings about the weakness of Government's fiscal policy but the Prime Minister never heeded his advice. The main point of contention was Government's intention as part of its fiscal strategy to make redundant 1800 workers without providing for their retraining for special work or otherwise. The private sector could not absorb them. All this was happening at a time when Government had failed to settle its long-standing salaries dispute with the public sector trade unions. One would have thought that these two senior ministers were speaking from the Opposition benches. Clearly such behaviour constituted a breach of the doctrine of collective responsibility whereby ministers are bound by decisions taken in Cabinet and in this case the budget proposals had the blessings of Cabinet before they were presented to Parliament.

I had an early Monday morning visit from the Prime Minister who advised me on the behaviour of two of his Cabinet ministers in Parliament three days before and how he intended to deal with such behaviour. Later in the day the two ministers sought an audience with me because, in their terminology, an emergency had arisen. At the time I was watching a game of cricket at Queen's Park between St. Lucia and Dominica in the Windward Islands Youth Tournament. After the first two sessions of play I returned to my office, and one would have thought that the honourable gentlemen had been watching my movements, as they were quick on my heels. They were accompanied by one of their colleagues, Tillman Thomas, a barrister who had been incarcerated without trial during the Bishop regime and was now Representative of St. Patrick East and Parliamentary Secretary in the Ministry of Legal Affairs. Although I was aware of their unorthodox performance in Parliament, admittedly I was taken by surprise when they informed me that they had decided to quit Government and handed me their letters of resignation. I in turn pleaded the cause of stability and tried to persuade them to think again. But their minds had been clearly made up. Earlier that day the Prime Minister had asked them to publicly retract the sentiments they expressed in Parliament three days previously or resign. They chose the latter. Brizan, who was more vocal than Alexis, intimated to me that his father would turn in his grave if he offered an apology to Herbert Blaize. They also resigned from the New National Party. In solidarity with his two colleagues, the Hon. Tillman Thomas also resigned from the Party and gave up his Parliamentary Secretary portfolio. Having closely monitored the work and attitudes of Cabinet members, and fully cognizant of the personal ambitions of some of them I came to the conclusion that these gentlemen would have resigned eventually. They grasped the opportunity when Blaize sought an apology from them, and, it seemed, this incident was the occasion rather than the cause of their resignation.

The disintegration of the Union Island accord was no longer in doubt. The opinion in some quarters that it was really a ploy to ensure that Gairy and his GULP were kept out of Government was gaining ready acceptance by an increasing number of people who had welcomed the initiative previously. One of the casualties of these disturbing movements was Marcel Peters, Leader of the Opposition and representative of St. Andrew North East who by then was a virtual independent in the House of Representatives. He seemed to have removed himself from the GULP when he had defied his political leader by accepting the post of Leader of the Opposition. This position gave him the constitutional right to advise the Governor General on the appointment of three senators in the thirteen-member Senate. Thus changes in the leadership of the Opposition invariably meant changes in the Senate in respect of senators appointed by the Governor General on the advice of the Leader of the Opposition. Phinsley St. Louis and Kenny Lalsingh notified me on January 30, 1987, that they were working together as opposition in the House of Representatives. They further informed me that they had been holding discussions with the Hon. Marcel Peters, Leader of the Opposition. Five days later I received the Opposition Leader who came to inform me that he had been having "fruitful discussions" with the other two opposition members. On February 13, Peters resigned as Leader of the Opposition and I appointed Hon. Phinsley St. Louis to replace him. Similarly when Brizan, Alexis and Tillman Thomas crossed the floor and joined the ranks of the Opposition, St. Louis stepped down as Leader of the Opposition and the path was clear for me to appoint Hon. George Brizan whom I thought was the one most likely to command the support of the majority of members on the Opposition benches.

By mid-1988 the body politic was severely bruised. This was exacerbated by resignations no less than by Blaize's deteriorating health. While a patient at the St. George's General Hospital, Blaize's condition worsened and he was flown to Walter Reed Army Hospital in the U.S.A. for further medical attention. It was acutely felt throughout the country that the end of his political career was near. Some were of the view that he should advise the Governor General to dissolve Parliament and call new elections. Others expressed the hope that he would be able to soldier on until the life of the current parliament expired. But there was unanimity in the thought that the name Herbert Augustus Blaize would no longer appear on the ballot paper.

While all the political meanderings were taking place, Dr. Keith Mitchell, the youthful and energetic Minister for Works who had earlier distanced himself from Dr. Francis Alexis, his one-time political leader, assumed the role of General Secretary of the New National Party. This gave Mitchell an opportunity to travel throughout the tri-island State and interface with as many people as possible from all walks of life. He got to know the electorate, and gained an insight into their own thoughts and expectations. Equally, and perhaps more importantly, the electorate, especially the members of the ruling NNP, availed themselves of the opportunity to get to know the man, Keith Mitchell, and to assess his sincerity and sense of purpose. As Minister for Works he had done a most commendable job in bringing electricity to the remotest of the rural areas. Rural electrification rose from 45% in 1986 to 95% in 1989. His road improvement programme with specific reference to feeder roads won him the admiration of friend and foe alike. He was doubtlessly a man of action. He was always on the move, visiting projects, meeting the people and trying to ascertain their needs at first hand. He was not a desk-bound minister. Prime Minister Blaize had been giving Mitchell every support and encouragement for the worthwhile initiatives emanating from the Ministry of Works. Whatever his political opponents might say about him there was no denying that he was easily approachable, he was industrious, and he had the knack of getting on well with people.

A political party convention always arouses great interest. It is an occasion for reflection. It is also a time for projecting plans for the future. The social aspect of these conventions must not be glossed over. For the co-mingling of the party stalwarts from all the constituencies provides a forum for exchanging ideas, for learning from the experiences of others, and for eating and drinking together. It is usually an all day meeting when delegates from all the constituencies assemble from early morning in exciting expectation particularly to hear the speech of the Party Leader who invariably is also the Prime Minister, or the Leader of the Opposition depending, of course, on whether he sits on the government benches or the opposition benches in Parliament. Sometimes they get a bonus by listening to a keynote address from a guest speaker who, more often than not, is a political leader from one of the other Caribbean territories. This does not mean that people outside politics do not deliver the lead speech. Resident diplomats also attend these conventions as it is an opportunity to feel the political pulse of the country, to observe the mood of the participants, and to take note of what new plans the party may have in store and to assess what impact these may have on Government policy. To a great extent, the rest of the country anxiously awaits any new pronouncement which, when translated into Government policy, may well affect Grenadian citizens as individuals or as members of some specific group or non-profit-making organization.

Because of Blaize's protracted illness the NNP convention which had been originally scheduled for December, 1988, had to be postponed to January 21, 1989. The entire country was anxiously awaiting the outcome of this very special convention which was most likely the last before General Elections. Would there be any surprises? Any important announcement? These were the questions being asked. There was great speculation that the Party Leader would give some hint as to when the next elections would be held. Most people thought it would be appropriate to hold elections just after the CARICOM heads of Government meeting which was to be held in Grenada under the chairmanship of the Prime Minister of Grenada during the first week in July. This speculation gained much currency because of Blaize's ill-health.

The delegates from the fifteen constituencies were present in full strength. There were also some from overseas representing the party support groups abroad. Each of our political parties has its own support group of Grenadians resident overseas. They are particularly active in New York and London where there are large numbers of Grenadian residents, and one of their main functions is to raise funds for their party especially at election time.

One of the key issues on the agenda was the election of a party leader. In normal circumstances this agenda item would cause no flurry on the convention floor. But coming as it did in the wake of so many parliamentary defections, and because of the leader's growing physical discomforts, it was bound to be accompanied by a heightened degree of emotion and excitement. All indications were that a tough contest was in sight. Barring the voluntary resignation of the leader, it was customary for him to be re-elected at the annual party convention. People outside the party would not at all be surprised if Blaize had announced that he was demitting office as political leader and Prime Minister. However, once he allowed his name to be put up for the leadership contest one would normally expect that he would be re-elected. If this was the feeling outside the convention hall, it was certainly not so within the hall where the majority of delegates had other ideas. Indeed, when the vote was taken for the selection of a leader, Keith Mitchell, the General Secretary of the Party, emerged victorious. One could well imagine the consternation of the Blaize supporters at the convention. Blaize, of course, in his usual manner seemed unruffled, and appeared to have accepted his defeat with grace. He showed no sign of anger or resentment, though he had never expected Mitchell to contest the party leadership against him. He felt betrayed and this was re-echoed by his party supporters, because Blaize was beginning to see in Mitchell the makings of an astute and committed politician. What was more he had been pleased that Mitchell remained loyal to him, while others abandoned him at a time when they should subdue their personal ambitions and instead pull together for the common good of the party and the country.

Should the Rt. Hon. Herbert Blaize continue as Prime Minister? That was the question. Not unexpectedly, the view was expressed that the Governor General should automatically replace Blaize by Mitchell. In all my public life I have never known myself to operate as a robot, and as Governor General was always guided not by the opinion of a few, but by the provisions of the Constitution, the supreme law of the land. Nowhere in the Constitution is mention made of political parties, and the Governor General is under no obligation to function in accordance with the dictates of any political party. The Constitution places the responsibility on the Governor General to appoint as Prime Minister "a member of the House of Representatives who appears to him likely to command the support of the majority of the members of the House."

Notwithstanding the results of the leadership contest at the latest NNP convention, Dr. the Hon. Keith Claudius Mitchell did not appear to me likely to command majority support in the House of Representatives. In any case Mitchell who continued to serve in Government as Minister of Works showed no interest in the Premiership. Nor did I have any representation

from members of the House of Representatives with respect to withdrawing their support from the incumbent Prime Minister. In a display of
magnanimity Mitchell in his acceptance speech as Party Leader made it
known to the convention that he would continue to give loyal support to the
Prime Minister who he expected to stay on as Head of Government until the
next general elections. He would be pleased to continue serving as Minister
for Works, or in any other capacity in accordance with the wishes of the
Prime Minister. He reminded his listeners of their responsibility to give
ready support to the Prime Minister and the Government. Mitchell also
sought the help of those present in mobilizing the electorate as he prepared
to lead the party into the next elections.

Some attorneys posing as experts in constitutional law and evidently not
blessed with a heavy load of clients' business found the time to make silly
emotional noises to the effect that a constitutional crisis existed in Grenada.
Some misguided and ill-informed journalists joined the handful of lawyers in
their cry that our country was facing a constitutional crisis. As far as I was
concerned there was no constitutional crisis in the country, there was no
danger looming on the horizon, and therefore there was no need for me to take
any pre-emptive action to avert any danger which was more imaginary than
real. So Blaize soldiered on as Prime Minister. He made no statement to the
nation or to the press on the outcome of the party convention, and he refused
to comment on his own future. He immediately had Ben Jones, his trusted and
loyal friend and colleague, appointed Deputy Prime Minister with effect from
January 31, 1989, thus by-passing the more youthful and exuberant Mitchell.
This appointment gave a clear signal to the nation that the Prime Minister was
determined to carry on, and at the same time sent an equally clear message to
Mitchell that Jones was the second in command in Cabinet and in the
Government. Without doubt Blaize was gradually becoming a lame duck
Prime Minister. Because of the uncertainty about the political future and in the
knowledge that parliamentary elections could not be very far off prospective
investors were beginning to put their plans on hold. George Brizan, who had
earlier parted company with the NNP and subsequently became Leader of the
Opposition, was busy with the help of Francis Alexis and others organizing a
new political grouping entitled the National Democratic Congress. In January,
1989, Nicholas Brathwaite was elected as Leader of the National Democratic
Congress. Doubtlessly, he would be a candidate for the Carriacou and Petit
Martinique constituency at the next election whether or not Herbert Blaize
was contesting. With great interest I watched this political drama unfold.

The annual CARICOM Heads of Government meeting was due to take
place in Grenada from July 3 to 7. The Prime Minister of Grenada was the

current Chairman of CARICOM, and he was looking forward to a successful summit under his chairmanship, which he no doubt perceived as a crowning glory during his premiership. It was in the interest of all the parliamentarians that this meeting should come about without any hitches, and there seemed to have been a voluntary cessation of bickering and defection, at least for the time being. For parliamentarians on both sides of the House the holding of such a meeting in Grenada was not a divisive issue, and their co-operation was readily forthcoming to ensure that the visiting delegations were well received and looked after.

The weather forecast for Wednesday, June 28, was a good one with the barometric pressure above normal. Bright sunshine would prevail with no chance of rain. The civil service delegations were already in Grenada for preliminary meetings in preparation for the summit. Alas! By mid-morning the day turned out to be grim as shock waves were felt in the hearts of most Grenadians. As if the horrendous events at Fort George in 1983 were not enough, Grenadians had to bear yet another massacre at the same venue some six years afterwards. Grafton Bascombe, a senior police officer on secondment from St. Vincent who up until Monday, June 26, was Assistant Commissioner of Police in Grenada, walked into the office of Cosmos Raymond, Acting Commissioner of Police, and fatally shot him at point blank range. Bascombe then proceeded to the office of the Deputy Commissioner of Police where a meeting was being held. There he wielded his gun, shooting at and wounding Deputy Commissioner Collis Barrow and Assistant Superintendent Daniel Searles. Both men had to be rushed to the nearby hospital. In the process, trigger-happy Bascombe shot dead John Butler, an American diplomat. The other two people in the room, Superintendents Darius and Sullivan, and another American diplomat escaped unhurt, Darius just barely. Bascombe was then apprehended and taken to the Criminal Investigation Department where he died of a heart attack. I was in audience with Mr Frank Leukaran, Director of the local office of the Organisation of the American States, when I received the incredible news. I was moved to bring the audience to an abrupt end. Work seemed to have halted instantaneously as a cloud of sadness rested over my residence. Some of my staff were actually in tears. They specially remembered Raymond as a kind but firm man during his three-year stint as my aide-de-camp.

Butler was a young affable American diplomat who was respected and well liked by the Grenadian community. His untimely passing evoked torrents of condolences from the general populace. His body was flown to the U.S.A. for burial. Because of the Heads of Government meeting that was to be followed immediately by the state visit of the President of Guyana, Raymond's funeral could not take place before July 16.

Amid the shock and grief that Grenadians were yet again experiencing the public service technocrats already in Grenada for the CARICOM meeting continued their work peacefully as they prepared the various briefs and papers for consideration by the Heads of Government. Prime Minister Blaize and I had a long discussion on the extent to which the unfortunate events on Fort George would affect the forthcoming summit. We both concluded that the meeting should be held as scheduled, and we saw no reason why the senseless slaying at Police Headquarters should have any adverse bearing on the meeting particularly in terms of security. All logistics preparation was proceeding apace unfettered and unhindered. The people in this "right little tight little island" (to re-echo the words of our late statesman, Theophilous Albert Marryshow) were looking forward to welcoming the Caribbean leaders and would certainly rise to the occasion, as they were wont to do in circumstances like these, and ensure that the summit was a resounding success. But Prime Minister James Mitchell of St. Vincent and the Grenadines thought otherwise. He was shouting from the rooftops that because of the recent unfortunate occurrences at Fort George it would be unsafe to hold the meeting in Grenada. And as if he was some latter day expert on Grenadian affairs, he went out of his way to get his colleagues to agree to move the meeting from St. George's. He did not have his way. Prime Minister Herbert Blaize firmly rejected the posture and proposal of his Vincentian counterpart and gave every assurance to the regional Heads of Government that what had happened at Fort George was an isolated case and had no adverse effect on security. He reiterated his invitation to them and re-assured them that it would be perfectly safe to come to Grenada. Blaize was right. Mitchell's prognosis was dismally faulty.

The CARICOM meeting was a huge success. The Prime Minister of St. Vincent was in attendance and he could bear testimony to its success. The opening session at the packed auditorium of the Grenada Boys' Secondary School set the mood for the week-long conference. In a colourful and impressive inaugural ceremony under the chairmanship of Roderick Rainford, Secretary General of the Caribbean Community (CARICOM), the audience was treated to speeches which struck at the chords of Caribbean unity and which were all punctuated by wit and good humour. All thirteen member States of the Community were represented, twelve by their Heads of Government. The Prime Minister of Antigua and Barbuda, and outgoing Chairman of the Conference, the Rt. Hon. Vere C. Bird, Sr. was unable to attend. His Deputy Prime Minister represented him.

The Rt. Hon. Herbert Blaize delivered the opening address in his capacity as Chairman of the Conference. His genuine and cordial words of welcome dispelled all doubts about the efficacy of holding the meeting in Grenada. He warned that in order to ensure survival in the global village there was no other choice for Caribbean people other than mutual co-operation and joint efforts. He reminded his colleagues and the rest of his audience that it was necessary to reconfirm that West Indians were one people, with the same heritage, the same history, the same culture and the same destiny. Their alternatives for the future were very clear: "Common prosperity through joint efforts to tackle widely regional problems or mutual self-destruction through confrontation." For His Excellency Desmond Hoyte, the President of the Co-operative Republic of Guyana, the occasion was a nostalgic one. As he addressed the audience on familiar ground he could not resist the pleasant temptation to put aside briefly his prepared text and reminisce on his teaching years at the Grenada Boys' Secondary School and the spontaneous friendliness and hospitality of the Grenadian people. His mind must have gone back to the first day of term when masters in full academic robes walked in dignified procession to take up their positions on that very stage from which he spoke for the opening exercises of the new school term. Speeches were also delivered by Prime Minister Michael Manley of Jamaica, Prime Minister Kennedy Simmonds of St. Kitts and Nevis and Prime Minister A. N. R. Robinson of Trinidad and Tobago. Over and over the heads stressed the importance of Caribbean integration on all fronts. For the solving of national and regional problems which were becoming more and more complex they advocated a joint approach embracing Government, the private sector, the trade unions, the professionals, the Church, and other non-governmental organizations.

Their very comprehensive conference agenda covered four main areas: economic, financial and trade co-operation within the Community and Common Market; external economic and political relations; functional co-operation; and institutional development within the Community. They noted with satisfaction the progress made towards the establishment of a Caribbean Court of Appeal to replace the British Privy Council as the final Court of judicature. In a move to strengthen the integration process and to further stimulate the growth of democracy in the region the Conference agreed to establish an Assembly of Caribbean Community Parliamentarians. This proposal was passionately presented by The Rt. Hon. L. Erskine Sandiford, Distinguished Prime Minister of Barbados. The Assembly would be a deliberative body without legislative powers, and it would not encroach on the sovereignty of Member States. It would be a new forum for serious discussion of regional issues, and will act as a fillip in the formation of regional public opinion. At the end of the Conference the Heads issued the Grand Anse Declaration. This declaration was designed to advance the integration movement and embodied a work programme with specific initiatives to be implemented within four years. In this Declaration they pledged themselves to the fulfilment of all remaining obligations of the Treaty of Chaguaramas by July 4, 1993, the twentieth anniversary of CARICOM.

The camaraderie among the CARICOM leaders at a dinner which my wife and I hosted in their honour matched the conviviality which they had experienced two days earlier in the same venue at a reception following the opening session of the conference. The Heads had an opportunity to meet a wide cross section of Grenadians as well as other Caribbean people who were visiting for the conference. The working sessions of the meeting were held behind closed doors at the Ramada Renaissance Hotel on Grand Anse beach. The meeting was a triumph for Prime Minister Blaize who was chairing such a conference for the first time. Ominously and sadly it might well be for the last time as well. He was pleased that there was no security problem and his guests enjoyed their stay in comfort and safety.

My wife and I were on hand to welcome the President of Guyana and Mrs Hoyte, our house guests for the next four days. Undoubtedly this State visit of President Hoyte was a further step towards strengthening the relationship between Georgetown and St. George's. The heavy and persistent rainfall throughout the visit did not prevent the President from strictly observing the programme that the local authorities had prepared for him. It was decided that the visit would officially start with a parade of police and other uniformed groups and a cultural performance at the Alston George Park in Victoria on the morning of Saturday, July 8. The inclement weather apart, our guests admittedly enjoyed the scenic drive along the west coast from St. George's to the small but crowded town of Victoria. The rain drenched field and the continuous pouring rain caused the abandonment of the parade and a curtailment of the cultural performance. After two brief speeches and the presentation of dignitaries to the President and Mrs Hoyte we moved to Diamond Plantation House, the Perottes residence, for refreshments. This house, perched on a hill in the middle of the plantation, commands a most gorgeous view of the ocean, of the plantation and of the town of Victoria. We then continued up the coast road to the northern and historic town of Sauteurs where we made a brief stop at Leapers Hill where the warlike Caribs had jumped into the sea rather than surrender to the invading French. Our next stop was at rural Morne Fendue where we were entertained to lunch in yet another plantation house, the home of Mrs Betty Mascoll. Our onward journey then took us to the bustling market town of Grenville on the east coast where we visited the large nutmeg processing station to learn how the nutmegs were treated before export. The removal of the mace which clothed the outer shell of the nutmeg, the cracking of the shell to get to the kernel fascinated some of the President's entourage who had thought that the mace was a separate and distinct plant from the nutmeg. Although the mace and the kernel are sold as separate entities, they are extracted from one and the same plant.

Grenada has a very good network of roads. Apart from the coastal road which could take one right around the island, there are several roads criss crossing the interior. So instead of continuing along the east coast road we cut across the country along the Grand Etang route so that the President and Mrs Hoyte might have a good view of our forest reserve area and at the same time get a glimpse of life in rural Grenada. We stopped briefly at the Grand Etang lake before continuing on our journey back to St. George's. In the evening Prime Minister the Rt. Hon. Herbert Blaize and Mrs Blaize entertained President Hoyte and Mrs Hoyte to a private dinner at their Mt. Royal official residence. On the following day, Sunday, the Hoytes attended a cultural show held in their honour at the Grenada Boys' Secondary School auditorium. In the evening they were the honoured guests at a state dinner at my residence.

The Hoytes were kept very busy on the last day of their visit. The President had a two-hour session of talks with Prime Minister Blaize, while Mrs Hoyte went on a shopping expedition. In the afternoon President Hoyte met the parliamentarians and addressed them in a joint session of the Senate and the House of Representatives in the parliamentary chamber at York House. He later held discussions with Hon. George Brizan, Leader of the Opposition. After a short rest the President and Mrs Hoyte were escorted to the Balisier Hotel at Richmond Hill where Guyanese nationals resident in Grenada hosted a reception in their honour. It was an opportunity for the honoured guests to meet and converse with their own nationals, and at the same time observe at first hand the interaction between Guyanese and Grenadian nationals in a social setting. The following morning the President and I exchanged gifts before he left for Point Salines Airport. With a police guard of honour and appropriate music supplied by the band of the Royal Grenada Police Force, my wife and I headed the list of dignitaries saying good-bye to our distinguished and honoured guests.

Dr. Keith Mitchell, the man who had done so much to pursue an electrification programme which brought electricity to almost every village in Grenada, Carriacou and Petit Martinique seemed to have been experiencing strained relations with the Prime Minister since the sensational NNP convention in January. Mitchell suddenly found himself almost powerless to deliver as the Ministry of Finance became extremely tardy in providing the necessary funds for completion of his programmes. However, Mitchell would not give up. He maintained, if not heightened, his visibility among the people. In his capacity as political leader of the ruling party, he sought and obtained an audience of me on Thursday, June 1. He seemed determined in a spirit of reconciliation to strengthen the party. That was his immediate concern. The following day I received Hon. Daniel Williams, Minister for Health and Representative of St. David's constituency, who discussed with me his own political future against the background of the current political situation. He seemed rather disillusioned and intimated that he had taken a decision not to contest the next general elections. Mitchell, the new leader of the NNP, held party meetings on June 4 and on July 12 thus assuming full control of the party. Blaize was absent at both meetings.

The time had come for the burial of Cosmus Raymond. He was accorded a state funeral with full honours. He was obviously a man of the people as evidenced by the mammoth crowd at the funeral. Monsignor Cyril La Montagne, Vicar General of the Catholic Church in Grenada, was the chief celebrant at the mass and he was assisted by two other priests. Also in attendance on the altar was Fr. Clement Francis, the Venerable Archdeacon of the Anglican Church and school mate of the deceased. My wife and I headed the congregation which included the Prime Minister and members of Cabinet, members of the diplomatic corps, a contingent of American armed service personnel, the British military attaché based in Barbados and former Grenada Police Commissioners, Holder from Barbados and Toppin from Trinidad and Tobago. Eulogies were given by Senator Lawrence Joseph and Superintendent Bernard of the Grenada Police Force.

Now that the Heads of Government summit, the State visit and the burial of Cosmus Raymond were out of the way, the political factions resumed their posturing as they worked through their own political agenda. The Prime Minister fired the first salvo when on July 20 he relieved Keith Mitchell of his ministerial responsibilities as Minister for Works, and also advised me to revoke the senatorial appointment of Lawrence Joseph. He further advised me to appoint Senator Ben Andrews as Minister for Works. Meanwhile, on that same day diplomatic relations were established between Grenada and the Republic of China on Taiwan. This, of course, virtually meant the severing of diplomatic relations with mainland China. In fact it was not long after, on August 7, that the People's Republic of China formally declared that it had broken off relations with Grenada.

The day after he fired Mitchell from Cabinet, Blaize announced the formation of The National Party under his leadership with Ben Jones as deputy. That was on July 21. While this was not entirely unexpected, this latest action of the Prime Minister gave rise to a certain measure of confusion in the minds of people, especially the floating voters, who were not affiliated to any particular party. Some began to ask whether a TNP government was in control of the affairs of the country. Others began to wonder whether Blaize and the rest of his dwindling Cabinet had caught the defection fever and removed themselves from the NNP on whose ticket they had contested the last general elections. Still others were of the view that new general elections should be called immediately. But for most people life went on as usual. Mitchell showed his displeasure at recent actions of the Prime Minister when he attempted to table a motion of "no confidence" in the Prime Minister and the Government at the next sitting of the House of Representatives which was scheduled for Friday, August 4. By letter dated July 26 Mitchell sought the Speaker's permission to have his "no confidence" motion put on the Order Paper. Two days later the Speaker replied to Mitchell giving him reasons why he could not comply with his request: The notice was too late for inclusion on the Order Paper. In accordance with Standing Order No. 22 the notice should have been sent to the Clerk of Parliament, not to the Speaker. The Speaker went on to be critical of the contents of the resolution itself. He thought that the preamble to the resolution bristled with opinions instead of facts. He advised Mitchell that in such matters the opinions of political parties held no sway.

One diplomat whose heart seemed troubled about the delay in holding elections was Ford Cooper, the United States Chargé d'Affairs. His requests for audience with me dramatically increased as he sought to find out how soon elections would take place. I was at pains to enlighten him on the relevant provisions of our Constitution and to emphasize that it was the Prime Minister's prerogative to advise the Governor General to dissolve Parliament and issue the necessary writ for the holding of new elections at any time during a government's term of office. The five-year term would begin on the day when Parliament met for the first time after general elections. Further, in accordance with our Constitution the Prime Minister could call elections up to three months after the end of the five-year period but not beyond. The timing of elections was not a matter for the United States Government, and I could not understand why he was so concerned about the holding of elections when there was no breach of the Constitution in this regard.

The cracks in the Cabinet immediately began to deepen when Blaize announced the formation of his new party, The National Party. Two Cabinet ministers reacted swiftly. Daniel Williams and Grace Duncan resigned their ministerial positions and openly declared that their loyalties were with the NNP and not TNP. This also meant that the Government had lost two more supporters in Parliament. In his letter of resignation dated July 25, 1989, Williams pointed to recent occurrences in Government and to the non-observance of the conventions of Cabinet. He was by no means specific about the occurrences or the conventions which made it uncomfortable for him to continue to serve as a Cabinet Minister. Three days later on July 28, Grace Duncan resigned from Cabinet with immediate effect. She had heard "with great consternation" the Prime Minister announcing the formation of The National Party. She stated categorically that she would support fully any motion of no confidence in Prime Minister Blaize moved by any member of Parliament. Herein lay Blaize's dilemma. He was definitely leading a minority Government. Dissolution of Parliament was certainly not one of his options. He wanted to carry on to the very end of his term as if he was under divine direction so to do.

Grace Duncan, a close ally of Mitchell, suddenly stepped up her field work in an effort to ensure fidelity and solidarity among party supporters and at the same time to woo new recruits to the party. Indeed, bearing in mind that parliamentary elections could not be far off, Duncan immediately moved to the campaign trail. Daniel Williams, though not as active in the field, nevertheless put his full weight behind Mitchell and supported him unreservedly. On the morning of Thursday, August 3, I received Hon. Dr. Keith Mitchell and Hon. Grace Duncan who brought me up to date on the political situation from their own perspective. Dr. Mitchell also informed me that the party was planning to hold a convention in Grenville on September 10.

No amount of damage control could repair the gaping fissures in the Cabinet. Divided loyalties, personal ambitions, and an obstinate leadership were the major determinants in the gradual disintegration of the Union Island Accord. Emerging from this fragmentation were three political factions which, five years earlier, had moulded themselves together in an apparent show of unity to ensure that Gairy would not be returned to power. If there was any doubt or denial then about the purpose of the Union Island Accord, subsequent events had clearly erased any perceived purpose that might have been ventilated then. The Accord had run full circle. Its obliteration was complete. It was quite clear that the three factions the NNP,

NDC and TNP had their gaze firmly fixed to the next national elections. Given the teething troubles surrounding the Accord which had become progressively tenuous and the subsequent ease with which it was broken, it was obvious that the binding of the parties on Union Island for peace and unity was neither sufficiently genuine nor divinely inspired as some people imagined. It was simply a marriage of convenience. For no sooner elections were over than successful candidates began vying for positions, and, at least three of them had leadership ambitions.

From all indications, the political forecast for the month of August was one of gathering gloom particularly for the Prime Minister and his Cabinet colleagues. The immediate future was fraught with challenges and uncertainties. The threat of a no confidence motion in Parliament was real and Blaize was aware of this. Courageous as he was, he knew that to go out of office through the no confidence route was to lower his self-esteem, and to suffer an outright rejection by his erstwhile colleagues. Blaize was a man to finish the course, however challenging, however rough and uneven and, contrary to expectations in some quarters, he had no intention of stepping down before the life of the current Parliament expired. Rumour of a no confidence motion against the government swept through the entire country. It was believed that members of the House of Representatives were anxiously awaiting the next sitting for the political showdown. No one expected Blaize to survive a no confidence motion, and he himself could see the writing on the wall should such a motion appear on the Order Paper in the name of any member of the House.

But Blaize got yet another respite. In accordance with the calendar of national events, August was designated as Festival Month. It was a time when visitors and Grenadians resident abroad converged on Grenada, Carriacou and Petit Martinique for vacation. It was a time for fun and frolic particularly during the first half of the month when there were three main festivities. During the first weekend in August there was the annual Rainbow City Festival in Grenville, while Carriacou was buzzing with activities in connection with the annual regatta. In Grenada the week long carnival competitions and fetes culminated in the street parade of the bands on the Tuesday of the second week in August. The political life of the country became almost dormant on these festive occasions. Prime Minister Blaize spent the bank holiday weekend at his private residence in Carriacou. When I met him in Carriacou he appeared to be very relaxed. It was the occasion of the 25th Annual Carriacou Regatta which I declared open in the presence of an exceptionally large crowd, many of whom had come home from distant lands specifically for this Silver Jubilee celebration. A plaque in honour of

Linton Rigg, the man who started these annual regattas, was unveiled by the Prime Minister. In the evening Prime Minister and Mrs Blaize hosted a buffet dinner at their home for dignitaries and other specially invited guests. This was an opportunity for me to meet a number of influential residents of Carriacou. An hour-long private meeting with the Prime Minister preceded my embarkation at Laureston Airport for my return to Grenada where I was scheduled to deliver the key-note address at the thirty-second Convention of the Caribbean Credit Union Confederation later in the day.

The Prime Minister returned to his official residence in St. George's three days after to ponder, among other things, on what his next move would be in order to avoid a humiliating defeat in Parliament. Meanwhile the Parliamentary Opposition was waiting until the carnival was over to fine tune their strategy as to how they should proceed in Parliament. Blaize, like his Carriacou and Petit Martinique constituents, was never enamoured with the celebration of carnival in August. Carnival in Grenada, Cariacou and Petit Martinique was traditionally a pre-Lenten festival held on the two days preceding Ash Wednesday. In the early 1970's Government shifted carnival to May and later to August in the middle of the rainy season. However, the people of Carriacou and Petit Martinique have maintained the old tradition, and have continued to celebrate carnival as a pre-Lenten festival.

The rationale behind Government's decision to change the date was that the August carnival would draw an enormous influx of visitors to Grenada, particularly from Trinidad and Tobago, and this made good economic sense. Further, this would give a boost to our tourism industry and the hotels stood to benefit. This never materialized. One need only check the records at our various hotels, large and small. The number of people coming from Trinidad and Tobago was neither enormous nor by any stretch of imagination could be described as an influx. The incidence of heavy rainfall has caused the cancellation of some of the carnival activities over the years, and it was not unusual for national carnival committees to seek Government subsidies because of loss of revenue. Until and unless we could create a carnival spectacle which would attract a truly international audience, we would have to be satisfied with a number of Grenadians resident abroad visiting home at carnival time to live at the homes of relatives and friends, not at hotels. But Blaize's main objection to shifting carnival from the two days before Ash Wednesday to a date in August was that the predominantly Christian people of Grenada, particularly the youth, lost all sense of the significance and meaning of the Lenten season. Unfortunately, he could not get his Cabinet to go along with him. I too was never supportive of the decision to move carnival from its pre-Lenten slot on our calendar of events. I was Secretary to the Cabinet when the idea was first mooted and I was never convinced by the arguments put forward then in favour of the need to change. One of the reasons given was that the pre-Lenten date was too close to that of Independence celebrations on February 7. There was no prepared Cabinet submission on the matter. In fact, it was taken up *ex agenda* and it seemed the conclusion was based on emotion rather than on sound reasoning. Over the years the shift of the carnival celebration adversely affected the strict observance of Lent. Prime Minister Blaize and I discussed this matter on several occasions and we were of one mind on the desirability of bringing back carnival to its original position. After my first year and during my remaining years in office the depth of my feelings on this issue manifested itself in my refusal to accept invitations to the various carnival shows.

Since the on-going dislocation in his Cabinet, Prime Minister Blaize drew much closer to me. Our meetings were more frequent and they lasted for a much longer duration than hitherto. He not only kept me informed about the general state of affairs in the country, but also sought my advice and help on many matters which perhaps should properly come under the purview of his senior public servants. He often began by saying to me, "I want to draw on your vast and varied experience." I perceived that he was becoming lonelier, perhaps also losing faith in his chief advisers, and I promised to give him whatever help I could. The fact that his office was now located at his official residence was a disadvantage, because his presence was no longer felt within the public service environment, and his visibility as Head of Government was reduced considerably.

What was uppermost in his mind was the probability of the premature dissolution of Parliament. I took the unusual step to advise Prime Minister Blaize that the way to get out of his dilemma was to prorogue Parliament. His initial reaction was that he would have to think about it. Within a couple of days he informed me that he would take that route. Meanwhile, my wife and I had planned a vacation in Canada. We were due to leave on August 16. I knew that if an election were imminent, I would have had to cancel my vacation plans and remain at home. I also knew that if a crisis, political or otherwise, were to arise during my absence, I would have to abandon the rest of my vacation and return home as quickly as possible. Blaize had carefully studied the Constitution and was satisfied that he could use the prorogation device and stay on until the end of the year. He confidently advised that I could proceed on my vacation as he had no intention of calling elections before the end of his five-year term of office. The day before I left for Canada, communication between Governor General's House and Mt. Royal was stepped up considerably. Sir Hudson Scipio, who was to be my deputy during my absence, came to see me twice that day. We spoke of the gradual erosion of political power as was then experienced by the Prime Minister. In the circumstances I deemed it expedient that Parliament be prorogued on Wednesday, August 23, 1989. I instructed him to sign the proclamation proroguing Parliament on the appointed day during my absence from the State. This was kept a closely guarded secret. The proclamation was prepared not in the Attorney General's office as was customary, but in my office. After carefully vetting it I left it in the safe hands of my personal assistant and I accordingly informed Sir Hudson.

From the time I embarked on the British West Indian Airways (BWIA) flight on August 17 to start my vacation I tried hard to clear my mind of all of Grenada's problems. As my vacation progressed my mind became vacant in terms of the political ramblings and posturing I had left behind. However, in the evening of Friday, August 25, out of sheer curiosity, I rang Prime Minister Blaize from my hotel room to find out how the prorogation of Parliament was received. The Prime Minister seemed to be in a jovial mood. In his usual style he said to me that those chaps needed to know the meaning of prorogation. Many of them thought that Parliament was dissolved and were eagerly awaiting the announcement of the date for elections. The chaps to whom the Prime Minister made reference included political activists and newspaper columnists. The other bit of news he relayed to me was that a new political party was announced and in his own words "the POPP or something or the other." He went on to say that the leader of this new party was some fellow who had been in the employ of the IMF. He added, "I believe he was an island scholar. You might have taught him. I am sure you know him." Blaize obviously never took a serious view of that party. Nor did I. The birth pangs of the party were too much for its leader to endure and it died in its early infancy.

I was very pleased to learn that all was quiet at home. I never gave further thought to what might be happening on the home front, but continued to enjoy my vacation in Jasper and Banff before returning to Grenada on September 6.

Blaize outwitted his parliamentary colleagues by silencing Parliament. He did it with constitutional rectitude. This latest action of his never aroused animosity. It did not provoke any demonstration. Life in Grenada went on as usual. Blaize must have endured a great deal of physical and mental anguish during his tenure of office. Nevertheless, despite his health problems the right-thinking people of Grenada still trusted him as the man most suitable

"DISTINGUISHED GUESTS AT THE GOVERNOR GENERAL'S RESIDENCE"

*Above*, President Ronald Reagan

*Below*, Her Majesty Queen Elizabeth II

"DISTINGUISHED
GUESTS AT THE
GOVERNOR
GENERAL'S
RESIDENCE"

*Left*, The first USSR
resident Ambassador
to Grenada

*Below*, U.S. Secretary
of State George
Shultz and Mrs Shultz

*ove*, At a vocational institute in Taipei

*ow*, On an experimental farm in Taiwan

"TAIWAN 1990"

*Above*, At the Taipei Trade Centre

*Below*, Official dinner party held in honour of Sir Paul and Lady Scoon

"AT HOME ALONE"

Sir Paul on the verandah of Governor General's House

"AT HOME ALONE"

*Above*, Meeting visitors in formal mode

*Opposite*, Sir Paul and Lady Scoon as host and hostess

"AT HOME ALONE"

Relaxing together in their beloved garden

for the premiership. From their standpoint, the young aspirants were not ready yet. His theme song was "Bind Us Together Lord" and he ordered it to be sung in almost every function in which he officiated.

Keeping the ship of state on an even keel was not an easy matter for a man whose Cabinet had been depleted of so many promising young men. The Prime Minister was not even sure whom he could trust in the upper echelons of the civil service. It was against this background that he came to depend more and more on me. Hence our frequent meetings in the latter half of 1989. There was no doubt in my mind that the burden of office was beginning to take a toll on him. When I told him that I was seriously thinking of demitting office, he advised me to tarry a little longer. Blaize did not attend the Commonwealth Heads of Government Meeting in Kuala Lumpur in mid-October. On November 5, The National Party was launched at Seamoon in St. Andrew's.

During the week beginning November 12, rumour was rife around St. George's that I had resigned as Governor General. The rapidity with which the rumour made its way through the city prompted Keith Mitchell to seek an appointment with me to find out whether there was any truth in it. The truth was that I was leaving the state shortly for a brief visit to Jamaica. I was going to Kingston primarily to be the guest speaker at the Annual Banquet and Induction Ceremony of the Professional Societies Association of Jamaica whose invitation I had gladly accepted. My association with the professional bodies of Jamaica went back to the 1970's when I served as Deputy Director of the Commonwealth Foundation in London. As part of its remit the Foundation encouraged and supported the growth of professional organizations in the Commonwealth, and Jamaica had received a sizable grant for the establishment of a Professional Centre. The purpose of these centres in the developing countries of the Commonwealth was twofold. Firstly, they provided a home for some of the professional societies who were unable to operate a secretariat on their own. Secondly, they facilitated the healthy and desirable practice of the multi-disciplinary approach to problem solving at the national level or otherwise.

While in Jamaica we were the guests of Their Excellencies the Governor General Sir Florizel and Lady Glasspole at King's House, their official residence. My first call was on Prime Minister Michael Manley. This was followed by a visit to the College of Arts, Science and Technology (CAST) where I held discussions with Dr. Sangster, the Principal, toured some of the departments, and met the Grenadian students. We then moved on to the Mona Campus of the University of the West Indies where Pro Vice-Chancellor Robinson warmly welcomed us, and showed us around.

Before leaving the campus I had a short meeting with the Grenadian students. Here, as in CAST, the students expressed the need for some form of diplomatic representation in Jamaica. This would provide consular and welfare services to the Grenadian community in Jamaica, especially the students. We also met the Registrar of the University, Grenadian-born Byron Robertson and other senior officers who together with the Vice Chancellor informed us as to the mission of the University and its plans for the future. Our next call was on the Rt. Hon. Edward Seaga, Leader of the Opposition who would be remembered with affection for his generosity and the statesmanlike qualities he had displayed during our problems in 1983.

Back at King's House my wife and I boarded an army helicopter for the fifteen-minute flight to Ocho Rios on the north coast. Mr Seaga was kind enough to invite us to lunch at Carinosa Gardens, his own tourism facility. He could not be present himself because of pressing matters which were engaging his attention in Kingston. However, the luncheon was ably hosted by Hon. Dr. Neville Gallimore who had visited Grenada shortly after the 1983 intervention by United States and Caribbean Forces.

We got back to King's House just on time to be able to take a rest before our major appointment at the Pegasus Hotel in the evening. Before the two hundred guests sat down to dinner there was great conviviality during the hour long cocktail reception, and it was an opportunity for me to meet as many of the professional people as possible. In my after dinner speech I addressed the gathering on the role of the professional in society. We left Jamaica on the following day.

On our return journey we disembarked at Antigua, where we were met by Their Excellencies Governor General Sir Wilfred and Lady Jacobs who very kindly invited us to be their guests at Government House. We could only spend one day in Antigua, as I felt that my presence was needed at home. How long could the Prime Minister cope with his increasing loneliness, it was difficult to tell. The political band- wagons were in full gear with the creation of new political parties, while public servants nervously awaited salary increases which seemed further and further away with every passing day. But most importantly the life of the present Parliament was due to expire in mid-December, a mere three weeks away. The announcement of a date for parliamentary elections could not be too far off. In these circumstances, the Governor General should be at home.

Our one-day stay in Antigua was taken up mainly in touring the countryside. Accompanied by Sir Wilfred we visited English Harbour and other historical and tourism sites. I was very impressed with the distribution of the hotels on the island. Whereas in Grenada our hotels dominated the southern St. George's area with the Grand Anse beach as the focal point, by contrast in Antigua they were widely scattered. I also had the distinct impression that the Antiguans really understood how important tourism was in terms of the economic development of their country and would do nothing to jeopardize the growth of the industry. We left for Grenada in the late afternoon.

Blaize's internal problems were far from over. He might have restrained his parliamentary colleagues by closing the door of Parliament in their faces, but he could not thwart the forward march of the unions who had been negotiating salary increases for months. Agreement was reached at last between the Government of Grenada and the unions representing public workers. This agreement was signed by both parties on October 4, and it provided for the payment of the new rates of salary with effect from November. Backpay was to be paid on December 1. The agreement as it stood could not be honoured by Government, the simple reason being that Government did not have the $25 m required to meet this commitment. No provision had been made in the national budget to cover an expenditure of this magnitude. The money which the Government was hoping to get from abroad was not forthcoming. The hapless Prime Minister in his capacity as Minister for Finance had to suffer the indignity of making a statement on television and radio that the new payments due to public workers could not be met on schedule. Needless to say this announcement was received with consternation and bitter disappointment. On the following day, Friday, December 1, the public workers including the teachers held a mass meeting and decided to take strike action immediately.

The week-long strike met with mixed reaction. There were those who felt that the Government's recalcitrance and dilatoriness was responsible for the current impasse. Others were of the view that, given the Government's impecuniosity, the public workers were unreasonable. Whatever the divergence of opinion it was a fact that the government was broke. What is more there was an economic downturn in the country. With the steady migratory wave of parliamentarians from one side of the House to the other, and because of the forthcoming elections which were still to be announced, prospective investors adopted a wait-and-see attitude, while the local private sector preferred not to venture into the unknown. The managers of Barclays Bank and the Grenada Bank of Commerce seemed rather concerned about the parlous state of the economy and sought an appointment to apprise me of it. They painted a gloomy picture of what was in store for us.

On Thursday, December 7, I received a delegation from the three Unions then on strike. Under the leadership of Mrs Luret Clarkson, President of the Public Workers Union, the delegation briefed me on the steps which led to the strike action. Their membership was anxious to get back to work, and they sought my intervention behind the scenes in order to bring about an amicable end to this long drawn out issue. There was one light moment during our meeting when Mrs Clarkson reported that in the midst of serious discussions at the Prime Minister's official residence, the Prime Minister posed the question to her and to Mr Hudson Mcphail: "Why don't you two go and preach?" Mrs Clarkson in particular felt very offended, but Prime Minister Blaize obviously did some homework before meeting the delegation. In fact Luret Clarkson and Hudson McPhail were both brought up in the same religious denomination, the Plymouth Brethen (or Gospel Hall as it was more popularly known), and later they both preached in the same church until Clarkson went over to the Pentecostal religion where she continued her lay preaching. Blaize was evidently aware of their religious practices and when he put the question to them he was subtly trying to convey to them that they would be better off preaching the word of God than harassing him for money.

Blaize was not a man to renege. He never gave up exploring various avenues to find the money to meet this very special commitment. Friday, December 8, was an eventful day. The good news was that the week-long strike had been called off. This agreement came out of a meeting between the Prime Minister and the union leaders earlier that day. Blaize felt confident enough to seek parliamentary approval for the expenditure to cover the salary increases for public workers. He knew that the Opposition would not object to such a request because they feared the wrath of the unions at a time of impending elections. It was for this reason that I signed a proclamation summoning Parliament for a special session on Thursday, December 14.

Parliament accordingly met at the usual place and at the usual time. On this occasion, however, there was none of the pomp and ceremony associated with the opening of a new session of Parliament. There was no Throne Speech to be read and there was no need for me to go down to the House on that day. Instead, The House of Representatives met in special session to grant approval for the Minister for Finance to raise the money from whatever source in order to pay public workers increases in salary. There was much mud-slinging in the House as each member tried to outdo the other in the apportionment of blame, all aimed at the Prime Minister who nevertheless had his way. He got his measure approved, and he was now free to conclude the negotiations he had started with Cable and Wireless for the purchase of the Government's shares in the telephone company, thus enabling him to meet his commitment to the public workers before Christmas. The new date for the payment of the back pay was announced as Monday, 18.

Political sparring for the impending elections had already begun. Blaize's reaction was that they would all run out of steam by the time the election date was announced. Amid all this it was to Blaize's great credit that he was able to keep the country calm and secure. Christmas took precedence over everything else, and the season had begun in earnest. I had already started my Christmas visits to hospitals, senior citizens' homes, and other community and social welfare organizations. On December 15, the day after the special session of Parliament, I had an hour long dialogue with the Prime Minister at his official residence. He felt relieved that he was able to find the money to pay public workers, but he felt saddened at the propaganda that he had the money but was refusing to pay. Some union members went out of their way to describe him as a dishonest man. This was a vicious, unwarranted and malicious attack on the integrity of the Prime Minister who could not be faulted for moral rectitude. When I met him on that day he seemed to me a tired man. Yet, despite this, he pointed out to me that he had some important matters on his desk which he had to look into before leaving his office that night, not least of which was the preparation of his speech for his party convention in two days' time. Uppermost in his mind was the setting up of a Commission of Enquiry to investigate the operations of certain Government Boards and Statutory Corporations. He sought my assistance in identifying capable personnel for membership of the Commission.

When The National Party held its convention at the Grenada Boys' Secondary School auditorium on Sunday, 17, the Rt. Hon. Herbert Blaize, Prime Minister and founder of the Party, was elected political leader amid popular acclaim. All the political parties then had their leaders in place, and, although the Prime Minister was still tight-lipped about the date for new elections, it was manifestly clear that the race for York House had begun. Constitutionally elections had to be held in three months' time. On the following day in continuance of my Christmas visits to institutions I made my way to the Princess Royal Hospital in Carriacou. This hospital is perched on the Belair Hill which affords a most commanding view of Grenada to the south and the Grenadines to the north. I also took the opportunity to visit the administrative building in down town Hillsborough where on a one-to-one basis I offered to the public workers present my best wishes for a happy holiday season. It was there I learnt that Prime Minister Blaize had telephoned the Chief Administrative Officer to find out whether the public officers in Carriacou were being paid their backpay. I understood he was very pleased when he got a positive reply to his query. Evidently the backpay issue had been a source of great worry for him.

One never knows what a new day will bring. Just before 9 o'clock on the morning of December 19, Inspector Alleyne, the senior police officer at the Prime Minister's Mt. Royal residence telephoned me on behalf of Mrs Blaize to say that there was an emergency and my presence was needed. This was a most extraordinary call from an inspector who had told the orderly answering the phone in the first place that he had an urgent message for the Governor General. Quite frankly I feared the worst as I briskly walked across the narrow pathway to Mt. Royal. On my arrival I was taken to the Prime Minister's bedroom where he was lying on his bed fully clothed with his boots on, speechless and motionless. In the bedroom with him were his wife, a daughter, three grandchildren and a brother. Two police officers stood close by. Valerie, their daughter was in deep tears. His expiration seemed perilously close and indeed within minutes he seemed to have breathed his last. He was about to leave for the hospital where Dr. Alister Budhlall had ordered him to go earlier that morning, but he collapsed and was unable to get out of his bedroom. The fact that he had been ordered to hospital as a patient was no bar to his enthusiasm: he had been telephoning people up to about 8.30 that morning, all in connection with work. Included among those to whom he had spoken were Hon. George McGuire, Minister for Education, and Ambassador Lamuel Stanislaus, our man at the United Nations. The day before he had presided over an executive meeting of his party. When Dr. Budhlall arrived, his second visit for the morning, he pronounced the Prime Minister dead. After offering condolences to Mrs Blaize and other family members I returned to my residence and I immediately gave orders that the manager of the radio station report to me as a matter of urgency. Within half an hour I was on radio telling the nation of the Prime Minister's death and of my intention to appoint a new Prime Minister before the end of the day. I also ordered that the national flag be flown at half mast on all government buildings and invited the private sector to fly their flags at half mast as a mark of respect. At the same time I sent a dispatch to Her Majesty the Queen to inform Her of the Prime Minister's passing. Mr Blaize was the chief of Her Majesty's Grenada Ministers and also one of the Queen's Privy Councillors.

The death of Herbert Augustus Blaize created a void in the political life of Carriacou. He first entered Parliament as Representative for Carriacou and

Petit Martinique in 1957, and held on to this seat until his death in 1989, except for the revolutionary period and the year after when Parliament was in abeyance. But even then his constituents still regarded him as their natural leader to whom they could always turn for guidance and advice. He was always there ready and willing to take up the mantle of leadership after times of crisis in Government or in the country. On two such occasions, in 1961 after the infamous squandermania crisis and twenty-three years later after our sordid flirtation with communism, Blaize received a mandate from the people to restore integrity in public life and to bring back stability and orderliness to the country. He accepted this mandate, thus courageously defying all his critics who at one time or other were ready to discard him as a political liability. During his long years in politics, and particularly as Head of Government he had a moderating influence that so often helped to resolve conflicts and transform impending chaos into stability and orderliness. Blaize was undoubtedly a man of great moral courage, perseverance and Christian fortitude and was imbued with a rare selfless passion to serve his fellowmen. He might not have had the charisma of many of his contemporaries, but his clarity of thought and the ease with which he used the English language endeared him to the hearts of many. Though a committed Christian and a regular and active worshipper, he was never ostentatious about his religion, and could never be accused of contriving to be overly religious in order to gain political mileage.

Blaize knew and understood the contents of the Constitution, and in his capacity as Head of Government he never attempted to depart from its provisions in arriving at decisions or to bend the rules in any way for the sake of political expediency. He absolutely respected the independence of the Judiciary, and he did everything within his power to sustain that independence which he regarded as sacrosanct. Unlike so many other Caribbean political leaders he did not enter politics through the Trade Union route. However, he saw the need for trade unionism and showed no hostility to it. Rather he encouraged organized labour. His aim was to maintain the best traditions of the country while admonishing his countrymen that the way forward was through their own efforts, their industry and their perseverance. He constantly reminded them that economic and social advance depended not on the receipt of largesse from abroad, but on the extent to which we, as a people, were prepared to make the maximum and optimum use of our scarce resources.

His fiscal policy was based on the maxim: "never spend more than you earn." As Prime Minister he kept the portfolio of finance, and in the role of Minister for Finance he kept a close watch on the cash flow at the Treasury and very often was forced to put on hold or to reduce expenditure which had been approved in the national budget. This, of course, incurred the wrath of some of his ministers. The frugality so clearly noticeable in Blaize's own lifestyle was brought to bear on his fiscal policy. In our conversations he often quoted Mr Micawber from *David Copperfield*:

"Annual income twenty pounds, annual expenditure nineteen nineteen six, result happiness. Annual income twenty pounds, annual expenditure twenty pounds ought and six, result misery."

In his foreign policy Blaize sought to maintain good relations with Grenada's traditional friends. He actively supported the work of international organizations such as the United Nations and the Commonwealth in which Grenada held membership. He firmly believed in the regional integration movement and felt that Grenada's interest lay in integrating with the subgrouping of the Organisation of East Caribbean States (OECS) as well as with the wider grouping of the Caribbean Community (CARICOM).

Mindful of the vulnerability of small island states, and mindful also of the local difficulties and anxieties in recent times, Blaize threw his fullest support behind the Regional Security System. Blaize might not have accomplished all that he had hoped for during his five years as Prime Minister. Quite arguably some might even conclude that he had no vision. However, there was no doubt in my mind during those years that he was a man with a mission. He more than any other in Parliament understood the strengths and weaknesses of the Grenadian society. He came into office when agriculture was in sharp decline and commodity prices were low. Nevertheless, he felt that the growing abandonment of agricultural lands should be brought to an end and people be encouraged to grow more food and to eat what they grow. He, therefore, saw the need to revitalize agriculture. In June, 1985, he signed a US $5 million loan with the World Bank for the financing of agricultural rehabilitation and diversification. He also secured for the farming community a U.S. $1.9 m line of credit which was managed by the Grenada Agricultural Bank. From the French Government he was able to get a grant of one million francs to finance two stud centres– one at Beausejour in St. George's and the other at Carriacou., and a farmers' education and training centre at Mardigras. The Food and Agriculture Organization (FAO) provided technical assistance for forestry development. A Pest Management Unit was set up and became fully operational.

Cognizant of the financial burden farmers had to bear in cultivating their holdings Blaize quickly moved to offer duty free concessions on vehicles imported for agricultural purposes. In February, 1988, export duty on cocoa, nutmegs, and bananas was abolished. Approximately four million dollars were put back indirectly into farmers' hands through their producer organizations. As far back as 1909 these export duties had been on the statute books, and only in 1975 was there a slight reduction in the exaction of these mandatory levies. Meanwhile there was an increase in the wages of agricultural workers, and in-service training for agricultural extension officers was intensified. In 1986 Government made some six thousand bags of fertilizer available to vegetable and cane farmers under a fertilizer subsidy scheme at one-third the market price. As a result of a fruit fly survey Grenada was declared fruit fly free and was subsequently able to export its fruits freely to the United States of America. This gave a great fillip to the local fruit growing industry.

The area of fisheries was not forgotten. Loans provided by the International Fund for Agricultural Development (IFAD) and the Venezuelan Investment Fund were used to improve marketing facilities with specific reference to storage capacity. Existing fish centres were refurbished and new ones established in the towns of Gouyave, Victoria, Sauteurs, and Grenville as well as in Carriacou and Petite Martinique. These improvements made it easier for the domestic consumer to buy fish and at the same time helped to stimulate export. The Artisanal Fisheries Loan Revolving Scheme managed by the National Commercial Bank helped fishermen to purchase boats, engines and fishing gear.

The tourism industry regained its buoyancy. Cruise ships resumed their regular calls to St. George's resulting in an unprecedented growth in one-day visitors to our shores in marked contrast to what obtained during the revolutionary years when these ships designedly by-passed Grenada. For example in 1985 there were 174 cruise ship calls as compared with 80 calls in 1983. Significantly, 1985, the year of return to democratic rule was also the year when cruise ships began to call regularly at Carriacou. There were ten such calls that year. Similarly, there was a welcome increase in the number of stay-over visitors. This pleased Government ministers no less than the stakeholders in the industry, especially the hoteliers, as they all saw tourism as the engine of economic growth which would bring in much needed foreign exchange in the short term and with its multiplier effect bolster the economy in the long term. The yachts also began to return in large numbers. Grenada had come into its own again with the restoration of democracy and all its cherished freedom, and tourists again felt that with its charm and beauty it was a safe and worthwhile place to visit. In 1984 39,400 stay-over visitor arrivals were recorded, the highest since 1972. Grenada was again becoming a favourite destination and by 1985 there was an increase of some 33% over the 1984 figure. Government appealed to Grenadians to make some significant contribution to the revitalized tourism sector of the economy, and offered generous duty-free concessions for the construction of hotels with a minimum of twelve rooms. Grenadians took up the challenge, some at great sacrifice given the prevailing high interest rates on bank loans. With the on-going encouragement from government, a number of mini-hotels rapidly appeared on the landscape, thus easing the shortage of accommodation facilities for stay-over visitors. The Tourism Authorities quickly embarked on a drive to improve the main tourist attractions, and a branch office of the Grenada Board of Tourism was established in Carriacou to help promote the development of the industry in the sister isles of Carriacou and Petit Martinique. The Board of Tourism also aggressively redoubled its marketing efforts both in Britain and in North America, and there was growing expectation that sooner rather than later many of the larger airlines would include Grenada on their itineraries.

In the field of education the Blaize administration followed the lead of the Interim Government by continuing to tackle the manifold problems posed by an educational system which was recently battered by ideological shock waves, and was still in a state of parlous disarray, shocking ill-discipline and utter confusion in terms of matter and method in teaching and in terms of the locus of authority. With a continuing high rate of resignations from the teaching service, the level of untrained teachers in the classrooms continued to rise. This was reflected in poor examination performances particularly in English and Mathematics at all levels. Many schools were in a state of disrepair and urgent measures had to be taken to make them more amenable for both learning and teaching. With the establishment of a Schools Maintenance Unit some effort was made to maintain school buildings, particularly the primary schools, which had suffered the worst neglect over the years. Indeed, with the continued financial assistance from USAID, extensive renovation was done on over twenty schools in the first three years of the administration. Teachers were returning to Grenada. Under the USAID programme, funding was provided for the pursuit of tertiary education in the United States of America. At the same time, USAID funding also provided numerous short-term training programmes to Grenadians, particularly those in mid-career. In an effort to reduce unemployment, a skills training programme was instituted. The business community was very helpful in this, leading to the emergence of a strong partnership between the public and private sectors. A skills training centre was identified in every parish. Meanwhile, the American Institute for Free

Labour Development initiated a skills training programme to train some 180 carpenters, plumbers and masons. A Curriculum Development Unit was also set up in the Ministry of Education. The principal task of this new Unit was to ensure that the curriculum was relevant to the needs of the country and satisfying to the all round needs of the students. It was, therefore, not surprising that subjects like Principles of Business, Principles of Accounts, Home Mangement and Commercial Arts became firmly entrenched in the curriculum of secondary schools. Drama, Music and Sport began to be regarded as integral parts of the school curriculum, thus surrendering their old familiar label of extra curricular activities. The introduction of a School Broadcast Programme was a welcome aid to learning. So, too, was the fully equipped and modern Audio-visual Unit acquired by the Ministry of Education. At the Crochu Roman Catholic School an experimental computer based educational programme was launched, the success of which clearly manifested itself in the unusually excellent results gained by the pupils of that school in the Common Entrance Examinations which served as a yardstick for placement in the secondary schools.

New programmes were developed using the approach of the World Health Organization to primary health care. The Ministry of Health initiated and developed preventive health programmes which were thought to be most effective in dealing with health problems in Grenada. Radda Barnen, a Swedish Aid Agency, made a significant contribution towards the health care programme by refurbishing and rebuilding health care centres throughout the country, and in some cases building new ones in areas where none previously existed. The presence in Grenada of Project Hope, an American organization, was timely, and the work it did in spearheading major developments in national health care was invaluable. With a $2.1 million grant from USAID and an additional $1.3 million in medical equipment and supplies by private donors, Project Hope was able to recruit specialist physicians, train health personnel including nurses and nurse practitioners, provide much needed health supplies, upgrade laboratory operations and equipment, and improve the collection of medical data and other health records. Project Hope was very concerned about the future manpower needs of Grenada. Dr. Wilhem, who managed the local operations of Project Hope, had the foresight to recruit Grenadian and other West Indian doctors on contract to fill vacancies in the hospitals and elsewhere in the health field. In fact, his earlier connections with the University of the West Indies served him in good stead as he sought to assist Grenada in developing adequate medical manpower. The salaries paid by Project Hope were attractive. The hope was that on termination of the contract these doctors would be willing to stay in Grenada and accept the local salaries. By then the reputation of these doctors would have been so well known that it should not be difficult for any of them to start a private practice lucrative enough to be able to top up the local salary. USAID also funded the construction of a new mental hospital in Mt. Gay. This modern and well-equipped hospital replaced the Richmond Hill Mental Home which had been accidentally bombed during the October, 1983 military activities.

By 1986 the American Government had generously approved aid to Grenada in the order of $74 million. Generally, the purpose of this aid was to resuscitate our ailing economy and to revitalize the political and institutional base of our country. We all had high expectations about rapid economic growth based on foreign and private investment, but we soon had to lower our sights as the level of such investment was disappointingly low. However, all was not lost as much progress was made in infrastructural development, relevant structures were put in place, and important policy initiatives were launched. Hopefully, positive improvements in development activities would follow. Three USAID Economic Support Fund grants totaling $17 million were released in 1986. Closely linked to fiscal and other policy reforms, these grants went a long way towards restoring economic stability. In the private sector liquidity was restored to the commercial banks, mainly through reduced borrowing by Government. Money from the Economic Support Fund was used by Government to meet its obligations to the commercial banks and to reduce its credit requirements. This had the effect of making credit more easily available to the private sector. Under this funding, budgetary support was given to government by meeting the local costs required for public sector projects and for the payment of United States goods to be used in these projects. In order to reduce Government's dominant role in the economy, certain policy reforms had to be undertaken. Governments are not very good at spearheading commercial and other business activities. Stunted by political interference, government enterprises are too well known as breeding places of indolence. Low productivity, over-staffing, inability to meet financial obligations, lackadaisical attitude of workers, and lateness for work are the hallmarks of these public enterprises which lack the profit motive anyway. Thus the privatization of major state-owned enterprises was a prerequisite in the thrust towards a buoyant market oriented economy. There was a gradual divestiture of state owned agricultural lands and a new fiscal reform programme was instituted, and transparently so. The relaxation of foreign exchange control, revision of the investment code, elimination of the monopoly to import cement, the removal of income tax and the advent of Value Added Tax (VAT) all contributed towards a heathier economic environment. Interest rate ceilings were raised and price controls on locally produced goods were removed.

The nation wide road repair programme which was started in November, 1983, continued under the Blaize administration. The main objectives of the programme were to expand road patching in Grenada and Carriacou, to rehabilitate primary and farm roads, and to continue to provide employment for some four hundred unskilled workers. With the financial assistance of USAID the American firm of Morrison-Knudson resurfaced two segments of roads connecting the Point Salines Airport to St. George's city centre as well as the Grand Etang road from St. George's to Grenville. Other Aid funded activities undertaken were the purchase and installation of 12.5 miles of low tension conductor wire and 220 poles to facilitate the provision of electricity. In 1986 an additional generator (1.8 to 2.1 megawatts) was purchased and installed to meet current and projected power demand and alleviate load-shedding. In the area of solid waste, the Grenville sanitary landfill was relocated and, under the auspices of USAID, three compacter trucks as well as three hundred trash bins were provided. Also, training in landfill management was given. At the same time new pumps and equipment were made available to pump sewerage away from St. George's harbour to eliminate pollution. In the line of communication a new transmitter and antenna for Radio Grenada were installed, and a new telephone exchange system for the Westerhall district in the parish of St. David, thus facilitating automatic dial telephone service between lines within the Westerhall area with connections to the St. George's exchange, and ensuring direct distance and international dialling. USAID also provided approximately US$750,000 to renovate four factory shells in the Frequente Industrial Park and to construct a new building with a capacity of 20,000 square feet of additional factory space. In this way the Frequente Park was expanded and developed to meet the needs of both local and foreign manufacturers. In an effort to strengthen the Grenada Industrial Development Corporation (GIDC). USAID also financed the services of an experienced investment promotion and development advisor and gave financial support to the Corporation to stimulate its investment promotion efforts.

Prime Minister Blaize fully understood that the successful growth of the private sector was essential for sustained economic development. He quickly realized that the private sector needed all the help they could find in order to build up their management structure, to rebuild their confidence, to enhance their profitability and to expand and develop their human and other resources. Blaize felt that the private sector should be included in any scheme for financial assistance and that they should be given every opportunity to make an input into any national development plan which Government might wish to formulate. So he encouraged a better working relationship between the public and private sectors. While with the assistance of USAID under its Economic Stabilization Grant liquidity was restored to the banking system. Blaize limited government borrowing, raised the interest rate ceiling, and eased exchange controls. These measures helped to maintain liquidity and facilitated commercial and productive activities. Being aware of the frustrations and difficulties of the private sector in the recent past, USAID was quick to take the cue from the Prime Minister and offered generous assistance to private sector organizations. The Grenada Chamber of Commerce was given management training support through the regional aid project with the Caribbean Association of Industry and Commerce. A grant of some $90,000 was made available to the International Executive Service Corps (IESC) for technical assistance to indigenous businesses. The newly established Grenada National Development Foundation through an aid grant of $724,000 was able to support the development of small businesses. The Foundation had the capability to provide loans to small entrepreneurs and tradesmen who normally did not have access to commercial bank credit. The small business sector swiftly and dramatically gathered momentum, and in a short space of time the ranks of the entrepreneurial class had swollen as many Grenadians especially the young suddenly realized that they were capable of doing something worthwhile on their own initiative in order to make a living. Therein lay the significance of the Grenada National Development Foundation. Undoubtedly, the Foundation gave a measure of hope to the poor struggling man or woman who over the years had been marking time in his or her small business enterprise striving to eke out a decent living. The American Institute of Free Labour Development (AIFLD) also received a grant in the order of $966,000 to assist in free trade union development and skills training. An additional $200,000 was given for funding small community self-help projects throughout the country.

We live in an imperfect world, and there is no political system that is ideal. From time to time democracy can show an ugliness that is obnoxious, particularly when we have within it people who think that the country's wealth is for the enjoyment of themselves and their families to the exclusion of that group of people whom politicians and social scientists like to call the masses. Also, in the absence of vigilance, the freedoms associated with democracy can be easily transformed into licence and then democracy becomes its own worst enemy. At the other end of the spectrum is communism which takes away the dignity of the individual and treats every man ,woman and child as a bit of state property to be used as the authorities think fit. There are other political systems in which power is concentrated in the hands of one man or in the hands of a few. In either of the two last cases, the citizenry is subjected to misery, corruption and unfair practices in daily living depending on the idiosyncracies of the political leaders many of whom are either absolutely corrupt, or brazenly brutal, or both.

Blaize abhorred communism. He was a great believer in democracy and strongly upheld the freedom of the individual. He was neither corrupt nor brutal. His guiding motive was service, not power. His constant prayer was that Grenadians would truly bind themselves together as one people, one family. He left behind a legacy of honesty and integrity in public life.

# 13

## Appointing a Prime Minister

I had the unenviable task of appointing a Prime Minister to succeed the Rt. Hon. Herbert Augustus Blaize, and I had to do this with a minimum of delay in order to ensure that there was no break in the governance of the country. Further, the transition should be a smooth one in strict accordance with our democratic traditions. With the passing of Blaize the Government could count on only five seats in the House of Representatives while the feigningly disparate group of Opposition members numbered nine. Speculation was rife as to whom I should appoint as the new Prime Minister. Soon after the sad news of Blaize's demise, some ingenuous media people stationed themselves at my main gate no doubt to observe the traffic to and from Governor General's House in an effort to be the first to spot the newly appointed Prime Minister. They maintained their ground for the entire morning with no luck in their mission. Business went on as usual within my office. In fact, a number of people passed through the gate, but the newsmen must have been puzzled. The first to arrive was a prominent lawyer who had a pre-arranged appointment. His visit had nothing to do with the Prime Minister's death.

Admittedly it was an unusually busy day at the telephone for my personal assistant who was trying to get hold of certain people whom I wanted to see or with whom I wanted to speak. Among those I summoned to my office for separate discussions were Ben Jones, Deputy Leader of The National Party, George Brizan, the Leader of the Opposition, Dr. Francis Alexis, former law lecturer at the University of the West Indies and leading authority on constitutional law on the island, Keith Mitchell, Political Leader of the New National Party, and Nicholas Brathwaite, Political Leader of the National Democratic Congress. Between the hours of 11 a.m. and 3 p.m., including the luncheon hour, I had consultations with these men not for advice as to whom should be appointed Prime Minister but rather to apprise them at first hand of the promise I had earlier made to the nation that I would be making an appointment before the end of the day. I expected co-operation and support from all and sundry, not least from themselves. As the nation plunged into mourning it was a trying time when the stability of the country should take precedence over selfish political motives.

During these consultations the view was expressed that the new appointee should call elections without further delay. Indeed, one person went so far as to suggest that I should make this a condition of appointment. Well knowing that no such conditionality should be attached to the appointment of a Prime Minister, I listened politely. However, I felt obliged to emphasize that the new Prime Minister would call elections at what he considered to be the most appropriate time, and as always, in accordance with the relevant provisions of the supreme law of the land, our Constitution. I rather suspected that some of the politicians were already feeling the strain of electioneering which they had started all over the country in anticipation of a January poll.

In the wider community some people held the view that because the majority of members of the House of Representatives were in Opposition, one of their number should be appointed Prime Minister. Others felt that the Deputy Prime Minister should automatically get the nod from the Governor General for this position. Still others postulated that in all the circumstances the Governor General should dissolve Parliament and call new elections. This divergence of opinion did not weigh heavily on me. I had already given much thought to the selection of a successor earlier that morning when I solitarily traversed the narrow pathway from Mt. Royal to my residence. In the circumstances, as Governor General, I had no constitutional authority to call elections at my own bidding. There was no constitutional crisis in the country, and the death of a Prime Minister did not necessitate the immediate calling of elections. Thus I could not invoke the doctrine of necessity. Further, the constitution never made any provision for a Deputy Prime Minister to be automatically appointed to the office of Prime Minister if and when the latter became vacant. Interestingly, nowhere in the constitution was reference made to political parties, and the Deputy Prime Minister was a creature on which the constitution was equally silent. When I heard that an overly enthusiastic high ranking official, who perhaps thought that the Government belonged to Mr Blaize's colleagues, had announced on radio that the Cabinet was due to meet in emergency session after lunch to discuss funeral arrangements, I was furious. I had to ask the goodly gentleman: Whose Cabinet? I also ordered him to desist from making pronouncements about funeral arrangements. Any such statements would emanate from my office until I appointed a new Prime Minister who in turn would advise me to appoint ministers of his choice.

In making an appointment to the Office of Prime Minister I had to be guided by the relevant provision in the Constitution. However, on the surface there appeared to be no clear-cut case of someone in the House of Representatives who might confidently command the respect of the majority of members of the House. Therein lay my problem. That apart, I had openly made a promise to appoint a new Prime Minister before the end of the day. There was, therefore, no question of postponing the issue. Although it was my prerogative to appoint a Prime Minister in my own deliberate judgement, I felt it necessary to take a few moments in quiet solitude for sober reflection and contemplation in order to read the mood of the Grenadian people before making so important a decision in these unusual political circumstances. I was also mindful of the fact that whoever was appointed would have a short time to prepare for general elections which could not be delayed beyond March 28 – three months after the five years from the time Parliament first met following the 1984 elections. In my view, too, the opposition forces in the House of Representatives, well knowing that elections were nigh, would not seek to oppose any new appointee to the high Office of Prime Minister. In any case it was my perception that the leading figures among the Opposition groups would hardly be interested in leading a government for such a short period of time. From their standpoint it would be more satisfying and presumably more beneficial to proceed with their feverish preparations for elections rather than dissipate their energies on the burden of running a Government which would be short-lived.

Of the fourteen elected members of Parliament, I thought Hon. Ben Jones was the one most likely to command the respect of the majority in the House of Representatives, even though he was leading a party which then had only five parliamentary seats including his own. I, therefore, called Mr Jones, invited him to form a Government, and made him take the oath of allegiance to Her Majesty the Queen as well as the oath of office. That was about 4.30p.m., and it was his second visit to my office for the day. On this occasion he came through the main gate, and, on leaving, he was provided with a security man. Before administering the oaths I made this short statement which was widely circulated in the media:

"This morning I announced the very sad news of the passing of the Rt. Hon. H. A. Blaize, the Prime Minister. As a result of his passing it was left to me to appoint a new Prime Minister. This, of course, is a great responsibility, but it is one which I alone, according to the Constitution, must discharge. In the present circumstances, I delayed the appointment for several hours, because I thought it prudent to take soundings and to consult before taking a decision. I have now made up my mind, but

I want to point out that in making up my mind I had to be guided by the Constitution of Grenada which I hold very sacred and also, and this is very important, I had to think in terms of the peace and stability of our country. As I have said before, several times before, whatever I do in this office as Governor General, I take into consideration first and foremost the national interest.

And so, I have decided to ask Mr Ben Joseph Jones to be Prime Minister of our country. And again let me repeat, that I think I have made the right decision and so I am going to ask Mr Jones to take the Oath of Allegiance to Her Majesty the Queen as well as the Oath of office.

I want to appeal to all the people of Grenada to give every support to the new Prime Minister, and also I want to ask all Grenadians to remain calm at this sad moment and I expect the ready support of all citizens of this country. In a very short time we have to go to the polls. Grenadians will be given an opportunity at the polls to elect a Government of their choice, and between now and then I expect that all concerned will behave with responsibility, with decency and as true Grenadians for the peace, stability, and prosperity of our country."

Jones immediately selected his ministers, who took the prescribed oaths before me on the following day. The Prime Minister had little or no room to manoeuvre given the current distribution of membership in the House. He, therefore, reappointed the Cabinet of Ministers who were in office at the time of Mr Blaize's death, but gave some of them added responsibilities.

Born in rural St. Andrew's on August 5, 1924, Ben Jones received his early education at the Belair Presbyterian School where he showed great academic promise. He served in the Windward Islands Battalion of the South Caribbean Force of the British Army for two years before migrating to the Dutch colony of Aruba for employment with the Lago Oil Company. There he met Herbert Blaize and became one of his most trusted friends. Undoubtedly Jones was endowed with a good brain, which he put to good use. Fired with ambition, Jones decided to pursue studies in law. From Aruba he made his way to London where he first enrolled at Chiswick Polytechnic and attended classes there for two years in order to acquire certain academic requirements necessary for reading law. He obtained membership in Gray's Inn and enrolled with the Council of Legal Education, but he was not satisfied simply to study for the bar examinations on his way to becoming a barrister. He wanted a law degree as well and in 1962 he annexed the LL.B. from London University. In that same year he was qualified as a Barrister-At-Law. On his return to Grenada in 1964, he entered private practice and shortly afterwards was appointed Magistrate of the St. George's Magistrate Court. After the attainment of Statehood by Grenada in 1967 Jones sought and obtained a transfer to the Civil Service as a Senior Assistant Secretary. He organized and was responsible for the Division of External Affairs in the

Premier's Office. This was the precursor to the full-blown Ministry of External Affairs in independent Grenada. His stay in the civil service was short. He seemed more interested in serving his people in a political capacity.

Jones first entered politics in 1967 when he was named an Opposition Senator. In fact he served in the Senate from 1967 to 1979 when the revolutionary regime abandoned Parliament. In the intervening years he had offered himself as a candidate for one of the St. Andrew's seats, but was never able to get past the post before the other contestants. Sir Eric Gairy, who had great admiration for him tried unremittingly to woo him over to his Grenada United Labour Party. Jones first had to witness the fall and rise of parliamentary democracy before he could capture an electoral seat and so ensure a place around the horseshoe table in the House of Representatives. That was in the December 1984 elections. When the Cabinet was appointed Jones was named Minister for External Affairs and Legal Affairs.

Affable and friendly, Ben Jones could move freely with people of all political shades. I have never known him to be confrontational, although he could make some hard-hitting speeches in Parliament and during electioneering campaigns. He had had a good record of community work in St. Andrew's parish. In and out of active politics he got himself involved in community efforts. Himself a tennis player, he quietly contributed towards the development of tennis in Grenada generally and in St. Andrew's in particular. For many years he was President of the Grenada Lawn Tennis Association and served in a similar capacity in the Windward Islands Lawn Tennis Association. Avid reader that he was, Jones had proven himself to be a first class public speaker. His diction, his clarity of thought and his simplicity in the use of words all manifested themselves in his beautiful and engaging delivery.

The immediate concern of Prime Minister Jones was his preoccupation with preparations for the State funeral of his friend and mentor, The Rt. Hon. Herbert Blaize. The 71-year-old late Prime Minister was accorded a State funeral with full honours. On Friday, December 22, at the St. George's Anglican Church the funeral service took the form of a concelebrated Eucharist with the Venerable Charles A. Adams, Archdeacon of St. Vincent and the Grenadines, as chief celebrant. In the absence of the Bishop of the Windward Islands, it devolved upon Archdeacon Adams, Vicar General of the diocese and most senior clergyman, to officiate at the funeral. It was an impressive array of clergymen processing to the altar of this historic church. The local Anglican clergy, headed by Venerable Fr. Clement Francis, Archdeacon of Grenada, was well represented. The Catholic Bishop of St. George's-in-Grenada was there. So, too, were the heads of the Methodist and Presbyterian churches and the Salvation Army. Also in the procession were visiting clergymen including the Chairman of the Barbados Council of Churches, Grenadian-born Fr. Paul Lashley. Assembled in the choir loft was a massed choir made up of the choirs of the Anglican, Roman Catholic, Methodist and Presbyterian Churches in St. George's as well as the National Folk Choir and A Group of Us. There were three organists in attendance.

The church was filled to capacity, and many more people had to follow the service from outside. From early morning hundreds more had filed past the body as it lay in State in the Chamber of Parliament at York House. Among the diverse and mournful congregation were Caribbean Prime Ministers, other representatives of regional Governments and of regional and international organizations, Ambassadors and High Commissioners and other members of the diplomatic corps. By Her Majesty's command I represented her at the funeral. I read the first lesson, while the President of the Senate, Dr. John Watts, read the second. An appreciation of the life of the late Prime Minister by His Excellency Dr. Lamuel Stanislaus, Grenada's Ambassador to the United Nations, held the unwavering attention of the huge congregation. The superb eloquence of Dr. Stanislaus and his certain and indisputable knowledge of the departed Prime Minister, "his near and dear life-long friend," made him the fittest person to deliver the eulogy. At the conclusion of the obsequies in the St. George's Anglican Church the body of the late Prime Minister was taken on its final journey to Carriacou for burial. This took place on Sunday, December 24, at Brunswick cemetery just outside the town of Hillsborough. Carriacou held a funeral Eucharist at Christ the King Church in Carriacou similar to the one held in St. George's two days previously. The resident priest officiated, and the church choir in their ceremonial uniform sang lustily. The Royal Grenada Police Band was in attendance. I was again invited to read a lesson and Dr. Stanislaus gave a stirring eulogy.

The people of Carriacou turned out in large numbers to pay their last respects to the man who had served them so selflessly, so faithfully and so well for so long. As the funeral procession left the church and wended its way through the streets of Hillsborough, on-lookers stood silently in deep reverence. The cortege stopped briefly in front of the Blaize's residence as if to wave a fond good-bye. On Main Street flags were flying at halfmast on Government buildings. But what was most touching was the manner in which the boats in the harbour paid their respects. Nearly all of them had a black flag hoisted at half mast, and the sailors and other occupants on board stood at attention as the cortege passed by. The music played by the Police Band, the slow march of the police officers and the general orderliness of the procession all contributed towards making the occasion solemn and impressive. The Last Post was sounded at the graveside.

Of all the political systems, I give my vote to democracy without any reservations. The manner in which I was able to transfer power to Ben Jones in somewhat difficult and unusual circumstances bears testimony to the strength of the democratic process. The country remained calm, there was no protest, and my decision was accepted by all the political parties. Grenadians from all the political parties mourned the death of Herbert Blaize and paid sincere tribute to him. His demise brought together for a while all the political parties, whose leaders temporarily sank their political differences in a display of respect and reverence for the departed Prime Minister. What was even more remarkable about all this was that the death and burial took place within the six days prior to Christmas day, normally a time of great festivity and abandon. Once the last rites had been performed at the burial, Grenadians addressed themselves yet again to the merriment of Christmas fully realizing that nothing they could do or say would bring back the Prime Minister. But the Roman Catholic Church of which Mrs Blaize was a devout member felt obliged to pay their own tribute to the late Prime Minister. Thus on Friday, January 12, as a mark of great respect, the Roman Catholic Church held a concelebrated requiem mass at the Cathedral of the Immaculate Conception for the repose of the soul of this Christian gentleman. The Bishop of St. George's-in-Grenada, His Lordship the Most Reverend Sydney Charles, was the chief celebrant.

When Ben Joseph Jones assumed the role of Prime Minister, he well knew that his main objective was to prepare for general elections, and perhaps his main aim was to win the forthcoming elections. The majority of citizens did not expect anything spectacular from the premiership of Mr Jones, bearing in mind his unusually brief stay in office. Thus he could not afford to dissipate his energy by starting new projects while at the same time trying to complete some of the work that Mr Blaize had begun. This was certainly a tall order for a man who was suddenly plunged into the deep and sometimes unclear waters of the premiership with diminished manpower in his cabinet. Meanwhile, the Supervisor of Elections advised me that all preparations were in place for the forthcoming elections, and his office was ready to act once the election writ was issued. I could not, of course, issue the election writ without first being advised by the Prime Minister about the date of the election. But what I did issue, following discussions I had with the Attorney General and the Supervisor of Elections, was a proclamation bringing into force the electoral list for the forthcoming elections. By then everyone had realized that the elections were nigh. The issuance of this proclamation simply heightened speculation about the imminent announcement of the actual election date.

Life in the tri-island State went on as usual. I continued to receive a steady flow of visitors at Governor General's House. Among those visiting was the new Chilean Ambassador who presented his letters of credence. Mrs Judy Starling, daughter of the late Sir Laurence Lindo, who acted as Governor of the Windward Islands in 1959, came by with her husband for some nostalgic moments as she viewed the interior of the house and later walked through the garden. I received representatives from the world of sport, from business, from agriculture, from regional and international organizations and from foreign governments.

In the rival political camps patience was on the wane while restlessness was beginning to fill the breach. The clamour for elections was growing louder and clearer, but all in good humour. There was no suggestion of violence from any quarter, nor was there any semblance of unseemly behaviour in any constituency. But the impatience of the political leaders began to show. On Monday, 21, I received a three-man delegation from the New National Party (NNP). The delegation was led by Dr. Keith Mitchell and the other members were Lawrence Joseph and Daniel Williams. They expressed great concern about the Prime Minister's dilatoriness in naming a date for elections, and pointed with grave disapproval to some of the decisions the government had taken and were continuing to take. As to naming the election date, I felt obliged to remind them that this was the Prime Minister's prerogative, and no respectable Prime Minister would allow anyone to dictate to him on the question of calling elections. Rather in our democratic society the Prime Minister would be guided by the provisions of the Constitution. On the matter of taking far reaching decisions, I could not accept such sweeping statements, well knowing that any decision taken by any government would be approved by some and not by others. If the decisions fell within the ambit of the law and the Constitution I did not have a problem.

Swift on the heels of the NNP, yet another three-man delegation, this time from the Grenada United Labour Party (GULP), came to see me the following day. Herbert Preudhomme headed this delegation and the other members were Dr. Wellington Friday and Dr. Jerry Seales. They came full of complaint, and as if they had compared notes with the earlier delegation the substance of their complaints was not dissimilar. First they handed me three documents from their political leader and President, Sir Eric Gairy. In discussions they also expressed grave concern about certain far-reaching decisions the Government appeared to have taken. They considered the current Government as a purely caretaker Government. But I could not conceal my astonishment when they informed me that if their party came to power they would not honour certain agreements and financial obligations of the current Government. I thought that such disclosure was unbecoming of men who were aspiring to high public office, and I classified their attitude as nothing more than puerile. I told them that any new Government assuming office should honour the commitments of the outgoing Government if only for credibility.

These three wise men who so faithfully and dutifully made representations on behalf of their political leader expressed unease about the composition of the electoral list. Yet they could not tell me exactly what was wrong with it. I reminded them of the method of registration used in the past and went on to make a comparison with what currently obtained and asked them to draw their own conclusions in an objective manner. I was not convinced that anything was wrong with the electoral list. Nor could I discern loop-holes in the method of registration which was a vast improvement on what obtained before 1984. The delegation admitted that there was some merit in the new style method of registration that brought the Registration Officer face to face with the person to be registered. However, three days later Mr Herbert Preudhomme was again at my doorstep, this time accompanied by Mr Derek Knight QC, to further discuss the registration of voters. The gist of the matter was that they wanted certain names added to the list. I could give them no comfort, and advised them that the Supervisor of Elections had to abide by the rules at all times.

On that same day Friday, January 26, Derek Knight, Attorney for the GULP, went into the Ministry of Health which was located at the extreme end of the Carenage. This visit was not a friendly one. Nor was it a normal visit for business transaction.

Mr Knight demanded the keys for the building following a Court Order that unhappily had not been challenged by the Legal Department. He and others actually occupied the building, and so work was disrupted. Whether such precipitate action was taken to embarrass the Government and thus gain political mileage for the GULP was open to question. The matter was dealt with by the Court of Appeal later in the morning and all was well again, at least for the time being. An application for a stay of execution was granted by the Court. This building, Progress House, which had been confiscated by the People's Revolutionary Government, was the head office of Sir Eric Gairy's Grenada Manual and Mental Workers' Union. The Ministry of Health had been housed in this building during the revolution and continued its operations there after democracy was restored. The building was constructed during the Gairy administration of 1967/1972 after the Union had bought a piece of prime land from the Government. At that time the Head of Government and President of the Union was one and the same person. The previous Government had earmarked that portion of land to accommodate in part a ministerial complex, but they were too slow to move. No sooner than Gairy assumed office in 1967 he sold the land to the Union. With the demise of the revolution in 1983 the whole question of freedom to own property was highlighted. Owners of confiscated property immediately began to bombard Government with massive claims for compensation, and even in cases of restitution of property to the rightful owners, claims for loss of use or for arrears in rent were submitted. It was a real dilemma for the Blaize administration with its slender financial resources. Added to this financial blitz were the demands for compensation in respect of lands acquired prior to the Revolution by the Gairy administration under the Acquisition Law. A commission was appointed to examine the validity of those claims and to make recommendations. Progress House, of course, was not to be left out. For the most part, restitution and/or compensation was recommended. But everyone knew that Government would be hard pressed to make good these claims. It was against this background that the Grenada Manual and Mental Workers Union took Government to court for its pound of flesh, and it was rather ironical that its president wearing another hat was the architect-in-chief of the acquisition of lands for which compensation was yet to be paid. But through his attorney he was pressing on for compensation and arrears of rental even to the extent of calling a halt to the work of the Ministry of Health.

The activities at the Ministry of Health did cause some anxiety. The last thing I wanted at this point in time was any form of confrontational politics, however mild. I summoned the Commissioner of Police who gave me a full-scale report on the matter and reassured me on the state of security in the country. I held consultations with the Attorney General and later that same day I received the Prime Minister who briefed me on the Ministry of Health matter and on the state of the country generally. I was satisfied that there was no cause for alarm.

Meanwhile a breath of fresh air was coming out of South Africa. Over the years the scourge of apartheid had sapped the creative energies of black South Africans and mercilessly robbed them of their dignity and self-esteem. For as many years Grenada like the rest of the Caribbean had joined freedom-loving people everywhere to renounce the iniquitous and degrading system of apartheid as practised in South Africa. Apartheid was condemned in every international forum, and in many a massive demonstration in the world's capital cities, not to mention the powerful homilies and writings of the more enlightened religious leaders. The people in the Caribbean, who bore close affinity to the majority of South Africans, had always demonstrated a sense of oneness with their black brothers and sisters in South Africa and reached out to them in solidarity of spirit. When on February 2 at the opening of Parliament in Cape Town President de Klerk, in a rare display of humanity, and seized by political inevitability, lifted the thirty-year old ban on the African National Congress and announced the imminent release of Nelson Mandela, ripples of joy went through the Caribbean. The Grenadian people paused to take note and to rejoice. The President also lifted restrictions on some thirty other organizations, including the Communist party. He further announced the release of political prisoners, the suspension of the death penalty and the abolition of emergency restrictions on the media. Nine days later the 72 year old Nelson Mandela was released from prison after twenty-seven years. For the majority of people in South Africa this act of humanity signalled a future of hope. The dismantling of apartheid could not be far off.

Coming as they did during the observance of Grenada's sixteenth anniversary of Independence, these developments in South Africa added zest to the usual pomp and ceremony of the local celebration. I took the salute at the Queen's Park parade where the sharply dressed police and other uniformed groups went through their paces with exceptional smartness and alertness. Prime Minister Jones, who gave an excellent address at the main ceremony in the presence of several diplomats and other visiting dignitaries, must have been very pleased not only with the large attendance but also with the mood of the crowd. In his speech, while paying tribute to the life and work of the late Prime Minister, he struck forcibly at the chords of patriotism and exhorted his listeners to unite in love and harmony as one family in order to achieve the national goals of higher productivity and an improved quality of life. He made reference to the events which were unfolding in South Africa. To the disappointment of many he did not announce the date of the forthcoming elections. Instead, he called for free and fair elections. H.M.S. Phoebe under the command of Commander D. J. Smith was in port for the celebrations. So also was a Venezuelan frigate.

On the morning of Saturday, February 10, I received Prime Minister Jones who advised me that he had chosen Tuesday, March 13 , as election day. Jones appeared to be in good fettle and brimming with confidence. I tried to figure out what prompted him to choose Tuesday rather than, say, Thursday, and March 13, an already significant date in our history and not some other date.

Then it came to mind that Gairy, whose party was contesting the elections, never liked doing important business on a Tuesday, and I knew for sure that he would avoid travelling on a Tuesday. "Never on a Tuesday," I would always remind my senior staff in my Cabinet Secretary days. I wondered whether Prime Minister Jones knew of this peculiarity on the part of his rival, and had taken it into consideration in selecting Tuesday as polling day. As for March 13, did he want to claim a convincing win on that date in order to take away some of the "glory" from the glorious revolution of March 13, 1979? Whatever the criteria used, Jones continued to be in a happy mood as he launched his electioneering campaign, or as he called it, a political crusade at Queen's Park the following day. In front of a huge crowd Jones in a hard hitting address announced the date of General Elections as Tuesday, 13 March, adding that he had already advised me to issue the Elections Writ. This announcement was received with great enthusiasm by those in attendance, and no doubt by the contending political leaders who were listening to their radios at home. Part of Mr Jones's strategy for the launching of his campaign was to bring home from Trinidad the world renowned calypsonian, Grenada-born *Mighty Sparrow* who entertained the crowd at the "political crusade." It was left to be seen to what extent the enthusiasm so prevalent throughout this initial crusade would be translated into positive outcomes for Mr Jones on polling day.

Rapidly the entire country, including Carriacou and Petit Martinique, was gripped by elections fever. Frankly I was rather sceptical about the preparations, if any, Jones had made for the elections from his party perspective. To some people, The National Party was a fall out of the New National Party. To others, it was a rehash of the old Grenada National Party (GNP). Jones made the mistake of gathering around him a number of old GNP diehards of yesteryear, each jockeying to be his chief adviser. Many of these individuals were out of touch with the thinking, needs, and aspirations of the youthful population which made up a large percentage of the voters. The days of condescension were over. Youth was begging for a chance to show its mettle and to make some meaningful contribution to nation building. What was really needed was the building of bridges so that the collective wisdom of the old and the exuberance and talent of the young could combine to bring the best out of the Grenadian man and woman. The National Party was a new party with an old image. It lacked vision no less than the will to succeed. The party had to be built on a more solid and secure base, and more importantly it needed to penetrate into the rural heartland of Grenada if it were to capture a significant number of votes on election day. Jones himself had a rural background. He was friendly, kind and eloquent, but from the standpoint of political leadership he lacked the savvy to organize, to mobilize and to get things done. He struck me as being a leader with an inordinate number of lieutenants around him but with insufficient foot soldiers. When it dawned upon Jones that it might be necessary to seek help from outside to organize his campaign strategy he discovered that he had missed the boat. He approached sources who had already been committed to the NNP. All along Jones had apparently been lulled into a false sense of security by those who made him believe that the name of the late Prime Minister Herbert Blaize, if featured prominently and constantly in the campaign, would produce an unusually high number of votes for the TNP.

Jones's election campaign was based on the performance of the Blaize administration, the spirit of the late Herbert Blaize, and integrity and honesty in public life. None of these could sufficiently woo the electorate who were more interested in the bread and butter issues of the day. It was quite clear to any election watcher that The National Party under the leadership of the incumbent Prime Minister was entering the contest ill-prepared, disorganized, and disoriented. There were no effective party organs in place, particularly at the constituency level where in some cases it was difficult to find a suitable and willing contestant. It might be argued with some justification that Jones should not be entirely blamed for this state of unpreparedness. Obviously, Blaize had not laid the groundwork for elections, even though he must have known he would have to call one in three months' time, if he had lived. In the absence of any efficient mechanism at the constituency level, The National Party had to resort to a recruitment drive for candidates through the personage of Sir Hudson Scipio, a high-ranking member of the party and Speaker of the House of Representatives. It was difficult to tell what criteria Sir Hudson used in his recruiting efforts. But one thing was certain. It was a great strain on this devoted and faithful party member who, no longer blessed with youthful endurance, had to traverse the villages and towns in his quest of prospective candidates. Needless to say he was not altogether successful given the still born birth of The National Party and the conflicting perception of the political future of Grenada between Sir Hudson on the one hand, and those he was trying to woo on the other.

The other main political parties were not without their problems. Their common problem lay in the difficulty of finding a full slate of suitable candidates to contest the elections. The Grenada United Labour Party (GULP) never had the confidence of the newer, younger voters. Nor did it ever regain the confidence of those who had abandoned it, although it must be admitted that there were pockets of strong and unflinching support perhaps sufficient to carry the day for the party in three or four constituencies. Gairy was still the supreme boss of the party and every candidate had to give blind allegiance to the party boss. Under the leadership of Keith Mitchell, The New National Party (NNP), the remnant of the old (NNP) which had its birth in Union Island, did not have sufficient time to repair the damage done to the party. Further, many of the prospective voters perceived Mitchell, rightly or wrongly, as a man who could not be trusted because, as they claimed, he had stabbed Blaize in the back in the leadership contest at the party convention of January, 1989. The National Democratic Congress (NDC) like the (TNP) was a splinter group from the original Union Island NNP. While the Congress Party appeared to be better prepared than either Mitchell's NNP or Jones's TNP yet there were misgivings among certain influential party members about handing over the leadership to Nicholas Brathwaite. Many inside the party thought it was a cowardly act on the part of George Brizan, the former party leader. On the other side of the coin, public opinion seemed to indicate that Brathwaite's administrative experience and stature would enhance the chances of an NDC victory at the polls. In any case, despite the reservations of certain party members, Brathwaite was appointed party leader unopposed at the 1989 convention. The other parties did not have a ghost of a chance of being declared winner in any polling station, let alone any constituency.

On Nomination Day, February 23, seventy-six candidates were duly nominated to contest the fifteen seats in the House of Representatives. In the intervening period between Nomination Day and Election Day, the intensity of the campaign increased with motorcades, blaring loud speakers, colourfully displayed posters of all shapes and sizes, various meetings in favourite spots in every constituency, door to door soliciting of votes by party workers, presentation of candidates to householders who for one reason or other would not leave their home and follow the campaign trail. In Grenada electioneering meetings are generally held in the open air. I could not escape the full blast of the microphone or the thunderous applause and shouts of approval as candidate after candidate pontificated on the policies his party would pursue if and when given the mandate by the electorate. The roving resonant microphone attached to vehicles conveyed glowing messages about parties and their candidates on a daily basis. I must confess that I would have given my vote to the chirping of the birds rather than to the contrasting blasting noise of the early morning microphone along the normally quiet Upper Lucas Street. However, it was through all these means that I was able to get information about the parties and their candidates.

By Sunday, March 11, the electioneering campaign had reached fever pitch proportions and related activities had taken on a carnival like atmosphere. Ben Jones, the incumbent Prime Minister and Party Leader of TNP, had been playing the Blaize card very hard indeed, but admittedly without much success.What Mr Jones's advisers failed to grasp was that elections are not won by extolling the virtues of dead men. Elections are about the living. They are about the presentation of good and honest men and women who could pursue a realistic programme and direct policies for the common good. Issues such as employment, healthcare, education and the environment were of now of great importance to the Grenadian voter.

A review of the election manifestoes revealed that there were no major differences either in philosophy or programme as put forward by the contesting political parties. If indeed there were any differences, they were really differences in degree rather than in kind. The Maurice Bishop Patriotic Movement (MBPM) with a strong socialist bias came nearest to presenting the electorate with a manifesto with a difference. While the political philosophy of the MBPM was never clearly articulated, it was expected by the populace in general that they would endeavour to continue to toe the New Jewel Movement party line with their own brand of socialism, as they had been doing since the formation of the Party. Because of recent history, this was not acceptable even to those who had earlier supported Bishop. Many young Grenadians had abandoned hope of a socialist path after their traumatic experience of the death and destruction that befell the People's Revolutionary Government, and were not inclined to enter upon a similar experiment under the MBPM. Moreover, the leadership of the Party had no national appeal and most of the stalwart supporters had dissociated themselves from the Party. The leader of the party was Terence Marryshow, a medical doctor, trained in Cuba. He was a grandson of the late Theophilous Albert Marryshow, one of Grenada's heroes and "father" of the short lived West Indian Federation (1958-1962). In the current political climate the name Marryshow did not help, and the young doctor had neither the intellectual stature nor the charisma of Maurice Bishop. The Deputy Leader, Lyle Bullen of Carriacou, an entrepreneur from a business family, was more capitalist than socialist in his outlook and way of life.

The torridity of the campaign had no effect on the functioning of Governor General's House. I was absolutely confident that the elections would be fair and free and that there would be no associated violence. I was equally confident that once the elections had ended people would accept the results and abandon the rigidity of divisions along party lines.

Polling day came and went without incident. Perhaps this was Jones's great achievement during his brief premiership. He had constantly called for free and fair elections, and through his campaign style and his frequent exhortations he worked towards that end. After dinner my wife and I stayed up to hear the preliminary results which were being announced on radio from York House in St. George's as they came to hand. In her usual meticulous and thorough manner my wife jotted down the results of every polling station on a form she had specially prepared for that purpose. At that time I was more concerned with the overall results in each constituency. My worst fears were confirmed when the results showed that no single party received an absolute majority of seats. Of the 15 seats at stake the National Democratic Congress captured 7, the Grenada United Labour Party 4, the New National Party 2 and The National Party 2. As anticipated, the MBPM failed in its efforts to secure a single seat.

Some self-appointed pundits thought that I had an enormous problem on my hand. Others called it a crisis and claimed that I was powerless to appoint a new Prime Minister. Still others, describing the day's polling as inconclusive, went so far as to suggest that I should take upon myself to call fresh elections, though they did not venture to say what section of the Constitution gave me such authority. Hard as they might try I knew they could not find any such section. I did not think the results of the elections constituted a crisis, and without delay I began to formulate in my mind what seemed to be the best way forward.

In all the circumstances it appeared that the Leader of the National Democratic Congress (NDC), Nicholas Brathwaite, was the man most likely to command the support of the majority of members of the House of Representatives. To appoint Brathwaite as Prime Minister was to run the risk of the formation of yet another minority Government. But I thought it was worth taking such a risk. For one thing power meant so much to some of the winning candidates that they dared not attempt to bring down a fledging Government having just gone through a long and costly campaign; and there was no guarantee that they would retain their seats in a freshly called election. Also, with the knowledge that one of the successful GULP candidates had breathed a sigh of relief and raised a great hosanna of joy when Gairy's personal defeat in the South St. George constituency was announced, I had a gut feeling that once a Government was formed one or more representatives outside the ruling party might wish to support the Government.

While all this was going through my mind I heard nothing from Prime Minister Jones who, if he were resourceful and sufficiently alert, might have been able to mobilize the successful NNP and GULP candidates around him with a view to forming a new Government. Brathwaite, the NDC leader, did not show up in St. George's until the afternoon of March 15. He was still in Carriacou basking in the glory of his handsomely won election victory there, when he should have made his way to St. George's on the first flight on March 14 in readiness for a possible call from me. Jones, then, had a glorious opportunity to take the initiative in an effort to keep the premiership. But he failed to grasp that opportunity. On the other hand, perhaps Jones was really not interested in getting together with the NNP and the GULP to form a government. During the electioneering campaign, he had made it quite clear that it would be a sorry day for Grenada if either the NNP or the GULP were to win the elections.

It was Dr. Keith Mitchell, Political Leader of the NNP and successful candidate for the North-West St. George Constituency, who seemed to have been most proactive in trying to effect an arrangement whereby the NDC would be denied any chance of forming the next Government. He himself would settle for the role of Deputy to Ben Jones. To my utter astonishment, Mitchell telephoned early on the morning of March 14 to say that eight of the successful candidates had grouped together and decided to form the next Government and they were coming to my residence to so inform me.

The day went by and the disparate eight never sought an appointment to see me. All that happened was that I received a further telephone call from Mitchell who advised me that they were due to hold a meeting among themselves before coming to see me. By the following morning rumour had begun to spread her ugly wings to add more uncertainty and confusion to the minds of people. There were meetings and rumours of further meetings, accusations of political intrigues and displaced loyalties were being levelled left, right and centre. The regional media were beginning to show intense interest in what they referred to as the political stalemate in Grenada. By then I realized that the grouping of the eight was a well nigh impossible accomplishment although Mitchell and others were trying desperately to keep the plan alive.

It is not usual for Governors General to make pronouncements on political matters in public , but I felt impelled to do so at the earliest opportunity even on the ides of March. Without any foreboding I went to the St. Joseph's Convent mid-morning on Thursday, March 15, to open an exhibition of arts and craft. My visit was fully covered by the local press and radio. In my brief address I took my audience by surprise when I referred to the current political situation in the country. I gave the assurance that I was on top of the situation and I stated categorically that I was going to appoint a Prime Minister the following day. My remarks were swiftly and faithfully reproduced throughout the region. On return to my office I summoned Edwin A Heyliger, the Legal Adviser , and instructed him to prepare the necessary Instrument of Appointment. In the afternoon we went to Sauteurs where we attended a church service and reception which were part of the "St. Patrick's Week" celebrations. Later my security officer informed me that after the service many little groups stood outside the church chit chatting about the political situation, some calling for a coalition Government, others for new elections but all wondering what the Governor General would do. I was also informed that Nicholas Brathwaite had flown from Carriacou to Grenada on the midday flight and had a meeting with Prime Minister Jones.

On Friday, 16, I summoned Prime Minister Ben Jones to my office. He arrived promptly at eleven o'clock in the forenoon. I gently reminded Mr Jones that it was three days after elections and I warned him that I was ready to act with respect to the formation of a Government. I went on to advise him to resign, and made it quite clear to him that if he failed to do so I would revoke his appointment as Prime Minister. Meanwhile Heyliger, as Legal Adviser, was in my Personal Assistant's office getting the Revocation Order typed. Using his better judgement, Jones immediately resigned. The road was quite clear then for me to send for the person who in my own deliberate judgement could command the support of the majority of the elected members. Minutes after Mr Jones took his leave, my office was able to arrange for his resignation to be announced on the mid-day newscast. At the same time it was announced that I would appoint a new Prime Minister before the end of the day. Efforts were still being made to get the eight together. A meeting was held in the office of a prominent barrister, but the big meeting which was scheduled for 11.30 a.m. at Mt. Royal, the official Residence of the Prime Minister, proved abortive, as two of the principal actors did not show up.

I immediately called in Brathwaite and asked him to form a government. He complied without any reservation, and seemed confident that he could count on non-party support in parliament. At two o'clock in the afternoon in the presence of his party colleagues and the media Mr Nicholas Brathwaite was sworn in as Prime Minister. After taking the prescribed Oath of Allegiance and the Oath of Office Brathwaite made some brief remarks promising to give of his best at all times and seeking the co-operation and support of all. I then abruptly closed the ceremony with these words: *"There is work to be done. Let us get on with it."*

In less than an hour after the swearing-in ceremony Dr. Mitchell wanted to know what would be the position if the eight came to see me. I told him that there was no consolation prize, and I could neither accommodate nor entertain them. They would first have to bring down Mr Brathwaite's Administration, and they could only do that in Parliament.

# 14

## *Demitting Office*

NICHOLAS Alexander Brathwaite had the rare distinction of becoming Prime Minister on his first attempt at the polls. While he was new to frontline politics he was by no means a green horn in the art of administration. Born in 1925, Brathwaite received his early education at the Grenada Boys' Secondary School, the premier school on the island. Like Herbert Blaize before him, he had to cross the sometimes difficult passage between Carriacou and Grenada by schooner at least twice per term in pursuit of a secondary education. Brathwaite's career was essentially in the field of education, except for a spell of seven years when he migrated to work as an oil refinery operator in the Dutch West Indian island of Curaçao. On his return to Carriacou from Curaçao, he resumed his work in education continuing through the ranks to become head teacher of Dover Model School Carriacou, Assistant Inspector of Schools, and still later Senior Tutor of the Grenada Teachers College. Meanwhile he proceeded to Jamaica where he successfully completed a course of studies at the University of the West Indies to annex the Bachelor's degree in Education. In 1968 he was appointed Principal of Grenada Teachers' College and one year later was elevated to the post of Chief Education Officer. Brathwaite served in that capacity until 1974 when he went on secondment to the Commonwealth Secretariat to take up the job of Regional Director of the Commonwealth Youth Programme based in Guyana.

In his capacity as Chairman of the Advisory Council that I had set up in November, 1983, Brathwaite performed the role of *quasi* Prime Minister with distinction. Pragmatic in approach, he brought to his new role a level of humility and selflessness. Under his Chairmanship, everyday life in Grenada was brought back to normalcy, and he worked to ensure that our democratic institutions and freedoms were restored.

After celebrating with his constituents in Carriacou, Brathwaite arrived in Grenada to assume control of government. In a sense he was about to bat on what appeared to be a tough wicket. On the day when Prime Minister Brathwaite solemnly took the oaths of allegiance and of office, the prospects of a working majority in Parliament were not bright for him. It was Brathwaite's team of seven against the rest who numbered eight. A minority Government loomed large.

But luck was on Brathwaite's side. Within a matter of days his parliamentary team increased by one. On Monday, March 19, three days after the Prime Minister was sworn in, I received a letter from Mr Edzel Thomas, the victorious GULP candidate for the St. John's constituency, informing me that he would support Mr Brathwaite in Parliament. He further intimated that it was his intention to become a member of the National Democratic Congress (NDC). This meant that he was going to take his exit from the GULP under whose banner he had entered the electoral race. This did not surprise me as I was told by a very reliable source and close relative of Thomas that he had jumped for joy when Gairy's personal defeat at the polls was announced on election night.

For the next few days I was busily engaged appointing ministers, and parliamentary secretaries, and senators as recommended by the new Prime Minister. Before a representative gathering of church leaders, senior government officials, the business community , the diplomatic corps and the Hon. Chief Justice, I administered the prescribed oaths to the new ministers and parliamentary secretaries on Wednesday, March 21.

Some more good fortune came the Prime Minister's way when Ben Jones and Alleyne Walker, the two successful TNP candidates at the polls, decided to throw in their lot with Brathwaite and his NDC colleagues, and to support them in Parliament. Unlike Edzel Thomas, they continued to hold their TNP membership cards and maintained their party loyalty. Jones was named Minister for Agriculture and Walker was made a parliamentary secretary. I administered the oath to both men on Thursday April 22. If there was any lingering doubt about the newly appointed Government's tenure of office, such doubt was effectively dispelled by the entry of Thomas, Jones and Walker. Their governmental appointments quietly brought to an end any speculation that the Government might be short-lived by the passage of a no confidence motion in Parliament. The new Government could now settle down to the serious business of governing without the anxieties and uncertainties that the election had brought in its wake.

Ben Jones had quietly defied all the self-appointed emissaries who rushed to his doorstep on the morning after the elections seeking his support to form a government. Jones told me that at the crack of dawn he was approached by a newspaper editor who was soliciting his support to be part of a coalition government consisting of the eight successful candidates from TNP, GULP and NNP. On the heels of the newspaper editor was a prominent NNP member from Grenville with a similar quest. His legalistic persuasion could not sufficiently convince Mr Jones. The next to knock at Mr Jones's door were two successful NDC candidates. Mr Jones politely told them that he would rather see their political leader. Then came a GULP member also resident in Grenville. With all his medical skill he was unable to inject the necessary remedy to get Mr Jones to make up his mind to work with the other two parties. Jones failed to show up at meetings which had been arranged to discuss the formation of a government to include the GULP, NNP and TNP. Jones was too busily engaged in consulting his party diehards who in their never ending dreamland could not see anything on the political landscape except the fading outline of their own party. However, Brathwaite and Jones met on the afternoon of March 15. They discussed the formation of a new government with special reference to the possibility of NDC and TNP working together. Neither Jones nor Brathwaite was interested in forming a coalition government between NDC and TNP. Brathwaite, nevertheless, was willing to accommodate a joint relationship, and this was acceptable to Jones whose subsequent decision to accept a ministerial appointment in the new government was a clear indication that he preferred to work with Brathwaite's NDC rather than with the other parties. His political colleague, Alleyne Walker, had openly declared that he would follow Mr Jones in Parliament. It was not surprising then that Mr Walker accepted a junior ministerial post in the government.

I appointed Mrs Winifred Strachan, the successful GULP candidate for the St. Andrew's South East constituency, as Leader of the Opposition. She in turn advised me on the appointment of three senators in accordance with Section 24 (2) (b) of the Grenada Constitution. This, too, was Strachan's first appointment since plunging into the unpredictable waters of politics. Like Prime Minister Brathwaite, she had made her contribution to education over a period of some thirty years. As a specialist teacher in Home Economics she ascended the professional ladder to the headship of the Domestic Arts Institute before gaining appointment to the post of Supervisor of Home Economics and School Feeding in the Ministry of Education. Her job was to co-ordinate and oversee the teaching of Home Economics in the schools, and to ensure the effectiveness of the school feeding programme in the primary schools. She co-authored the book, *Home Economics in Action*, which was widely used in the schools. Mrs Strachan was a volunteer social worker in St. Andrew's parish and a member of the Methodist church where she was a lay preacher.

On the morning of April 6, I made the journey to York House to open the first session of the new Parliament, and to read the traditional speech from the throne at a joint sitting of the Senate and the House of Representatives. This colourful ceremony always attracted non-resident ambassadors and high commissioners as well as the resident diplomatic community. Because this was a speech prepared by a new government, the seats in the diplomatic section of the gallery were filled to capacity as the diplomats came out in unusually large numbers to hear the contents of the speech, and to get to know the new faces in Parliament. Specially invited guests were the Speakers of the parliaments of Barbados, Trinidad and Tobago, St. Kitts/Nevis, and the British Virgin Island (Tortola), and the Clerk of Parliament from Jamaica. The Throne Speech, outlining the Government's legislative programme for the year, had nothing in it which was fundamentally different from similar speeches in more recent times. As one observer remarked, the NDC was only a branch from the NNP sapling that had been hurriedly planted at Union Island only six years previously, but subsequently badly nurtured. In the speech the Government affirmed its belief in the rule of law, confirmed its obligations to international and regional institutions in which Grenada held membership, and gave the assurance that it would unflinchingly foster the growth of relationship with friendly countries.

From mid-March to mid-April I was busily engaged ensuring that all appointments to Parliament, to the Cabinet, and other state institutions were properly made, and that appointees took the prescribed oaths before assuming office. By the end of March the executive arm of government was in place and functional under the leadership of the Prime Minister. The legislature was fully constituted in accordance with the relevant provisions of the Constitution. The judiciary, too, had to be fully manned. With the resignation of Chief Justice Sir Samuel Graham, it became necessary to appoint a successor without delay. Mr Carol W. J. Bristol, QC, a long-standing practising barrister, was appointed to replace Sir Samuel. On the morning of April 12, I administered the oaths of office and of allegiance to the newly appointed Chief Justice in the presence of the Prime Minister, the Attorney General, and the judges of the High Court.

The most urgent task facing the new administration was the preparation and presentation of the national budget for fiscal year January to December, 1990. While budgets should be normally presented in December, there is a statutory obligation to do so no later than April of the fiscal year. Although all the basic work on the 1990 budget had been done by the technocrats in the Ministry of Finance, nevertheless time and circumstances did not allow an earlier presentation. Further, it could be argued that the then Prime Minister did not have the moral authority to present the budget. Furthermore, in the prevailing political situation I would not have given him the certificate authorizing him to do so. In the forenoon on Thursday, April 19, Hon. George Brizan, Minister for Finance, proudly entered the chamber of the Honourable House of Representatives with his brief case for the presentation of his first ever budget. The imposition of new taxes is always a frightening prospect on budget day, and everyone was waiting anxiously for Mr Brizan to reveal the contents of his black briefcase. In a speech lasting three hours and nine minutes he allayed all fears by announcing that there would be no new taxes. Instead, the emphasis would be on better arrangements for collecting taxes. Of course, the matter of greater efficiency and effectiveness in the collection of revenue was nothing new. In my public life I had heard similar statements from several ministers responsible for finance, and perhaps long after I retire into private life I shall continue to be treated to the same refrain. One of the characteristics I have discovered in the majority of our politicians is that they have a natural propensity to talk profusely but lack the political will to act. Through fear or cowardice (or both) they often reduce themselves into compromising positions when it comes to following through on measures they themselves have approved. Productivity would improve in the government service only when ministers understand their limitations and civil servants begin to observe with due diligence and loyalty their non-partisan role in the governmental machinery bearing in mind that their duty is to serve the public at large, rather than any political or other sectoral interest. Communication between the political directorate and government employees is facilitated by the extent to which there is a clear understanding of each other's role. From my own experience in the civil service, and more particularly from my vantage point as Governor General, it has become clear that poor communication in the Government service leads to frustration, animosity, vindictiveness, lack of trust and falling productivity.

The voices of the people's representatives were certainly heard in the historic 1990 budget debate. It was historic because it was the first time ever that the entire debate was carried live on both radio and television. This was a departure from the practice of broadcasting only the speeches of the Minister for Finance and the Leader of the Opposition who more often than not was the shadow Minister for Finance. The fact that people could sit in their homes and see or listen to their representatives making their contribution to the budget debate was a good boost for democracy, the growth of which was a priority of both the previous government and the present NDC administration. The debate was concluded in the House of Representatives on Friday, May 18. Thus the month long debate gave an opportunity to every member of the House to air his or her views.

In our Christian society, after the solemnities of the Lenten season of compassion and self-denial, we welcome with joyful hope the radiance of Easter. The year 1990 was no exception. Easter Sunday fell on April 15. On that day the churches were filled to capacity, with many of the worshippers making their annual pilgrimage to church for worship, but religious observance apart, Easter was a time for cultural activities, fun and frolic. The village festivities, beach picnics, boat rides, yacht races, weddings and church harvests were all held during the Easter week-end and beyond. The annual St. Mark's day celebrations took me yet again to the town of Victoria, some fifteen miles from St. George's. As I had done so many times before, I declared the celebrations open. These festivities got bigger and bigger with every passing year, and they provided an opportunity to put on display the cultural and other talents of the people of the parish. In an effort to forge cultural links and to strengthen the already existing bonds of friendship and co-operation between Taiwan and Grenada, the hard working resident ambassador His Excellency Liu Polun persuaded his authorities at home to send to Grenada a team of acrobats. The visiting acrobats put in a guest appearance at the St. Mark's day celebrations. They attracted huge crowds at all their performances and I attended their major display at Queen's Park in St. George's.

But amid the April festivities and while the Finance Minister's budget speech was still on the table of the House of Representatives for debate, disaster struck just after 10 p.m. on Friday, April 27. At one end of the Carenage dozens of Grenadians were disembarking from the pleasure boat, *Rhum Runner*, which had berthed in front of the fire brigade building after a birthday cruise along the west coast for a well-known St. George's barrister. In utter bewilderment they were greeted by a ball of fire emanating from the other end of the Carenage, followed by the blaring sirens and thunderous roar of the fire tenders as they raced to the scene of the fire that spread with amazing rapidity. The Georgian buildings which housed several government departments submitted in complete surrender to the flames. Despite their best efforts our firemen and their equipment were no match for this great conflagration which had engulfed the financial complex to bring about complete destruction of the Ministry of Finance, the Treasury, the Inland Revenue Department, the Post Office and the Government Printery.

I stayed up late pondering on the ramifications of such a disaster. The Prime Minister reported to me immediately with deep concern about ascertaining the cause of the fire. The Commissioner of Police also apprised me of the latest situation. On the following day I was conducted by the police on an inspection tour of the burnt area where the debris was still smouldering. It seemed miraculous that the Public Library and the more modest building which accommodated the Audit department had escaped. I sent a telegraph to the Queen informing her of the fire. Prime Minister Brathwaite held an emergency Cabinet meeting to discuss the fire and its implications for sustained productivity in such an important section of the governmental machinery. He also decided to seek help from Britain's Scotland Yard to investigate the cause of the fire. In a broadcast to the nation Prime Minister Brathwaite admonished his listeners to be calm. He promised a full investigation to determine the cause of the fire, and he announced the launching of a rebuilding fund. He struck at the chords of patriotism when he urged his fellow citizens to put the disaster behind them and concentrate on the rebuilding of a structure which would rise phoenix-like from the ashes by dint of their concerted effort, their perseverance and sacrifice. A two-man team from Scotland Yard quickly arrived in Grenada and, to the relief of all, ruled out any probability of arson as the cause of the fire. Their findings suggested that the fire started in the roof of the main treasury building through worn and defective electrical wiring.

This unexpected disaster was a great setback for the new Government that had just begun to feel its way and constituted a nightmare for the dislocated civil servants who had to get the administrative machinery in motion again with the minimum of delay. They were able to salvage from the rubble the great safes which were left intact despite the heat from the raging flames. Alternative accommodation had to be found for scores of employees. The Grenada Co-operative Nutmeg Association had recently constructed a massive building on the Lagoon Road about two miles away from the burnt out complex. Fortunately, this building came in very handy and Government rented it to relocate the Ministry of Finance and the Treasury. The Printery went to the old West Indian newspaper building on Hillsborough Street that the Gairy administration had bought some years before. The General Post Office first moved to the unoccupied St. James Hotel in the heart of St. George's, then to Burns Point to occupy a building belonging to the Port Authority. It has often been said that Grenadians always rise to the occasion, and the co-operation, hard work and tolerance of the general populace both in the private and public sectors give credence to this assertion. But, above all, the political directorate and the civil servants were worthy of high commendation for their joint efforts in speedily resuming service to the public. This great St. George's fire figured prominently in the Prime Minister's "state of the nation" address on July 3 marking his first one hundred days in office.

As if the St. George's fire was not enough, in the early hours of the morning on Wednesday, July 25, Grenada was in the grip of tropical storm Arthur with winds of about 50 miles per hour. Grenadians had been warned the day before to prepare for the first storm of the season, which was about 190 miles south-east of Grenada at latitude 10.5 N. All sporting events, including a match between Jamaica and Grenada in the Shell Football Competition, were postponed. Doors and windows were battened down, fishing boats and other small craft were pulled up well beyond the beach line. People were reminded of the buildings designated as shelters in the event of storms and hurricanes. Grocery shops suddenly became unusually busy as people flocked into them to purchase essential items for storage at home. While the chances of Grenada being struck by a hurricane were minimal, Grenadians were still very conscious of the severe damage in lives and property wrought by hurricane Janet in September, 1955. Grenada had never got into a state of preparedness for that hurricane and the warning was taken lightly. Since then we have never had a visitation from a hurricane, but year after year during the hurricane season Grenadians are on the alert with eyes and ears glued to their televisions and radios following the hurricane path with a depth of interest hitherto unknown in a island country which still prides itself as being outside the hurricane belt.

Storm Arthur brought with it very heavy rainfall but little or no thunder and lightning. Most of the damage occurred mainly in the south and south-east of the island. Rooftops were blown off, banana trees tumbled to the ground, and there were landslides of varying magnitude in many parts of the island. The River Road district in St. George's was the worst hit area in the south. The St. John's River which normally flows through the River Road area somewhat lazily availed itself of the excessive water from Arthur to overflow its banks and to destroy cars which were parked on the roadway.

My residence did not escape the fury of the storm. The driveway strewn with debris and fallen branches of trees proved unmotorable for several hours. Yet again the house leaked like a basket. I shuddered to think what might have happened had it been a full-blown hurricane with winds of 75 miles per hour or more. The staff at my residence deserved high commendation for the speed and efficiency with which they did the mopping up operations once the storm had subsided. The orderlies worked assiduously to clear the driveway to make it motorable once again, while the domestic staff put in an extra effort to restore a certain measure of aridity to our living quarters.

What had happened at Governor General's House during the passage of Arthur showed up the Ministry of Works in a bad light and pinpointed the abysmal neglect and lukewarm attitude of the Public Works Department towards the House. And this was not for lack of complaint at both technical and political levels. Successive governments seemed not to be able to appreciate the significance of this two-hundred-year old building, the premier heritage house on the island. Of all the ministers including prime ministers with whom I have had to deal, only Gairy and in a later administration, Keith Mitchell, Minister for Works, showed a genuine appreciation and understanding of Governor General's House not by lip service, but by action.

The Leader of the Opposition, Mrs Winifred Strachan, had a running battle with party leader, Sir Eric Gairy, who in his typical way was bent on controlling every move she made with respect to her parliamentary duties. While remaining faithful to the party and acknowledging Gairy as the undisputed political leader, she would not brook any interference with her constitutional role. In this regard she refused to accept directives from him, as for example in the choosing of the opposition senators. Being new to parliamentary practice and procedure, she had thought it prudent to seek her leader's advice on the matter of strategy in making her contribution to the budget debate. But she got no help of substance from him. This was the first and last time she consulted him on matters pertaining to her parliamentary duties. Quite frankly, I thought Gairy was a spent force by then, and had little or nothing to offer by way of contributing to a budget debate. Presiding over executive meetings of the party Gairy embraced the opportunity to hurl provocative remarks at Strachan who in turn replied appropriately on every occasion. The relationship between the two deteriorated to such an extent that Strachan withdrew herself from further executive meetings of the party in order to avoid further clashes with her party leader.

Gairy's reaction was to suspend Strachan from the party. This did not go down well with the top echelons of the party, but there was nothing they could do for fear of suffering a similar fate. Gairy was still the boss. As party president for life he never missed an opportunity to remind his followers by word or by deed that he was still alive and in control. Strachan sent a message to Gairy that the party had a constitution, and he could not suspend them so arbitrarily. He received this message with scorn and paid absolutely no heed to it. Instead he tried his level best to get members of the executive to distance themselves from Strachan, but without success. His pettiness propelled him to order them not to accept Strachan's invitation to the official and historic opening of the office of the leader of the opposition. For the first time an office was provided for the leader of the opposition. This initiative was the brain-child of the Brathwaite administration, and it was in keeping with the best traditions of parliamentary democracy. Gairy subsequently tried to make peace with Strachan, but to no avail. Strachan continued to maintain her distance from Gairy and nobody was brave enough to come between her and her parliamentary duties. Strachan called on me frequently and, among other things, kept me fully informed about what seemed to be an irreversible break down in communications between herself and her political leader.

Dr. Lawrence Gibbs, a young medical practitioner, who had been a successful GULP candidate in the recently held elections, could no longer accept Gairy's arrogance. Nor could he close his eyes to Gairy's paternalistic attitude towards members of the executive who were treated more and more like little children who had to be carefully nurtured and kept under strict control. As early as May 7, less than three months after winning his parliamentary seat, Gibbs resigned from the GULP "in the national interest." The following day Gairy reacted by telling the media that Gibbs's resignation was no loss to the party. Gibbs then crossed the floor of the House of Representatives and became a member of the NDC.

On the occasion of Her Majesty's official birthday on June 16, Mrs Venetia Blaize, widow of the late Prime Minister, was honoured by the Queen with the award of Dame Commander of the Most Excellent Order of the British Empire ( DBE). It was a fitting tribute to a woman who had stood alongside her late husband in all seasons during his political career, and particularly during his term as Prime Minister.

Economic growth was key to the survival of the new government. The weakness of the economic base was exacerbated by the fire that burnt down the Treasury complex, and later by the ravages of storm Arthur. The Government firmly fixed its gaze on tourism, agriculture and small-scale industries. It was felt that a marriage between agriculture and tourism would facilitate growth in both sectors of the economy. More specifically, farmers would grow more food for consumption at the hotels and restaurants. Agricultural diversification was the hue and cry of the day, but the implementation of such a policy was easier said than done. An educational programme aimed at bringing about attitudinal change in farmers and extension officers should be a precursor to any serious attempt at agricultural diversification. The mere destruction of traditional crops to be replaced by cash crops might be expedient in the short term but might prove senseless in the long term. If this and nothing more is what agricultural diversification entails then we might be in for a rude awakening when these traditional crops are again fetching high prices on the world market. A case in point was the felling of nutmeg trees on the Belvidere Estate to plant bananas. That was utter folly and it was the most senseless ministerial directive which came to my notice during my tenure as Governor General. I thought the minister was grossly ill-advised, if advised at all. Before nutmegs were grown in commercial quantities in Indonesia, Grenada had taken pride of place in being the largest nutmeg producer in the world, and Belvidere Estate had gained the distinction of being the largest nutmeg-growing plantation not just in Grenada, but in the world. Nutmeg had always been synonymous with Grenada, and it was grossly insensitive even to contemplate the destruction of one nutmeg-bearing tree, notwithstanding the prevailing slump in world prices. On the other hand, the future of the banana industry in Grenada and the other Windward islands of St. Vincent and the Grenadines, St. Lucia and Dominica was insecure. The nicety of preferential treatment in international trade was being questioned, and such accommodation as given to bananas from the former colonies was being challenged. This challenge grew so rapidly that it led to serious lobbying in Washington by the banana producing countries of Central America and their agents in the U.S.A. The government of the U.S.A. naturally felt obliged to throw its weight behind its suppliers who had been raising strong objections to preferential treatment for Caribbean bananas. The mandate of the World Trade Organization (WTO) of which Caribbean countries are members does not include preferential treatment. This reputable world body would do nothing to bend its rules. Nor would it make exceptions even in cases of small and impoverished island states, such as ours. The rules might have to be changed. But whatever happens, Grenada would be well advised not to depend on preferential treatment for bananas or, for that matter, any agricultural product in future international trading. Grenada was never really a leading banana producing country. Although some bananas had been grown from the early twentieth century, large scale production came into prominence after hurricane Janet had dealt a heavy blow to the island's agriculture flattening most of the plantations, including the banana fields. To make up for the loss in revenue as quickly as possible, and bearing in mind that after just nine months of planting, the banana begins to bear fruit, it was then decided to grow bananas on a large scale for regular export to the British market. The production of bananas was therefore in the vanguard of agricultural rehabilitation. The Grenadian farmers were really producers of nutmegs and cocoa for export, but the rehabilitation of these crops would take a longer time.

Agriculture got a well-needed boost from the assistance given to the State by the Taiwanese. By 1990 diplomatic relations between Grenada and the

Republic of China on Taiwan were deeply rooted. From the outset the Taiwanese authorities had established an agricultural mission which ever since has been working to restore confidence in the farming community, to demonstrate the production of new varieties of crops including horticultural products, and to encourage farmers to diversify their crops. On their demonstration farm at La Sagesse in St. David's could be seen a variety of fruit and vegetables as well as a fairly large collection of flowers. Field days brought farmers from all over the country to observe methods of production, to gather information and to visualize for themselves what their own farms could achieve in terms of higher yield and higher prices. The members of the agricultural mission worked closely with the Ministry of Agriculture in pursuance of the Government's declared policy of agricultural diversification. They also visited the agricultural holdings of fruit and vegetable farmers, especially those who were willing to take the plunge into the production of some of the new varieties grown at the La Sagesse demonstration farm. The more industrious farmers linked with hotels to supply them with products such as water melon (a new variety which the Chinese introduced) and cherry tomatoes which were always in great demand. There has been a growing market for cut flowers both at home and abroad and in close association with the local horticultural society the agricultural mission promoted the cultivation of flowers. The mission also believed that fresh water fish farming was a feasible prospect in Grenada and could bolster the country's strained economy. Thus they set up a fish farm in Telescope, St. Andrew's, for the production of shrimp and tilapia with the hope that Grenadians would come to realize that fish farming was a lucrative business and would start their own fish farms. The impact which the Chinese agricultural mission has made and continues to make on Grenada is not without significance as the country tries to move towards a more diversified agricultural economy.

Tourism development was a top priority for the Nicholas Brathwaite administration, despite the very limited resources for marketing Grenada as a destination. Efforts were concentrated on improving the tourism product with special reference to infrastructural development in some of the main tourism areas. The government continued in the footsteps of its predecessor by granting generous concessions to prospective hoteliers, including a ten-year tax free period on profits. On June 23, 1990, tourism got a fillip when American Airlines touched down at Point Salines Airport for the first time This inaugural flight, which was greeted with great jubilation at the airport, marked the beginning of a daily flight to Grenada out of San Juan, Puerto Rico. The airplane would turn around for the return hour and a quarter flight to San Juan from where passengers could easily make their connections to various parts of mainland U.S.A. Two new hotels, La Source and Rex Grenadian, were built and opened for business in the south of the island during the NDC regime.

On August 9, I travelled to Seamoon in St. Andrew's to turn the sod for the construction of a new industrial complex similar to the one at Frequente in St. George's. The Seamoon Industrial Park was financed by a loan in the sum of U.S. $1.4m from the Caribbean Development Bank. This amount was to be used for constructing four factory buildings and one administrative centre to cover land space amounting to 33,000 square feet. USAID contributed U.S. $250,000 for the provision of the infrastructure facilities and the fencing of the compound. This was an exciting venture, not just because it was happening in a rural area, but more importantly because such a complex had great potential for job creation in a parish where many jobs had been lost with the closing down of operations at Pearls Airport and the transfer of all aviation activities to Point Salines in St. George's. The Seamoon industrial complex would bring some measure of hope to the young people of St. Andrew's who had been steadily increasing the ranks of the unemployed. Leading the way in agricultural production on a parish basis, St. Andrew's, more than any other, was well poised for the development of agro-industries.

Carnival 1990 was held in mid-August against the backdrop of some anxiety of an impending tropical storm. Of course, the possibility would always exist that carnival in August could be marred by persistent inclement weather. On carnival Monday, August 13, Grenada was placed on a storm watch for tropical storm, Fran, which was located some five hundred miles south-east of us. But not even a threatening storm could stop the carnival. In fact nothing in Grenada seemed to be able to stand between the revellers and their carnival. Happily, it became quite clear by midday on Tuesday 14 that Fran was bypassing Grenada, and so the storm watch was discontinued and carnival went on in the afternoon as planned.

Prior to the general elections on March 13, 1990, I had firmly made up my mind that I would demit office at about halfway through the Government's term. This would take me to the summer of 1992. I thought the most convenient time for change would be July/August. I had discussed all this with my wife who warmly supported me. We wasted no time in planning and preparing to move into our private home in St. Paul's, just a five minute drive from Governor General's House. Moving into our home was gradual and passed almost unnoticed. Some of our personal belongings had been packed in cardboard boxes and had not seen the light of day since

September, 1978, when they were removed from our London residence for forwarding to Grenada. Needless to say we had some breakages in our chinaware which we had no cause to use during our years at Governor General's House.

The month of October always brought back sad memories of the 1983 carnage at Fort George. At noon on Friday, October 19, I laid a wreath at Fort George in the area where Prime Minister Bishop and others had been executed. Just prior to the wreath laying, with friends and relatives of the deceased in attendance, the Most Rev. Sydney Charles, Bishop of St. George's in Grenada, officiated at a short memorial service.

Thanksgiving Day, October 25, was a bank holiday. This holiday had its genesis in the intervention of United States and Caribbean forces to restore order in the country as a first step towards the full return to democracy. On the Sunday immediately preceding Thanksgiving Day my wife and I attended an ecumenical service at the St. George's Anglican Church when I read the first lesson from 1 Chronicles 16 v. 34-36. This was a service organized by the Grenada Council of Churches. On the day itself I took the salute at Queen's Park during the parade marking the seventh anniversary of the intervention. On parade were the police and other uniformed groups such as St. John Ambulance Brigade, Boy Scouts, and Girl Guides. Also participating was a contingent from *U.S.S. Jesse Brown* which had specially come for the observance of Thanksgiving Day. Prime Minister Brathwaite in his address appealed to the good sense of his listeners to redouble their efforts at national development and national reconciliation. A short message from President Bush was read by the Chargé d'Affaires of the American embassy in St. George's. In the afternoon my wife and I were present at the Grand Anse campus of the St. George's University for its annual observance of Thanksgiving Day. This was in honour of the nineteen American soldiers who had lost their lives in combat during the 1983 military engagement in Grenada. In my short address I yet again thanked the American Government and people who had come to our rescue through the instrumentality of their armed forces in one of our darkest hours, thus averting what might have been an even more massive massacre than the one perpetrated on October 19. I particularly thanked the relatives of the nineteen fallen soldiers. Some of these relatives were in the audience. They had come to Grenada for the occasion. I also expressed the hope that the supreme sacrifice of those nineteen men in the cause of freedom would not have been in vain. I took the opportunity to appeal to my own countrymen for greater vigilance, greater tolerance, and a redoubling of concerted effort in our quest for peace and prosperity. Under the strains of sombre music supplied by the Royal Grenada Police Band I laid the only wreath at the foot of the memorial monument on which were inscribed the actual signatures of the nineteen dead.

Persistent inclement weather on the morning of November 11 did not put a stop to the observance in the St. George's Market Square in commemoration of those servicemen who had died in active service during the two world wars. This is a hardy annual which is attended by the top ranking officers of State led by the Governor General himself. The crucial point in the ceremony is at 11 a. m. when the cannons resound from Fort George to mark the beginning of the two-minute silence for the dead in both world wars. It was at this very solemn moment that the rain suddenly increased, and, oh what a blessing I received! By the time I got back to my residence I was severely drenched. During my years as Governor General I had never been so ill-treated by the weather, although many a time I have had to stand in the rain to take the salute at the march past or to inspect the uniformed groups on parade. My wife and I entertained the ex-servicemen at our residence afterwards, as indeed we had been doing every year.

The month of December was always a very busy month. In 1990 despite the problems occasioned by a tropical storm and a great fire in St. George's the merriment at Christmas time was by no means diminished. Nor was the religious fervour of our predominantly Christian community. In fact there was an increase in the number of Christmas parties, concerts and other forms of entertainment. Our attendance at lunches, dinners, cocktail receptions, concerts was taken in our stride during this festive month. The Carols by Candlelight observance was held in Grenville for the first time on December 19. It was well worth journeying to Grenville for the occasion. Some six years previously I had invited to my residence a small group of music lovers headed by Lauren Ramdhanny of St. Andrew's to form a committee to promote the singing of carols at Christmas time. The idea of Carols by Candlelight was put to me by Bruce McLeod of Trinidad where he was the moving figure behind such activities. My musical guests were enthused by this idea, and I immediately inaugurated them as the committee of Carols by Candlelight. This committee had been working diligently to revitalize carol singing and had done a commendable job by bringing Carols by Candlelight to every parish in Grenada to the extent that the people of St. Patrick's had begun to organize their own programme. Hopefully, other parishes as well as Carriacou and Petit Martinique would follow in that direction.

Christmas festivities notwithstanding, I was obliged to go down to the Parliament building on Friday, December 21, to read the traditional speech from the Throne marking the second session of the fourth Parliament. Accompanied by my aide-de-camp I took the twenty-minute flight to Carriacou in the afternoon to be on time for the opening of the annual parang festival. The following morning I embarked on the coast guard boat that had berthed alongside the Hillsborough jetty waiting to take me to Petit Martinique. Senator Deroche, Parliamentary Secretary for Carriacou and Petit Martinique Affairs, accompanied me on the journey. Also on board the coast guard vessel was Col. Nestor Ogilvie, Commissioner of Police. A contingent of police officers were on board all ready for their parade in Petit Martinique. I took the salute at the street parade that attracted many of the inhabitants. This was novel for many of them who nonetheless enjoyed the spectacle of such a parade on their own front door. While in Petit Martinique I was shown some development projects with particular reference to the roads where there was modest improvement. On my return to Carriacou I visited the Princess Royal Hospital where I was received by the resident doctor and the matron. Walking through the wards I stopped to speak to each of the patients.

Driving along I was able to observe the roads which, sad to say, were in a horrible state of disrepair. Following a short visit to the administrative building where I met public officers and extended season's greetings, I then made my way to the home of Dame Venetia Blaize to present her with her warrant of Dame Commander of the Most Excellent Order of the British Empire. Having completed this last official act I left Dame Venetia's home immediately for the airport where I took the last flight for Grenada.

During the month my wife and I went on our customary visits to hospitals, homes for senior citizens and children's homes culminating in our traditional visit to the General Hospital in St. George's on Christmas morning where we walked through the wards bringing Christmas cheer to the patients. We could not help noticing the unprecedented number of patients with injuries from road accidents. We then exchanged greetings with the doctors and nurses whom we had joined for a Christmas drink. I also availed myself of the opportunity to say farewell and extend best wishes to the matron who was due to retire at the end of the month.

In a speech lasting four and a half hours, George Brizan, Minister for Finance, presented his U.S.$296,000,000 budget for fiscal year 1991. That was on Thursday, December 27. The budget debate continued into the New Year with speeches from every member of the Opposition –some serious, others amusing, and still others below the standard expected of a parliamentarian, but in every case they were playing up to the gallery and to their constituencies as the debate was broadcast live on both radio and television.

If ever there was a prize for longevity in speech it would have to go to Dr. Keith Mitchell, the member for St George's North-West, who took up the entire day on January 3 to make his contribution.

One of the main items on the budget was the re-introduction of income tax. This was a complete reversal of Blaize's fiscal policy when he replaced income tax by value added tax (VAT) on goods and services. Theoretically the imposition of value added tax seemed fair and reasonable and at the outset it was welcomed by those on whom income tax had fallen heavily. However, our basically agricultural society with a plethora of small shops particularly in the rural areas was not attuned to this new style taxation, and more significantly the small businesses and the populace generally were not educated in the ramifications of value added tax which called for a fair measure of paperwork. The Blaize administration, therefore, had to amend the VAT law constantly and this did not help the situation. Rather it made the VAT system even more complicated, particularly for the small shops around the corner as well as the smaller ones in the rural districts. In fact, by January, 1991, VAT looked more like an additional customs levy. All this confusion in the tax system led Brathwaite to seek expert advice on fiscal performance with special reference to the feasibility of the value added tax and the re-introduction of income tax. The message was loud and clear: "Bring back income tax."

The upshot of all this was the resignation of Ben Jones from the Government. Jones was not happy about the re-introduction of income tax. That apart, he felt rightly or wrongly that he had not been taken into the fullest confidence of the Government. His resignation from the government benches came on January 4, the day after Mitchell had made his marathon speech in Parliament criticizing the budget proposals on every front including errors in some of the mathematical calculations. In his turn Jones now adorned his opposition garb and from the other side of the House was highly critical of the budget particularly as it related to agriculture and fiscal policy. Although Jones had joined the government's ministerial team he, nevertheless, remained very close to his own party stalwarts who were so inflexible as to consider the reversal of any of Blaize's major policies as revolting. Jones felt unable to dismiss out of hand the feelings of his party supporters. Strangely enough, his colleague, Alleyne Walker, who had indicated earlier his determination to follow Jones's leadership in joining the Government, did not remove himself from the government benches. He continued to the end serving in a junior ministerial position.

Meanwhile there was what seemed to be an irreversible break in communications between Winifred Strachan and her party leader, Sir Eric

Gairy. She had ceased to consult him on matters pertaining to her parliamentary duties. But continuing to behave as if Strachan was his personal representative in Parliament Gairy became very peeved when contrary to his expectations he had not been consulted on the opposition's contribution to the budget debate. On January 21 Strachan sought my advice as to her future relationship with her political leader. This was somewhat awkward for me as even in the privacy of my office I felt unable to give any advice which smacks of politics, more so to a politician seeking advice involving her party boss. Having worked so closely to Sir Eric in the past as his Cabinet Secretary I could bring my experience to bear in advising Mrs Strachan how to deal with him. At least so thought Mrs Strachan who added that all seemed to have been well between us during those years. I confirmed that Mr Gairy (as he then was) and I always had a cordial relationship and that was because I always maintained my distance and neither he nor his ministers could complain about the quality of my job performance. In the course of our conversation I pointed out to Mrs Strachan that I had never asked any favours of Gairy, I never played up to him as I had seen so many others do. Indeed I never adorned my office walls with his photograph even though his office was in close proximity to mine. In my work as Cabinet Secretary I had always made a sharp distinction between government and party and our relationship then was one based on mutual respect. I went on to tell the Leader of the Opposition quite bluntly that I could not advise her how to deal with Sir Eric, if only because he had no constitutional authority. However, I reminded her that she ought to know how Gairy had gone out of his way to vilify me in meetings of his party executive, all because he could not have his way since his return to Grenada in January, 1984, from his exile abroad. I had never once called him for consultations or advice on any matter. During the election campaign at a meeting in the South St. George constituency he went so far as to name me as one of the first casualties on his attainment of power. He told the crowd that I would have to leave office immediately after the general elections. He was so sure of victory at the polls. I took all this in my stride, but totally ignored him. In my view he was trying his utmost to bring the office of Governor General into disrepute. He was bent on getting another term as Prime Minister, but by then Gairy was a broken reed, and his health had started to fail. I recalled the occasion when he attended a cocktail reception hosted by the ambassador of the Republic of China on Taiwan. It was brought to my attention that the Grenada flag was flying in the front of his car – strange moments of nostalgia! I beheld this funny spectacle myself. After a lengthy conversation with Mrs Strachan I could see that she was much more relaxed than she was when she first entered the room. I simply advised her to get on with her parliamentary duties as Leader of the Opposition and as representative of her constituency. In this regard her political leader could not stand in her way.

The year 1991 did not start brightly for the government. Prime Minister Brathwaite had his hands full. There was a spate of rumours circulating in the country. Among them was the imminent pulling out of Grenada by American Airlines. By Saturday, January 5, Radio Barbados carried a newscast to the effect that the airline was withdrawing its flights from Grenada, Colombia and Curaçao. This immediately clouded the tourism industry with sighs of despair, although neither the Government nor the airport authority had received any notification from the airline. Happily for all concerned, American Airlines continued to fly the Miami / Grenada route. The other bit of rumour flying around was that Brathwaite was on the verge of resigning as Prime Minister. This rumour spread so swiftly and so intensely that Brathwaite had to make a national broadcast to dispel this rumour whose origin was unknown, but which was calculated to introduce a certain measure of instability into the country. On Wednesday, January 16, Grenadians received the shocking news of a fatal accident along the west coast in Concord, St. John's. Just after 8 a.m. a huge boulder made its descent from the hillside and landed on top of a mini-bus that was travelling on its way to St. George's. The bus was flattened by the impact, it caught fire and eight of the nine occupants died on the spot. The ninth later died in hospital. Within an hour of my receiving the news I went on radio to express sympathy to the bereaved relatives. When I visited the site of the accident the following day I was told by the villagers that there were a few other loose boulders which might be dislodged involuntarily at any time. They obviously considered the loose boulders a source of danger. On my return to St. George's I went to the fire station to view the chassis of the wrecked bus.

During the month of February Prime Minister Brathwaite had to deal with what became known as the Radio Health Scandal. Radio equipment addressed to the Ministry of Health was cleared at the Customs in the usual way by ministry officials. No sooner had the goods reached the ministry than tongues began to wag. There was no provision in the ministry's budget for such expenditure, although the ministry first contended that it was to provide music to the staff while at work. This departure from the norm in the civil service was difficult to swallow. Both within the civil service and in the wider community there was widespread allegation that the radio equipment was for the use of a private radio station. The media took up the matter, which was investigated by a Government-appointed committee who came down heavily on the hapless acting permanent secretary for incompetence and misappropriation of funds. In her innocence the permanent secretary claimed that she was only carrying out a ministerial directive. The Prime Minister, who discussed the matter with me on more than one occasion, was clearly embarrassed. I warned him that this problem would escalate if steps were not taken urgently to diffuse it, and he was advised to revoke the minister's appointment immediately. In a small country like ours there would always be people who know the truth about any matter of topical interest. Brathwaite was slow to act. Things came to a head on Thursday, February 28. The Prime Minister on his own volition came to hold further discussions with me on the Radio Health Scandal. I reiterated my earlier advice to Prime Minister Brathwaite, and he promised to get back to me within twenty-four hours. The Prime Minister telephoned me just before nine o'clock that evening advising me to expect a letter of resignation from Hon. Kenny Lalsingh. Shortly afterwards, Hon. Francis Alexis, Attorney General, called to say that Mr Lalsingh was coming to Governor General's House to deliver his letter of resignation. He was told that the letter should be left with the guard at the gate. During my sojourn at Governor General's House no visitor, not even a minister of government, was allowed to get past the main gate after six o'clock in the evening except by invitation. Communication between the main gate and the house had always been very good, and Lalsingh's letter came to hand soon after it was delivered at the gate at twenty-five minutes after nine. I personally saw to it that the resignation was announced on the local radio half an hour later as a news flash, and in the 7.15 newscast the following morning Lalsingh's resignation was the dominant news item.

Among the visitors I received in the New Year were Rod and Kathy Muir from Australia. For Kathy it was a visit to her former home where she lived as a child. She had pleasant memories of her stay in Grenada and particularly in Government House (as it was then called) when her father, Sir Ian Turbott, was Governor of Grenada. She was happy to show her husband, Rod, where she once lived. She welcomed my invitation to walk around the grounds and to take some photographs.

On Tuesday, March 15, I received the Rt. Hon. Lynda Chalker, the British Minister for Overseas Development and Foreign and Commonwealth Affairs. She came by to see how Grenada had been progressing since the restoration of democracy. We had far reaching discussions ranging from unemployment to drugs, the performance of the economy to the role of non-governmental organizations and the proposed political unification of the Windward Islands. I had always felt that the proposed political unification of the Windward Islands was a non-starter. Similar initiatives in the past either had been short-lived or had never gone past the drawing board. I was never impressed by the unification train as it steam rolled its way through the Windwards with stops at the capital cities to deposit its all too familiar cargo of rehashed rhetoric in an atmosphere of pomp and splendour. As Governor General I declined the invitation to be present at the opening ceremony of the Grenada meeting of the unification committee. The fact that in other territories the Governor General had taken part in similar exercises was no yardstick that I should follow suit. Notwithstanding the "well-intentioned" speeches by Prime Ministers and other senior ministers I was not convinced that the politicians were genuine about giving up their territorial power for the sake of regional integration. More importantly the proposal of Windward Islands unification did not come from the people, but rather from a few technocrats and even fewer politicians.

Grenada lost two of her distinguished daughters during the month of April. Miss Louise Rowley, OBE the first female permanent secretary in Grenada and indeed in the English-speaking Caribbean, died at her home after a short illness. After a brilliant school career, Louise Rowley entered the civil service at a time when there was grave discrimination against women in terms of pay and job security. But because of her brilliance and her determination to excel she was able to make her way to the top. There could be no denying that she had a most distinguished career in the civil service. It was she who taught me the niceties of public administration when, after years of teaching, I sought and was granted a transfer to the administrative arm of government. Her tutelage covered not only procedural matters but also confidentiality, loyalty, and civility towards the public at large. As her deputy in the Ministry of Social Services which embraced Education and Health I was able to draw on her vast and varied experience in public administration. I learnt more from Louise Rowley than I would have ever learnt from the new-fangled and frequent short courses and seminars which provide so little for the mind and lack stimulation for constructive action.

When I called on Louise Rowley about a fortnight before I was due to take up my new appointment, she presented me with copies of the Colonial Regulations and the Financial and Store Rules and said to me, "Now, you go and study these as your homework for the next two weeks." I wondered what one of my recalcitrant students would have thought if he were within hearing distance. Miss Rowley placed great emphasis on filing, so often did I hear her admonishing members of staff that the file told the story. It is no wonder, then, that during my first week in office she thought that I should become acquainted with the files and the filing system. In fact, on entering my office on the very first day I was greeted by a bunch of files which were left on my desk for my perusal.

Dame Venetia, widow of Prime Minister Blaize, died in a New York hospital on April 7 and was buried beside her husband in Carriacou six days later. Prime Minister Brathwaite and representatives from the different political parties attended the funeral with the Royal Grenada Police Force musical band in attendance. Because of my absence at the funeral I took the opportunity on a later journey to Carriacou to visit the Blaize's family home and offered condolences to the children.

On this my latest journey to Carriacou we experienced unusually bad weather, and it was the roughest aircraft landing I had ever experienced when we got to Laureston Airport that morning. The main purpose of this my trip was to bring birthday greetings to a centenarian, Mrs Mary Palmer, who lived in the village of Brunswick. I presented a telegram from the Queen and a bouquet of flowers from my wife and me. During my years in office I always enjoyed visiting these centenarians on their special day when family and friends looked forward to the telegram from the Queen extending birthday greetings.

At the invitation of the Government of the Republic of China on Taiwan my wife and I left Grenada on the morning of Saturday, April 27 for what was to be our longest journey since assuming office. The nearest I had got to Taiwan before was when I visited Malaysia during my Commonwealth Foundation years. Adrian Hayes, Chief of Protocol, was travelling with us. Hayes was an efficient and experienced foreign service officer whom I personally selected to accompany me in preference to a more junior officer whom the Ministry of Foreign Affairs wanted to palm off on me. This official visit to Taiwan was serious business and I would have the best available protocol officer accompany me. Two years previously Hayes had accompanied our Foreign Minister to mainland China.

Our aircraft was right on target in terms of time, having touched down in Miami just after midday where we were met by the Airport Protocol Officer who saw us through immigration and customs with the minimum of delay, even though the luggage was long in coming through the chute. Outside the Customs area we were met by Mr Ting-Yu Yu. Mr Yu was the Deputy Director of the ROC Co-ordination Council for North America office in Miami who saw us off on American Airlines. We left promptly at 1.55 p.m. However, after taxiing to the take-off position the plane had to return to the gate because it was carrying too heavy a load and so was denied permission to take off. All in all we were almost two hours late, thus arriving at Los Angeles at 6.20 p.m. rather than at the scheduled time of 4.35 p.m.

Mr Preston Deng, the Deputy Director of the CCNA in the Los Angeles Office, was at the airport to meet us. We were taken by limousine to the nearby Stouffer Concourse Hotel for the night quite exhausted after the day's journey. The following morning we attended holy mass at St. Anastasia's church about ten minutes drive from the hotel. After mass we were taken back to the hotel where we had just enough time to pack our bags in readiness for our onward journey. Mr Cheng Huang, Director of Service Division of CCNA in Los Angeles, who was to accompany us to the airport was already in the hotel lobby. Awaiting our arrival at the airport was Mr Shih whom we had met the night before. Mr Shih and Mr Haynes checked us in. We then said our goodbyes and proceeded to the Dynasty Lounge to await departure. But before that my wife and Mr Hayes failed the test on first count while passing through the security post. There were loud beeps. It turned out that my wife's bracelets and Mr Hayes's belt buckle were the source of the embarrassment. The fourteen-hour flight to Taipei was delightful.

Our aircraft touched down at the Chiang Kai-shek International Airport at exactly 8 p.m. on Monday, April 29. Dr. Hoang Sieou-je, the Director of the Protocol Department, met us on the aircraft and immediately escorted us to the terminal building where the welcoming party headed by the Vice President and Mrs Ling were awaiting us. After the exchange of greetings and the presentation of a beautiful floral arrangement to my wife, we left in a motorcade for the Grand Hotel. It was raining. On reaching the city boundary, we were joined by several police outriders who escorted our motorcade to the hotel. I learnt later that outriders were not allowed on the highway. At the Grand Hotel, which was going to be our temporary home for the next few days, we were overwhelmed by the generosity and sincerity of the welcome. Dr. Hoang briefed us on the week's programme.

I was up as early as 5.45 a.m on my first whole day in Taipei, despite the fact that we had turned in just before midnight after the long haul from Los Angeles. After breakfast, accompanied by Mr and Mrs Hoang of the Ministry of Foreign Affairs, we left the hotel for the Premier's office to call on Premier Hau Pei-tsun. Here again we were warmly received, and during the thirty-minute session the Premier showed great interest in Grenada and he took the opportunity to quiz me thoroughly on our system of government, our cultural pursuits, our education system and our economic activities. The Premier had invited the press and photographers to cover our meeting. Also in attendance was the Vice-Minister of Foreign Affairs. At the end of our discussions we exchanged gifts.

Our next stop was at the Taiwan Handicraft Promotion Centre where we looked at exhibits on two of the four floors and made some purchases. What we saw was a very impressive display of high quality products. Promptly at 10.15 we left the Handicraft Promotion Centre for the Council of Agriculture where His Excellency Yu Yu-hsien, Chairman of the Council, received us. During our meeting the Chairman was flanked by his senior (highly qualified) technocrats. We were treated to a very good briefing which was reinforced by a film. I then asked a number of questions on the current state of agriculture before the Chairman and I exchanged gifts. The shift from subsistence farming to a viable and sustainable agricultural industry was impressive.

After lunch we continued with our round of visits. At the Ministry of Economic Affairs we were received by His Excellency Vincent C. Siew, Minister for Economic Affairs, who briefed us on the economy of the country before showing us a documentary on its economic development. Before taking leave of the minister we exchanged gifts.

We then made our way to the Taiwan World Trade Centre. It was a pleasure to meet Mr Wu again. Some months before we had met in Grenada. As Director of the Centre he welcomed us and then invited us to watch a short film on the operations of the Centre. We walked through two floors of exhibits which constituted an impressive array of products all made in Taiwan. The Centre is a fantastic organization catering to the needs of both exporters and importers. It consists of exhibition halls, a hotel and conference room facilities. All aspects of prospective investors' business can be done from the Taiwan World Trade Centre with help from a team of knowledgeable and efficient professional men and women.

Back at our hotel we were able to take about an hour's rest before leaving again to call on Vice President Li Yuan-zu and Madame Li and then to be their honoured guests at an official dinner. The Vice President was most interested in our local products, particularly nutmegs, but we also discussed the differences and similarities in the composition and working of our respective governments. We exchanged gifts before moving to the dining room. Among the dinner guests were Ministers of Government and their wives and the Dean of the diplomatic corps, the Ambassador of Haiti. My wife and I had met all the guests before we sat down to dinner. Everybody wanted to know something about life in Grenada, and notwithstanding the great distance we had travelled, I must admit that at the very outset we felt at home among sincere friends. In his after dinner speech the Vice President welcomed us most warmly and pointed to the ties of friendship existing between our two countries. He expressed the wish that we would enjoy every moment of our stay in Taiwan. He ended his speech by proposing a toast to Grenada. I replied suitably, stressing the importance of the growth of friendship and co-operation between our two countries, and pledging the support of my government in Taiwan's quest for recognition and membership in international organizations.

We set out at 8.45 o'clock the following morning for Martyrs' Shrine where I was scheduled to lay a wreath. On arrival I was met by the Vice Minister for Foreign Affairs. The laying of the wreath was a short but impressive ceremony. In the first place I had a special escort of military police on motorbikes from the hotel to the Shrine. At the ceremony, the military band was in attendance. Within the precincts of the Shrine, soldiers had lined the route on which the short procession headed by the Vice Minister and myself passed with measured steps as we proceeded to the cenotaph. Ahead of us were the wreath bearers who had taken up their places near the cenotaph. The huge wreath was borne by two military men to the cenotaph and I then stepped forward and placed my hands on it.

We then visited the Chiang Kai-shek Memorial Hall where we paid our respects by bowing before the large statue in the middle of the Hall. Here again we saw a short film depicting the history of the Hall and of the man in whose memory it was built. This was followed by a conducted tour of the building.

A visit to the Taishan Vocational Training Centre followed. We were well received by the Director who showed us a documentary film on the Centre, and took us on a tour of the various classrooms where we observed the students at work. Here, as indeed everywhere else we went, we were presented with souvenirs. The campus is situated in a very salubrious and quiet area conducive to serious studying and teaching.

We then had a two-hour respite at the hotel before leaving again to call at the Employment and Vocational Training Administration, Council of Labour Affairs. Here we were welcomed enthusiastically by Mr Cheng Chung-Sheng, Director General, and his staff who briefed us on the work of the organization before we were invited to watch a short film that underscored quite vividly the operational side of the organization.

A visit to the nearby Ministry of Education followed. There we were greeted by His Excellency Mao Kao-wen, Minister for Education, whom I had met the previous evening at the Vice President's dinner. Apart from my personal interest in education I was curious to know to what extent education was responsible for the phenomenal economic growth that Taiwan had been experiencing. With the emphasis on science and mathematics at all levels of the educational spectrum together with the stiff

competition for places in the most renowned schools I became convinced
that their education system and practice were geared towards economic
growth, and there was no doubt in my mind that the corollary between
education and economic growth was real in Taiwan. After watching a film
on the current state of education in the country, the Minister and I
exchanged ideas on education. As an erstwhile classroom practitioner and
educational administrator I listened with more than passing interest to what
the Minister had to say about the development of education in Taiwan. Six
years of primary education are followed by three years of junior secondary.
The cut off point for compulsory education was the end of the final year at
Junior Secondary. The entrance examination for those desiring to pursue
academic studies at the senior secondary school was very demanding, and
the competition was fierce. Thus from the level of junior secondary school
students had to work extremely hard and were under great strain to achieve
high grades because of their own ambition and partly because of their
parents' high expectations. Primary and secondary school teachers were
exempt from the payment of income tax. This was an incentive to lower the
rate of attrition, thus ensuring the maintenance of a high level of teacher
performance and the provision of a sound basic education to the nation's
children. However, the Minister admitted that this incentive was a bone of
contention with other teachers and professionals in the government service.
The commitment of teachers, the co-operation of parents, the high
motivation of students, well-equipped schools, and the relevance of
educational practice to national goals and aspirations all combined to make
the educational system of Taiwan efficient and effective.

We returned to our hotel for just over an hour before leaving again to call
on Dr. Frederick F. Chien, Minister for Foreign Affairs and Madame Chien at
the Ministry of Foreign Affairs at six o'clock and then to a dinner in our
honour at the same venue. The Minister recalled his early meetings in
Washington with the late Prime Minister Herbert Blaize concerning the
establishment of diplomatic relations between our two countries. We also
discussed the progress of the relationship as well as the agricultural
agreement signed between our two countries and the presence in Grenada
of an agricultural mission from his country. After an exchange of gifts, the
Minister and his wife invited us to the ante-chamber of the dining room for
drinks and to meet the other dinner guests before proceeding to dinner. The
guest list was made up of senior government functionaries some of whom
we were meeting for the first time. In his after dinner speech, the Minister
referred to the role I played in restoring democracy to Grenada. In my reply
I thanked him and Madame Chien for their gracious hospitality and

generosity. I reiterated that the government and people of Grenada would do every thing within their power to strengthen and sustain the relationship between our two countries, the establishment of which was most welcome by the general populace of Grenada.

We set out at eight o'clock the following morning on the eighty-mile drive to the Window on China. This was a magnificent tourist attraction where you could see the main historical, cultural and economic aspects of China in miniature – from airport to shipyard to the wall of mainland China to the forbidden city and much more. A private enterprise the Window on China was beautifully kept and obviously well managed. The exhibits, all in the open air, evoked great interest on our part, but it was cold. Nor did the persistent wind and rain help to raise the level of the temperature. A very kind and efficient tour guide began by showing us a film depicting and describing what we were going to see in the open air, and kindly provided us with some warm overcoats for the tour.

Our next stop was at the Titan Corporation, a small to medium garment factory. On our way we saw a funeral procession with music and the lot. Our motorcade reduced its speed and in fact almost came to a halt as I was fascinated by the way this funeral procession took to the streets. I must admit that I did not find anything particularly mournful in this procession nor did I find the music sombre in any way. I was witnessing a funeral march in a culture different from mine, and conducted in a religious setting which was not concordant with my own religious persuasion. This was a learning experience. At the garment factory we were enthusiastically received both by management and workers. After a brief welcome speech by the Director of the corporation to which I appropriately replied we were treated to light refreshments before touring the factory from the designing room (well equipped with computers) to the finishing room where the garments were carefully ironed and packed away neatly for distribution. Most of them, we were told, were for export. Again what I discerned here was a healthy and purposive attitude to work, orderliness and sound management. The authorities at Titan Corporation were generous with gifts to us. I was deeply touched by the guard of honour of workers at the factory gate on our way out.

After lunch we visited the National Palace Museum where we were warmly welcomed by the director who briefly outlined the work of the museum and presented us with a couple books on the collection at the museum. We were then taken on tour of the exhibits by a very efficient tour guide. Only Chinese exhibits were on display. We watched these exhibits with such absorbing interest that we had time only for the porcelain and jewellery floors. The museum was obviously a great educational tool. It was not surprising, therefore, to see so many school children of all ages with their teachers there.

From the museum we left for what I considered to be the highlight of my visit to Taiwan, namely, a call on His Excellency the President of the Republic, Dr. Lee Teng-hui. We spent half an hour with the President who expressed his desire to see the relationship between our two countries grow. Our main topics of conversation were agricultural development and the role of education in economic growth. He made reference to the work of the distinguished West Indian scholar and Nobel Prize winner for economics, Sir Arthur Lewis, who was his personal friend.

In the evening we were dinner guests of Dr. and Mrs Hoang Sieou-je who had been with us all week. We dined at the Hoover Theatre restaurant where we had a delicious Chinese meal and saw a great show inclusive of acrobatics, singing and dancing lasting seventy minutes. A special welcome to us by the Master of Ceremonies evoked loud and enthusiastic applause from the audience. Other guests at our table included Dr. and Mrs Huang. Dr. Huang, a businessman, was planning to take a group of potential investors to Grenada later in the year. He had also been in touch with our Foreign Ministry offering his services as our honorary consul in Taiwan. Also at our table were Mr Wang of the Ministry of Foreign Affairs and Mrs Wang. Mr Wang had escorted us earlier to the Window on China in place of Dr. Hoang who had to be present at the President's office for presentation of credentials by a new ambassador. No sooner had we returned to the hotel when I received a telephone call from Grenada informing me that my private car was involved in an accident and was badly hit from behind. This did not make sleep less sound.

The following day, Friday, May 3, we left the hotel at ten minutes to nine o'clock for Taipei Domestic Airport where we took the flight C 1273 for Kaohsiung in the south of the island. The picturesque and varied scenery from the air was enthralling. On disembarkation we were whisked off to the Ambassador Hotel, and immediately afterwards we embarked on a very packed programme of visits in the south of the island. Within minutes we were at the China Steel Corporation where we were greeted by the Vice President of the company who also briefed us on the company's operation. This briefing was re-enforced by a bus tour of the company's complex under the control of a most articulate and knowledgeable tour guide. Here, too, we were offered souvenirs.

Close by was the China Shipbuilding Corporation. This was our next stop. We watched a documentary film and then went on a tour of the works. We were told that business was on the up swing after a slight lull. Under construction was a frigate for the Taiwanese Navy. This was a source of joy and pride to both management and workers. It was the first such assignment given to the Corporation. The building of a ship like this would have been contracted out to the Americans as was customary. Everyone with whom I spoke in the shipyard was elated over the prospects of a national frigate soon to be commissioned from their own dockyard. I inwardly shared in their joy and pride as we made our way to Crab's House Restaurant for lunch.

After lunch we visited Fengshan Tropical Horticultural Experiment Station. This agricultural station had embarked on experiments leading to fruit improvement and diversification. We were conducted on a tour of the farm, and were treated to an excellent talk on the work of the Station. A visit to Nantze Export Processing Zone brought us in full view of a variety of products manufactured for export. This was a duty-free zone. Dr. Huang Chi huei, Deputy Director General of the Export Processing Zone Administration, kindly and patiently responded to questions as he led us on a tour of the building which housed not only offices but exhibition halls, and where visitors could make duty free purchases. We had dinner at the exotic Long Life Restaurant before returning to the Ambassador Hotel.

We checked out of the Ambassador Hotel early on Saturday morning, and by twenty minutes past eight we had set off on the forty-minute drive to Pingtung City Farmers' Association. Here we received a great welcome from the farmers, all smartly dressed in their suits. From the outset I was forcibly touched by the composure, the self-confidence, and the dignified appearance of the farmers, not to mention their broad smiles. The President of the Association in a welcome speech extended the hand of friendship, and declared that he and his colleagues were extremely happy that a visit to their Association was included in my itinerary. He went on to outline the work of the Association. I thanked the President for his warm and sincere words of welcome and congratulated the farmers on their hard and steady work which doubtlessly enhanced the level of agricultural production in Taiwan. Light refreshments were served and I availed myself of the opportunity to meet informally with many of the farmers present. We then visited the City Fruit and Vegetable Market where farmers sell their produce in bulk between the hours of 3.30 a.m. and 8 a.m. We also visited the Meat Corporation where we observed pig auctioning.

At the Pingtung Junior College of Agriculture we had a tour of the campus and we were luncheon guests of the President of the College, Dr. Carson Kung-hsien Wu and Mrs Wu. We then continued on our way to Kenting. We were driven straight to the Headquarters of Kenting National

Park where we had a briefing session before touring the park. This was
followed by some sight-seeing in this growing tourism area. We spent the
night at the Caesar Park Hotel where we were accommodated in the
President's suite. Back at the hotel we had a Chinese lunch before setting off
on the hour-long drive to Kaohsiung Airport. We returned to Taipei at
approximately 3.30 p.m. and back to the Grand Hotel. After dinner we
packed our bags in readiness for our departure on the following day.

We had no engagements on the morning of Monday, May 6. Since our
arrival in Taipei this was the first time we were able to have a late breakfast
and to relax in our hotel suite for at least a couple of hours. Accompanied by
the Vice Minister of Foreign Affairs we left the Grand Hotel at midday for
the Chiang Kai-shek International Airport where we were met by
Dr. Fredrick Chien, Minister for Foreign Affairs. At the airport there was a
guard of honour of military personnel who paid the usual respects before I
was escorted to the VIP lounge where an official party headed by the Vice
President was awaiting my arrival. At the conclusion of a short conference
in the VIP lounge my wife was presented with a gorgeous floral
arrangement. We then expressed our gratitude for a most enjoyable and
fulfilling stay in Taiwan and said our final good-bye before boarding the UA
844 flight for the long haul to San Francisco. There we were met on arrival by
Chinese officials from their trade office in San Francisco. We were invited to
a Hong Kong style restaurant where we enjoyed a delicious Cantonese meal.
At the San Francisco Airport Mr Hayes took leave of us. He was catching a
flight for Miami where he was due to make a connection with British West
Indian Airways (BWIA) on the following day for his return journey home.
Esmai and I were having an extended nine-day stay in the U.S.A. visiting with
our son and daughter and their families in Maryland and Houston
respectively. We returned to Grenada on Wednesday, May 15.

The next eight weeks were very busy ones. It was the season of
graduations, a time when secondary school students who completed their
course of studies received their certificates. The schools liked holding their
graduation exercises under the patronage of the Governor General and the
students looked forward to receiving their certificates from his hands. More
often than not I was invited to give the keynote address. It was impossible for
me to attend all the graduations in any given year, but my wife and I tried to
be present at as many as possible. These graduations are important
occasions to students, parents and teachers, and they are fully covered by the
media. For most parents, graduation is a costly exercise, but they go all out
and make the necessary sacrifices to ensure that their sons and daughters are
smartly dressed and well adorned in their graduation ring (which is an

expensive item). I have always thought it rather odd not to see the teachers in their academic robes while the school leavers were splendidly attired in gowns and mortar boards.

I was also involved in a number of social and other activities associated with non-governmental organizations such as St. John Ambulance Brigade, the Jaycees, the Grenada Cocoa Association, the St. John's Fishermen Association and the Police Passing Out Parade. I also received midyear visits from a number of non-resident ambassadors and high commissioners and representatives of international organizations. A week-long meeting of the OECS heads of government was held in Grenada from Monday, June 17. I met them at a reception held in their honour at the Ramada Renaissance Hotel. The one sad note for me was the passing of Lionel Maloney, our Commissioner of Prisons. It was with deep regret that I learnt of his death which occurred on June 6 at the Queen Elizabeth Hospital in Barbados. He had given sterling service to Grenada and had transformed the Richmond Hill Prisons into a most disciplined institution with a hardworking and responsible core of prison officers. He was a dedicated and industrious man who truly executed his duties without fear or favour.

The costly and much talked about Maurice Bishop murder trial concluded in July, 1991. It went on for some seven years – starting with the preliminary investigations in the magistrate's court by Senior Magistrate Lyle St. Paul, followed by the long drawn out trial in the Grenada High Court under Acting Chief Justice Denis Byron, and finally the sitting of the three- man Appeal Court under the Presidency of Sir Frederick Smith. It was a trial that evoked much public interest both at home and abroad. From time to time the trial had to be adjourned to enable the Court to deal with a number of constitutional motions all aimed at stalling the proceedings and giving the accused a faint glimmer of hope that the case might be abandoned.

On Monday, July 8, the Appeal Court met for the final hurdle in this dramatic criminal hearing. The Court adjourned without going into the judgement. There was tight security in the precincts of the Court as well as in the Coyaba Hotel where their Lordships were staying. The proceedings continued on the following day when the Court dismissed the grounds of appeal dealing with the constitutionality of the Court, the appointment of Chief Justice Byron and the selection of the jury. As the appeal case proceeded there seemed little or no chance that the sentence of death would be quashed. In fact, one of the Justices of Appeal said that if he were the jury Rayburn Nelson (who had turned Crown witness) would have been convicted and not set free, and the three who were given long jail terms would also be sentenced to death. On Friday, July 12, 1991, the Court concluded its judgement. The sentence given by Chief Justice Byron was upheld. One woman and thirteen men were to suffer death by hanging from the gallows, and three other men were to serve long jail terms in the order of 45 years each for Richardson and Joseph and 30 years for Mitchell.

In a radio call-in programme two days afterwards 121 people felt strongly that the fourteen sentenced to death should face the gallows while only four callers wanted the sentences commuted to life imprisonment. Letters, telegrams and telephone messages from far and near seeking clemency for those sentenced to death began to reach me, and these increased with every passing day. Most of these petitions were from overseas, and three notable ones were from world renowned Mother Teresa of Calcutta who had previously visited Grenada, and from two illustrious sons of Grenada, namely Sir Sidney Gun-Munro, former Governor General of St. Vincent and the Grenadines and the Rt. Rev. Cuthbert Woodroffe, former Archbishop of the West Indies. As usual my staff was very good in screening telephone callers who wanted to speak to me about the upshot of the trial or who wanted to put in a plea for clemency. In this connection they put me on to only three callers and they were right on target. Amid the calls for reprieve I could discern three categories of people making these requests. Firstly those who had deep convictions against the death penalty, secondly the defense lawyers for one reason or the other, and thirdly people immersed in the leftist way of life. For my part I knew it would be very painful for me to sign warrants for the expiration of these prisoners, some of whom sat at my feet in their formative years. However, I had taken an oath to execute the duties of my office and uphold the Constitution without fear or favour. In the circumstances, I felt I had to act strictly in accordance with our Constitution and our laws.

On Thursday, July 25, Hon. Joan Purcell, Chairman of the Advisory Committee on the Prerogative of Mercy, advised me that the death sentence should be carried out. It was my understanding that Purcell was at one with the members of her committee in this regard. In keeping with the provisions of Section 73 of the Constitution the committee consisted of six persons. With the advice of the Prime Minister I had appointed Joan Purcell, Minister for Tourism, as the designated minister and Chairman of the committee whose role was to advice the Governor General on the granting of pardon to prisoners. Two members, the Attorney General and the Chief Medical Officer were *ex-officio*, and the other three members were appointed by me by instrument in writing under my hand on the advice of the Prime Minister. In the case of a death sentence the Chairman would hold a meeting of the Advisory Committee on the Prerogative of Mercy to seek their advice, but after obtaining such advice, she in turn would decide in her own deliberate judgement whether to advise me to exercise any of my powers under Section 72 (1) of the Constitution to alter the sentence in any way. Thus the chairman, otherwise called the designated minister, is not obligated to act in accordance with the recommendation of the Committee when tendering advice to the Governor General. That is the Law. That is the Constitution.

The following day I signed the death warrants and later summoned Winston Courtney, the Commissioner of Prisons, to my office where I handed them to him. The plan was to hang the fourteen in three or four batches the following week. Courtney advised me that everything was in place for the execution. The gallows were in good working order, the hangman was identified and a Roman Catholic priest was standing by to say the final prayers.

Then there was a dramatic turn of events. I was relaxing at my private home in St. Paul's on the morning of Saturday, July 27, when suddenly I observed a car coming through the gate. It stopped half way down the driveway. A gentleman got out of the car and started to walk towards the house. I soon recognized him to be Dr. Francis Alexis, the Attorney General. When I invited him into the house, I could see a somewhat worried look on his face. Whatever was going through his mind he obviously regretted that he had to be the one to approach the Governor General unannounced in his private home on a Saturday morning. No doubt he felt that all this could have been avoided.

After apologizing profusely for coming into my presence unexpectedly, the Attorney General went on to advise me of the agonizing state of both the Prime Minister and the Minister of Tourism who was also the Chairman of the Committee on the Prerogative of Mercy. According to Alexis, the Prime Minister could not see himself facing up to the execution of so many people during his tenure of office, and for the time being he would like to see a stay of execution. I was greatly surprised when Alexis disclosed that Joan Purcell was sitting in the car in my driveway .She evidently did not have the courage to face me after having advised me just a few days previously that the death sentence be carried out in respect of the fourteen condemned prisoners.

My morning visit to my private residence came to an abrupt end. No sooner than Dr. Alexis and Mrs Purcell left my premises, I received a call from the Prime Minister who advised me to effect a stay of execution. I immediately left for Governor General's House and had the Commissioner of Prisons report to me with the signed warrants. Courtney acted promptly. He returned the warrants to me, and I told him that he should not take any further action on the matter of hanging until he received fresh directions.

During the following week my wife and I were involved in activities marking the 75th anniversary of the Anglican High School. But the week-long anniversary celebrations did not overshadow the Maurice Bishop Appeal Case which continued to be a matter of topical interest. There was much speculation as to when the fourteen condemned criminals would face their death by hanging. There was even much unsolicited advice as to the order in which they should make their appearance at the gallows. There was a strong wave of opinion in favour of the Court's ruling. The defense lawyers thought differently. They filed a motion with the Grenada High Court that the execution be stayed and that there be a retrial. The Court of Appeal sat as a matter of urgency and threw out the motion

On Sunday, August 4, my wife and I accompanied by Sir Ellis Clarke, former President of the Republic of Trinidad and Tobago, attended holy mass at the Blessed Sacrament Church in Grand Anse. Father Oliver Leavy, an Irish priest of the Kiltigean Order, was the celebrant. Instead of preaching on the scripture reading of the day he was insensitive enough to deliver a sermon on capital punishment. He clearly stated that he was against capital punishment. In a democratic society it should not surprise anyone if there was a diversity of opinion on any matter. But when a priest chose to use the pulpit in an effort to impose his views on his congregation and openly made reference to the outcome of the Bishop Murder Trial I thought it was cheap and in bad taste. The congregation was made up of people of differing opinions on that matter and who understood the true import of capital punishment. To speak so condescendingly on such a sensitive issue in the presence of the Governor General and the parents of one of those murdered on October 19, 1983, was a bit repugnant. It was not the time, nor was it the occasion for such a homily. He was completely off the mark. Mr and Mrs Creft, the parents of Jacqueline Creft who was brutally murdered on Fort George on that dreadful October day, were among the congregation. Mrs Creft was visibly upset and she had to be restrained by her husband not to get up and answer Fr. Leavy. From where I sat I could hear her expressing her disgust. It was the sort of sermon that would drive people away from the church. In a telephone conversation later that day I felt obliged to report the matter to Bishop Sydney Charles, the head of the Roman Catholic Church in Grenada.

Four days later I received Joan Purcell in her capacity as Chairman of the Committee on the Prerogative of Mercy. Apparently she had got over the embarrassment that kept her away from me when she elected to remain in her car half way down my driveway a few days earlier. Having regained her self-confidence she was able to approach me face to face to advise me to commute the death sentence to life imprisonment. On this occasion I did not act as promptly as I did when she first advised me to pursue the sentence of death as pronounced by the Court. I allowed five days to elapse before I signed new warrants commuting the death sentence to one of life imprisonment. I wanted to make sure that I would not have to recall the new set of warrants. Meanwhile in his audience with me on Tuesday, August 13, the Prime Minister and I held discussions pertaining to the fourteen condemned prisoners. The Prime Minister confirmed that he could not face the spectre of fourteen people suffering death at the hands of a hangman. The last Grenadian who suffered the penalty of death was Charles Ferguson for a gruesome murder in La Poterie, St. Andrew's. That was in 1978, thirteen days after I assumed the office of Governor General. It fell on me to give orders for the hanging of Charles Ferguson as stipulated in the death warrant which had been previously signed by my predecessor. Since then there had been no judicial hanging in Grenada. Prime Minister Brathwaite took the extraordinary step to announce in a special national broadcast that the sentence of death meted out to Coard and his colleagues was commuted to life imprisonment. The reaction from the public was one of mixed feelings He fell short of saying that it was a cabinet decision. The Cabinet had discussed the question of a pardon for the fourteen convicted on three occasions although there was no written conclusion. At first Cabinet was firmly in favour of carrying out the sentence of death, even though there was a tiny minority against it. On the second occasion there was a tremendous amount of wavering among Cabinet members on this issue. For the third time the Prime Minister took the matter to Cabinet there was an almost complete turn around when members took the view that the death sentence should be commuted to life imprisonment.

The whole question of a pardon for the thirteen convicted men and one woman was clumsily handled. In all my public life I had never witnessed such vacillation on the part of a government. Entwined with this indecision was an apparent lack of knowledge or understanding or both of the sections of the Constitution pertaining to the Committee on the Prerogative of Mercy with specific reference to the role of the chairman of the Committee. If only our politicians would follow procedures based on rules and regulations, let alone the Constitution, time wasting in official quarters would be eliminated, and our governments would be more efficient and more respected. Admittedly, I was very embarrassed to have to recall documents on which I had painfully affixed my signature all because of the hollow advice I had first received. But when the Prime Minister went on national radio and gave the impression that he was granting a pardon I thought it was time to start packing my bags as there was nothing more I could usefully do to protect the integrity of my office. Given the number of enquiries my office received after that Prime Ministerial broadcast it was clear to me that the perception among listeners was that the Prime Minister was the one responsible for granting pardon to prisoners. During my years in office I had granted pardon to a number of prisoners including some on death row without any fuss or bother and without any reference to any of the Prime Ministers. I liked doing this on special occasions as, for example, on Independence anniversaries and on the visit to Grenada of Her Majesty the Queen. In fact, on September 20 I went on to grant pardon to eight other convicted prisoners by commuting their death sentences to life imprisonment.

Heads of governments of East Caribbean States (The OECS Authority) met in Antigua on August 15 and re-admitted Grenada to the regional Court system. I immediately signed a proclamation giving effect to Grenada's re-entry and sent it to the Government Printery for an extraordinary publication in the Government Gazette on the same day. On the following morning at eight o'clock I administered the prescribed oaths to newly appointed Judge Lyle St. Paul and magistrates in the Court of Grenada and the West Indies Associated States. All this was of great significance as it marked the complete restoration of the Constitution, and I felt an acute sense of relief and satisfaction.

For the rest of the year I was very busy receiving outgoing and incoming ambassadors, launching appeals for funds for worthy causes, opening national and regional conferences and festivals, and attending events organized by non-governmental organizations. On Sunday, November 3, deposed President Aristide of Haiti visited Grenada. He was accorded a welcome normally reserved for an official visit of a Head of State. Aristide later called on me. He had discussions with the Prime Minister, held a press interview, and spoke at a rally in the town of Grenville before taking his departure to continue his whistle tour through the Caribbean. Grenada, like the rest of CARICOM and so many other countries, still regarded Aristide, this former Roman Catholic priest, as the constitutional Head of State of Haiti.

On November 7, Laureston Wilson Jr., who had given years of loyal, devoted and distinguished service to his homeland under trying circumstances for most of the time, took leave of me upon relinquishing the post of Director of Finance to proceed on retirement. The month of December demanded much of my time and energy. Well knowing that this was going to be my last Christmas as Governor General I accepted more invitations than I did in the past at this time of year and our annual

Christmas party was bigger than ever. During the month my wife and I did much more than making our usual round of visits to institutions such as children's homes, hospitals, and homes for the aged and for the handicapped and preparing and delivering my Christmas message to the nation. Apart from all this we attended a special event, Assembly '91, a Catholic extravaganza held at Queen's Park in St. George's. We were present at the well-attended open air mass that was concelebrated by Bishop Charles, Bishop Guilley of St. Lucia, the Pope's representative who flew in from Trinidad for the occasion and all the priests of the local diocese. Wednesday, December 11 was the day appointed for the ceremonial opening of a new session of Parliament and I went down to the House to read the traditional Throne Speech at a joint sitting of the Senate and the House of Representatives.

By January, 1992, my mind was clearly made up about demitting office during the course of the year. While carrying out my official duties I began to make preparations to leave. We had been spending more time on weekends at our private home. Although I had warned the Prime Minister that I was going to demit office about the middle of the year, it was not until March 31 that I discussed the exact timing of my departure with him. He told me that at the next weekly meeting of Cabinet he would apprise members of my impending departure. By then I had received word from Buckingham Palace that the Queen had granted my request to demit office on July 31, 1992 and that a farewell audience had been arranged for me for Thursday, July 23.

At midday on Monday, April 6, in a very brief statement I announced my retirement on radio and television. Cabinet was still in session when I made this announcement. I chose the time very carefully as I wanted the public to hear it from me first rather than from any other source officially or unofficially. At once tributes began to flow into my office, and there were several callers to my personal assistant as they started to arrange farewell functions for me. Calypsonian, Robert Grant, who was also a practising lawyer and ardent farmer, composed and recorded a calypso in my honour. Three days after announcing my retirement I had a surprise farewell reception at Queen's Park, the premier recreation ground in Grenada. It was on the occasion of the two-day annual intersecondary schools athletic sports meeting when the best athletes from each of our secondary schools vied for athletic supremacy. This was the most popular athletic sports meeting in the country, and during my tenure of office I officially opened each of them and witnessed some of the events in the late afternoon. At the conclusion of the 1992 games the great jubilation among the winners, the students of the St. Andrew's Anglican Secondary School, ceased temporarily to allow the principals of the school, through Mrs Lyndonna Webster ( Principal of Westmorland School), to pay tribute to me and to thank me for my support and encouragement over the years. After receiving a memento I replied suitably expressing the hope that this annual event would grow from strength to strength.

At the invitation of Dr. the Hon. Francis Alexis, Minister for Legal Affairs and Attorney General, I paid a farewell visit to his ministry. This visit took the form of a comprehensive tour of the legal complex to include the Judges chambers, the magistrates courts, the law library, the registry and the Attorney General's office. Two presentations were made to me in the Attorney General's office – one from the staff (a plaque) and the other from Dr. Alexis himself (two copies of his published works).

Non-governmental organizations arranged specific farewell functions for my wife and / or me. These included the Red Cross, the Girl Guides Association, the Grenada Football Association, the St. John Ambulance Brigade, and Partners of the Americas. Other organizations like the Catholic Teachers Association used the occasion of their annual conference which I officially opened to wish me all the best in my retirement and to present me with a gift. So too did the Grenada Union of Teachers, and the Duke of Edinburgh Award Scheme. On Friday, 19, the diplomatic corps hosted a most delightful and delicious dinner in our honour at the Spice Isle Inn and gave us a lovely parting gift. On Sunday, June 21, at the invitation of the Anglican Parochial Council we worshipped at the St. George's Anglican Church where the Venerable Archdeacon Clement Francis and members of the congregation bade us fond farewell and presented us with a gift. We were the honoured breakfast guests at the rectory afterwards.

Several influential individuals who wanted to express gratitude for what I had done for Grenada especially during our crisis periods called on me. Among them were Pastor Nord Punch, Head of the Seventh Day Adventist Church in Grenada, Mrs Winifred Strachan, Leader of the Opposition., and Mr Everett Woodroffe, a St. George's businessman. I also received a number of delegations from non-governmental organizations who wished us well and presented us with gifts. Included in this category were the Society for the Deaf, the Grenada branch of the Institute of Management Network of Civil Servants in the OECS, the St. Joseph's Convent, St. George's and the Carols by Candlelight Committee. The Chairman and members of the Public Service Commission were not to be undone. They too called on me to say farewell.

My wife and I had to restrict our appearances at graduation exercises because of our extremely busy schedule. However, I did find the time to give the main address at five graduation ceremonies and present the graduation certificates. At the Grenada Boys' Secondary School, my alma mater, a special presentation was made to us by Dr. Barry Rapier, Chairman of the Governing Body. During the graduation ceremony at St. Andrew's Anglican Secondary School which some years previously had conferred upon me the title of honorary Old Boy of the school, I received good wishes for a happy retirement and a gift.

On the morning of Tuesday, 30, Esmai and I embarked on the early morning flight for Carriacou to say goodbye to the people of Carriacou and Petit Martinique. After breakfast at the Cassada Bay Hotel we journeyed to Windward to take the half hour trip by boat to Petit Martinique. At the Roman Catholic school the staff and pupils with their parents as well as other adults in the community had assembled to bid farewell to us in song and dance. In the afternoon in Carriacou at the Hillsborough Secondary School some 140 people came out to extend best wishes for happiness in our retirement. In both Carriacou and Petit Martinique I thanked the people for their loyalty and support during my years in office, and expressed the hope for a brighter future. We received gifts in appreciation of our years of service. It was a memorable one-day visit to Carriacou and Petit Martinique,

It was at Gouyave, my hometown, that I was particularly touched by the nature of the farewell accorded us. It was a splendid affair at the St. John's Anglican School where I had received my early education under the tutelage of Arthur Randolph Leopold Miller. People of all walks of life from St. John's parish including some of my teachers had assembled there. So, too, were prominent Gouyave people who no longer resided in Gouyave. Also present were my mother and my sister and other relatives. It was a homecoming organized by my home people. On our arrival we were greeted by a guard of honour of uniformed scouts who then escorted us to the building. The function was held with clockwork precision. We were entertained in song by the Youthquake group of singers who already had two overseas performances to their credit, the first being to Ireland through the instrumentality of the then parish priest, Father Oliver Leavy. A saxophone solo was beautifully rendered by the young and talented schoolboy, Dwight Matthew, who went on to annex the island scholarship based on his performance in the Cambridge A level examinations. Carlos Thomas, a young teacher, entertained us with a calypso, and Jerome McBarnette, Grenada's leading baritone, gave us a solo performance. Brief speeches were made by Hon. Edzel Thomas, parliamentary representative for the parish of St. John and Senator Carlyle Glean. But it was left to Justice Lyle St. Paul, the main speaker to give the tribute. I was then presented with a beautiful plaque depicting the main industry of Gouyave, fishing. In my reply, I recalled my boyhood days in Gouyave and thanked the people for honouring me thus and for their presence. We then all repaired to the St. Rose Modern Secondary School for refreshments which were lavishly served.

On the morning of July 14 the police under the leadership of Commissioner Colonel Nestor Ogilvie paid tribute to me. This took the form of a one-mile march from Police Headquarters to Governor General's House with the police band in attendance. The large contingent of police officers and men resplendently dressed in ceremonial uniform took up their positions in the driveway in front of the main entrance to the house. I then inspected them before taking the march past. After a brief display and kind words of tribute and presentation of a gift, I thanked the police profusely for all their courtesies, their support and their work during my term of office.

The following evening the combined staff of my residence including the office staff got together to bid us farewell. So many of them wanted to speak. Others were visibly sad. While thanking them I admonished them to maintain the best traditional standards of the office and of the house and to give their fullest loyalty and co-operation to my successor, Mr Reginald Palmer, whose appointment had been announced on July 6.

The big farewell was at York House in the parliament chamber at a joint meeting of the Senate and the House of Representatives and in the presence of dignitaries and a wide cross section of the public. The police formed a guard of honour in the courtyard as they were wont to do whenever I made my annual visitation to Parliament to read the Throne Speech. On my arrival I was paid the usual compliments and then I inspected them for the last time. In the chamber glowing tribute was paid to me and my wife by Prime Minister Nicholas Brathwaite, Leader of the Opposition Winifred Strachan, Ben Jones and Senator Derek Knight. I replied with feeling.

At the end of the ceremony in Parliament I held a small reception at my residence for parliamentarians and their spouses.

My wife and I left for the United Kingdom on Saturday, July 18, primarily to be received by the Queen in farewell audience on Thursday, July 23. The rest was vacation but I terminated my appointment with a three-day visit to Lourdes in spiritual rapture and thanksgiving towards the end of July when my resignation took effect. In a pre-recorded message to the people of Grenada I said the following on July 31:

"Ladies and Gentlemen,

As I step down from the office of Governor General I would like to thank you, all of you, for your loyal support, for your various acts of kindness and for your loving words of encouragement throughout my term of office. There are many of you I can single out for special mention, but it would be imprudent on my part to do so, as I know that there has been a silent majority of all walks of life who deep down in their hearts have been wishing me well and have been praying constantly for my wife and me. I wish also to publicly thank all of you who in any way expressed your appreciation of our work and extended best wishes on our retirement.

For me it was a privilege and a pleasure to serve during those fourteen eventful years, and I have no regrets. My faith in our people has grown stronger with the passing years, and my great hope is that our country will one day soon come out of its present economic difficulties and all our people will be able to enjoy a higher standard of living, with greater employment opportunities, better health facilities, improved educational standards, and a wider and improved spread of social amenities. This accomplishment is not beyond our scope, if we approach our manifold problems as a united people with a strong commitment to produce and to advance. Let us look around the world and examine carefully what has been achieved by people who have had little or no natural resources, but by dint of hard work and a commitment to nation building have been able to make remarkable economic and social progress.

As an independent country we can no longer depend on grants from other countries in order to carry out our basic functions. The signals are clear that if we want to succeed we must rely on our own efforts, bearing in mind our limitations and making the best possible use of our resources both human and natural. In all this we cannot afford to be idle. Nor can we afford to dissipate our energies, to waste our natural resources, and to constantly engage in unnecessary wars of words with one another. For while we are talking, people in other parts of the world are doing, they are performing, they are working in order to build their own communities and their own countries and to enhance their personal growth.

I see the role of the Non-governmental Organizations as vital to the economic and social development of our country. Working with these NGO's was indeed a pleasure and I should like to pay tribute to the large number of dedicated Grenadians and friends of Grenada who give so much of their time and expertise and resources in keeping the NGO's alive, and many of them at great sacrifice. Some of them work for long hours without any thought of reward. These people serve our country with honour, and in a personal way I want to take the opportunity to say to them, 'well done' and to wish them Godspeed in all their future undertakings.

It is my hope also that the development of sport and culture will continue to receive more and more support and encouragement. It is imperative that our young people in particular engage increasingly in sporting and cultural activities if we are to ensure a well-ordered and disciplined society now and in the future. I commend all those who are working so zealously to promote sport and culture in our country.

All in all I see a bright future for our country. The realization of that bright future depends on us as a people, spiritually renewed and determined to build, never to destroy.

My best wishes go to my successor in office and I am confident that you will give him all the courtesies that befit this high office. Let us look to the future with confidence and hope that we unite as one people under God. Good-bye and good luck and God bless you."

# 15

## *Reflections*

I had always thought that the job of Governor General was a lonely one. It did not take me long to confirm this view. My experience as Governor General was like living in a gilded cage that was well protected against entry. In this situation I was thus denied participation in the good old Grenadian pastime of friends dropping by at any time and without prior notification. The ordinary everyday chores of life were also gone. It was, for example, out of the question for me to be engaged in gardening – something I do with passion now that I am once more a private citizen. My temporary and intermittent releases from the cage were something of a ritual. It was not like simply going through the main door, getting into your car and speeding away, or taking a quiet stroll along one of our tranquil streets of St. George's. Oh no! My every move was carefully programmed and calibrated with a number of other individuals, particularly those with direct responsibility for my security and welfare as head of state.

One of the cardinal rules in the cage was that the occupant should always be on time. Thus whenever I had to attend any function, a punctilious well-dressed gentleman known as the ADC would telephone my bedroom to remind me that we should leave in ten minutes. Walking down the staircase, I could hear the car already revving ready to go.

The ADC always ensured that I return to the cage on time. For example if we were attending a cocktail reception that was due to end at 8 p.m., the ADC would give me the nod, at five minutes to the hour. That meant that it was time to say good-bye to the host and hostess. Throughout the function, any function, the ADC has his eyes glued on me. At least two security men would accompany us always travelling at a discreet distance immediately behind my car.

Apart from the official cars, we had our personal car. As Head of Security for the country, the Commissioner of Police, advised me not to drive. Thus for all my years in office, I never touched the steering wheel of a vehicle. My wife, on the other hand, insisted on driving herself when her travels did not relate to official government business. Her reasoning was that she was not in office and should not expect government to be responsible in any way for her private movement. She therefore almost always drove on her own without any form of security during our years at Governor General's House. The major exception was a short period in 1983 when I was able to convince her that it was unwise for her to venture out alone.

After my first month in office, I reviewed the security arrangements pertaining to my movements and made certain changes. Under my new security arrangements, whenever we were going to the homes of close friends and relatives we went in our private car driven by our official driver but without flag, without ADC, and without security. For Church on Sundays while driven in the official car we had no one except the driver. In fact, it was only for official functions that we had the ADC and security. These arrangements remained unchanged during the entire revolutionary period.

I had always taken the view, some might say naively, that the Grenadian people would not harm me. That I should harm no one is one of my basic tenets in life. In a small and normally peaceful country as Grenada, too much security for high ranking personages can send the wrong signals The only time I felt my life threatened was when I had to take cover below the settee in the dining room on that dreadful night of October 25, 1983, to escape the advancing bullets. It was not safe to remain in our bedroom or indeed anywhere upstairs our residence.

During the revolutionary days there was a sharp contrast between the multiplicity of security personnel surrounding the Prime Minister and his ministers and the paucity of those attending on the Governor General. Whatever might have been the rationale for beefing up the security detail for the Prime Minister and other government ministers, I always considered my security to be adequate. It was only after our irregular difficulties in October, 1983, that security was stepped up, both in my residence and around my person. Thus, at the Blessed Sacrament Church in Grand Anse on a Sunday morning, we were always accompanied by the ADC, and the church was surrounded by at least four armed soldiers from the Caribbean forces, and for sometime wherever I went I was accompanied by members of the Caribbean forces. However, once democracy was restored, security was never a problem and I never really felt that that my personal safety was in any danger when I traveled around the country. Many a visitor to the island expressed surprise when they observed how I went about with the minimum of security or with no security at all.

During my early days in office, my wife was preoccupied with reorganizing the work schedule of the domestic staff and improving the physical décor and replacing, not without veiled opposition from the Treasury, cutlery, drapes and other domestic items that were no longer in keeping with standards expected at a Governor General's residence. In the absence of so many basic domestic amenities, we were forced to use our own personal belongings on certain occasions as our predecessors were wont to do. The lighting in the main reception room was horrible. My wife remembered too well that there was a beautiful chandelier hanging from the high ceiling. No one seemed to know at what point the chandelier was removed. We were determined to place two chandeliers in that room. We sought and got advice from an interior decorator, an English lady, living on the island. When we put a request to the Ministry of Finance for funds to purchase two chandeliers, the request was turned down promptly. This was during the first year of the People's Revolutionary Government. The thinking was that the chandelier was a piece of bourgeoisie apparatus. Perhaps in my attempt to be as forthright as possible, I had made a tactical error. It is conceivable that if I had asked for funds to improve the lighting in the reception room and not specifically for a chandelier, I might have been successful. But in our determination to better equip the main reception room, we bought two small chandeliers while on a visit to Britain, and with some judicious juggling of our budget my office was able to pay for them.

Throughout my stay at Governor General's House, it was always a hassle to get anything done for the improvement of the residence and the grounds. Fortunately both my wife and I had been civil servants and were accordingly knowledgeable of the way in which the civil service operated. I had to be constantly assisting my office staff in responding to the negative vibes of the mandarins of the Treasury and to the bumptious and unreasonable technocrats of the Ministry of Works. I hope that my successors in office would be spared the problems and frustrations that I had encountered in the maintenance of the beautiful two-hundred-year-old House and in the provision of amenities. The treatment of the Governor General's House as just another government department which must await its turn in the long queue for repairs and upkeep is preposterous and quite unacceptable. The State has a duty to provide the highest standard of accommodation for its Governor General, its Prime Minister, its Chief Justice and its Ambassadors and High Commissioners abroad.

It was clear to me that politicians and civil servants alike either did not understand how important it was to maintain high standards at Governor General's House or they did not care. Or if they did, they behaved as though they were powerless to act. Eric Gairy and Keith Mitchell were the proven exceptions. As Prime Minister and Minister of Works respectively, both men undoubtedly showed a commitment to provide for the House's upkeep in a manner befitting the role the occupant held in the nation's constitutional system. The attitude of ministers towards Governor General's House was clearly demonstrated when I asked to rebuild the Governor General's bathhouse on Grand Anse beach. The bathhouse had been destroyed on the morning of the Revolution, March 13, 1979. The People's Revolutionary Government never rebuilt it, no doubt on ideological grounds. During the Interim Government, there was so much restoration and refurbishment to be done throughout the country that I took the altruistic view that work on my residence and the bathhouse should await the coming into office of a democratically elected government. My friends told me that it was a mistake on my part. However, as a servant of the people, I was not convinced that it was a mistake, especially as I then had the sole right to exercise executive authority.

Government's reaction to my request for rebuilding the bathhouse was surprising. To my astonishment I learnt that when the matter went before Cabinet, a senior member questioned why the Governor General should have a bathhouse. The same member went on to recommend that the land on which the bathhouse once stood should be leased for the expansion of an existing hotel. That recommendation was later approved. I had refused to sign the deed for the lease of the land to expand the hotel facility, but since relinquishing office I observed that the expansion had taken place. Up to this time the Governor General is without a bathhouse.

When I assumed office there was no Act fixing the emoluments and other conditions of service of the Governor General. Nor was there any such law with respect to the Governor prior to independence, although the first local Governor was appointed in June, 1968. Neither the first local Governor nor my predecessor received a pension after leaving office. One of my first requests to the Prime Minister was for the introduction of a Governor General Emoluments and Pensions Act. Gairy readily agreed to do this. There was, however, a delay in taking the matter to Parliament because he wanted to do something similar at the same time for parliamentarians. In fact both bills were prepared by the Attorney General's office and sent to Parliament for the first reading. Shortly afterwards, the revolution occurred and both bills died with Parliament. I then had to pursue the matter of my pension and gratuity with Maurice Bishop. Despite the stubborn resistance of the learned revolutionary Attorney General, the Prime Minister was decent enough to sign a People's Law providing for a pension and gratuity for the Governor General.

I worked alongside six Heads of Governments and established an Interim Government wholly appointed by me. Of the six heads of Government, four were democratically elected and two seized power by force of arms. Four of them had the benefit of university and/or professional level education. From my own experience I must point out that the level of formal education does not necessarily bear strict concordance with the level of political performance.

Of the democratically elected Prime Ministers, the flamboyant Eric Gairy was the odd man out in so far as higher education was concerned. Although his formal education had been limited to the primary school, he was a politician *par excellence*. Gairy knew Grenada well, and he seemed to understand the needs and aspirations of the people. He was obviously endowed with the gift of mass psychology that he successfully used to entrench his political leadership. But like so many other leaders in developing countries, he remained in office too long. Despite his great faith in Christianity, Gairy seemed to have forgotten that man's pilgrimage on earth was a short and uncertain one. His main objective was to remain Prime Minister until death. He expected everyone to pay obeisance to him. However, many of his supporters began to desert him in his later years. Through his successful political agitation in 1951 for better working conditions, he had mitigated the hardships that the Grenadian poor had been suffering for years at the hands of the plantocracy. He opened up several doors for young Grenadians particularly in the field of education. He encouraged the growth of tourism, and, through expansion in the public service, created new job opportunities.

Herbert Augustus Blaize lacked the flamboyance of Gairy and the charisma of Bishop. A man of integrity and honesty, he governed by the rules and made no attempt to bend the law. He had great respect for the institutions of State. His main objective was to restore the old Grenadian values in society and to bind all Grenadians together. Very adept at bringing orderliness in public life, Blaize appeared to be scared of rising public debt. He was a good father figure, and in my view he was the best politician available to lead Grenada after our traumatic experiences of 1983. Grenada needed an experienced and mature leader, well seasoned in the art of governance. However, his deteriorating physical disability eventually got the better of him. Throughout his term of office, the young Turks who surrounded him had their own agenda, and there was an ever-widening gap between themselves and Herbert Blaize.

Ben Jones's stay in office was short lived. A man of honesty he was very articulate and capable of making a fine speech. But he was not a ball of fire nor was he a great initiator. His was a holding premiership while the country prepared for general elections.

Nicholas Brathwaite was a good administrator and a good thinker who lacked the charisma of the politician. He, too, was a man of integrity who was committed to work for Grenada's all round development. Brathwaite, however, was disappointed and let down by unwarranted, and in my view, unfair and uninformed criticisms from at least one of our newspapers. He was too easily upset by criticism especially from the media. He was equally upset by any kind of violence. As a newcomer to politics he found it difficult to cope with certain elements in the party and in the Cabinet. He stepped down as Prime Minister before his tenure of office was due to expire.

Maurice Bishop was the most charismatic of all the Prime Ministers. Youthful and articulate he had the capacity to sway his listeners and convince the youth of the nation, in particular, that he was on the correct political and ideological path. It was not by accident that he seized power by ousting the democratically elected Eric Gairy by force of arms. Bishop had been preparing for years to do this, from the time of his student days in London. His mission was two-fold, firstly to get rid of Gairy and secondly to overthrow the established political and economic order by imposing a Marxist / Leninist regime on the unsuspecting Grenadian people. On his return to Grenada in 1969 from London where he qualified as a Barrister-at-law he wasted no time in mobilizing individuals and groups whose loyalty to Gairy had turned sour. He very cleverly infiltrated the civil service, the police, the teachers and the nurses to name a few. He got a hearing from several people in business He warmed himself towards the church, particularly the Roman Catholic church of which he was a member. While all this was going on, in his anxiety to hold on to power Gairy reacted by taking certain draconian measures which further alienated the people and caused him to continue to lose friends and supporters. In preparation for his second objective Bishop formed a network of like-minded people in the Caribbean, especially young professionals who were of the same ideological slant as himself. Fidel Castro was his mentor. Bishop then ventured into the socialist and communist world to make new friends.

Once in power, Bishop ruled by the gun. He controlled the local media which he effectively used not only to belittle Gairy but also to spread his new ideology and to suppress any opposing views. Grenada was *de facto* a one-party state. He never lived up to his promise of early elections. Nor did he pay compensation still outstanding for lands which were acquired during the Gairy administration. Instead he confiscated more property and never paid for them. But the greatest blow he inflicted on the people was the curtailment of freedom of speech. Dissenting voices were only clandestinely raised. Anyone who publicly spoke against the Revolution ran the risk of being jailed without trial. It was no surprise that many Grenadians left and relocated in other countries. As he became more confident Bishop began to distance himself from institutions and individuals whose support he readily got prior to the revolution and during the early days of his self-acclaimed premiership. He tried hard to muzzle the church, but with little success. The church suffered great stress and strain under Maurice Bishop but it was too powerful to crumble. In the end his glorious revolution failed. His own comrades blamed him for the failure, executed him, and made sure that his mortal remains would disappear without trace. This was a sad end for a man who misread the mood of the people and was unable to grapple with the ambitions of his own comrades.

General Hudson Austin, a weary and confused man, took control with the help of a Revolutionary Military Council (RMC) after Bishop's cruel death. Educationally he did not reach the proficiency level of any of the Prime Ministers. Austin knew his limitations and had nothing of substance to offer during his six-day rule. Nevertheless, he continued rounding up known Bishop's supporters, many of whom went into hiding. Austin did not have a clue about the governance of a country. He did not know where to begin.

Over the past thirty years politics dominated Grenadian life. It was politics not so much of issues but rather of personalities. Any discussion on the politics of Grenada revolved around the personal characteristics and activities of the Prime Minister and his Cabinet ministers. When it comes to politics so many of our good Christian people put aside the Christian virtue of love for neighbour and instead hate with a vengeance. In the case of Gairy, people either loved him passionately or hated him profoundly. This love / hate relationship swept through the home, the work place and even the church. This same unhealthy attitude to work was based on selfishness and greed. The governments must also take some of the blame, because their actions sometimes add cracks to the divisiveness in the society. Our governments, all of them, have tended to give special favours, including jobs to party supporters, and in many cases they forgot that they were servants of all the people. Politicians of ruling parties are most unhelpful and inconsiderate to those who might have opposed them in general elections. Yet over the years we have heard passionate calls for unity, for forgiveness and reconciliation from those who, by their very actions spread hatred in the community. Exhortations about peace and justice and excellence are quickly overshadowed by intolerance, vindictiveness and political expediency. From my own experience in public life, I know that many of these calls are based on emotions or self-interest. This I consider hypocrisy, whether these calls come from politicians, private sector interest groups or certain individuals, when they know full well they are not living out the true Christian doctrine of love of God and love of neighbour.

In my first national broadcast after the arrival of the American and Caribbean Forces in 1983, I called for reconciliation well knowing that it would take a long time to achieve given the grief and sadness generated by the horrendous events of October 19, 1983.

Where are the bodies of Maurice Bishop and others who were gunned down on Fort George on October 19, 1983? This is a question which is still seriously and quite appropriately asked by relatives and friends who in their disgust affirm that they will never be satisfied until the bodies are given up for burial. One can quite understand their grief and concern. I, too, shared that concern when on the day after the massacre, I asked the leader of the Revolutionary Military Council to produce the bodies for a Christian burial. Despite the initial assurance I received from General Austin on the morning of October 20, based on unofficial reports I received from Pat MacLeish, by the end of that day I was convinced that the dead bodies would never be found. I am still of that view. Yet there are still those who erroneously believe that the bodies are held in custody somewhere in Grenada. Some went so far as to suggest that the Americans took away the bodies. One widow had written to me seeking her husband's body which she understood was locked up in a room at Governor General's House. I could only offer her comforting words. I have never had any interest in dead bodies. I prefer to remember people as active and smiling, not as lifeless corpses.

When the Americans were led to a grave in Calivigny (near Camp Calivigny, one of the leading security areas of the People's Revolutionary Army), they found some burnt bones which I was officially notified could not be positively identified. This was the end of that saga. If the comrades in jail were manly and truthful enough, they would volunteer to tell the nation exactly what happened on October 19, 1983 pertaining to the dead bodies with special reference to their subsequent removal and disposal. Were they all burnt and buried at Calivigny? Were some burnt and buried on the Prison Grounds? Were others taken to sea for burial? Only General Austin and his RMC can answer these questions and more .The comrades must clearly give a step-by-step account of what exactly happened to the dead bodies.

While there were sporadic signs of growth during my term of office, there still remained some disturbing symptoms of low economic performance by the time I was ready to step down from office. True, there has been an upsurge in the construction industry since the traumatizing events of 1983 both in the public and private sectors. This has been evident by the building of roads and the construction of homes particularly by Grenadians who, after residing in the United Kingdom for several years, had returned home to spend the rest of their lives. New hotels had been built, thus increasing the number of beds in the hotel industry. There was some steady progress in the tourism industry but much more needs to be done by way of making our natural assets as well as the talents and skills of our people more marketable. Because of the fickle nature of tourism, there is a danger in neglecting other sectors of the economy as for example, agriculture. To do this would be to enhance, to our detriment, the flow of people from the rural parts of the island into St. George's, thus bringing enormous pressure on infrastructural facilities in the capital. This, of course, can lead to undesirable social practices.

Rural depopulation and the consequent decimation of the rural economy will be a matter of great concern to successive governments. Until and unless they do something positive, apart from lip service, for the improvement of the rural economy they will be inviting social discontent and economic instability in the country as a whole. This is an area that needs urgent attention. Tourism development, for example, should no longer be concentrated solely in the southern part of St. George's. Hotels and other tourism facilities should be developed in other parts of the country, thus making it possible for youngsters to find gainful employment in the rural areas. Any plan for rural development must, however, be couched in such language as to be easily understood by the people themselves. But a mere plan is not enough. Government must implement it.

Successive governments did little or nothing to resuscitate the agricultural industry. They talked much about it. Too often government formulate policies which they label economic policies, but which in truth and in fact have a political twist. It has always seemed to me that in formulating policies our politicians have uppermost in their minds the level of political mileage that can be accrued. However, I am still to see an agricultural policy that aims at making agriculture more attractive to young people, and at convincing them that they can make a decent living by engaging in diversified agricultural pursuits. The Taiwanese have made some stalwart efforts in demonstrating what is possible in agriculture by introducing some new crops and some new methods of farming, but their efforts and enthusiasm have not been matched by the commitment of our own Ministry of Agriculture.

Agriculture had received a massive body blow from Gairy's policy of "land for the landless." From the outset it was quite clear to me that the business of acquiring large tracts of farm lands and dividing them into small portions was politically motivated and damaging to the economy. Gairy very cunningly selected the lands to be acquired. His main aim was to put his political enemies out of business, thus forcing them to relocate. More importantly, he wanted to bring more of his supporters into areas where he had not been faring well in elections. This more than anything else was the basis on which the newly acquired lands were distributed. In a very personal way, Gairy always took the trouble to make a deep study of elections results.

Bishop's policy of "idle lands for idle hands" was even worse. While Gairy acquired property under the Acquisition Law, Bishop simply confiscated people's lands, one for political reasons, the other on ideological grounds. In both cases the policies failed dismally, and in both cases agriculture declined abysmally. It is going to be a difficult task for any government to revive our agricultural industry, given the lack of financial resources and the growing scarcity of agricultural labour. But something has to be done to increase agricultural production. The soil is still rich, the weather pattern is still conducive to prolific growth, and it is imperative that the agricultural industry produces the necessaries to enable the people of Grenada to feed themselves.

The manufacturing sector is still in its infancy. As an agricultural country, Grenada needs to move rapidly into agro-industries including the processing of herbal products for medicinal and other purposes, poultry products and milk. Efforts at arts and craft are too simplistic and the sameness of the finished products as displayed in the tourist booths clearly demonstrates the state of infancy of the industry. The human capital is the most important element in economic growth. We need to be more action oriented. Governments in association with their private sector partners should be more proactive in setting the stage for our people to be more productive in the work place and to be able to spend their leisure time more constructively.

A review of our educational and training needs should be undertaken as a matter of urgency. Much has been said and written elsewhere about the relevance of our educational system. Much more has been written by both educationists and non-educationists about the necessity of revamping the educational system. I have observed over the years that many people express their opinions to support their own vested interest. But nothing has been done to take a serious approach to making constructive changes to the system except for holding the odd seminar or, to be more fashionable, the grand consultation. All this talk about education has led to more and more interference in our schools. Over the past two decades our schools have been bombarded by all kinds of fanciful innovations which add little to the students' minds. The role of the Principal has been progressively eroded as the control mechanism shamelessly shifts from the Principal's office to the office of some functionary in the Ministry of Education. I have repeatedly warned that our schools cannot be operated by remote control. The real learning process must take place in the classroom and on the playing field, and thus the onus of running the school must rest on the shoulders of the Principal and his teaching staff. With the shift of the control mechanism more and more will the Principal be summoned to meetings by the establishment in the Ministry of Education, and the paper work will evidently increase with the answering of all kinds of questionnaires from the Ministry.

The school has become the whipping boy of every non-governmental organization or interest group. As far as these organizations are concerned, everything which is of some special interest to them must be included on the curriculum. Thus curriculum reform becomes a simple process of constantly adding subjects to the course of studies. Is it not more sensible to stick to a core of subjects and let everything else revolve around them rather than adding new-fangled courses to the curriculum with less time for the tried and tested subjects of real educational value? The proliferation of subjects on the curriculum does not add one iota to the quality of education. It is my contention that such a practice can sap the productive energies of the most well-intentioned and talented teacher. In a small country like ours with scarce natural resources it is important that we use education to seek economic empowerment. The development of human resources is the key to the future development of Grenada. Teachers must not be allowed to dissipate their energies through unreasonably large classes, overcrowded timetables, and undue interference from elements outside the classroom. In an ever-growing competitive world, it is important that we aim at high quality education in our schools. Reflecting on my own schooldays I have learnt so much on family life, on moral and spiritual values, on work ethics, on community living from my headmasters who would take five to ten minutes after the morning act of worship to address matters of the kind. Two men who had a profound influence on my life were Arthur R. L. Miller, my primary school head teacher, and Rawle S. Jordan, my secondary school headmaster. The values they taught me I did not find in any textbook. I see no reason why the inculcation of moral and spiritual values cannot be an integral part of any subject on the curriculum. Every teacher must be an exemplar of moral and spiritual values.

We now live in a society where we hear so much of children's rights but very little of children's responsibilities, where we hear about liberalization and little or nothing about obedience and respect for authority. I contend that children must be offered every opportunity to live out their childhood and grow to realize their full potential. However, under no circumstances should children be made to feel that they have a right to frustrate the authority of their teachers and parents. It is the duty and responsibility of parents and teachers to ensure that those under their care live up to certain standards of discipline which an orderly society would expect of them. If the educational authorities are not sufficiently vigilant, or if they are not prepared to work hand in hand with the school Principal, we will soon be faced with an increasing number of unreasonable parents descending upon our schools to question what they consider the severity of the discipline meted out to their children. The next stage will be confrontation with the teachers who will inevitably be subjected to a barrage of abusive words, if not physical manhandling. When this happens students will feel that they could challenge the authority of the teachers. May we never see the day when our nation's schools become the bastion of ill-discipline and violence as is happening in some developed countries.

During my years in Office, Grenadians suffered unyielding tension. Surrounded by an aura of uncertainty, we had to face the awesome challenges of political transformation. On top of all this the country mourned the loss of two sitting Prime Ministers, Maurice Bishop and Herbert Blaize. The resilient people of Grenada have come out of their anxieties and difficulties better equipped to deal with political crises, and better educated in comparative political philosophy. They have had first hand experiences of socialism and communism. They were part of the beginning of the dismantling of the communist Empire. It is in Grenada it started. The ease with which Grenadians embraced democracy after a period of enforced flirtation with communism was eloquent testimony of their longing for their democratic way of life. Indeed, it was a triumph for democracy itself.

Grenada is securely back in the democratic fold. It is left for us to be constantly vigilant as we strive to maintain and uphold our democratic freedoms. Our leaders must know their limitations. We may have equal voting rights in various international organizations. This, however, does not confer upon us a licence to behave as if we are a big and powerful country when communicating with our people in Grenada. We must all know our limitations and behave with humility. What we need to do is to concentrate on improving our human resources through education and training and to protect our environment. If we can do this and make a concerted effort to live and work more harmoniously we shall become a first class nation despite our small size and paucity of economic resources. I see a bright future for Grenada in which an increasing number of its citizens will have the urge and commitment to serve for our nation's betterment.

\* \* \*

Ever since the demise in 1962 of the four-year old Federation of the West Indies, Caribbean governments have made and continue to make worthwhile attempts to accomplish some semblance of closer co-operation. The constraints of geography, the unevenness of economic capability between the islands, and the reluctance of our political leaders to surrender even a modicum of their power base are stumbling blocks on the road to meaningful Caribbean unity. If, indeed, the race for regional integration is to be won, then the question in the minds of Caribbean nationals should be "What can we do to make Caribbean unification a reality?" rather than "What is there in such a process for us?" Reframing the question in this manner will require at the highest levels considerable statesmanship and vision for the region's future amid the increasing challenges of globalization.

The sub-grouping of the Organisation of East Caribbean States (OECS) comprising the Windward and Leeward Islands has produced a glimmer of hope. The frequent meetings of organizations like the OECS Authority (the Prime Ministers and Chief Ministers), and use of a single currency by all the East Caribbean countries point to strides that have been made in the right direction. So too is the staging of sporting competitions and cultural festivals at the sub-regional level. The expressed intention of introducing free movement of people within the OECS countries is also a healthy sign. It is hoped that these initiatives will impact on the efforts of the larger Caribbean Community (CARICOM) grouping which comprise all the English- speaking territories including Guyana and Belize.

But all these are official or governmental initiatives. It would seem that Caribbean togetherness must be expressly fostered by the Caribbean people at large. To achieve this our people must be educated to think West Indian. We must begin to look at ourselves as West Indians rather than just Trinidadians, Barbadians or Grenadians. Any movement for the forging of a truly great West Indies must involve the people and be sustained by the people. A regional non-governmental organization transcending insular boundaries and with a clear commitment to promote Caribbean unity is the way forward. Such an outfit would succeed in its goals and efforts only if it enjoys wide support from regional governments. Its impact should be felt not only at the professional or business level but also, and perhaps more critically, among the vast majority of our people who live in our towns and villages. They are the natural agents of change and they must be allowed to play an integral part in transforming our national societies into a Caribbean entity.

The 1983 initiative by the OECS, Barbados and Jamaica to restore law and order in Grenada was a commendable manifestation of Caribbean unity. But it was only partially successful. Some territories through their leaders missed a splendid opportunity to show the world that Caribbean people could unite. Indeed, the utterances of some of the leaders who opposed the intervention in Grenada were the causation of unnecessary divisiveness at a time when solidarity and cohesiveness were most needed.

West Indies cricket and the University of the West Indies are two powerful unifying forces in the Caribbean. But there is still the field of culture in all its ramifications and manifestations to be explored more fully and more fruitfully as a means of helping people realize their fullest potential as West Indians. Our Caribbean identity, our West Indian-ness, is deeply rooted in our rich cultural diversity fashioned by the quirks of history and refined by the commingling of successive migratory waves to the region. Our cultural heritage must not be utilized merely as a cheap commercial commodity to entertain tourists. Therein lies the danger of cultural dilution. Moreover, viral infiltration is always a possibility when we put aside our drums for the adoption of electronic devices. Our children have a right to grow in the knowledge of every aspect of West Indian culture. It is vital they know, understand and appreciate their history. To this end I would strongly advocate, as a matter of urgency, the establishment of National Archives in all our territories to save our records and preserve our past for the present and future generations.

Caribbean politicians do not always see themselves as servants of the people they represent. In fact, more often than not, their actions seem to indicate that they consider themselves as masters rather than servants. It is, therefore, in the interest of our political leaders to so manage their successes at the polls as not to cause post-electoral chasms among the populace. Once parliamentary elections are over the onus is on the successful candidates to demonstrate that they represent persons who voted for them as well as those who did not.

The electorate must be given a chance to serve in accordance with their ability, aptitude and integrity. Democracy is compromised when after elections our political leaders dispense with the services of competent persons in order to make way for party activists. The spirit of representation lies at the very heart of our parliamentary democracy in the postcolonial era. It is hoped that this same spirit will subdue the appetite of our own elected Prime Ministers, for the dispensation of political patronage. The practice of appointing Senators, and still worse Ministers, from among those who have been rejected by the electorate is an affront to the niceties of the democratic process. While our constitutions may be silent on this, Prime Ministers and Leaders of Opposition must be wary of this kind of political manipulation which can be interpreted by some as a wily device to reward the party faithful, by others as a tool to increase their political foothold in certain constituencies. On the other hand, where there are no constitutional restrictions on senatorial or ministerial appointments of defeated candidates, Presidents and Governors General are in duty bound to accept the appropriate recommendations and act upon them expeditiously. Indeed, if in their righteousness they seek precedent in this regard, they do not have to go far. They can find such within the Caribbean Community. All the CARICOM states have written constitutions. Thus Presidents and Governors General are guided by these constitutions in the performance of their duties. Personal concepts of morality cannot be allowed to efface the provisions of the constitution or delay constitutional sanction.

Nearly all the CARICOM States are monarchies with Her Majesty Queen Elizabeth II as Head of State and represented locally by a Governor General. Trinidad and Tobago and Dominica have ceremonial Presidents, while Guyana opted for an executive President. In the past Governors General worked in total isolation; in fact they only met one another in London when Her Majesty invited them there for some special occasion. It is refreshing to note that from 1994 Governors General and ceremonial presidents have been meeting annually (each year in a different territory) to discuss matters of common interest. The first meeting was held in Barbados under the chairmanship of Her Excellency Dame Nita Barrow, the Barbadian Governor General. Collectively these men and women are a rich source of knowledge and experience waiting to be tapped and acted upon. It is hoped that Prime Ministers in the region will take seriously the reports that come out of these meetings.

During my tenure of office there had been much talk about constitutional reform. For some, such reform constitutes a change from a monarchical to a republican form of Government. For others, it means putting a seal on the length of time any one person can serve as Prime Minister. For still others, constitutional reform is synonymous with a change from the Westminster model of "first-past-the-post" to proportional representation. The constitutional instruments in our Caribbean lands bear striking resemblance to one another. There can be no denying that they have served the people of the Caribbean well. Democracy continues to be healthy and strong in the English-speaking Caribbean.

The problems in the Caribbean are basically economic. Constitutional reform *per se* will not solve these problems. Changes that involve the creation of new structures of government might be costly, thus imposing further financial burden on taxpayers. I am yet to hear any compelling argument supporting the viewpoint that constitutional reform is initiated in the name of greater efficiency at governmental level or in response to popular demands. More often than not, it is undertaken to meet the narrow political goals of the ruling elite and their supporters. Rather than lower the economic pressures which they now face, radical changes to the constitutions of these vulnerable small island states, might well increase the level of impecuniosity which is proving more and more difficult to eradicate. Instead, proposals for constitutional change must seek to further protect our citizens and to enhance peace and justice as experienced in everyday life. It might be instructive to remind the protagonists of constitutional reform that government must be able to pay for itself. It is pointless adopting expensive constitutional models from other parts of the world if, in the end, independent Caribbean countries would find it difficult to refrain from the practice of going abroad with their begging bowls for aid with marked persistency. The emphasis should be on economic reform coupled with a greater determination to make the maximum use of our scarce resources.

In the case of Grenada our electoral process has never been marred by violence. The orderliness of general elections has never been in doubt. But there is a case for electoral reform with particular reference to the role and appointment of the Supervisor of Elections. The 1984 Electoral Law that brought about changes in the pattern of registering voters and the introduction of ID cards for voters also envisaged a permanent electoral office with a permanent staff including the Supervisor of Elections. But the Constitution, which is the supreme law of the land, makes provision for the naming of a public officer as Supervisor of Elections. In practice, this officer holds appointment in conjunction with his substantive post. This situation can no longer be acceptable and must be changed. Being Supervisor of Elections is a full time job that must be done efficiently and well. The office holder must be prepared at short notice to deal with an avalanche of pressing demands that might appear almost overnight. Finally, the job is sufficiently demanding and important to require an officer who does not have to split his time between two posts. It would seem that there is also a case for electoral reform with a view to finding ways of improving the whole electoral process, including the work of the Boundaries Commission, the compilation of the voters' list and the operations of the Parliamentary Elections Office.

The office of Governor General is an institution of enormous importance and influence. As representative of Her Majesty the incumbent assumes a posture beyond reproach when it comes to dignity, moral rectitude and exemplary conduct. The Office holder, like the ceremonial President, must be ready to act in moments of crisis. When the Constitution allows him to take decisions "in his own deliberate judgement," he must do so firmly and promptly. In extreme cases, as was the case in 1983 when a governmental void existed in Grenada, he should be prepared to invoke the doctrine of necessity to restore peace, order and proper governance. As a symbol of stability, he must support good causes and strive for the moral and spiritual uplifting of the country. A culture of spirituality is a solid platform for the promotion of economic and social advance of any country. As chief guardian of the constitution, the Governor General must continuously exercise vigilance and be ready to warn the Prime Minister if at any time the latter appears to be acting beyond the constitutional limits or if some government functionary attempts to bend the constitution or the laws of the country. It seems to me that on demitting office the Governor General should never become involved in partisan politics. Instead he should assume the role of statesman ready to be consulted at any time by any faction in the community.

To maintain the high standard of service, it is necessary that Presidents and Governors General be provided by the State with appropriate conditions which are clearly defined. On no account should a Governor General be treated like a public officer in terms of emoluments and other conditions of service. Adequate and appropriate provisions in keeping with the dignity of the office should be made available for the recruitment of a suitable ADC, a high-calibre administrative staff and a competent domestic staff. The official residence and the grounds must be maintained in perfect condition at all times. The governments of the larger Caribbean islands have gone a long way towards the enhancement of the dignity of the office of Governor General. The smaller territories have lagged behind miserably. Governments of small territories certainly need to review conditions of service of Governors General not only while in office, but also in retirement. Their urgent goal should be to bring these conditions on par with what obtains in the larger territories not necessarily in absolute but certainly in relative terms.

\* \* \*

Service to one's fellowmen is the highest human attribute in quest of peace and justice. It is through service that we meaningfully experience the Fatherhood of God and the brotherhood of man. In serving others we bring comfort to the distressed, joy to the downtrodden and hope to many who are struggling against the tide of despair and frustration. By serving we embolden our own spirituality, and smooth away our troubles as we seek to find true fulfilment in life. For me, to serve is to love. Growing up as a boy I was constantly made to do errands for the sick and the elderly in my neighbourhood. At home and at school I dutifully complied with the frequent exhortations to respect everyone, to be kind and generous, and to share with others whatever little I had. These exhortations have remained with me in adult life. I continue to hold on to them doggedly, and I hope never to depart from them. At primary school my head teacher, Arthur R. L. Miller, always impressed upon me that the "S" in my surname stood for service.

# INDEX